Bits and Pieces

Bits and Pieces

A History of Chiptunes

Kenneth B. McAlpine

OXFORD
UNIVERSITY PRESS

OXFORD
UNIVERSITY PRESS

Oxford University Press is a department of the University of Oxford. It furthers
the University's objective of excellence in research, scholarship, and education
by publishing worldwide. Oxford is a registered trade mark of Oxford University
Press in the UK and certain other countries.

Published in the United States of America by Oxford University Press
198 Madison Avenue, New York, NY 10016, United States of America.

Library of Congress Cataloging-in-Publication Data
Names: McAlpine, Kenneth B., author.
Title: Bits and pieces : a history of chiptunes / Kenneth B. McAlpine.
Description: New York, NY : Oxford University Press, [2019] |
Includes bibliographical references and index.
Identifiers: LCCN 2018001620 | ISBN 9780190496098 (cloth : alk. paper) |
ISBN 9780190496104 (pbk. : alk. paper) | ISBN 9780190496135 (oxford scholarship online)
Subjects: LCSH: Video game music—History and criticism. |
Chiptunes—History and criticism.
Classification: LCC ML3540.7 .M33 2018 | DDC 781.5/4—dc23
LC record available at https://lccn.loc.gov/2018001620

For Shonagh, Wee Kenny, and Iona

Contents

Bits and Pieces

Introduction

Back in January 2015, I sat down with my two children to watch *The Jam Badge*,[1] an episode of the animated series *Hey Duggee*. Broadcast on CBeebies, the BBC's television station for younger children, the show revolves around the Squirrel Club, a Scout-like organization for young animals run by an avuncular brown dog.

As my children became absorbed by the characters' quest to preserve a basket of overripe fruit, I decided to put in a spot of quality second-screen time with the iPad in my lap, until, that is, I heard the familiar chirp of 8-bit-style music drifting from the screen. I looked up to see Duggee and the Squirrels assume the roles of Donkey Kong and Mario as the cartoon transformed into a take-off of Nintendo's arcade classic, while my daughter, who normally prefers tactile play with an impossibly proportioned blonde doll, pointed at the screen excitedly, yelling, 'Daddy! Daddy! Listen: It's Mario music!'

Any doubts I might have had about the currency of 8-bit music as a pop culture reference vanished in that moment. Music that works as a cutaway gag in a show aimed at four-year-olds is part of, or very near to, the mainstream.

Chiptune

The word *chiptune* has a wonderful, almost onomatopoeic quality to it; two short affricate syllables in quick succession that bring to mind the chirps of the microchip-based sound hardware of the home computers and video game consoles of the late 1970s and early 1980s. For those of us who grew up playing on that hardware, that sound has a definite nostalgic appeal. It was the sound of our childhood, a repetitive electronic soundtrack that was as much a backdrop to teenage life as were Iron Maiden and Depeche Mode.

Certainly, it was a nostalgic wink towards parents that Grant Orchard, the director of Hey Duggee, intended.[2] Like all really good children's television, the show is designed to be a shared experience, with the characters, situations, and humour working on many levels to engage and amuse parents just as much as children. The look and feel of the show shares many of the characteristics of those early 8-bit games, with flat, distinctive characters, and planar environments that that work without the need for any complex backstory. As the episode came together, Orchard thought that the gag just seemed like a good fit. A chase scene involving a monkey and basket of fruit? What else *but* Donkey Kong?

My daughter's reaction, though, suggests that there is something more than nostalgia at work, something about the music that transcends its video game roots. Just like the trend for retro gaming, which has been embraced by kids too young to have been born when that first generation of 8-bit machines was already obsolete, that 8-bit sound has currency with a new breed of musician through the *chipscene*, a vibrant lo-fi musical subculture that repurposes obsolete gaming hardware to make music.

That inventive repurposing of video game hardware and its embodied performativity distinguishes the contemporary chipscene from contemporary video gaming and aligns it more, perhaps, with other countercultural artistic movements, including alternative media, antiart, and punk,[3] but ever since it emerged as part of the Amiga music scene in the late 1980s, the term *chiptune* has always applied to a broad range of perspectives, approaches, styles, and sounds.

Even today, several diverse communities of practice exist, perhaps not all mutually exclusive, but certainly distinct, who, quite legitimately, self-identify as chip musicians, and whose approach to music making extends from low-level performance coding on 'old-skool' hardware through to the reinterpretation and live performance of classic video game scores by 8-bit cover bands.

As an exercise, I often set my students the task of trying to arrive at a concise form of words that captures our shared notion of what 'music' is. To their credit, they work hard, but in truth, it is an exercise in futility. Often, they arrive at definitions that are too restrictive and that exclude examples about which, by consensus, we all agree, or they focus on process to the exclusion of form, or vice versa. Attempting to unpick the definitions and broaden their scope usually dilutes them, often to the point of banality, demonstrating, perhaps, Martin Mull's comic adage that writing about music is like dancing about architecture.[4]

Trying to do likewise with chiptune poses a similar challenge: focusing on the process of composition, for example, can't hope to capture the diverse range of approaches that result in the 'chip sound', while basing a definition on the hardware and software platforms used to create the music can lead to some perverse exclusions—Nintendo's Game Boy, for example, has no dedicated sound chip yet played a pivotal role in the development of chip music.

Even trying to capture a comprehensive picture of the contemporary chiptune scene is not straightforward. Like any thriving community, it is multifaceted and comprises a number of tight-knit and sometimes exclusive cultures of practice, each with its own social values, hierarchies, and orthographies. Regardless of which corner of the chiptune world they inhabit, chiptuners are passionate and feel a very strong sense of ownership of their musical space and identity.[5]

There is, however, one element that connects all of these strands together: the imaginative way musicians embrace the hardware, and use software both to capitalize on its affordances and to push transgressively beyond its constraints. As such, exploring the emergence and evolution of chip music depends as much on an understanding of the elegance and sophistication of low-level machine code and computer architectures as on the aesthetics and form of the works themselves.

But while technology plays an important part in the story of chip music, so too do the other areas of computer and electronic music that have influenced it and have in turn been shaped by it. Situating the chiptune phenomenon in its historical, cultural, and musical context, then, requires an interdisciplinary perspective, an approach that is quite common in the study of digital cultures.[6]

Roots and Routes

I have chosen to navigate this complex terrain with a 'roots and routes' approach,[7] drawing on musicology; youth and subculture studies; game studies; software and platform studies; the history of computing; and domestication and diffusion studies to examine the communities and cultures in which chip music is grounded (the roots), and the different evolutionary pathways that have led to the contemporary scene in all its forms (the routes).

I'm going to begin that journey with a platform approach. Just as it would be unusual to consider the evolution of keyboard music without reference to virginals, spinets, harpsichords, and pianos and how their sound and actions influenced the composers who wrote for them, we can't really explore the emergence and evolution of the chip sound and the practice of writing music on vintage hardware without considering the machines and their software, and the different ways different musicians have used them as creative tools.

This part of the story begins with the music of 8-bit video games, which was, after all, the primary reason the hardware was initially conceived. I will examine four home computer platforms: the Atari VCS, which was the machine that brought video gaming from the arcades into people's homes; the ZX Spectrum, a machine that, despite its technical limitations, almost single-handedly created and drove the UK gaming market throughout the 1980s and whose single-channel 1-bit beeper perhaps represents the ultimate in lo-fi digital music making; Commodore's C64, an 8-bit powerhouse whose sound chip offered possibilities that were more in line with a hardware synthesizer than a games machine; and Nintendo's NES, the machine that reintroduced console gaming following the US video game crash of the early 1980s. I will explore the context into which these machines were launched and examine how their technical architectures and the demands of the games that were written for them shaped both their music and the process of sound chip composition.

The approach here will be predominantly musicological, but I would like to qualify that slightly. While we can, of course, examine the music to understand the stylistic influences that helped to shape the sound, often such analysis doesn't tell us very much. Those early video game soundtracks drew on a rich range of source material, everything from baroque to blues and taking in everything in between. Sometimes those influences were driven by the narratives of the games, so that the music might provide context and flavour, but in many cases young coders, keen to turn around their games quickly and with little appreciation or regard for copyrights, just reached for the nearest sheet music to hand or arranged whatever vinyl was spinning in the background as they coded.

Stylistic analysis also doesn't paint a complete picture. Video game music is, at least in part, functional; just think of the 'attract mode' of many arcade games, nonplayable demos used to entice the quarters of prospective gamers like a midway caller drumming up trade for a ringtoss stall.[8] It is a type of media music, whose form and structure is determined, to some extent, by factors that lie outside the music itself: the constraints of the hardware, for example, or the need to balance the music with the gameplay. In this book's opening chapters, therefore, I examine some of the games that defined the platforms, or that exemplify their characteristic sound, and show their impact on the development of chip music.

It is also necessary to broaden our sense of what constitutes musicological study when it comes to video game music. Those early video game soundtracks were typically written in machine code and reproduced in real time by a sound chip, usually a *programmable sound generator* (PSG). In some respects, the machine code is equivalent to a traditional musical score, since it captures the musical detail and can be interrogated to provide insights into the music, but there is one important difference. A musical score is an efficient way of communicating the macro elements of music, but it relies on a performer interpreting those high-level musical directions and imparting the sort of unnotated expressive nuances that truly animate it. When the performer is a PSG, all of that musical expression must be hard-coded in advance. Every aspect of musicality depends on the composer having both an overarching sense of musical development and the ability to translate it into machine code, the technical language of machine expression.

Those video game composers, like the early pioneers of computer music at MIT and Bell Labs, were technologists-as-artists, and the technology was both the means of realizing creative ideas and the motivating force for creativity.[9] These composers' creative fingerprints can be detected as much in their code as in the music itself. Typically, PSGs offered little in the way of musical expression, usually only a few channels of polyphony and a prescriptive palette of simple waveforms, technical restrictions that posed a challenge to musicians. Programmable sound generators imposed constraints that mapped out a territory of musical possibilities that lay waiting to be explored and perhaps transformed.[10] In response, an explosive period of creativity arose from this digital frontier as game programmers and musicians—often one and the same—used creative coding to coax the hardware into performing feats of musicality it had never been designed to achieve.

Those early days of video gaming were replete with tales of ingenuity, and I will explore some of these in the following chapters, but the approaches that were adopted to broaden and expand the musical capabilities of PSGs were not without cost, and their application often imparted a unique characteristic to the sound. Over time, those characteristics came to define the aesthetic, if not the style, of the 8-bit computer soundtrack. It is only by examining the hardware and how it shaped and supported the games that were created for it that we begin to appreciate the challenges—both creative and technical—that were presented to those early game designers, and the routes through which the chip sound evolved. These chapters, then, explore both the process of writing music directly in machine code and the emergence of that 'chip sound'.

Minimalism ... to the Max!

But while constraint was a certainly powerful driver, the relentless march of technological progress also offered musicians new avenues for creative expression. In a wonderful scene in *Bill and Ted's Excellent Adventure*,[11] Beethoven, transported from nineteenth-century Vienna to San Dimas, California, in 1989, finds himself in a music store and begins to improvise around Mozart's *Rondo a la Turca* using the autoaccompaniment patterns of the electronic keyboards he finds there. The resulting fusion of classical themes and electronic rock sounds illustrates beautifully a moment of technology-inspired creation.

From the mid-1980s on, the introduction of next generation hardware and more user-friendly interfaces coupled new possibilities with new users who wanted to use their computers in different ways. Music trackers provided a more accessible interface than did machine code and memory monitors for musicians who wanted to compose and perform music on home computer platforms, and the quality of the raw sound sources improved as Frequency Modulation (FM) and sample-based synthesis began to appear in home computer systems via Commodore's PAULA chip and a range of plug-in sound cards for IBM compatible PCs. The profile of the game composer began to change, and game soundtracks evolved to take advantage of the growing number of channels and the timbral range that these new sound chips offered, becoming more cinematic but in the process losing some of that distinctive charm.

By the early 1990s, CD-ROM technology made it possible to stream full-bandwidth digital audio recordings direct from disk. In the same way that an industry drive towards filmic realism and shifting audience expectations normalized colour cinema in the 1940s and 1950s, bringing an end to the era of black-and-white film and its brooding unreality,[12] so too PSG music disappeared from video game soundtracks, to be replaced by more complex MIDI (Musical Instrument Digital Interface) arrangements, sampled loops, and licensed commercial tracks on CD-ROM.

PSG music, however, wasn't dead.

Software piracy had long been a problem for the games industry. At a time when most computer games were distributed on floppy disk and analogue cassette, many schoolchildren established themselves as illicit software distributors, using twin-deck tape recorders to duplicate games and trade them with friends at the playground. The industry responded, trying to dissuade casual piracy using a range of more sophisticated copy protection routines. Games that were once traded on tape in the playground began to be traded on bulletin board systems or on 'cracked' floppy disks; those that had been hacked to remove the copy protection software.

The programmers who worked to crack the copy protection began to leave digital calling cards, usually a graphical tag and a music track, which were displayed as a loading screen as the game booted. Although these first appeared on the Apple II in the late 1970s, it was with the Commodore 64 and then with the Amiga and the Atari ST that these calling cards began to increase in complexity and sophistication, evolving from graffiti-like messages to fully animated sequences with custom fonts and scrolling text effects.

The code to execute these crack-intros, or *cracktros*, had to be both compact and efficient so that they would fit in the boot sectors of the floppy disks they were distributed on, and PSG music, with its simple waveforms and sequences, lent itself perfectly to this end. Cracking crews began to compete with one another to demonstrate both their coding virtuosity and their graphical and musical creativity, competition that eventually transcended its illicit beginnings and evolved into the *demoscene*, a distributed online community of digital arts practice dedicated to the production of complex audiovisual displays.

With its roots in illegal software cracking, the demoscene was, and remains part of the digital underground.[13] Countercultural, with a strong noncommercial ethos and a culture of sharing, cracking crews riffed on the audiovisual vocabulary and grammar of video games; however, this second wave of chip musicians, freed from the need to create music that functioned as game music, could explore more experimental musical territory. Coders, artists, and musicians worked hard to squeeze every ounce of performance from the host machine, taking the hardware very close to the point of collapse in the pursuit of generating the most complex and vibrant real-time presentations possible. From this community of practice came *compos*, competitions, many of which continue today and which celebrate the point where technical and artistic virtuosity meet.

This was the era from which the term *chiptune* emerged, coming into use in the early 1990s. Before then, chip music was just one of a number of terms, including *micro music*, that had been used to describe music created on microcomputer systems.[14] However, with the advent of the Amiga, whose 4-channel 8-bit hardware sampling made it possible to create music with a very different character from that of the PSG music of older systems, the Amiga tracking community began to adopt the prefix 'chip' as a designator to distinguish music written in the style of those 8-bit PSG tunes, using short, single-cycle samples of synthetic waveforms from other styles.

In chapters 5 and 6 of the book, I will explore that reinvention of chip music. In chapter 5, I will discuss the notion of interface and how the emergence of soundtrackers in particular changed the way chip music was conceived and written, while in chapter 6 I will link chiptune, via the demoscene and software cracking, to the first generation of computer hackers and explore how a culture of digital collectivism and competition not only allowed the chip sound to continue but also offered a means for technique and workflow to be shared and for informal support networks to emerge.

Everybody Loves Chips

During the 1990s, a third wave of chiptune musicians began to emerge. Unlike the musicians of the demoscene, who were interested in exploring the limits of the hardware on which they worked, this new generation embraced the chiptune sound and aesthetic above all else, using the hardware as instruments and repurposing them for self-expression. *Nanoloop* and *Little Sound DJ*, both custom ROM cartridges for the Nintendo Game Boy, brought together the ease of use of a step sequencer or tracker interface with familiar gaming controls and a cheap handheld console to create an expressive but lo-fi digital music production system that could be busked just as easily as it could be incorporated into a live or studio rig.

Around this time, recording studio hardware was being virtualised,[15] and was being incorporated into software sequencers for desktop platforms, and musicians naturally linked the technologies, modding consoles to provide high-quality audio outputs that enabled them to sync and link consoles, feed signal processing chains, and use chiptune sounds and elements in other multilayered and multitextured compositions. Chip music was reborn with a new, harder sound, less influenced by video gaming than by other contemporary musical sounds: dubstep, house, glitch, and reggae.

Around chip music has grown all of those things you might expect of a vibrant musical scene. Small gigs coalesced into chip festivals. Online record labels, *netlabels*, emerged to distribute the music to a growing legion of chiptune fans and to sell the merchandise that comes with fandom. Boutique synthesizer manufacturers started building hardware and software instruments to cater to the growing band of musicians who wanted to write music in the 8-bit style but without the hassle of hacking antique hardware, an approach the scene has dubbed *fakebit*.

As this musical subculture has grown, chip music has begun to rub shoulders more and more with the mainstream. Live rock bands playing cover versions of video game tunes, crossover acts, movie soundtracks, television advertisements, and major exhibitions all suggest a growing acceptance of chip music, alongside 8-bit video game art and animation, as a legitimate form of cultural and artistic expression. Even Iron

Maiden, those stalwarts of the New Wave of British Heavy Metal, have embraced the sound, launching their 2015 album *Book of Souls* with an NES-style game, complete with a chip-style 8-bit arrangement of the band's song *Speed of Light* that plays in the background.[16]

To explore this dimension of chip music, we have to delve into the events and personalities that surround the music, its performers, and its fans. I'll present direct perspectives from those who have been a part of the chip community in all its forms and at different points in time, so as to explore the very different attitudes and outlooks of those who are rooted in video games, those who come from the demoscene, and those who have adopted the chiptune aesthetic as a form of self-identity and expression.

In chapters 7 through 9, I will explore the different aspects of the contemporary chipscene, not just live performance of original music on obsolete hardware but also the economies that have grown up around it; the different ways the chip sound has been interpreted and reexpressed and how that sound has been incorporated into more mainstream forms of musical expression. Chapter 7 examines the Game Boy and how it turned chiptune from a desktop activity into something that could be taken onstage. Chapter 8 explores the growth of netlabels and events to support the performance and distribution of chip music, while chapter 9 focuses on the reinterpretation of classic video game music, from Nintendocore bands riffing on vintage NES themes to YouTube artists performing a cappella versions of the same. Finally, in chapter 10, I will conclude by looking at that uncomfortable point where the chipscene meets the mainstream, and I will consider what the future might hold.

Where Do You Get Your Crazy Ideas From?

The comedian Richard Herring runs an award-winning podcast, *Richard Herring's Leicester Square Theatre Podcast*, in which he engages fellow performers and public figures in conversation, allowing listeners simply to indulge in the delights of eavesdropping on a meandering colloquy between two interesting—and invariably entertaining—people. Herring has a stock of refreshingly puerile emergency questions that he rolls out in each episode, which serve to break down the barriers between audience, interviewer, and interviewee and which he asks without prejudice. As a result, his interviews are affectionate, forthright, fascinating, and very funny.

Herring is an insider in the world of comedy and he makes no secret of his fondness for his interviewees. He has no agenda other than to find out more about them and engage them in dialogue. In that comfortable, open space, his questions unearth some fascinating insights. Famously, when he asked the British national treasure 'What's it like to be Stephen Fry?'—a question that had been posed by the twelve-year-old son of Herring's producer—it prompted Fry to reveal how he had attempted suicide the previous year with a lethal cocktail of pills and vodka.[17]

Yet it's an approach that hasn't always worked. Herring had the opportunity to pose a question to the legendary comic Richard Pryor before he died. Herring says:

> The thing comedians are consistently asked is: 'Where do you get your crazy ideas from?' It's a dumb thing to ask and is pretty much impossible to answer.
>
> Thinking Pryor would understand that a comedian would never seriously ask another comedian this facile question, I thought it might be funny to do so. Surely he'd come back with a funny and knowing response and maybe congratulate me on my subversiveness and acknowledge me as his equal and heir. But he clearly missed my post-modern irony because he replied wearily and correctly, with dismissive brevity: 'From life'.[18]

Yet wouldn't we all, secretly, like to ask exactly that of those whose work we admire, so that we might better understand the relationship between artist and artefact? While there is a romance around creativity, the idea that creative works are somehow plucked from the ether is just plain wrong. Romance tells us nothing of the experience, expertise, innovative play, and hard work that shape creative practice, and in this book I hope to shed a little light on the nature of how all four have collectively shaped the direction, the practice, and the sound of chip music.

Over the last few years, I have had the pleasure of meeting and chatting with all manner of interesting people, from the inventor of Mattel's Autorace, the world's first handheld video game, through to the teen musicians who are even now hacking and making music with gaming hardware that was already obsolete years before they were born. I have asked all of them where they get their crazy ideas from, and what is presented here is the distillation of their responses, woven together into the story that follows.

We begin with a two-player arcade game that used blocks for graphics ... and for sound.

The Atari VCS
The Rise of the Machines

It all starts with *Pong*.

Pong wasn't the first arcade game. In fact, Pong wasn't even the first arcade game with sound, but it managed to do something that none of its predecessors had: it domesticated video gaming.

Before Pong, the domain of the video game was very firmly the university computing lab; the hardware required to run games ran to tens or hundreds of thousands of dollars and lay beyond the reach of even the most committed home enthusiasts.

It was one such lab, Brookhaven National Laboratory in Upton, New York, where, in 1958, William Higinbotham decided that the annual open day needed livening up. Working on a Donner Model 30 Analog Computer, Higinbotham created *Tennis for Two*, a two-player bat-and-ball game that was displayed on a five-inch oscilloscope and controlled using two rotational dial controllers with buttons that provided the game's only auditory feedback, a satisfying mechanical click during play. Although the graphics were limited to a streak of green light bouncing back and forth over a vertical net, the motion of the ball was smooth and believable, and the game was addictive. Hundreds of visitors queued out the door and along the corridor for a turn to play.[1]

Three years later, Digital Equipment Corporation (DEC) gifted a prototype PDP-1 computer to MIT. The PDP-1 was housed in the Kluge Room on the second floor of Building 26 and straightaway became a hub for MIT staff and students.[2]

Jack Dennis, a member of the computing faculty, allowed his undergraduates quite a bit of latitude when it came to developing software for the new machine, an approach that was rewarded with a number of notable innovations, including the world's first word processor, the literally named Expensive Typewriter.[3]

There was a lot of discussion amongst the students about how best to use the computing power that the PDP-1 offered, and that talk turned quickly to games. Steve 'Slug'

Russell, Martin Graetz, and Wayne Wiitanen, three computing undergraduates, were keen to develop something that would push the new hardware to its limits: 'Wayne said, "Look, you need action and you need some kind of skill level. It should be a game where you have to control things moving around on the scope, like, oh, spaceships. Something like an explorer game, or a race or contest … a fight, maybe?" "SPACEWAR!" shouted Slug and I'.[4] And thus was born the shoot-'em-up.

Working alongside the trio was Peter Samson, an engineering undergraduate, who had developed a scrolling star field, the Expensive Planetarium,[5] that was used as a backdrop in the game. Samson was also a keen musician. A lover of Bach, he had developed an interest in computer music while working with Jack Dennis on the TX-0, the PDP-1's predecessor at MIT.

Initially, Samson devised a music compiler that converted high-level commands into monophonic pitch sequences, an experience he describes as like playing 'an absurdly expensive musical instrument on which you could improvise [and] compose'.[6]

When the PDP-1 arrived, he began work on developing an enhanced version of his music compiler, extending its capabilities to provide four simultaneous channels of 1-bit sound from the hardware.

Data entry was text-based, with music entered as strings of characters punched on eight-channel paper tape in FIO-DEC code, a proprietary ASCII-style code that was used to encode text characters for input and output.[7] Although experimental computer music was happening elsewhere—Max Mathews, for example, had developed his MUSIC 1 system at Bell Labs in 1957[8]—the execution of the music often required lengthy precalculations, taking hours of computer time before it could be played. Samson's compiler was one of the first that synthesised sound in real time, and to demonstrate the capabilities of his new Harmony Compiler, he began transcribing Bach fugues into code.

The music of the PDP-1 was raspy and coarse, but it was a new and compelling voice, and, although it would be a few more years before this voice echoed in the virtual space of video games, it hinted at how those games might sound.

Meanwhile, the reputation of *Spacewar!* had spread as the game found its way to the other computer labs across the country that ran PDP-1s. One of these was the lab at the University of Utah, where the game caught the attention of a young electrical engineer called Nolan Bushnell.

Convinced that there was some commercial potential in the game, Bushnell spent the best part of the next decade trying to make a version of it simple enough to run on cheap and easily accessible hardware. He moved to California and took a job in Ampex's advanced technology division, working on the game in his spare time with his friend and colleague Ted Dabney. The result was *Computer Space*, which Bushnell and Dabney sold to a relatively unknown arcade manufacturer, Bill Nutting Associates, in 1971.[9]

To keep costs low, Dabney had designed the Computer Space prototype around a domestic television display, using a state machine made of 7400-series transistor-transistor logic chips and diode arrays for the graphics and bringing an aural dimension to the gameplay with a range of monophonic beeps, rocket thrusts, missile screams, and explosions.

The game was built into a fibreglass cabinet, whose funky metallic paintjob and flowing curves are as of-the-moment as Bootsy Collins's star-shaped shades and bass guitar or the iconic Rover that chased Patrick McGoohan across the Welsh sands in the classic TV series *The Prisoner*.

As innovative as the hardware design was, Computer Space proved to be just a little too complex for its time, and it wasn't a commercial success,[10] selling fewer than 1,000 units on a production run of 1,500. Undeterred, Bushnell proposed a remake of the game but demanded an ownership stake in Nutting Associates in return. Nutting refused, and Bushnell and Dabney left, each investing $250 in their new video game company, whose name, Atari, was taken from the ancient Chinese game Go, a position similar to a check in chess, where one player's stones are under imminent threat from their opponent's.

Bushnell and Dabney looked to Ampex to source engineering talent for their new firm, poaching Al Alcorn, who had worked with them there as a trainee, by telling him that Atari had a contract with General Electric to supply a home video game.[11] That nobody from General Electric ever called to check on progress didn't ever occur to Alcorn—he was too busy developing the prototype of Atari's new bat-and-ball game, Pong.

Alcorn threw himself into the project. He improved on Bushnell's initial design brief, adding a scoring system and complex ball dynamics. He purchased a $75 black-and-white television from Walgreens,[12] and he added some crude sound effects:

> Now the issue of sound.... People have talked about the sound, and I've seen articles written about how intelligently the sound was done and how appropriate the sound was. The truth is, I was running out of parts on the board. Nolan wanted the roar of a crowd of thousands—the approving roar of cheering people when you made a point. Ted Dabney told me to make a boo and a hiss when you lost a point, because for every winner there's a loser. I said, 'Screw it. I don't know how to make any one of those sounds. I don't have enough parts anyhow'. Since I had the wire wrapped on the scope, I poked around the sync generator to find an appropriate frequency or a tone. So those sounds were done in half a day. They were the sounds that were already in the machine.[13]

Almost by accident, then, the shape of video game sound had been defined, and it was square.

Out of the Tavern and into the Lounge

With a Pong prototype up and running, Bushnell decided to test the game on the customers of Andy Capp's Tavern, a bar in Sunnyvale, California. He installed the machine alongside a Computer Space cabinet that was already in play there. Pong's simpler, competitive two-player gameplay made it an instant hit, and the machine quickly became a social hub; players would load up on food and drinks and watch others when they weren't playing themselves. A fortnight after they had installed Pong, Alcorn got a call from the manager at Andy Capp's to say that the machine had stopped working. When he went to investigate, he opened the coin box and quarters spilled out; the jammed coin mechanism had clearly caused the problem.[14] Pong was literally a victim of its own success.

With a hit on their hands, Atari pushed Pong into full production, and by the end of 1974 had filled orders for more than 8,000 cabinets. Hungry for success, Bushnell began to look for new markets to exploit. Arcade video games were lucrative, but they were largely displacing older gaming technology, diverting the flow of coins from electromechanical pinball machines to video game cabinets without significantly increasing the overall take.[15] Bushnell realized that he could do just that by taking Pong from the tavern to the living room, and in 1975 Atari partnered with Sears and released a domestic version of Pong.

Sensing a buck to be made, other manufacturers jumped in with their own versions of the game, causing a wave of competition that turned into a flood with the release of General Instrument's AY-3-8500 Ball & Paddle integrated circuit, a commodity chip designed by two engineers from Glenrothes in Scotland that allowed all comers to enter the video game market with their own repackaged bat-and-ball games.[16]

One machine, however, stood out from the rest. Fairchild's Channel F Video Entertainment System (VES) was no single-play home Pong clone; it was based around a core console that could load and play different games from swappable cartridges. Inside was a programmable microprocessor, Fairchild's own 8-bit F8, running at 1.79 MHz; 64 bytes of core RAM; and 2 kB of video RAM, supporting a 128 x 64 pixel display.[17] Sound was limited to just three discrete beep frequencies at 120, 500, and 1,000 Hz, and although these could be modulated to provide different tones, the sound generator was used mainly for special effects.

Bushnell loved the concept and appointed a group of engineers led by Jay Miner to design a similar console, one he hoped would be a VES-beater. The development team didn't have the in-house chip design expertise of Fairchild, so they licensed one from rivals, MOS Technology, the 6507, a cut-down, cheaper variant of the company's 8-bit 6502.

Designing the hardware to support the processor wasn't a problem, but the cost of tooling up to manufacture the machine in sufficient quantities to go head to head with Fairchild was. Atari found itself cash-strapped and had to be bailed out. Its saviour was Manny Gerard, the executive vice president of Warner Communications, who, with Bushnell, in 1976, drew up an agreement on the back of a restaurant napkin for a $32 million Warner buyout of Atari.[18]

Warner's cash injection enabled Atari to complete its Video Computer System (VCS; fig. 1.1), and the console launched late in the summer of 1977.

FIGURE 1.1 The Atari VCS 'Woody', which launched in the summer of 1977.

Racing the Beam

In the mid-1970s, RAM was prohibitively expensive, costing tens of thousands of dollars per MB.[19] Thus, to keep the VCS cost-competitive, the designers were forced to devise a hardware architecture that relied on memory as little as possible. That meant coming up with a radical approach to the display.

Nearly every console and computer uses a *framebuffer*, an area of RAM that's used to cache a full image of the display in memory before uploading it in its entirety to the screen. Even a monochrome display similar in size to Fairchild's would have required around 1 kB of video memory to store each complete frame of data in a framebuffer, pushing up the cost of the system beyond Bushnell's target price point.

Atari's solution was novel, although many programmers would perhaps describe it in more pejorative terms. Rather than sending a complete image of each frame to the screen, Atari created a graphics chip that removed the need for a framebuffer by building the image directly, a line at a time, on the cathode ray screen as its electron gun slewed from side to side, carrying out the game processing in the moments that the electron gun was turned off as it transitioned between vertical lines. The cost saving on video memory shifted the responsibility for the video display from hardware to the game code, a complex process that is still known in game programming folklore as *racing the beam*.[20]

Alongside this complex display mechanism were two independent audio circuits, also synced to the display, whose output was multiplexed with the display components and sent to the television speakers via a radio frequency modulator. This was the Television Interface Adaptor (TIA; fig. 1.2).

The oscillators on the TIA were basic, providing just one bit of resolution, that is, they could be either fully on or fully off, with nothing in between, but they were capable of producing a range of different pitched and noise tones.

Now it might not be immediately obvious that flipping the state of a sound generator between its fully on and fully off positions could generate anything other than square waves, let alone a range of different tones, but by sending different sequences of ones and zeroes, that is, a *binary waveform*, to the digital-to-analogue converter, quite a variety of tones is possible.

The most obvious way of generating an audio wave at a particular frequency on a 1-bit device would be to send the sound generator a stream of ones followed by an equal number of zeroes. Repeating this cycle over and over creates a continuous tone whose period, and therefore frequency, is determined by the number of ones and zeroes in each cycle. Increasing the number of ones and zeroes increases the period and so lowers the pitch, and vice versa. The result is a *square wave* (see fig. 1.3).

FIGURE 1.2 The TIA chip from Atari's VCS.

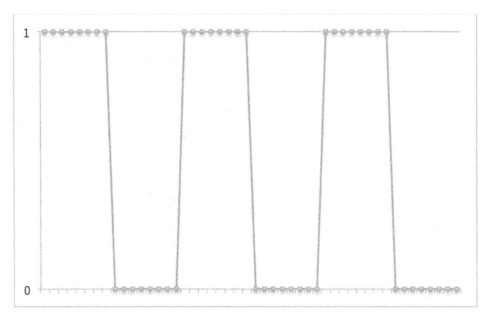

FIGURE 1.3 A square wave is formed by sending a 1-bit sound device a repeating sequence of ones followed by an equal number of zeroes.

The square wave is not, however, the only waveform that you can create this way. Suppose that, rather than sending an equal number of ones and zeroes to the speaker, you send a sequence of ones followed by three times as many zeroes. This is a *pulse wave* (fig. 1.4), an asymmetrical version of the square wave, with a sound that is similar to but distinct from it. In this case, 25 percent of the pulse is made from ones, and the rest from zeroes, so we say that the pulse wave has a duty cycle of 25 percent.

You could further reduce the number of ones in each cycle to create smaller and smaller duty cycles, varying the frequency spectrum and tone of the sound, until you send the sound generator just a single bit followed by a sequence of zeroes. This signal is a *binary impulse* (fig. 1.5), and it contains all possible frequencies in equal strength, something that is characteristic of noise.

This was the approach taken in the TIA to create different timbres; by sending the chip different combinations of ones and zeroes, it could create a range of these binary waveforms.

To save on memory, rather than store a series of complex binary waveforms in RAM, the TIA generated them in real time using a nine-stage *linear feedback shift register* (LFSR); a simple computing device made up of a series of memory registers, it calculates its next input as a linear function of its current state before shifting the contents of each register to the next in series and outputting the state of the last register in the chain.[21]

In general, an LFSR generates its next input bit by reading, or *tapping*, the state of the current registers and calculating their sum using an exclusive OR (XOR) operation,

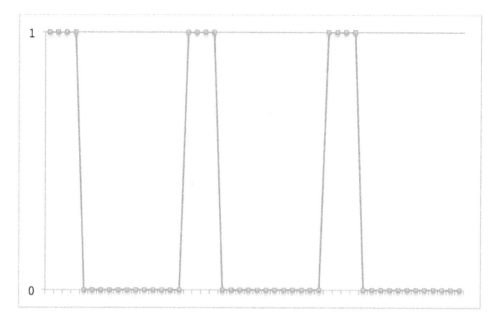

FIGURE 1.4 A pulse wave is formed by sending a 1-bit sound device a repeating asymmetric sequence of ones and zeroes. In this instance, there are three times as many zeroes as ones, creating a pulse wave with duty cycle of 25 percent.

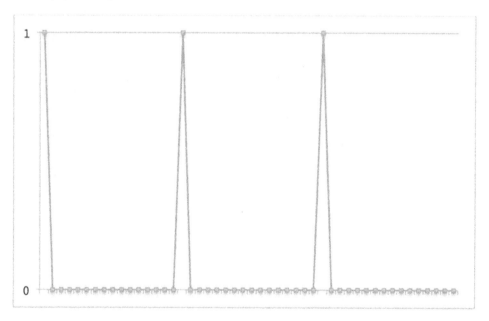

FIGURE 1.5 Sending the speaker a one followed by a series of zeroes generates an impulse. Sequencing a series of impulses one after the other creates a binary impulse train, a buzzy tone that contains all harmonics at equal strength.

resulting in a continuous bitstream that depends on both the initial state of the registers and the way they combine to form the new input. Inevitably, of course, the output sequence of the LFSR must repeat at some point, because there are only a finite number of ways its registers can be configured—2^n for an n-stage register, in fact—and, because the next input of the LFSR is determined by the current state, as soon as it hits a state that has appeared before it is fated, like Sisyphus, to repeat the same sequence of events over and over.

But how quickly should that repetition come around? Those 2^n possible states of the shift register certainly suggest an upper limit for the output sequence, but in fact the longest sequence an n-stage LFSR can produce has the length 2^n-1, since the all-zero configuration will always result in zero as the next input, generating the trivial sequence 0000000 . . .

These maximum-length sequences, or *M-sequences*, turn out to have a number of very useful properties. In particular, they share many characteristics with randomly generated sequences, although of course they aren't really random at all—the sequence is entirely deterministic. This is what's called a *pseudorandom sequence*, and it's close enough to true randomness to create a sound that's very similar to white noise when it's used to flip the state of a speaker in sequence.

The TIA uses a nine-stage LFSR to generate its binary waveforms, meaning that its sequences can extend to a maximum of 511 bits before repeating. By tapping different registers, the TIA can generate binary waveforms of varying length that range from silence to noise. It uses a pair of 4-bit audio control registers, AUDC0 and AUDC1, one for each of the two channels, to select the different LFSR taps, as detailed in table 1.1.

The shifts in the LFSRs are synchronized to a frequency select circuit, which generates clock pulses from the horizontal video sync counter. A **phase-alternating line** (PAL) system, with 312 video scanlines operating at 50 Hz, gives a master clock of 31.2 kHz, while NTSC systems, with 262 scanlines operating at 60 Hz, have a master clock of 31.44 kHz: a PAL VCS will play slightly flat compared to an NTSC console.

This clock frequency is then sent to a frequency divider circuit, which uses a 5-bit frequency register to divide down the master clock to give 32 possible pitch values, arranged as a subharmonic series.

The actual frequency of each tone depends on two factors, the 5-bit frequency register value and the length of the sequence generated by the LFSR—longer sequences increase the period of the waveform and so decrease its frequency. Setting the audio control register to 1, for example, generates an output sequence of length 15, giving an upper frequency of 2,096 Hz and a lower frequency of 65.5 Hz for an NTSC VCS, and 2080 Hz and 65 Hz for a PAL model. Similarly, setting the audio control register to 4 generates a square wave, specified by the bit sequence 10, resulting in an upper frequency of 15,720 (15,600) Hz and a lower frequency of 491.3 (487.5) Hz. Table 1.2 shows the tuning chart for Distortion 1, a 15-bit-long waveform generated by tapping the shift register on bit numbers 2 and 3.

There are a couple of things to note here. First, the differences in the master clock signal result in different sets of useable pitches for PAL and NTSC consoles as some tones are flattened closer to neighbouring pitches. This, though, is really just an issue of nomenclature. More significantly, some tones—see pitch numbers 27 and 28, for example—double up pitches, although just as significantly, neither tone is particularly close to the desired pitch.

TABLE 1.1. The 16 audio control codes used to select the TIA's binary waveforms, or *distortions*, and the associated LFSRs that are used to generate them.

Distortion type	Mechanism	Description
0 & 11	Sets the output value to continuous high	This setting generates a bias signal, driving the speaker to a static position of maximum displacement while activated. This can be used as a 4-bit sample playback engine.
1	Generates a 15-bit output sequence using a four-stage shift register with taps on the third and fourth bits.	This setting generates a complex pitched tone with qualities similar to those of a classic sawtooth wave.
2	Generates a 465-bit output sequence by clocking the Distortion 1 sequence to the Distortion 6 output sequence, with the Distortion 1 output updating every time the Distortion 6 sequence transitions from high to low or vice versa. The effect is to extend the duration of each output bit by a factor of 18 or 13.	Distortion 2 generates a low-pitched rumble.
3	Combines a five-stage shift register, with taps on the third and fifth bits, and the four-stage shift register of Distortion 1 to generate a 465-bit sequence. The five-stage register updates continuously. The 4-bit register updates only when the 5-bit register outputs high. The output of the four-stage register is used to generate the audio waveform.	This pulsing noise tone is the classic TIA 'engine' sound, used, for example, for the tanks in Atari's Combat.
4, 5, 12, & 13	Generates a 2-bit sequence of alternating high and low bits. When Distortion 12 or 13 is selected, the sequence updates every third clock tick, dropping the pitch to a lower frequency range.	These settings generate a classic binary square wave.
6, 10, & 14	Uses the five-stage shift register of Distortion 3 to generate a 31-bit sequence whose state flips from high to low and vice versa whenever the four least significant bits are equal. This generates a stream of 18 ones followed by 13 zeroes. When Distortion 14 is chosen, the sequence updates every third clock tick.	The asymmetric distribution of the bit sequence creates a classic pulse wave with duty cycle 58 percent.
7, 9, & 15	Generates a 31-bit sequence from the output of the five-stage shift register. When Distortion 15 is chosen, the sequence updates every third clock tick.	This setting generates a harmonically rich buzz tone, which provided the log sound in Activision's Pitfall.
8	Generates a maximal-length 511-bit sequence from the output of a nine-stage shift register with taps on the fifth and ninth bits.	The pseudorandom sequence generated from the nine-stage register is used as the TIA's white noise signal.

This isn't really an issue with divide-down tone generation per se; rather, it's a direct consequence of the TIA's limited implementation of it.

Divide-down frequency networks of this sort have a long history of use,[22] but most implementations rely on a very high-frequency master clock as the timing source and a

TABLE 1.2. Frequency table for Distortion 1, a 15-bit-long binary waveform, showing the corresponding discrepancy from equal temperament in cents.

Pitch number	Frequency (NTSC)	Pitch	Discrepancy (NTSC)	Frequency (PAL)	Pitch	Discrepancy (PAL)
0	2096	C7	2.48	2080	C7	−10.79
1	1048	C6	2.48	1040	C6	−10.79
2	698.67	F5	0.52	693.33	F5	−12.75
3	524	C5	2.48	520	C5	−10.79
4	419.2	G#4	16.16	416	G#4	2.9
5	349.33	F4	0.52	346.67	F4	−12.75
6	299.43	D4	33.65	297.14	D4	20.38
7	262	C4	2.48	260	C4	−10.79
8	232.89	A#3	−1.43	231.11	A#3	−14.7
9	209.6	G#3	16.16	208	G#3	2.9
10	190.55	F#3	−48.84	189.09	F#3	37.89
11	174.67	F3	0.52	173.33	F3	−12.75
12	161.23	E3	−38.05	160	D#3	48.68
13	149.71	D3	33.65	148.57	D3	20.38
14	139.73	C#3	14.21	138.67	C#3	0.94
15	131	C3	2.48	130	C3	−10.79
16	123.29	B2	−2.48	122.35	B2	−15.75
17	116.44	A#2	−1.43	115.56	A#2	−14.7
18	110.32	A2	4.96	109.47	A2	−8.3
19	104.8	G#2	16.16	104	G#2	2.9
20	99.81	G2	31.7	99.05	G2	18.43
21	95.27	G2	−48.84	94.55	F#2	37.89
22	91.13	F#2	−25.8	90.43	F#2	−39.06
23	87.33	F2	0.52	86.67	F2	−12.75
24	83.84	E2	29.85	83.2	E2	16.58
25	80.62	E2	−38.05	80	D#2	48.68
26	77.63	D#2	−3.39	77.04	D#2	−16.66
27	74.86	D2	33.65	74.29	D2	20.38
28	72.28	D2	−27.1	71.72	D2	−40.37
29	69.87	C#2	14.21	69.33	C#2	0.94
30	67.61	C#2	−42.56	67.1	C2	44.17
31	65.5	C2	2.48	65	C2	−10.79

much higher resolution for the divisors. Without either of these, the TIA didn't just have a limited number of pitches to choose from; many of them ended up being forced badly out of tune relative to their equally tempered counterparts. As a consequence, melodies played on the TIA will sound, if we are well-disposed towards the chip, exotic, and if we are not, utterly discordant. But spend a little time with the TIA, and its quirky voice grows on you. After all, equal temperament is, itself, a tuning compromise.

For the ancient Greeks and Renaissance scholars, the musical ideal was *just intonation*, a system of tuning based around the frequency ratios of the harmonic series.[23] Starting from the fundamental, the second harmonic, at a frequency ratio of 2:1, is exactly one octave higher. The next, at a ratio of 3:2, is a perfect fifth higher again. Lowering this note by an octave—halving its frequency—retunes it to within the same octave as the other two notes. Continuing like this, we can derive all of the notes of the just diatonic scale as shown in table 1.3.

Tuned like this, the scale sounds beautifully sonorous, but when we shift from the bottom C to the next note up, D, we begin to see the limitations of just intonation as a coherent system of tuning. The perfect fifth between D and A is now only 680 cents wide instead of the true 702 cents, like that between C and G, and it sounds dreadfully flat. An instrument tuned justly like this will sound mellifluous provided the music doesn't stray too far from the I, IV, and V chords of the root key, but the moment it starts to venture further afield it will sound awful.

The solution was to arrive at some sort of tuning compromise. Some notes of the scale were deliberately detuned, or *tempered*, losing a degree of pitch accuracy in order to get a better harmonic balance overall. As they prioritize different tuning goals, different tuning systems have different characteristic strengths and weaknesses.

The Pythagorean scale, for example, is built around repeated applications of the perfect fifth interval. The cycle of fifths is a concept familiar to many musicians. It captures a sense of natural harmonic motion and is often used to gauge the harmonic distance between chords. Considered as a set of discrete pitches, the cycle of fifths also provides a means of tuning the notes of a chromatic scale, since, if we start on any note and move successively up by a perfect fifth, we visit each note of the chromatic scale in turn before finally reaching the original note some eight octaves higher. We can then use this to form a single-octave scale by transposing individual notes up or down by octaves until all lie within the same octave range. Starting on C gives the diatonic scale illustrated in table 1.4.

TABLE 1.3. The notes of the just diatonic scale starting on C, with intervals measured in cents, a unit of measurement equal to one-hundredth of an equally tempered semitone.

Note name	C	D	E	F	G	A	B	C'
Ratio	1:1	9:8	5:4	4:3	3:2	5:3	15:8	2:1
Cents	0	204	386	498	702	884	1088	1200

TABLE 1.4. A diatonic scale can be derived from repeated applications of the perfect fifth.

Note name	C	D	E	F	G	A	B	C'
Cents	0	203.9	407.8	521.5	702	905.9	1109.8	1223.5

There is a problem, though. The frequency of that top C is sharp. It's around 23 cents too high—the octave we derive from repeated applications of the perfect fifth is around a quarter of a semitone wider than the true octave. The solution to this was quarter-comma meantone tuning, which compromised the tuning by flattening the fifths by one-quarter of a *syntonic comma*—the difference between four justly tuned perfect fifths, and two octaves plus a justly tuned major third, and equal to about 21 cents—so as to ensure that the major thirds are accurately tuned.

This system works reasonably well, but as before, because 12 perfect fifths, each flattened by a quarter of a syntonic comma, do not add up to an exact number of octaves, one of the fifths in the scale is forced very badly out of tune. This is the *wolf interval*, so called because the interval 'howls like a wolf' when played.[24]

Thus, although quarter-comma meantone tuning broadens the harmonic range of the instrument while maintaining the just tuning of the major thirds, it's still limited in the number of keys that are playable. This restriction lay behind the subsequent development of the *well temperaments*, for which J. S. Bach wrote his famous *48 Preludes and Fugues*, and, later, the *equal temperament*, as composers and players looked to broaden their harmonic range still further.

It's interesting to note, however, that although these new methods of tuning allow much greater flexibility of modulation, for equal temperament in particular, all of the component intervals except the octave are forced out of tune relative to just intonation, with the major third in particular becoming very sharp. It's something we don't consciously register, since equal temperament has become the cultural norm and our ears are conditioned to it from the moment we start to become musically aware, but while quarter-comma meantone tuning sounds very bad in a few keys, equal temperament is equally bad in all. Provided you don't have to move very far from the tonal centre, quarter-comma meantone tuning is arguably the better compromise.

The composers of the time understood this and worked to the strengths of the tuning systems they used. Interestingly, exactly the same happened on the VCS; programmers quickly learned to use musical patterns that avoided the notes that sounded 'off'.

During a presentation at the Game Developer Conference in 2011, David Crane, the cofounder of Activision, explained that Garry Kitchen, who developed Activision's *Pressure Cooker*, worked out which of the nine notes the VCS could produce were reasonably in tune and marked them on a Casio keyboard. They hired a professional jingle writer to compose a melody for the game, as transcribed and illustrated in figure 1.6, using only the marked notes.[25] The TIA forced the composer's hand but, by good fortune, forced it towards a classic major I-IV-V progression.

Although the TIA's tone generator was only 1-bit, it did offer 16 levels of volume control via two 4-bit volume registers, AUDV0 and AUDV1, one of which applied to each of the TIA's two channels. The digital output from the tone generator is passed to four transistors in series, each twice as large as the previous one and controlled by one bit each from the relevant audio volume register, using good old analogue impedance to vary the output level.

FIGURE 1.6 The two-channel intro and in-game sequence to Atari's Pressure Cooker is a simple repeating I-IV-V riff that avoided the problematic tunings of the TIA by restricting the pitches used in the melody to those that were reasonably close to equal temperament.

This combination of 1-bit generation and a 4-bit digital-to-analogue converter allowed for some quite sophisticated control. Although Distortion 0 and Distortion 11 are silent when activated, they are silent only because they output a continuous stream of ones, driving the speaker to a continuously activated but static state. By varying the audio volume register over time, it is possible to create custom 4-bit sound samples, but because this uses up quite a bit of the VCS's available storage space and puts a significant load on the processor, it was only ever used as a special effect to top and tail gameplay.

In fact, the effect was only ever used in two original VCS cartridges, Bit Corp's *Open Sesame*, a PAL-only action platformer based loosely on the tales of the *Arabian Nights*, and Atari's own *Quadrun*, one of the rarest VCS cartridges, since it was only available as a limited run by mail order through the Atari Club.

Quadrun chants 'Quadrun! Quadrun! Quadrun!' at the start of each level, the voice pitch-shifting up each time until it becomes almost unintelligible. Such were the demands on the system that the Atari's screen had to blank as the speech played because it used all of the power of the CPU and every spare byte of memory. 'I think some audio guy from the outside was trying to sell us some sort of audio tool that we didn't buy', programmer Steve Woita recalls. 'I guess that may've got me to thinking about putting voice in the game, so Frank Hausman had some weird tools that he and I worked on to do the audio compression. I did some weird 6502 tricks to pull off the voice. We got my voice data down to 700 or so bytes and then I would just pitch bend my voice more and more as you progressed through the game'.[26]

Later homebrew games—independent titles that were developed after the VCS was discontinued and were no longer constrained by such a tiny amount of memory—featured more sophisticated sampling. One notable retrofit is a hack of the 1982 arcade port *Berzerk*. Coded by Mike Mika, *Berzerk Voice Enhanced* adds speech samples from the arcade game, along with other tweaks to the colour scheme and artwork that give the game more of the feel of the original coin-op. It has far and away the best speech of any VCS game, such being the benefits of a little extra cartridge memory.

The Early Game Carts

The VCS launched in September 1977, and those kids lucky enough to find one under the Christmas tree that year would have opened the box to find the console, two joysticks, a pair of paddle controllers, and a copy of *Combat*, a simple player-on-player game that was very much in the mould of Pong and offered 27 different gameplay variants based around *Tank; Tank-Pong; Invisible Tank; Biplane*; and *Jet Fighter*.

Combat's importance lay not so much in its playability or originality as in the fact that it came bundled with the VCS, making it the first experience most players had of the system and, in turn, shaping their expectations of VCS gaming. The label '27 Video Games' on the cartridge cover suggested value and variety, and the two-player combat mode helped to establish the idea, helped along by the Atari Family Tree television commercial,[27] that it was a social device, something every generation of the family could enjoy together.

Combat's soundtrack featured only sound effects, playing up to the TIA's strengths but in the process establishing right from the outset that the VCS just didn't do music very well, something that Steve Wright, Atari's director of special programs, acknowledged: 'The 2600 was never designed to do music', he recalls. '[It was like] a piano with a bunch of broken keys'.[28]

In fact, of the nine original launch titles for the VCS, only *Basic Math*, an educational game that challenged the player to solve basic arithmetic problems—the challenge arising mainly from the use of the joystick to enter numerical values—featured any music at all. Two musical stings, one to reward a correct answer and one to signal an error, were used as the primary auditory feedback.

It was *Asteroids* in 1981 that introduced VCS gamers to the sound of in-game music, but even then it was little more than a repeating monophonic two-note theme that brings to mind the bass ostinato of John Williams's *Jaws Theme*. The music, simple as it is, is surprisingly effective. It increases in tempo as the game progresses, helping to pace the gameplay and increase the tension, similarly to Taito's arcade classic *Space Invaders*.

It was a formula that carried over to other popular cartridges. Imagic's *Demon Attack*, for example, uses the ascending notes of a major scale to signal player progress as each wave of demons attack, and Bit Corp's *Open Sesame* uses a series of ascending four-note modal motifs to impart a sense of growing urgency as the player climbs towards the cave at the top of the screen.

By 1982, the VCS had already played host to a number of arcade ports, and generally the games aped the functional nature of the arcade music it sought to recreate. Music was used mainly for intros and event-driven stings, and developers used the limited tonal and frequency range of the two-channel TIA to mimic the original musical themes from the arcades as closely as possible. Atari's *Pole Position*, for example, recreates the opening fanfare and the sound of the lights of Namco's coin-op but condenses the two treble parts of the coin-op into one and simplifies the rhythm slightly, while dropping its speech synthesis and the opening flourish to save memory.

It was fairly common for arcade ports to simplify both the graphics and the sound in the conversion process. At times, this had little impact on the game beyond losing a little musical detail while the strong gameplay shone through. The Parker Brothers' *Frogger* cartridge, for example, was universally praised for David Lamkins's two-channel rendition of the Frogger theme at the start of each level, but it still loses the in-game music during play. Coleco's *Mr. Do!*, on the other hand, strips both the music and the graphics of the coin-op back to such an extent that the VCS port bears little resemblance to the original, with only the isolated ascending notes of the major scale surviving to accompany the titular hero as he gathers cherries. The two-channel end theme in particular, with its loose timing and limited range of notes, highlights the limitations of the VCS as a music platform.

Gottlieb's coin-op, *Q*Bert*, an Escherian isometric platform game, used an MOS Technology 6502 chip, the bigger sibling of the 6507 that beat at the heart of the VCS, to generate the game's sound and a phoneme-based Votrax SC01 speech synthesizer to generate Q*Bert's famous expletives. Much of the arcade game's unique charm comes from the incoherent babble that is spat out of the speech synthesizer. According to David Thiel, the sound engineer responsible for programming the SC01's phonemes, trying to encourage the chip to produce coherent and recognisable speech was a long and frustrating process: 'We wanted the game to say, "You have gotten 10,000 bonus points", and the closest I came to it after an entire day would be "bogus points". Being very frustrated with this, I said, "Well, screw it. What if I just stick random numbers in the chip instead of all this highly authored stuff, what happens?" '[29]

What happened was a characteristic garble that matched Q*Bert's speech bubble perfectly. Without this, the VCS version loses much of its endearing character. Video Games magazine noted: 'those people who are going to be buying the Atari 2600 version may find themselves just a little disappointed', largely because the 'chatter of the original's voice synthesizer has, by necessity, been replaced by inarticulate squawks, while the music, with the exception of a few ineptly executed themes, has been totally excised'.[30]

Dig Dug took the idea of the game-synced soundtrack to a new level. Released in Japan by Namco in 1982 and distributed in the United States by Atari, the coin-op sees the eponymous character tunnelling in a subterranean world. Armed with little more than a bicycle pump, Dig Dug fights the fire-breathing, dragon-like Fygars and the Pookas, cute little creatures that resemble beachballs in sunglasses. The arcade game's cute graphics belie its aggressive gameplay, an illusion completed by the bouncy soundtrack that chirps away beneath the action. Video Game's review notes that the 'translation from the arcade original, if a little less detailed, is accurate. The sound track, featuring the infectious Dig Dug theme, is wonderful'.[31]

Yuriko Keino's music in the arcade version begins with a catchy intro sting as Dig Dug enters the playfield from the top right of the screen and tunnels down to begin the game. Figure 1.7 shows how the original score and the Atari VCS implementation compare. The Atari version is slightly slower and is pitched a major third higher. It also loses the two-bar intro to minimize the memory requirements. The flavour of the original track, however, is still there.

There is a real art to arranging music like this, a minimalistic distillation of the essence of the original track into just one or two channels, and Dig Dug manages to capture the spirit of the original track as well as the limitations of the hardware allow.

FIGURE 1.7 The original arcade (top) and Atari VCS (bottom) intros to Dig Dug. The VCS soundtrack is slightly slower, is pitched a major third higher, and loses the two-bar lead-in of the arcade version yet retains the overall feel of the track.

Indeed, the VCS tuning serves to emphasize the tritone interval in bar 3, giving it a little more bite before it resolves in the final bar.

Both versions tie the in-game soundtrack (fig. 1.8) to the player's movements, playing the music back only when the player moves the joystick and vamping with a warning siren when the player stands still for any length of time. There is one important difference, though: the arcade music maintains musical continuity, picking up the theme from where it left off when the player moves, while the VCS version restarts the theme from the beginning.

When all but one of the baddies have been dispatched, the music transitions into a double-time chase sequence of the main game theme, a device that would later be used by Koji Kondo in his Mario soundtrack.

Dig Dug succeeds where Mr. Do! and Q*bert fail because although it simplifies the soundtrack to suit the limitations of the VCS, it manages to hit the Goldilocks spot, neither simplifying so much that the musical detail and character of the original is lost nor burdening the system with such complex music that it struggles to cope and has to make concessions in other areas. Dig Dug uses both channels of the TIA to maintain a continuous two-channel soundtrack throughout the game, maintaining the sense of driving bass line and chirpy melody from the arcade and using 'voice-stealing'—dropping the melody line momentarily to free up a playback channel—to handle the synchronous in-game sound effects.

FIGURE 1.8 The main game loop from the arcade (top) and VCS (bottom) versions of Dig Dug. The concessions to memory can be clearly seen: the VCS theme is only four bars long, and the rhythm has been simplified, losing the bass pedal point in the process.

A New Dawn?

Although sales of the VCS and its cartridges were strong, by 1982 its hardware was looking decidedly dated alongside the competition, particularly that from newcomers like Mattel's Intellivision and the ColecoVision. Atari responded with a new console based on its line of 8-bit computers, which were also fighting to become popular gaming platforms in their own right.

The new console was named the Atari 5200 Super System to sow the idea in the minds of consumers that it was twice as powerful as the VCS, which, by that time, had been renamed the 2600.[32] The 5200 was intended to be the top-end machine in a new three-console line-up alongside the VCS and a new midrange console, the 3200. However, because the architecture of the 5200 was very similar to that of the Atari 400,[33] and thus easy to produce, it was fast-tracked, and the 3200 was quietly dropped.[34]

The 5200 was based around a custom MOS 6502C processor running at 1.79 MHz, meaning that although it was technically compatible with the 6507 processor in the VCS, the higher clock speed would have meant that games would run too quickly, and backwards compatibility was only possible with a plug-in adaptor that included its own 6507.

Graphics were handled by a combination of the Alphanumeric Television Interface Controller (ANTIC) and the Graphics Television Interface Adaptor. Sound was controlled using a new combined function chip, the Pot Keyboard Integrated Circuit (POKEY), which also handled input from the controllers.

The POKEY supports up to four audio channels, each with its own frequency, noise, and volume controls, and uses methods of tone generation and control similar to those of the TIA. An 8-bit frequency control register is used to control a frequency divider on each channel to determine pitch. The four frequency dividers can be clocked together to either a 64 kHz or 15 kHz master clock, but in addition, dividers 1 and 3 can also be clocked from the main CPU clock (1.79 MHz NTSC, 1.77 MHz PAL), with dividers 2 and 4 clocked from the output of dividers 1 and 3, effectively stacking the frequency dividers and allowing the POKEY to operate with two channels of sound at 16-bit frequency precision, or one 16-bit and two 8-bit channels in place of the default four 8-bit channels.[35]

A 4-bit volume control circuit is placed at the output of each channel. As with the TIA, POKEY allows for a fully-on waveform, which enables the creation of custom 4-bit samples by successively writing values to the volume control circuit while the fully-on waveform is being triggered.

The audio output of channels 1 and 2 can be routed through a high-pass filter, a D-type flip-flop and XOR gate, whose cutoff frequency is determined by the frequency divider of channels 3 and 4, and which compares the input with the sound in the reference channel, using this to set the cutoff frequency.

Compared to the TIA, the POKEY was a world apart: still distinctive yet more controllable and with a range of features that allows much more interesting music to pour out of it. Less successful, however, were the 5200's game controllers. The machine was shipped with a 360-degree noncentring analogue joystick, which was touted as offering more control than the old eight-way digital joystick controller that was offered with the Atari 2600.[36] The reality, however, was that the new joystick was awkward to use and very unreliable.[37] Poor build quality mated to an overly complex mechanical design left gamers frustrated, and although a number of aftermarket alternatives became available, the 5200's reputation was badly dented.

Many of its games were enhanced versions of VCS titles—*Super Breakout*, for example, an enhanced version of the VCS classic, came bundled with the system—and many potential customers looking for a more technically enhanced gaming experience migrated to the ColecoVision, whose bundled port of Nintendo's *Donkey Kong* was far closer to the arcade game than anything Atari could offer. The 5200 was discontinued in 1984 after just two years on the market, and the POKEY, which offered far more potential for musical expression than the TIA, and might even have given Commodore's mighty **sound interface device** (SID) a run for its money, was silenced without ever really being given the opportunity to sing.

Life in the Old Dog Yet

Atari was not alone in recognizing the limitations of the VCS as a platform. By mid-1982, several third-party manufacturers had begun to explore the possibilities of expanding its hardware by including additional memory and sound hardware on the game cartridges themselves.

The first of these was Starpath's Supercharger. Released in 1982, it was an expansion peripheral that plugged into the cartridge slot of the VCS and loaded games from audio cassette by connecting an audio cable on the side of the cartridge to the earphone jack of an external tape player.[38] With an extra 6 kB of memory on-board—almost 50 times that of the VCS's on-board 128 bytes—the Supercharger meant bigger games, better graphics, and better music.

The games for the Supercharger were generally enhanced clones of existing ones. *Rabbit Transit*, for example, fuses together elements of Frogger and Q*bert. *Communist Mutants from Space* borrows heavily from *Galaxians*. *The Official Frogger* picks up where the Parker Brothers title left off, providing a gaming experience much more like that of the original coin-op and including a varied selection of musical jingles that accompany gameplay throughout.

There were also some interesting original titles. *Escape from the Mindmaster*, for example, is a first-person perspective 3D maze game that uses interactive sound effects as a navigational aid, one of the first examples of sound being used as a key gameplay driver rather than as a reactive supporting element. *Dragonstomper*, a pre-*Zelda* RPG, is remarkably ambitious for its time and is perhaps the finest example of the genre on the VCS.

Around this time, Activision released *Pitfall!*, an action platformer in which the player controls Pitfall Harry, a character styled along the lines of Indiana Jones, who has to recover treasure from a crocodile- and scorpion-infested jungle.

The origins of the game are rooted in 1979, a time of unrest and disenfranchisement amongst Atari employees. Atari was making $100 million each year from cartridge sales and following the replacement of Nolan Bushnell by Ray Kassar at the head of the company had become much more corporate, something that was reflected in the dress code, which evolved from jeans and open-collared shirts to sharp pinstriped suits in a matter of months.

The engineers began to voice concern that Atari was losing touch with its creative roots. Kassar responded by dramatically cutting research and development budgets, telling the game designers that they were no more important to the success of the company than the people on the assembly line who put the cartridges together, and describing them as a 'bunch of high-strung prima-donnas'.[39]

Four of Atari's most successful game designers—Larry Kaplan, Alan Miller, Bob Whitehead, and David Crane—grew increasingly frustrated by the lack of recognition, both creatively and financially, and left to form Activision with music industry executive Jim Levy, whose approach was to promote the games like album releases and treat the programmers like rock stars.[40]

Before leaving Atari, Crane had been working on a technology that displayed and animated a little running man character and had been looking for a game to house it. At Atari, the emphasis had always been on bringing Atari's arcade games into the home. Activision didn't own or have the rights to any arcade hits, so Crane had no option but to design original game content to house the little running man.

The concept came about in 10 minutes, early in 1982. Crane sat with a pencil and paper and put his little running man on a path. Where was the path? In the jungle, of course! *Raiders of the Lost Ark* had been released the previous year and had taken the country by storm. The idea of hopping across crocodiles came from an old Heckle and Jeckle cartoon.[41]

The concept, a mash-up of pop culture ideas, was the easy bit. The technical challenge of developing that game concept on the VCS, however, was something else. Coding the game took around 1,000 hours, and the technical accomplishments extended beyond the flicker-free animation of Harry. Crane repurposed existing sprites for the background canopy of trees and for the swinging vines, and by using a procedural method to encode the levels, all 256 screens of the game could be squeezed into just 50 bytes of code.

With so much game packed into so little memory, it's remarkable that Crane had any room for music at all, but Pitfall! features a few key event-driven musical effects: the ominous opening riff to Walter Schumann's Dragnet punctuates Harry's demise, and a musical nod in the direction of Johnny Weissmuller's ululating jungle call can be heard each time Harry grabs a rope swing.

A sequel followed hot on the heels of an animated segment on CBS's Saturday Supercade that also introduced two new characters to the Pitfall family, Harry's niece, Rhonda, and Quickclaw, his cowardly pet mountain lion.[42] Crane wanted the gameplay of *Pitfall II: Lost Caverns* to extend the scope of the original, but Activision had really pushed the hardware of the VCS about as far as it could go. To take it further, Crane began to explore the idea of adding extra hardware inside the game cartridge.

He designed a new chip, the Display Processor Chip, a custom device that worked like a coprocessor, taking on many of the game's simple, repetitive calculations. It could generate three independent channels of music, summing multiple individual virtual channels to give an output mix and then feeding the resulting digital waveform into the volume registers on the VCS to create a lo-fi sampled music track on one of the TIA audio channels. Because this sample playback required just the one channel, it meant that all three channels of the music could play continuously without the need for note stealing if sound effects were required on the second channel.

The music in the game builds on that of Pitfall!, adding to the key event-driven musical cues with a continuous in-game soundtrack that arranges elements of the music from the Pitfall cartoon as the main game theme. The death theme is a dirge-like variation of the main theme, and an arrangement of the trapeze artists' favourite *Sobre las Olas* is used to accompany Harry's balloon flights.

'Right before we published someone asked if we had the rights to the music', Crane recalls. 'We had people humming the music into answering machines all over the country. Nobody knew. When I related this story that night to my wife, a classically-trained musician, she said "Are you kidding? That song is called 'Over the Waves', or 'Sobre Las Olas'"…. She went on to name the composer and said "I might have the sheet music around here"'.[43]

Without a doubt, Pitfall II was one of the most ambitious games the VCS had seen, largely thanks to the Display Processor Chip breathing new life into the ageing platform. Crane had hoped that the chip could be licensed to other manufacturers, but VCS cartridge sales slumped soon after the game's launch, and the demand disappeared. It never featured in another commercial release.

Atari, too, was beginning to recognize the importance of music in games. In March 1983, they hired professional composer Ed Bogas as a musical consultant.[44] A San Franciscan, Bogas had begun his musical career as a keyboard player with the psychedelic rock band The United States of America before moving into scoring for film and television, writing the music for the Peanuts series after Vince Guaraldi's death in 1976. His entry into the video games industry was very much a case of being the right person in the right place at the right time; when Atari licensed video games based on Charles Schultz's characters, Bogas was the natural choice to provide the music.

Bogas worked closely with the game designers at Atari. As is still common in video games, the music was added towards the end of the production once the gameplay and the visuals were reasonably complete, giving Bogas the time and the opportunity to reflect on how best to represent the experience of play. He brought an important level of musical insight to the role, recognizing that music that is designed to be played over and over again has to be rich but also nonintrusive. He began to play around with layers of sound that cycled over one another at slightly different rates, creating shifting musical textures that introduced variety without adding significantly to the memory requirements.

The first game to feature Bogas's work was *Snoopy and the Red Baron*, which sees the player controlling Snoopy sitting astride the roof of his kennel as he patrols a Defender-style scrolling landscape on the tail of the Red Baron. Stylistically, the music is a revelation. Clearly taking its lead from Peanuts, the title music features a rolling bassline that conjures up Guaraldi's *Linus & Lucy*, while the level start theme riffs on Wagner's *Ride of the Valkyries*. As inventive as the music is, however, the title music in particular suffers from the terrible tuning of the TIA.

The most significant aspect of this was not so much the soundtrack itself but what it represented. It signalled the growing influence of music on video games—proper music rather than just 'bleeps'—and Atari's hiring of an established film composer fully a year before Nintendo hired its first full-time composer, Koji Kondo, points to the beginning of the convergence between video game production and the studio model of movie production.

Before then, game development had been much less nuanced. Typically a single engineer would be given a rough play concept and would code the game, shading the squares on a piece of graph paper with coloured pencils to create the graphics and sequencing simple short melodies to provide the music. The first wave of professionalization of game design saw artists beginning to specialize in sprite design, starting with Imagic's Demon Attack in 1982.[45] The role of the professional game artist emerged as visuals evolved from the simple block graphics of games like Combat to the more sophisticated and suggestive sprites of Snoopy, who is instantly recognizable in the game, lending it a contextual authenticity that was rare in licensed games of the time.

Music was slower to follow suit, due in part to the prominence of graphics in showcasing and marketing games, but the role of the video game composer slowly began to professionalize too.

Ed Anderson, manager of manufacturing at Namco America, began pushing the idea of combining music and video gameplay in coin-ops as early as 1977, having grown frustrated with companies who 'used to just throw in the music on top without much thought. They would ask in-house if anyone played the piano and then they'd just drop in a few notes here and there. But consumers get wise fast and they hear so much music on radio, TV and the movies, and they can tell the difference. They want that professionalism in video games'.[46] His magnum opus can be heard in Exidy's arcade game *Venture*, which features multiple complex narrative musical sequences, arranged as fragments, that bring to mind the cartoon style of Carl Stalling of Warner Bros.

Game Over

From its launch, the VCS enjoyed a complex relationship with the arcades. On the one hand Bushnell had always been keen to break the link between video games and the sleazy image that parents associated with arcades, bars, and pool halls. On the other hand the success of the VCS depended on leveraging the reputation of game titles that had proven themselves in those same sleazy arcades. Of the nine titles available at launch, all but two had their roots in arcade games, either lifting or adapting elements from popular Atari coin-ops.

The quality of the games varied. The VCS port of Taito's *Space Invaders*, for example, the first cross-company arcade-to-home license, became the first 'killer app' on the platform, offering players a fairly authentic arcade experience at home, but even then the first signs of a classic bubble were beginning to show.

The phenomenal success of Space Invaders sowed the idea that anything that was packaged as a video game could sell, and poor-quality games based on the most tenuous of tie-ins started to find their way into stores. Atari, for example, released *Video Cube*, a video-game version of the Rubik's Cube, apparently confident that people would pay 10 times as much for the digital version of a puzzle that played better as a collection of plastic parts and stickers.

Nevertheless, Atari's hopes were high for its 1982 conversion of Namco's coin-op smash hit *Pac-Man*. Too high, perhaps.

At a time when Atari estimated that there were around 10 million VCS consoles in use, the company manufactured 12 million Pac-Man cartridges, confident that demand for the game would drive sales of both cartridges and consoles.[47] The licensing deal cost Atari $1 million, and they were keen to get the game to market quickly to capitalize on Christmas sales, so Pac-Man was fast-tracked.[48]

Atari programmer Todd Frye developed the game from a maze game prototype he had been working on when Atari acquired the game rights to Pac-Man. In an attempt to simplify the arcade game enough to realize it on the VCS hardware, Frye straightened out the rounded edges of the coin-op's maze and pills and dropped the Pac-Man theme with its flamenco-style half-step modulations in favour of a much shorter, featureless dirge at the start of play (fig. 1.9). The directional animation of Pac-Man was also dropped, and the ghosts, Inky, Blinky, Pinky, and Clyde, were not just indistinguishable but flickered as they moved, making playing the game a visually fatiguing experience.

Pac-Man had lost his personality. Although early sales were strong, racking up around 7 million units, that still left Atari with millions of unsold copies. In an article for Video and Arcade Games, Danny Goodman noted that the port was a challenging maze game in its own right.[49] But players expected, and had been sold, a game that was much closer to the original. Atari, in an attempt to keep players from migrating to ColecoVision to satiate their Pac-Mania, had run newspaper ads at the tail end of 1981 advertising an arcade experience, and VCS Pac-Man was but a pale imitation of the coin-op.

This may have been at the back of Atari's mind when it followed its adverts with a classic piece of marketing understatement in their 1982 cartridge catalogue, noting that Pac-Man 'differs slightly from the original'. Frank Ballouz, marketing manager for

FIGURE 1.9 Namco's original Pac-Man theme (top) and the VCS version (bottom).

Atari, was less coy: 'I took a look at this bullshit game and told Ray [Kassar] that no one's going to want to play it'.[50]

The critical reception was damning. Next Generation magazine described it as the 'single worst coin-op conversion of all time'.[51] In the rush to market, Atari was eroding a consumer confidence and brand loyalty that just a year earlier had seemed unshakeable.

Undaunted, Atari and Warner Communications pressed ahead with their next big-ticket release and looked towards movie franchise tie-ins, thinking that the public would eagerly buy into games that came with a ready-made image and recognition factor.

Steve Ross, then head of Warner and keen to build a relationship with director Steven Spielberg, felt confident enough of Atari's ability to shift cartridges to offer Spielberg a $25 million royalty for the video game rights to his next movie, *E.T.*, regardless of how the game sold.[52] The licensing deal was completed in July 1982, leaving just six weeks to design and code, manufacture, package, and market the game ahead of the Christmas rush.

It was a disaster.

Atari manufactured 5 million cartridges, and although the game sold strongly in the runup to Christmas, once customers actually started playing it and realized how bad it really was, nearly all of these purchases were returned for refunds. With a stockpile of millions of cartridges, Atari racked up $536 million in losses. With no hope of selling them, they were dumped in a landfill in the New Mexico desert and covered with concrete.[53]

The video game bubble had burst.

The ZX Spectrum
The Sound of One Bit

While the Atari VCS swept across America, it failed to make quite the same impact on the other side of the Atlantic. The VCS and other Pong clones, like the Grandstand series of television consoles, had a solid user base in the United Kingdom, but it was the launch of the first home computer kits towards the end of the 1970s that really caught the British imagination, tapping into its Heath Robinson (Rube Goldberg)–esque sense of technical creativity.

The UK has always had a strong hobbyist community, for whom the idea of carefully assembling and soldering the thousands of component parts that made up those early kits not only posed no problem but was actively appealing. It was against this backdrop that Science of Cambridge, later to become Sinclair Research Ltd, launched the Microcomputer Kit 14, or MK14 (fig. 2.1) in February 1978 as a 'minimum cost computer'.[1]

There is a definite sense of familiarity about the design of the MK14. The form factor and layout echoes Sinclair's calculators, and its conductive rubber keys would later provide the template for the ZX80 and ZX81. Although there was no on-board sound, an optional cassette interface added a 4.6 kHz square wave oscillator to generate audio tones as a means of data storage on external analogue compact cassette tape.[2]

Cheap though it was—the £39.95 price point was described by Practical Electronics as 'a landmark of … unassailable proportions'[3]—the MK14 looked primitive alongside its contemporaries, the Commodore PET and Apple II. Nevertheless, it sold well enough to justify a successor, named the ZX80 for its 3.25 MHz Zilog Z80 processor, with an added X to denote a magical X-factor.[4]

The ZX80 really was a landmark machine. Not only was it the first useable computer to retail at below £100, but it had a built-in keyboard and radio frequency modulator, which enabled it to be connected to a domestic television set for display. Sinclair

FIGURE 2.1 The Science of Cambridge MK14 had a form factor and interface that showed a clear lineage from the company's handheld LED calculators and was an important first step in the development of mass home computing. Image edited from an original supplied by Dan Birch.

incorporated the MK14's tape interface directly onto the ZX80's motherboard, providing two 3.5-millimeter jack sockets, labelled EAR and MIC, to read and write data from and to compact cassette tape. Although it was a great improvement over its predecessor, building a machine to such a tight budget inevitably meant that there were design compromises. With no video hardware to support the CPU, the display would frequently flicker and fade as the processor dropped video control to work on other tasks.

Following the broadcast of *The Mighty Micro*,[5] a ground-breaking television documentary series about the developing computer revolution, the BBC's Further Education Department began to take a real interest in the burgeoning home computer market and established the BBC Computer Literacy Project, a series of television and radio programmes that would be based around a BBC-branded microcomputer.[6]

The project was initially scheduled for launch in the autumn of 1981, which left little time for the BBC to develop its own microcomputer in-house. Instead, the BBC collaborated with another Cambridge-based firm, Newbury Labs, to draw up a specification for the BBC Microcomputer. This spec matched very closely that of Newbury's own NewBrain, the intention being, presumably, that Newbury Labs would pick up the BBC contract. As the project developed, however, it became clear that Newbury Labs was not going to be able to produce a machine to spec, and the company didn't tender.[7] The BBC was forced to postpone the Computer Literacy Project and broadened their search for a partner. Sinclair pitched the ZX81 (fig 2.2).

FIGURE 2.2 The Sinclair ZX81 became the first really successful microcomputer in the United Kingdom, selling through national newsagent chains.

Already under development before the ZX80 launched, the ZX81 used a simpler, cheaper chipset that contained dedicated video circuitry to address the ZX80's screen fade. A bigger ROM chip—8 kB to the ZX80's 4 kB—allowed Sinclair to extend the new machine's functionality, adding floating point operations and trigonometric functions. Aside from the cassette interface, which could be co-opted by POKEing the memory from BASIC or with machine code programming to output simple melodies, the machine still lacked any on-board sound hardware, although external peripherals, like the BI-PAK ZON X-81 Sound Module,[8] which allowed users to dabble with micro music making by adding a three-channel PSG and a built-in loudspeaker, were available soon after launch.

Sinclair lost out on the BBC contract to rival Acorn,[9] but the ZX81 was pushed hard by the national newsagent chain WHSmith, who had an exclusive contract to supply the machine for six months. It sold by the thousands.

Growing support from the popular press and a burgeoning mail-order games marketplace grew the market for the machine, so that when the ZX Spectrum (fig. 2.3) launched the following year, Sinclair had an established user base and an army of independent developers selling through a national network of retail outlets.

FIGURE 2.3 The Sinclair ZX Spectrum, the machine that kickstarted the home computer craze in the United Kingdom, taking it from the hobbyist market to the mainstream.

Free to specify its own components and price point, Sinclair was able to design a compact and powerful computer that was much more competitively priced than its rivals, undercutting the Acorn-designed BBC Model B by over £200 at launch.[10] With the Computer Literacy Project giving the machine free marketing by pushing the very idea of the home computer as a tool for learning, thousands of parents bought into the idea and gave the cheaper ZX Spectrum a home.

Even for its time, the ZX Spectrum was a simple machine. Available in two guises, both models had 16 kB of ROM and either 16 or 48 kB of RAM. It was Sinclair's first machine to feature a true on-board sound interface, albeit a rudimentary one. The introductory booklet that was bundled with the machine claimed, rather optimistically perhaps, that the 'ZX Spectrum can make sounds of an infinite variety'.[11] Most users, however, would have realized fairly quickly that the on-board 22-millimeter, 40-ohm 'beeper' speaker (fig. 2.4), which provided just a single channel of 1-bit playback across a 10-octave range, couldn't do much except 'beep'.

To compound matters, all of the sound commands were managed directly by the main CPU, a Zilog Z80A processor running at 3.5 MHz, and a custom Ferranti Uncommitted Logic Array chip, and so driving the speaker tied up the processor. This meant that while the Spectrum was beeping, it couldn't, without some very clever machine code programming, do very much else.

FIGURE 2.4 The 22-millimeter speaker from a 1983 Issue 4B Sinclair ZX Spectrum, which provided just a single channel of 1-bit sound.

BEEP

Little wonder, then, that few of the early Spectrum titles featured much in the way of sound. *Football Manager*, one of the first big commercial successes on the platform, is fairly typical of the period. Originally developed as a text-only game for the Tandy TRS-80, Football Manager was ported to the Spectrum to make use of its colour graphics and sound. Simple isometric block graphics are used to display cut-scene match highlights, punctuated by rudimentary sound effects at key points in the action: a random tone sequence when a goal was scored and a series of low-frequency blips to accompany attempts at goal.

Football Manager was written entirely in BASIC, Sinclair's version of which came preloaded into the machine's ROM. For many, this was their introduction not only to programming but also to computer music.

Spectrum BASIC offers a single audio opcode, BEEP, which takes two arguments, a duration expressed in seconds and a relative pitch, measured in semitones (or fractions of semitones) from middle C (C4). The code of example 2.1 plays a two-second tone on C4.

Using the BEEP command and the note values outlined in table 2.1, it is a fairly straight-forward, if tedious, process to transcribe simple melody lines into BASIC commands.

Each line of code in Spectrum BASIC is preceded by a line number for reference. Multiple commands can be combined in one line of code using a colon to separate them.

EXAMPLE 2.1. This Spectrum BASIC command plays a 2-second square wave tone on middle C.

```
BEEP 2,0
```

TABLE 2.1. Table of note numbers for the BEEP command.

Octave	Note numbers											
	C	C#	D	D#	E	F	F#	G	G#	A	A#	B
−1	−60	−59	−58	−57	−56	−55	−54	−53	−52	−51	−50	−49
0	−48	−47	−46	−45	−44	−43	−42	−41	−40	−39	−38	−37
1	−36	−35	−34	−33	−32	−31	−30	−29	−28	−27	−26	−25
2	−24	−23	−22	−21	−20	−19	−18	−17	−16	−15	−14	−13
3	−12	−11	−10	−9	−8	−7	−6	−5	−4	−3	−2	−1
4	0	1	2	3	4	5	6	7	8	9	10	11
5	12	13	14	15	16	17	18	19	20	21	22	23
6	24	25	26	27	28	29	30	31	32	33	34	.35
7	36	37	38	39	40	41	42	43	44	45	46	47
8	48	49	50	51	52	53	54	55	56	57	58	59
9	60	61	62	63	64	65	66	67	68	69		

EXAMPLE 2.2. Playing a major scale, starting on C, in Spectrum BASIC.

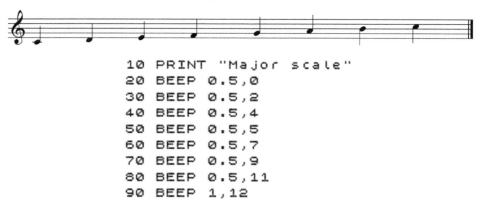

```
10 PRINT "Major scale"
20 BEEP 0.5,0
30 BEEP 0.5,2
40 BEEP 0.5,4
50 BEEP 0.5,5
60 BEEP 0.5,7
70 BEEP 0.5,9
80 BEEP 0.5,11
90 BEEP 1,12
```

To create a simple major scale starting on C, for example, the notes of the scale are listed one after the other as shown in example 2.2.

Of course, because the note values are encoded numerically, it is possible to use simple procedural methods to generate note sequences, just as Toms did with the random tone sequence in Football Manager. Here, the goal sting, outlined in example 2.3, is created using the Spectrum's RND function, which generates a random number between 0 and 1. Line 20 defines a function, $r(x)$, which uses RND to generate a random

EXAMPLE 2.3. Using the RND function to play a random note sequence between C4 and C7.

```
10 PRINT "Football Manager Goal"
20 DEF FN r(x) = INT (RND*x+1)
30 FOR n = 1 TO 5 + FN r(5)
40 BEEP 0.05, FN r(36)
50 Next n
```

EXAMPLE 2.4. The nongoal sound effects from Football Manager.

```
10 PRINT "Football Manager Shoot"
20 BEEP 0.15, -40
30 PAUSE 0
40 CLEAR
50 PRINT "Football Manager Save"
60 BEEP 0.25, -50
70 PAUSE 0
80 CLEAR
90 PRINT "Football Manager Miss"
100 BEEP 0.15, -30: BEEP 0.08, -40
```

integer between 1 and the variable value *x*. Lines 30 and 50 create a loop of between six and ten notes, and line 40 generates a 50-millisecond square wave tone on a random pitch between C#4 and C7.

The other sound effects in the game are all achieved using simple BEEP commands in low registers (see example. 2.4).

Rests could be programmed using the PAUSE command, but that caused the Spectrum to stop computing for a duration specified in display frames, each corresponding to around 20 milliseconds, tying up the processor and limiting its use as a background process.

Two into One Does Go ...

Spectrum BASIC, then, provided a very straightforward way for novices to control the sound hardware, and it was the way many musicians, myself included, trod their first, tentative steps into the complex and murky waters of computer music. But sound on the Spectrum was limited; it was about as low-tech as electronic sound can possibly get, and because it was an interpreted language—that is, programs were decoded and executed a line at a time—it was agonizingly slow. Nevertheless, with a bit of planning and the right sort of musical material, it was possible to move beyond simple monophonic lines to create at least the suggestion of an accompaniment part alongside the melody by switching sequentially between the two.

To illustrate, figure 2.5 shows the opening four bars of Beethoven's piano bagatelle *Für Elise*.

As written, there's a clear delineation between the right-hand melody line and the left-hand accompaniment. The two parts alternate, overlapping only on the first beat of

poco moto

FIGURE 2.5 The opening four bars of Beethoven's *Für Elise*.

poco moto

FIGURE 2.6 Arranging the score for monophonic playback.

EXAMPLE 2.5. Suggesting alternating movement between melody and accompaniment in Spectrum BASIC.

```
10 PRINT "Fur Elise"
20 BEEP 0.25,16: BEEP 0.25,15
30 BEEP 0.25,16: BEEP 0.25,15: BEEP
0.25,16: BEEP 0.25,11: BEEP 0.25,14: BEEP
0.25,12
40 BEEP 0.25,9: BEEP 0.25,-8: BEEP 0.25,-
3: BEEP 0.25, 0: BEEP 0.25, 4: BEEP 0.25,9
50 BEEP 0.25,11: BEEP 0.25,-8: BEEP 0.25,-
4: BEEP 0.25,4:BEEP 0.25,8: BEEP -.25,11
60 BEEP 0.25,12: BEEP 0.25, -8: BEEP 0.5,-
3
```

bars 2, 3, and 4, and the accompaniment is orchestrated as a series of arpeggiated chords. Dropping the first note of each of these left-hand patterns, as shown in figure 2.6, makes it possible to retain something of the character of the original piece while playing it in single notes. Of course, the tonal richness created by applying the pedalling as marked is lost in this monophonic arrangement, as is the dynamic marking of pianissimo, since there is no way to alter the level of the beeper. Nevertheless, you can maintain the suggestion of two simultaneous alternating parts using just a single channel of playback.

The translation into Spectrum BASIC is fairly straightforward. Using 16 (E5) as the starting pitch and a semiquaver duration of 0.25 second, corresponding to a tempo of 60 beats per minute, we get the code of example 2.5.

The potential of Für Elise did not go unnoticed by game developers. *Timebomb*, an unlicensed port of the coin-op game *Check Man*, for example, plays a similar monophonic arrangement one note at a time as the player character moves around the screen, and Perfection Software used it as the main title music in its first release, *Turtle Timewarp*.

This repurposing of existing musical themes was not uncommon in the early days of gaming. Most of those early Spectrum games were developed by an individual, often a teenager in a bedroom, in fact, who would create the graphics, gameplay, sound, and machine code single-handedly. Quick turnarounds often meant that the coder would adapt whatever musical material was close to hand and with little regard to copyrights.

Elite's *Chuckie Egg*, for example, features the melody from *Dance Little Birds (The Birdie Song)*[12] by the Tweets, itself a cover of Werner Thomas's accordion tune, as its title music. Interestingly, the melody modulates—not unpleasantly—down by a tone in the last two bars, the result, perhaps, of a transcription or encoding error. The game also features the *Romance d'Amour* each time a life is lost, a theme that is also used in both the arcade game *Phoenix* and in *Pheenix,* an early Spectrum clone by Megadoo.

Pyjamarama, the second of Micro-Gen's Wally series, was initially released with an arrangement of Gershon Kingsley's synth-pop hit *Popcorn* as the title music.[13] A second release of the game, which differed only in the title music and in the addition of a demo play sequence, fuelled speculation that Micro-Gen had run into copyright issues and been forced to undertake a rewrite. Certainly, the next game in the series, *Everyone's a Wally*, had an original theme tune, a live version of which was performed by Mike Berry and included on the B-side of the game cassette. However, the next Wally title, *Herbert's Dummy Run*, again used a borrowed soundtrack, this time in the form of *Baby Face*.[14]

Sweevo's World features a beautifully orchestrated carousel-style medley of marches, beginning with *Blaze Away*,[15] before moving into Sousa's *Washington Post March*,[16] while Firebird's *The Wild Bunch*, which is loosely based on exploits of the nineteenth-century gang of outlaws rather than Sam Peckinpah's 1969 film, raids Ennio Morricone's back catalogue, featuring the pipe organ theme *La Resa Dei Conti* as the musical segue into the game's showdown sequences.[17]

When I asked video game composer Ben Daglish about that wholesale lifting of material, he laughed and shook his head. 'Copyright?' he joked, 'What's that then? Listen, we had no idea as 15-year-old kids that copyright existed. Quite seriously, we really didn't. We had absolutely no idea that we weren't allowed to just take *Equinoxe 5*, or whatever, and put it in a game and sell it. To this day it amazes me that either Jean Michel Jarre never found out we were ripping off his music or he didn't care.'[18]

It was one such act of creative appropriation that lay behind Perfection Software's title *Fahrenheit 3000*. Perfection wanted a title theme that would make an impact as soon as the game loaded, and Peter Jones, one-half of the development team, suggested using Bach's *Toccata and Fugue in D minor*, which he had heard opening the movie *Rollerball*. Working from the sheet music of Sky's contemporary cover, Jones coded the five-minute beeper arrangement in BASIC, and his coding partner, Tim Williams, converted it to machine code for the final game.

What makes the music in Fahrenheit 3000 interesting isn't so much the arrangement, which doesn't quite stick faithfully to either the Bach or the Sky sources, as the choice of musical material itself. The opening statement of Bach's fugue (fig. 2.7) is a

FIGURE 2.7 The opening section of J. S. Bach's Organ Fugue in D minor creates a sense of two-voice polyphony by contrasting a repeated pedal note against a melody line.

sequence of semiquavers that alternate between the melody and an implied pedal point on A. The effect, particularly when played at speed, is to create a sense of two-voice polyphony by using the pedal note to continually reinforce that sense of the tonal centre against the melody, the simplest example, perhaps, of *virtual* or *implied polyphony*.

It's clear, particularly in the toccata section that opens the game, where concessions have been made in Jones's arrangement. The drama and the harmonic tension of the spread diminished seventh chord, which resolves back to the tonic major at the end of the opening section of Bach's toccata, for example, is completely lost when converted to a sequence of monophonic tones, but the remainder of the arrangement works well to create a sense of movement and implied harmony, and Jones incorporates elements of performance in the code, featuring rallantandi at the end of both the toccata and the fugue, an effect that was coded by systematically calculating note length augmentations.

Software Projects' *Jet Set Willy* features a similar technique in its arrangement of Beethoven's Piano Sonata no. 14, *Moonlight*. Using a pattern of broken octaves similar to the left-hand bass patterns of boogie-woogie piano, the arrangement (fig. 2.8) creates a sense of continuous movement between melody and accompaniment. The effect is striking, and it is easy to forget that there is nothing more complex at work than a sequence of monophonic square wave tones.

This approach, of sequentially alternating between melody and accompaniment to create a sense of two or more simultaneous parts separated in time, has its roots in the Baroque. In his *Prelude in B♭* from Book I of *The Well-Tempered Clavier* (fig. 2.9), Bach uses the same technique, delineating the right-hand triples from the staccato bass to provide both a sense of harmonic motion and melodic contour.

In this instance, however, Bach's approach is motivated more by the need to create dynamic contrast between these light, prancing figures and the denser and more dramatic chordal figures that follow than it is to suggest additional polyphonic lines. But in his Chaconne, for example, from Partita no. 2 in D minor for solo violin, BWV 1004, a wonderful example of musical architecture,[19] he again uses the technique, this time to explore alternate ways of voicing melodic and harmonic material given the physical constraints of the violin as an instrument.

On the Spectrum, Ben Daglish took the idea to its logical extreme with his soundtrack for Gremlin Graphics' 1987 Arkanoid clone *Krakout*, providing an implied bass, an accompaniment and melody, all played at breakneck speed. Part of the joy of working on a Spectrum, he recalls, was the sense of challenge it gave. It forced composers to look for ways to circumvent its limitations and find novel ways to introduce dynamic movement and musical interest.

FIGURE 2.8 Matthew Smith's arrangement of Beethoven's Piano Sonata no. 14 for Jet Set Willy uses broken octaves to imply a sense of accompanied melodic movement.

His earlier Spectrum port of *Thing Bounces Back* uses a similar approach but alternates between a bluesy bass vamp in broken octaves and a bright blues melody. The effect works in much the same way as a blues harpist alternating between vamping and soloing to self-accompany, making use of the listener's aural memory and strong sense of harmonic familiarity with the I-IV-V chord progression.

J. S. BACH

FIGURE 2.9 The opening two bars of Bach's Prelude no. 21 in B♭ from Book I of *The Well-Tempered Clavier* use similar intervallic jumps in rapid note sequences.

'It was just the obvious thing to do with a one-voice beeper', he says;

> once you've established the sequence, especially when it's an obvious chord
> sequence that an audience can pick up, and once you've gone round it a couple
> of times, then you'd sort of assume that people would still be hearing it. It's like
> a canon or something like that. Once you've established the bassline, you know
> that they're still hearing that in their minds while the melody plays. It only works
> for simple stuff, though, so there's only so far you can go with it. But yes, if you're
> using tropes, as it were, it's very effective.[20]

Going against the Grain

Although this inventive musical back-and-forth lifted the music of the Spectrum out
of monophonic rasps and dirges, it did little to challenge the machine's hardware.
Remember, calls to the beeper tied up the main processor, making in-game sound a real
technical challenge. Music, if it featured at all, was generally reserved for title screens,
and in-game sound effects were used sparingly.

Artic's *Invaders* was an unofficial clone of Taito's Space Invaders and features
graphics and a field of play that are nearly identical to the original coin-op. The soundtrack also mimics the original and uses a descending, four-note Dorian scale pattern
(see fig. 2.10) that repeats and gradually speeds up as the invaders are picked off one
by one.

This descending scale sequence plays continuously throughout the game, marking
the first use of a continuous nondiegetic in-game soundtrack on the Spectrum. So how
did Invaders achieve this feat? The solution was to think small.

FIGURE 2.10 The descending Dorian scale pattern from Artic's 1982 game Invaders.

Granular synthesis,[21] an approach to sound synthesis and manipulation, was posed initially by the Greek composer Iannis Xenakis, who built a composition, *Analogique B*, around hundreds of tiny fragments of magnetic tape.[22]

Conceptually, granular synthesis has its roots in quantum mechanics, the new physics of the twentieth century. Debate raged in scientific circles from the days of Christiaan Huygens and Isaac Newton as to whether light was a wave or a particle, until the early nineteenth century, when Thomas Young with his double-slit experiment was thought to have shown, fairly conclusively, that light behaved as a wave. Conclusively, that is, until Einstein's work on the photoelectric effect a hundred years later demonstrated beyond doubt that light really behaved like a particle.

Light, it seemed, behaved like a wave in some circumstances and like a particle in others, its behaviour changing, like a knowing child playing one parent off against another, depending on who was looking. This led to the concept of wave-particle duality. Einstein wrote:

> But what is light really? Is it a wave or a shower of photons? There seems no likelihood for forming a consistent description of the phenomena of light by a choice of only one of the two languages. It seems as though we must use sometimes the one theory and sometimes the other, while at times we may use either. We are faced with a new kind of difficulty. We have two contradictory pictures of reality; separately neither of them fully explains the phenomena of light, but together they do.[23]

Of course, the reach of the quantum doesn't really extend into the macroscopic world of sound, but conceptually, the idea of treating sound at some times as a continuous waveform and at others as a series of tiny sound quanta, or *grains*, opens up many interesting and creative ways of working. Time-stretch and pitch-shift, for example, which allow for the independent manipulation of tempo and pitch in recorded audio, depend fundamentally on the granularization of sound. Usually, these two parameters are inextricably linked: slow down the playback of a sound recording, and the pitch will drop proportionally. Granular synthesis enables the pitch and speed to be processed independently by applying the processing individually to sound grains before recombining them to construct the final sound output.

To investigate how Invaders uses sound grains to combine its in-game sound effects and continuous music soundtrack, we can disassemble the game code and examine its subroutines. The Z80 assembly details how programmer William Wray split the processor time between the main game events and the speaker, which would be flipped open for a single processor clock cycle and then closed, to create a binary impulse. By intelligently sequencing these impulses and building on the idea of virtual polyphony, Wray managed to create the illusion of multiple sound effects playing synchronously with the underscore.

Wray's routine uses a combination of prioritized scheduling, favouring the most prominent sound at any one time, and perceptual masking, to create the illusory continuity of tone across multiple channels played sequentially.[24] Aside from a slight lumpiness of the underscore caused by the prioritized sequencing of the soundtrack elements, and the curious omission of any sound effects for the player ship's laser fire, the game's soundtrack is very effective, not just referencing the original sound effects from the coin-op but also creating a real sense of continuous two- or three-channel sound.

It's in the Hall of the Mountain King

That idea was developed further by Matthew Smith, a figure who deservedly has a place in Spectrum folklore.

In 1983, the teenage Smith was loaned a Spectrum by the Liverpool-based publisher Bug Byte in order for him to develop three games. His first, *Styx*, was a fairly simple action maze game based around a single repeating screen that became progressively more difficult each time the player completed a level. His second game, *Manic Miner*, became a runaway success and introduced the Spectrum's first truly iconic character, Miner Willy.

Manic Miner was based on *Miner 2049er*, a platform game starring a Canadian Mountie, Bounty Bob, who has to navigate his way through 10 different screens before his oxygen runs out. Several elements of Miner 2049er appear in Manic Miner—the underground setting and the oxygen level as a timer, for example—but in creating Miner Willy, Smith injected a particularly British spin into the game, with a surreal humour to the level and character design and a Pythonesque boot that descends to squash Willy when the game is over.

To squeeze music into the gameplay, Smith granularized the melody, using a software interrupt to split the processor's time between the main game loop and the sound playback routine. Every cycle of the main loop, the program branches out to play a very short sound grain each time it executes. In a thematic nod towards the game narrative, Smith chose an eight-bar phrase from Grieg's *In the Hall of the Mountain King* as the music to accompany the gameplay and split each note into two, four, or eight grains (see fig. 2.11), leaving a gap of around 750 milliseconds between each, during which time all of the other code for the game was executed.

Smith also realized that rather than simply prioritizing sequential events, a granular approach made it possible to trigger sound effects simultaneously with the

FIGURE 2.11 Manic Miner's in-game melody. Each melody note is split into two, four, or eight sound grains separated by silence to distribute the processor load between in-game music and gameplay.

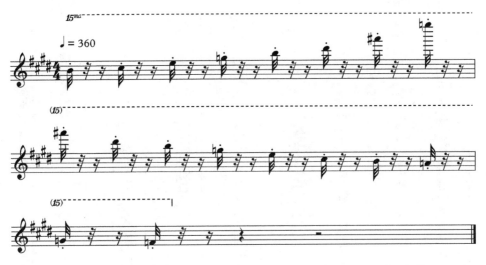

FIGURE 2.12 The jump sound effect in Manic Miner is an asymmetric sequence of melodic tones that display a distinctive rising and falling contour.

music by granularizing both and alternating between music and effect grains, slotting each fragment of the sound effect between those of the melody. Manic Miner has one main sound effect, the jump sound, notated in figure 2.12, which uses the familiar sound metaphor of the rising and falling pitch contour to suggest a sense of motion.

The sequence is offset from the melody and, when triggered, is interleaved with the in-game music, with each grain of the jump effect being triggered in the gaps between the melody grains (see fig. 2.13).

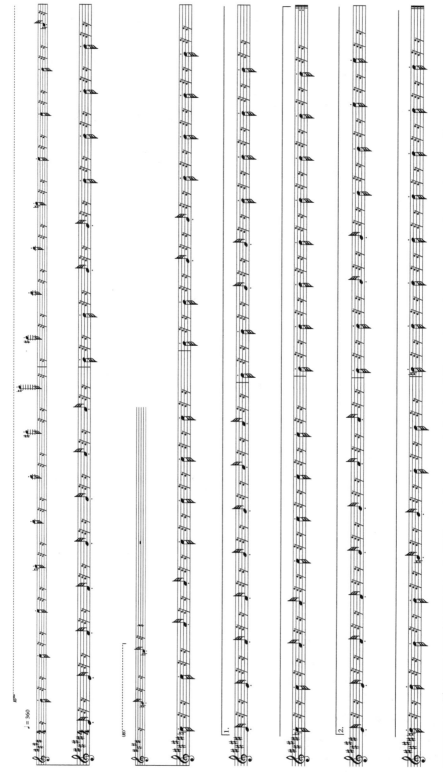

FIGURE 2.13 The jump sound is interleaved with the main in-game melody notes, falling on the semiquaver rests as shown. The jump effect can trigger at any point in the note sequence. This approach to virtual polyphony depends on the granularization of individual tones along with rapid alternation between different pitches.

Following the release of Manic Miner, granular in-game music became quite common. Smith used the technique again for the in-game music in Jet Set Willy. *Technician Ted*, a flip-screen platform game featuring the eponymous hero Ted Blewitt, a computer hacker who must complete twenty-one tasks before clocking off for the day, follows the musical formula of Manic Miner almost to the letter. The main title music is a monophonic version of *The Beautiful Blue Danube*, by Johann Strauss II, which also served as Miner Willy's main theme, while during the game a similar granular method is used to play the main thematic statement of Strauss's *Radetzky March* alongside synchronous object and jump sound effects.

Extending this idea further, it wasn't long before developers were using the technique to play two simultaneous musical lines by alternating between two grain pitches. *Rockman*, for example, features an arrangement of the first movement of Mozart's *Eine Kleine Nachtmusik*, although the use of 50-millisecond sound grains and lengthy intergrain silences results in an unconvincing polyphonic effect, in the same way that slowing a film sequence to below about 15 frames per second destroys the illusion of continuity of motion, and the viewer becomes aware of seeing a series of time-sampled images.

More successful was Imagine's port of the Konami coin-op *Yie Ar Kung Fu*, which uses the effect to play the main game stings in double octaves, and *Dynamite Dan*, which uses alternating and arpeggiated grain pitches to recreate Mozart's *Rondo a la Turca*. Durell Software featured two-channel granular music tracks on two of its 1986 releases, *Thanatos* and *Turbo Esprit*. The music on Turbo Esprit is a fine example of the technique, its Jan Hammer–styled melody complementing the Miami Vice–like gameplay perfectly.

All Aboard the Impulse Train!

Manic Miner is a rich seam that can be mined further still.

Not content with introducing a two-channel in-game soundtrack, Smith also coded a novel two-channel title tune. On loading, the game displays a dynamic title screen (see fig. 2.14), which shows the sun setting behind an idyllic clifftop house, below which an animated keyboard plays, pianola-style, the notes of a delightfully clangorous two-channel rendition of *On the Beautiful Blue Danube*. Although the music routine includes an algorithm that uses the note data to display the notes onscreen, the keyboard graphics use a short octave (C–E) to the left of middle C, making it almost impossible to use this as a visual point of reference for transcribing the music.

'The game needed music', Smith recalls, 'as I felt it was an integral part of the attraction. For the title song, I had an old, simple piano arrangement [of On the Beautiful Blue Danube] in sheet music, so it was easy to transcribe. I did everything as quickly as possible, got the loop running as fast as possible, but I never got too prissy about exact timings'.[25]

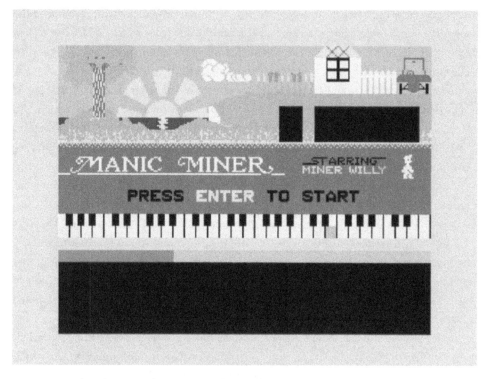

FIGURE 2.14 The title screen of Manic Miner, showing the short octave to the left of centre on the piano keyboard, making it nearly impossible to transcribe the music visually.

For that title music routine, Smith used binary impulse trains, storing the note data in memory as a series of ninety-five groups each containing three data bytes. Each triplet corresponds to a separate beat (or subbeat) in the arrangement, and each is encoded as a duration and a pair of pitch values, or more accurately, as counter values, which are used to calculate the period between successive impulses using the same sort of divide down synthesis that was used on the Atari VCS.

In Smith's music routine, the counter was updated on each cycle, so the timing of the music was determined by two factors: the clock speed of the Z80 CPU and the length of time the CPU took to execute each of the machine instructions in the loop. From these, Smith was able to construct a frequency table that mapped the notes of the musical arrangement to a series of counter values, and it was these values that provided the note data for his arrangement (see fig. 2.15).

He used two counters to calculate two simultaneous impulse trains, reading the counter values stored in the data triplets into two memory registers and using these to calculate the period between successive impulses, effectively interleaving the two impulse trains on playback to create two separate output channels. For single melody notes, he encoded the pitch as a pair of counter values separated by 1 to create a phasing effect. Chords are encoded as two distinct frequency values.

FIGURE 2.15 Matthew Smith's arrangement of Strauss's waltz *On the Beautiful Blue Danube.*

The phasing effect works well, creating a harmonically rich, time-varying tone on the single notes with a characteristic sweeping effect at the beat frequency. However, the chord tones, while interesting, are not entirely successful. Smith's routine lacks any amplitude enveloping, which means that successive notes tend to run into one another, losing any sense of articulation, which can be heard particularly from bar 25 until the end, when the sense of 3/4 time, already somewhat vague because of the very fast tempo, is lost, and, because of the use of the anacrusis on middle C as the main audible point of reference for the beat, the music takes on more of the character of common time.

More challenging still is the balance of harmonics. The monophonic notes, which are encoded as pairs of counter values separated by a single unit, create two very nearly synchronous binary impulse trains separated in frequency by only a few hertz. This results in a frequency spectrum that is very close to a harmonic series (see fig. 2.16).

When the two impulse trains are interleaved at distinct frequencies, this pseudoharmonic spectrum breaks down see (fig. 2.17). This spectral plot illustrates a major third interval. As before, the dark bands correspond to the harmonics of the lower tone in the interval and the light bands to the harmonics of the upper tone.

FIGURE 2.16 A spectral plot of the two near-coincident impulse trains, with frequency along the horizontal axis, and amplitude along the vertical, shows a pseudoharmonic series. The concordance between the harmonics of both tones makes it easy to identify a definite sense of pitch.

FIGURE 2.17 A spectral plot of two noncoincident impulse trains shows a more complex relationship: there is variability in the spacing between components and some clustering, leading to beating, giving a rough sound and making it very difficult to identify discrete pitches.

Unlike the near-coincident impulse trains, there is no regular structure to the frequency components. The spacing between spectral components is variable and includes a number of very closely clustered components, which introduces an unpleasant beating to the tone, and because each of the harmonics of each tone has equal magnitude, one of the key auditory cues we normally use to locate and identify pitch, the fundamental, which is usually the strongest of these frequency components, is ambiguous.

Like Alice's caucus race in Lewis Carroll's classic tale, which was run in a circle with no identifiable start or finish line, with no clear dominant frequency to use as a pitch reference in the sound's spectrum, every frequency component arbitrarily becomes the dominant one as the ear focuses in on different regions, creating a very vague and indistinct sense of pitch. The overall effect is to create a sense in the listener of a rough, complex tone rather than two discrete and distinct pitches.

Pulse-Width Modulation

In 1983, Quicksilva released *Ant Attack*, a survival horror game. Like *3D Monster Maze* on the ZX81, which introduced gamers to the first person perspective dino-escape horror game, Ant Attack took the Spectrum into new and interesting graphical territory. Although it wasn't the first video game to feature isometric perspective graphics—Q*Bert and *Zaxxon*, for example, both used isometric projections—it was the first Spectrum game to provide a true isometric field of play, beating *Knight Lore* by at least a year, and offered extra degrees of player control, creating a sense of agency and freedom of movement that was truly innovative for the time. The use of monochrome shading, although a detail imposed by the Spectrum's graphics hardware, contributed to the game's look and feel, lending it something of the character of a 1950s B-movie, a thematic nod that continued through to its sequel, *Zombie Zombie*.

Developed by Sandy White and Angela Sutherland, Zombie Zombie draws on George A. Romero's *Living Dead* series to create a dystopian cityscape in which the player must lure zombies to precipices so that they might fall to their deaths, if indeed 'death' is the mot juste here. Visually, Zombie Zombie is very similar to its predecessor, but its soundtrack is much more sophisticated. White's sound routine was the first to coax two independently tunable square wave tones from the Spectrum's speaker, a feat made possible by a technique called *pulse width modulation* (PWM).

As mentioned in chapter 1, sending different sequences of ones and zeroes to a 1-bit sound device allows the creation of a series of related wave shapes, from trains of binary impulses through to pulse waves of varying duty cycles. This idea can be taken one step further.

Although a digital tone generator might only be able to exist in two binary states, the same isn't true of any speaker cone that might be attached to it. That cone can't change its state discretely and instantaneously. When driven, it takes a short but finite time to reach maximum displacement, and it must move through all its intermediate states between fully off and fully on. The speaker behaves in a similar, though not identical, way as it returns to rest. This lag, the reluctance of the speaker to flip its state instantaneously, is known as *speaker inertia*, and it's a phenomenon that allows a 1-bit sound device to be creatively hacked to extend its capabilities.

Armed with a knowledge of the state transition times, by varying the amount of time that the speaker is driven relative to the time that it is not, in other words, by varying or modulating the width of the signals that are sent to the beeper, the speaker can be driven to intermediate points between fully off and fully on, simulating the effect of a continuous analogue voltage.

In an old visual gag that is referenced in the classic Looney Tune cartoon *Canned Feud*, Sylvester is lying supine on a settee. With each snore, he blows a feather into the air and sucks it back as he inhales. This illustrates PWM perfectly. A long, continuous wheeze pushes the feather to its highest point, and a similarly long gasp pulls it back to its minimum. Were Sylvester to exhale with shorter breaths, the feather would rise only part way. By varying the size of each portion of the snore, the feather could be made to trace out a complex dance between its points of maximum and minimum displacement.

The same can be applied to a speaker cone. A sequence of continuous ones, the precise number of which will depend on the size of the speaker cone, will overcome the speaker inertia and drive the cone to its maximum displacement, and a similar sequence of zeroes will allow the speaker to come back to complete rest. Knowing in advance the particular dance the speaker cone must perform to recreate a complex waveform, and by taking into account the clock speed of the processor and the length of time it takes to execute the instructions sent to it, it's possible to calculate the pulse trains, the precise sequence of ones and zeroes, that will generate the wave.

There are, as you might imagine, many ways to achieve this, but the most common method for the Spectrum was to use precalculated lookup tables to convert note frequencies to counter values that could be stored in memory and used to synthesize pulse trains in a way similar to the way Matthew Smith used the binary impulse trains in Manic Miner.

The sound routine in Zombie Zombie generates two channels of sound without any volume or timbral control and is based around an eighth-note quantization scheme, with longer notes consisting of multiple eighth notes at the same pitch triggered sequentially. The game features three main music sequences. The first (fig. 2.18) is a triumphal, march-like setting of *Ten Green Bottles*, which morphs in bar 9 into an unsettling arrangement in parallel augmented fourths, a reference to the common 1980s horror soundtrack trope, which used grotesque arrangements of children's songs or nursery rhymes.

The game also features a simple arrangement of Bizet's *March of the Toreadors* that plays on completion of the game, and a track that combines White's two-channel routine with the implied polyphony technique I explored earlier, combining bass and a simple arpeggiated accompaniment to create the suggestion of three simultaneous channels (see fig. 2.19).

In an attempt to completely circumvent the limitations of the Spectrum beeper, White also included a MIDI routine in the game, which outputs the game's music to an external MIDI-equipped synthesizer connected to the machine's peripheral interface via a custom MIDI circuit, the diagram for which was printed in the cassette inlay (reproduced in fig. 2.20). Unfortunately, White was only able to get the routine working reliably on his own Yamaha DX7 synthesizer, which had shipped with buggy ROM, a limitation that only came to light when he attempted to demo the game at a press conference while connected to a different synth and it didn't work.[26]

FIGURE 2.18 The main theme from Zombie Zombie. The theme moves from a triumphal march into an uneasy variation in parallel augmented fourths, drawing on classic horror soundtrack tropes.

There were other attempts to provide an enhanced soundtrack experience on the Spectrum. Most notable, perhaps, is *Deus Ex Machina*,[27] which features a synchronous soundtrack on compact cassette. As the game begins, a series of animated icons of the celebrity cast are displayed on screen as the player is urged by the velvety tones of Jon Pertwee to 'pause your player when I count you down, and recommence playing at the screen's request'. A trippy combination of ambient electronic music, narration, and recitative-like song follows, leading the player through an Orwellian experience that follows the lifecycle of a mutant generated by an all-powerful computer. Automata UK described the game as 'an epic "computer movie", a game/film/LP', and in execution it is not unlike an interactive concept album, with echoes of Wendy Carlos's soundtrack to *A Clockwork Orange*, particularly on side 2 of the soundtrack cassette.

The next major release to feature a two-channel PWM title tune was *Fairlight*, an isometric adventure game developed by Bo Jangeborg and Jack Wilkes. The music, a swords-and-sorcery-style track penned by Mark Alexander that was reused in the Commodore 64 title *Wizardry*, was the first public release of his Music Box routine.

FIGURE 2.19 The final theme from Zombie Zombie combines virtual polyphony and true two-channel sound to create a sense of three simultaneous channels.

The Music Box, branded around the pop duo Wham!, was given a full commercial release later that year under the Melbourne House label. Although the band had little involvement with the release, the licensing tie-in meant that Alexander was able to include five separate two-channel arrangements of Wham! hits, including George Michael's *Careless Whisper*.

For its time, the software was revolutionary, giving musicians an accessible platform on which to make multichannel music on their Spectrums, something that, before, had been exclusively the domain of the programmer. By allowing musicians to export their creations as stand-alone code, the software opened up creative opportunities for programmers to work more directly with musicians.

The interface of The Music Box will be familiar to anyone who has used a digital audio workstation. A main title screen leads directly into edit mode (see fig. 2.21), which presents two musical staves using a side-scrolling horizontal timeline layout, similar to the score editors of modern sequencers. Notes are entered directly from the Spectrum

FIGURE 2.20 The cassette inlay from Zombie Zombie showing Sandy White's MIDI interface design, an early attempt to hack an external hardware solution to the limited musical capabilities of the Spectrum.

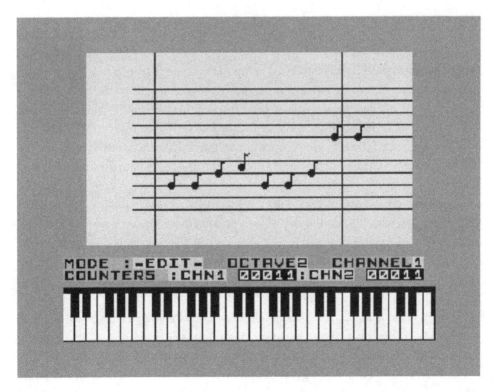

FIGURE 2.21 The Score Editor on Wham! The Music Box.

keyboard and displayed using a simplified form of music notation. By default, all music is written in C major in 4/4 time, and, as with Sandy White's routine, note durations are quantized to multiples of eighth notes. Editing is very straightforward, and there are precursors of sound trackers in the quantized structure of the note timings and in the mode of note entry.

The Music Box also provides a limited selection of percussive effects: a synth kick drum, modelled using a pitch-modulated square wave, and three editable enveloped-noise effects similar to the snare and hi-hat sounds on early Roland TR drum machines. These percussion effects are very processor-intensive, however, and tie up both playback channels, so although it is possible to create some interesting analogue-style drum patterns, this comes at the expense of any melodic or harmonic material.

The Music Box was capable of some quite complex and interesting music and featured the excruciatingly named *Whampiler*, an embedded compiler that output the music as an efficient machine code routine whose core is only 32 bytes long. Efficiency of code was everything in those early games. 'Often, developers would say that after all of the graphics and gameplay were in place there was just no RAM available for music,' Alexander recalls. 'I would beg to use the 192 bytes that were usually unused in the printer buffer, which provided just enough space for the music routine and a simple two-channel tune.'[28]

When Two Channels Just Aren't Enough

Around the time that Alexander's Music Box engine was seeing regular use, one of the Spectrum's most prolific and celebrated composers was beginning to develop his own approach to beeper music. Tim Follin, a young programmer from St. Helens in the Northwest of England, was introduced to Z80 coding by his elder brother, Mike, and together they took 1-bit sound to a whole new level.

In retrospect, Follin's earliest soundtracks showcase the incremental development of both his sound engine and his emerging musical style. The soundtrack for his first Spectrum game, *Subterranean Stryker*, is interesting only insofar as it demonstrates some of his engine's nascent capabilities. It features a monophonic line, which drifts stylistically and with little in the way of melodic coherence, the programming equivalent, perhaps, of a guitarist noodling on a fretboard. Beneath the notes, however, can be heard amplitude enveloping, a far from trivial task on a speaker that can be either on or off, and a phasing effect, creating a dynamically changing timbre, both features that Follin would continue to develop.

For his next title, *Star Firebirds*, Follin introduced a portamento effect, creating some quite dramatic pitch glides that bring to mind the soaring leads of Keith Emerson, but it was in *Vectron*, a 3D maze game inspired by the *Space Paranoids* sequence from Disney's *Tron*, that both the engine and Follin's musical style really begin to shine through.

The soundtrack in Vectron, transcribed in figure 2.22, achieves three channels of playback and begins with a phased, enveloped synth leading into an electronic fanfare, before a fast blues-scale riff, not unlike the percussive organ lines of Keith Emerson and Rick Wakeman, begins. The score then breaks style, directly referencing Wendy Carlos's original score from *Tron* in bars 14 and 16, before returning to a series of blues-scale sequences.

FIGURE 2.22 The opening to Tim Follin's Vectron. Note the reference to Wendy Carlos's theme from *Tron* in bars 14 and 16.

Follin published his three-channel music routine as a hexadecimal type-in program listing in Your Sinclair magazine.[29] making it freely available for use in noncommercial programs. The listing contains just 167 lines of code, and the entire routine, complete with note data, weighs in at just over 1 kB. The article noted that at the time, Follin was working on a new six-channel routine with chorus, bass, echo, portamento, and full attack-decay-sustain-release (ADSR) amplitude envelope, all elements that would turn up in his later soundtracks as his commercial music routine continued to develop.

In 1986, with the release of *Agent X*, Follin upped the channel count to five, although this came at the expense of some audio fidelity. With the processor pushed to its limits, the music was very lo-fi, something Follin acknowledged in an interview with Eurogamer, noting: 'It's hard to actually hear [the music in Agent X], I think I'd pushed the processor too far actually!'[30]

Follin's engine works by using five of the Z80's registers in a loop, all of which count down from a series of predetermined values to zero. When each loop is complete, it generates a pulse whose width determines the speaker level. The constantly shifting pulse widths affect both the level and timbre, adding 'noise', in the sense that the changing harmonic content introduces an undesirable roughness to the sound and causes tuning problems as the channel count rises.

That quality of sound, however, the grungy fuzziness, came to define the sound of the Spectrum for a generation of gamers, becoming an important feature of the 1-bit chip music style, in much the same way that the warmth of tape saturation came to characterize the sound of recorded music throughout the 1960s and 1970s to such an extent that modern software developers are now falling over themselves to create effects algorithms that degrade pristine digital recordings to simulate some of that analogue grit.

Early in his career, Follin had a degree of freedom that enabled him to express his own musical tastes and preferences in his scores. 'The motivation for making multi-channel sound', he recalls, 'was that I was really into chords and chord progressions at that point and was listening to a lot of early–mid Genesis'.[31]

That love of prog rock definitely shines through, particularly in the soundtrack for *Chronos*, which ends with an Emerson, Lake and Palmer–style flourish, but Follin was very capable of working across stylistic boundaries. His soundtrack for *Sentinel*, for example, uses sophisticated envelopes and arpeggiated entries across multiple channels to create a guzheng-like effect, simulating the sound and style of the Chinese zither, that is quite distinct from his other work. During his career, he adapted several arcade soundtracks, fusing his own prog-influenced style with the original themes in his arrangements of *Ghouls 'n' Ghosts*, *Bionic Commando*, and *Bubble Bobble*.

After moving to Manchester-based developer Software Creations in 1987, Follin found that the rapid pace of full-time development impacted his creative process, something he had always found trickier than coding and implementing concretised musical concepts. He began to suffer from writer's block, experiencing more and more 'blank days', at one point taking his work equipment home and composing the soundtrack to *Black Lamp* overnight just to get the music done on time.[32]

His musical legacy, however, particularly in terms of 1-bit chiptune, perhaps the most technically constrained approach, is huge. His work reached across multiple console and home computer platforms and brought prog rock changes and effects to the video game sound. He remains one of the finest beeper musicians, and his sound engines spawned several clones that are in use even now in the demoscene and 1-bit music communities. Imitation, especially on a technical level, really is the sincerest form of flattery.

The End of an Era

After a two-year run with only minor revisions, the Spectrum received a facelift in 1984 when Sinclair launched the Spectrum+. Housed in a larger case with moulded hard plastic keys, it was electronically identical to the earlier model save for a hard reset switch on the left-hand side of the machine, which shorted across the CPU reset capacitor. According to its designer, Rick Dickinson, the Spectrum+ was a turnkey product, made without the care and attention that went into the design of the original. So much so that when it became evident that the friction-fit keys of the prototype were prone to working loose and would take three weeks to reengineer, Sinclair's operations controller, David Chatten, ordered the production run to go ahead anyway. Within weeks, early adopters of the Spectrum+ and the similarly styled QL (for 'quantum leap'), began to report keyboard problems[33].

Meanwhile, Sinclair was working with its Spanish distributor Investrónica to develop a new machine. Investrónica had helped Sinclair adapt the ZX Spectrum+ to the Spanish market following a Spanish tax on all computers with 64 kB RAM or less and a law that obliged all computers sold in Spain to support the Spanish alphabet and show messages in Spanish. Led by the needs of the gaming public, who demanded more memory and better sound, the Spectrum 128 was launched at the SIMO '85 trade show in Spain in the second half of 1985 but didn't go on sale in the United Kingdom until January 1986, missing the important Christmas rush, largely because Sinclair still had a large stock of Spectrum+ machines sitting unsold in its warehouse.

The appearance of the ZX Spectrum 128 was similar to the ZX Spectrum+, save for a large external heat sink on the right-hand side of the machine. Internally, the most obvious change was the extra RAM, but the 128 also gained MIDI capabilities and a new three-channel PSG in the form of the 4-bit General Instrument AY-3-8912A. The onboard speaker of the 48K models disappeared in favour of a dedicated line-level audio output socket at the back of the machine.

The General Instrument sound chip was, perhaps, a safe choice for the Spectrum 128. By the time of its launch, it had been on the market for a number of years and had previously been used in a number of coin-op arcade machines, the Intellivision and Vectrex video game consoles, and the Mockingbird and Cricket soundcards for the Apple II. The chip had even seen service as an expansion board for Sinclair's own ZX81, and by the mid-1980s, expansion peripherals such as the Fuller Audio Box, the dk'tronics sound synthesizer, and the Music Synthesiser from William Stuart Systems offered an AY-chip sound expansion that gave the 48K Spectrum the same three-channel polyphony and synthesis capabilities of the 128.

To handle the new hardware, the 128 was shipped with an expanded version of Sinclair BASIC, which was housed in 32 kB of ROM; 128 BASIC introduced the PLAY command, which used three user-defined character strings to encode and control playback of the three tone channels on the AY chip.

The first games that most new 128 owners played were Ocean's *Daley Thompson's Supertest* and the graphical text adventure *Never Ending Story*, both of which were bundled with the computer at launch. They were reworkings of popular 48K titles. Both games made use of the 128's extra memory to get rid of the multiload routines of the originals, and in the case of Daley Thompson's Supertest, a button-smashing sports sim in the *Hyper Sports* mould, the programmers found space to introduce an extra four events: the javelin, the 100-meter sprint, 110-meter hurdles, and the triple jump. Ocean also made use of the new three-channel sound chip, featuring an arrangement of Vangelis's theme from *Chariots of Fire* as the main title theme and a collection of bluesy stings before and after each event.

Releasing 'enhanced' 128 versions of 48K games, as opposed to stand-alone titles, rapidly became the norm, but the level of enhancement was mixed. Some of the 128's launch titles featured extra game content but nothing to challenge the AY sound chip. Gargoyle Games, for example, released *Sweevo's Whirled*, an update of their isometric platform game, which had 50 additional rooms but the same beeper soundtrack as Sweevo's World. Odin's *Robin of the Wood*, by contrast, had gameplay that was unchanged from the 48K version but an enhanced soundtrack that spat out sampled speech alongside the three-channel music.

This wasn't the first time that a Spectrum had talked. External peripherals such as the Currah Microspeech and the Datel Electronic Vox Box provided phoneme-driven speech synthesis, and David Aubrey Jones had developed a sample-playback routine that debuted on Activision's *Ghostbusters* and featured again in System 3's *Death Star Interceptor*. The AY chip did not natively support sample playback, and the effect required direct manipulation of the chip's logical channel mixing system to achieve, but it improved greatly on the fuzzy, barely intelligible rasp of the beeper.

On the whole, though, the reaction from the public was lukewarm, and the machine was caught in a vicious circle. Developers were unwilling to commit to new titles until there was a proven market, and consumers were unwilling to invest in new hardware until titles were available that offered a significant improvement over their existing machines.

Without the push from developers, innovation dried up. The thrill that came from pushing at boundaries disappeared, and so did the personalities: 'When the

Spectrum 128k became available in early 1986', Mark Alexander recalls, 'the machine finally got a dedicated music chip and I produced an updated Music Box to use it. However, the technical challenge had gone and there were no barriers to break in programming someone else's sound chip, so this marked my departure from the world of Spectrum'.[34]

Sinclair never really recovered from the slow sales of the Spectrum 128, and the failure of other products, most notably the ill-fated Sinclair C5 electric vehicle and the QL, hit the company hard. On April 7, 1986, Sir Clive sold his entire computer product range and the Sinclair brand name to Amstrad for £5 million.[35] An attempt to develop the format was made with the release of the SAM Coupe in 1989, a Z80-based machine that offered a six-channel stereo sound chip and backward compatibility with the Spectrum 48K, but by then the days of 8-bit were already drawing to a close, and the machine was discontinued in 1992.

The Commodore 64
For the Masses, Not the Classes

We all love an underdog, and if the ZX Spectrum was a scrappy British pugilist, punching well above its weight, Commodore's C64 was, by contrast, a well-trained US heavyweight. Better built, better financed, and able to bring superior technical ability to the fight, the C64 was Dolph Lundgren's Ivan Drago to Stallone's Rocky Balboa.

Just as the Atari ST and Amiga, the Playstation and the Xbox, and iOS and Android have served as worthy opponents in successive rounds of playground Top Trumps, these two machines polarized a generation of schoolkids. Commodore users would point to the Spectrum's spongy rubber keyboard and garish colour clash with gleeful disdain, whilst those in the Sinclair corner would fight back with cries about the 'fat' graphics of the C64's MultiColor mode and the comparative lack of games on shelves.[1] News-stand magazines, most notably Zzap!64 and Crash,[2] both fuelled and were fuelled by this—mostly—good-natured rivalry. Neither side would concede an inch; except, that is, when it came to sound. In that respect, the 64 was nonpareil.

The PET, a Family Friend

The company that would become Commodore Business Machines was founded in 1954 as a typewriter service and repair company by Jack Tramiel, a Polish immigrant and Auschwitz survivor who had arrived in the United States in 1947.[3] Following a brush with insolvency when the Japanese entered the typewriter market in the early 1960s, Tramiel moved from typewriters to mechanical adding machines and then changed tack again, switching to digital calculators when the Japanese moved into adding machines a few years later.

Calculators suited Commodore well until Texas Instruments, who supplied Commodore with components, began producing calculators themselves at a retail price point that was lower than what it cost Commodore for the parts to build one.[4] In the ensuing calculator war, Commodore lost $5 million,[5] forcing an emergency $3 million investment by the Canadian financier Irving Gould, who had bailed out the company when it had run into financial difficulty before. Gould's cash injection saved Commodore and financed its purchase of MOS Technology, a semiconductor design and fabrication company based in Pennsylvania.[6]

Tramiel had seen how effectively Texas Instruments had been able to integrate their business upwards, growing their calculator operation from their existing expertise in chip manufacturing, and was determined that Commodore would never again be exposed to that sort of risk. He strengthened Commodore's position by integrating vertically downwards, taking the company's expertise in system design and expanding it into integrated circuits.

In 1976, two young engineers, Steve Jobs and Steve Wozniak, approached Tramiel to demo their new home computer, the Apple II, hoping that Commodore would buy the design and manufacture it.[7] Tramiel declined—he thought the deal too expensive—but he could see the shape of things to come and committed to developing a computer system of his own. Commodore announced the Personal Electronic Transactor (PET) 2001 at the Consumer Electronics Show in January 1977, claiming that it would be ready in time for the trade show in June that same year. That left just six months to design and build the prototype.[8]

The PET was built around MOS Technology's 6502 processor and was available with either 4 kB (2001–4) or 8 kB (2001–8) of 8-bit RAM. Housed in a pressed metal case that reflected Commodore's background as a manufacturer of office equipment, the smooth lines of the machine, which were shown in the cover image of the October 1977 issue of Popular Science, had the look of science fiction. And fiction was, to an extent, what that cover image was: Popular Science showed the world the prototype, and those smooth round edges were actually carved wood rather than fabricated steel.[9]

The PET was a hit, but the engineers at MOS had little time to bask in the glory. Almost immediately, they started work on a series of display chips, the 6562, the 6564, and the Video Interface Chip (VIC), a custom I/O chip that was primarily designed for use in arcade video games. Following the 1977 video games crash, the result of a market flooded with dedicated one-play Pong-style home video game consoles, it proved impossible to find buyers for the new VIC chip. Tramiel, though, was more convinced than ever that there was a market for a low-cost home computer 'for the masses, not the classes',[10] and instructed his engineers, Chuck Peddle and Bill Seiler, to design one for the winter 1980 Consumer Electronics Show in Las Vegas.

Their design, The Other Intellect (TOI), was intended to be a low-end computer for the home,[11] taking Commodore from specialist business machines into the growing and increasingly lucrative home computing sector. It was a well-specified machine, but its display was based around the 6564, a powerful graphics chip that required expensive static RAM to operate. It made the TOI much too expensive a prospect for the home user. In its place, a young engineer, Bob Yannes, showed Tramiel a prototype he'd been working on. Tramiel fast-tracked the machine and put the company's marketing strategist, Michael Tomczyk, in charge of a team of engineers he called the 'VIC Commandos'.[12]

The new machine, the VIC-20, had just 5 kB of RAM,[13] and 1.5 kB of that was reserved for the system, leaving just 3.5 kB of free user-addressable memory, which was barely enough to load a machine code compiler. The VIC chip, for which the machine was named, picked up some of the features of its more powerful siblings, getting the extended colour palette of the 6564 and the sound generator from the 6562.

Three tone channels offered 1-bit square wave generators, each with a range of three octaves, but all were clocked differently and pitched an octave apart to give a bass, alto, and treble channel. A 7-bit frequency register for each gave 128 different pitch values, but although this provided quite a bit more pitch accuracy than the TIA chip in Atari's VCS, the different master clocks on each channel could still lead to some interesting tunings across the voices; Atari's port of *Moon Patrol*, for example, was one of the rare games where the VCS version was in better voice than the enhanced soundtrack of the Commodore VIC-20.

A white noise generator, driven by a 16-stage LFSR, generates a binary noise pattern of length 65535, which can be modified using a 7-bit frequency register. All four available sound channels, the three square waves and the noise channel, could be passed through a 4-bit master volume control.[14]

Most of the games on the VIC-20 were a mixture of arcade ports and clones. The VIC-20 version of Dig Dug, for example, looks and sounds closer to the arcade original than the Atari VCS port; the extra memory and additional sound channels allow for a more faithful recreation of both the graphics and the music of the arcade.

Pac-Man also made an appearance on the VIC-20. HAL Laboratory, who held the home computer rights to Namco's games in Japan, had developed a port of Pac-Man for Commodore, but because Atari held the North American rights, the name was changed to *Jelly Monsters*. The large software sprites, monophonic rendition of the Pac-Man theme, and the authentic gameplay caught Atari's attention. Keen to show that they had learned their lesson from the VCS port, they sued both HAL Laboratory and Commodore and launched their own VIC-20 version, complete with a note-perfect two-channel theme tune.

Although the VIC-20 was undoubtedly much more musically capable than either the Atari VCS or the ZX Spectrum, it still sounded much the same. That third square wave channel gave a bit more depth to its sound, but the VIC-20 was still singing the same tune as everybody else.

If You See SID . . .

By January 1981, with the VIC-20 selling strongly, the engineers at MOS Technology were clamouring for a new project. 'We were fresh out of ideas for whatever chips the rest of the world might want us to do', recalls Al Charpentier, who was responsible for the design of many of the chips that had powered the VIC-20. 'So we decided to produce state-of-the-art video and sound chips for the world's next great video game'.[15]

Charpentier's team looked around at the most sophisticated hardware on the market and extrapolated from there to define all that the new MOS chips should be able to achieve. Thanks to Tramiel's philosophy of vertical integration, the design team had the luxury of a microchip fabrication facility on-site, meaning that component circuits could be test-manufactured and run quickly and cheaply, allowing for robust and rapid prototyping and debugging without having to worry about the other parts of the chip design.

While Charpentier worked on the graphics, Bob Yannes, the engineer whose proto-type had become the VIC-20, began work on a new sound chip. Unlike Charpentier, however, Yannes did not look to the competition for inspiration. 'I thought the sound chips on the market, including those in the Atari computers, were primitive and obvi-ously had been designed by people who knew nothing about music', he explains.[16]

Yannes's approach to design was one of efficiency. 'Any time I design something', he says, 'I want to use the minimum number of components possible. It's a personal challenge. If there's a spare [logic] gate in a gate package, I'll work to get rid of the entire package, because in working with a certain number of chips, I ought to be able to use up everything that's in them'.[17]

Although the design team were not under any particular cost pressure during development—Charles Winterble recalls that they had no formal budget accountability save for the buck that stopped with Tramiel himself[18]—they did feel the pressure of time, because Tramiel wanted to have the chips ready in time for the Consumer Electronics Show in January 1982. That pressure meant that rather than spending time compacting designs to minimize space, the chips were designed in a very modular way. Yannes had originally planned to have 32 different voices for his chip, using wavetable synthesis con-trolled by a master oscillator. 'The standard way of building oscillators', he explains, 'is to build one and then multiplex it until you have as many as you need. We just built an oscillator module and repeated it, because that was much faster than working out all the timing for the multiplexer'.[19]

The chip (fig. 3.1), now christened the Sound Interface Device (SID), continued the anthropomorphic naming convention established with VIC. Yannes had the freedom to include as many features as he could on its surface provided he could fit them in, and his design incorporated functions that suggest that he was not really designing a video game sound chip at all but a fully featured polyphonic synthesizer. Most tellingly, he included an analogue input pin on the SID which allowed external signals to be routed through its filter and mixed with the on-board sound channels, a feature Yannes had seen on Bob Moog's Minimoog and which extended the scope of the chip enormously. Two analogue-to-digital converters were also provided and were designed to allow the SID to interface directly with potentiometers; useful, perhaps, as front panel controls in a hardware synth setup.

Both the SID and Charpentier's VIC-II graphics chip were completed in November 1981. At a meeting with Charpentier and Winterble later that month, Tramiel decided

FIGURE 3.1 The MOS 6581 SID chip.

FIGURE 3.2 The Commodore 64 'Breadbin' model was housed in a case that was the same as that of the old VIC-20.

that the chips would go into a 64 kB home computer, and the designs for the new machine were laid out in just two days. The computer would use the same case as the VIC-20 and the same size circuit board to speed development and keep costs low. Five working prototypes were completed just before the new year, and the new Commodore 64 (fig. 3.2) debuted at the Computer Electronics Show in Las Vegas in January 1982.[20]

Not So BASIC After All …

The SID chip and its synth-like capabilities made the Commodore 64 the most powerful out-of-the-box music machine of its generation, but while the Spectrum BEEP command made it easy for the novice to code simple melodies and sound effects, Commodore's BASIC set the bar for entry very much higher.

Having hooked up the C64 to a television set or monitor, the user was confronted with a lilac screen and a flickering cursor beneath the one-word prompt READY. Getting the C64 to make any kind of sound at all involved POKEing numbers into several of the SID's memory registers, but while the C64 user manual that came bundled with the computer provided a chapter on getting started with programming sound on the machine and a summary of the main functions of the chip, a complete overview of the SID's functions and registers only appeared in the Programmer's Reference Guide, a document that most users would never see. At a time when Commodore were already shipping their business machines with version 4.0 of BASIC, a variant of Microsoft's 6502 BASIC, the C64 came with the reduced instruction set of version 2.0, which enabled Commodore to squeeze the interpreter into smaller ROMs, reducing costs in an area where it was presumed most home users wouldn't notice.

'That's because of what the SID chip could do, of course', explains Ben Daglish. 'It was a complex old thing, what with all the different waveforms and all the rest of it. And when they released the 64, well they rushed it out, didn't they? Commodore weren't going to extend the language to make it easy. The whole PEEK and POKE thing was always just a little bit of a hack'.[21]

In fact, sound wasn't the only casualty of that breakneck pace of development. The C64 also lacked dedicated BASIC commands to plot graphics, for example, leaving users with little option but to grapple with memory addressing and hardware registers, concepts that are more common to low-level assembly-language programming than to BASIC. It would take a fairly dedicated casual user to persevere.

Instead of simply calling up a sound or beep command, pages 80 and 81 of the user manual provided the eight lines of BASIC code necessary to create a simple tone.[22] The manual offered little in the way of technical explanation or, indeed, line spacing (see ex. 3.1).

EXAMPLE 3.1. Example sound program from the Commodore 64 User Guide.

```
5   FORL=54272TO54296:POKEL,0:NEXT
10  POKE54296,15
20  POKE54277,190
30  POKE54278,248
40  POKE54273,17:POKE54272,37
50  POKE54276,17
60  FORT=1TO250:NEXT
70  POKE54276,16
```

Line 5 of the program clears all of the writeable memory locations of the SID chip by POKEing a value of 0 into each register in turn. Line 10 sets the global volume to maximum. The next two lines define an ADSR envelope by specifying values that correspond to the attack/decay times and then the sustain level and release time. Next, two values, corresponding to the pitch of the tone, are written to memory, and a triangle wave is activated in line 50. The FOR ... NEXT loop in line 60 is used as a rough timer to define note length, before the note is turned off in line 70 by deselecting any of the waveforms. That's a lot of work to make a beep.

The SID's registers start at memory location 54272 (see table 3.1).[23]

The pitch of each voice is given by the contents of the first two registers, Freq LO and Freq HI, which combine to give the least and most significant bytes of a 16-bit pitch value. This gives a tremendously fine frequency resolution, far finer than can be differentiated even by a well-trained set of ears, laying to rest once and for all any memories of those horribly out-of-tune notes of old.

The code in example 3.2 demonstrates the C64's frequency range.

The registers at locations 54274 and 54275 are used to set the pulse width of the pulse waveform and so only have an effect on the sound when that waveform is selected. Again, the Pulse Width LO and Pulse Width HI values are combined to give a 12-bit control value, so the upper four bits of the Pulse Width HI register are not used at all. This gives 4,096 possible settings for the pulse width.

It's worth noting, however, that if, as in example 3.1, the SID registers are all cleared prior to POKEing control values into the registers, the default pulse width will be 0, and the SID will generate a continuous direct current, which, although it can be co-opted to play back sound samples by rapidly changing the volume level, will normally be inaudible.

Most games on the C64 used PWM to create a sense of dynamic timbral movement—listen to the opening melody of Rob Hubbard's *Monty on the Run*, for example—but PWM could also be driven harder, as it was on the ZX Spectrum, to create an LFO-style voice-level amplitude effect, which can be heard on Martin Galway's soundtrack to *Parallax*. The code in example 3.3 demonstrates the effect.

The next register essentially acts as a series of switches and uses each bit of the binary form of the byte POKEd to memory to toggle the associated function.

The GATE bit controls the function of the SID's envelope generator. Setting this bit to 1 triggers the envelope, causing it to run through its attack, decay, and sustain portions. Setting it to 0 triggers the release portion of the envelope. Only by selecting a suitable waveform, constructing an ADSR envelope, and setting this bit to 1 can the SID be coaxed into sound.

When the SYNC bit is set, the frequency of Voice 1 is locked to that of Voice 3, whose period is used to retrigger the period of the Voice 1 oscillator, creating a harmonically rich tone whose timbre can be altered by varying the respective frequencies of the voices.

TABLE 3.1. The control registers for the SID's three oscillators.

Memory location (Channel 1/2/3)	Data								Description
54272/ 54279/ 54286	FRQ_7	FRQ_6	FRQ_5	FRQ_4	FRQ_3	FRQ_2	FRQ_1	FRQ_0	Freq LO
54273/ 54280/ 54287	FRQ_{15}	FRQ_{14}	FRQ_{13}	FRQ_{12}	FRQ_{11}	FRQ_{10}	FRQ_9	FRQ_8	Freq HI
54274/ 54281/ 54288	PW_7	PW_6	PW_5	PW_4	PW_3	PW_2	PW_1	PW_0	Pulse width LO
54275/ 54282/ 54289					PW_{11}	PW_{10}	PW_9	PW_8	Pulse width HI
54276/ 54283/ 54290	NOISE	PULSE	SAW	TRI	TEST	RING MOD	SYNC	GATE	Control
54277/ 54284/ 54291	ATK_3	ATK_2	ATK_1	ATK_0	DCY_3	DCY_2	DCY_1	DCY_0	Attack/decay
54278/ 54285/ 54292	STN_3	STN_2	STN_1	STN_0	RSL_3	RLS_2	RLS_1	RLS_0	Sustain/release

This type of hard-syncing oscillator has been around since the early days of analogue synthesis and offers quite a range of tones.[24] It is a nonlinear operation, and the outcome depends on the waveshape of the slave oscillator and the relative frequencies of both the master and the slave. By varying the frequency of the master oscillator, the slave is retriggered at intermediate points in its cycle, creating unusual waveshapes and giving the synthesis method and, to an extent, the Commodore 64 a very distinctive sound. (See example 3.4.)

Similarly, setting the RING MOD bit in SID register 54276 replaces the triangle waveform with a ring-modulated combination of the outputs of Voice 1 and Voice 3.

As an effect, ring modulation will perhaps be best known to readers of a certain age as the means by which Brian Hodgson, one of the sound engineers at the BBC

EXAMPLE 3.2. A short program to cycle through the full frequency range of the SID.

```
10   REM FREQUENCY RANGE
20   PRINT CHR$(147)
25   PRINT "FREQUENCY RANGE DEMO"
30   SIDREG = 54272
40   REM INITIALISE SID REGISTERS
50   FOR X = SIDREG TO SIDREG + 24
60   POKE X,0: NEXT
65   REM SET VOLUME TO MAX
70   POKE SIDREG + 24, 15
75   REM SET ATTACK/DECAY
80   POKE SIDREG + 5, 190
85   REM SET SUSTAIN/RELEASE
90   POKE SIDREG + 6, 248
95   REM TURN ON TRIANGLE
100  POKE SIDREG + 4, 17
105  REM FREQUENCY RANGE
110  FOR F = 256 TO 65000 STEP 128
115  REM CALCULATE FH VALUE
120  FH = INT(F/256)
125  REM CALCULATE FL VALUE
130  FL = F - 256 * FH
135  REM SET FREQUENCY LOW
140  POKE SIDREG, FL
145  REM SET FREQUENCY HI
150  POKE SIDREG + 1, FH
160  NEXT
165  REM TURN OFF TRIANGLE WAVE
170  POKE SIDREG + 4, 0
```

EXAMPLE 3.3. A short program to demonstrate the effect of sweeping the pulse width control.

```
10   REM PWM
20   PRINT CHR$(147): PRINT "PWM DEMO"
30   SIDREG = 54272
40   REM INITIALISE SID REGISTERS
50   FOR X = SIDREG TO SIDREG + 24
60   POKE X,0: NEXT
65   REM SET VOLUME TO MAX
70   POKE SIDREG + 24, 15
75   REM SET ATTACK/DECAY
80   POKE SIDREG + 5, 190
85   REM SET SUSTAIN/RELEASE
90   POKE SIDREG + 6, 248
95   REM TURN ON PULSE WAVE
100  POKE SIDREG + 4, 65
105  REM SET FREQUENCY LOW
110  POKE SIDREG, 195
105  REM SET FREQUENCY HI
120  POKE SIDREG + 1, 16
130  FOR PW = 0 TO 4095 STEP 8
135  REM CALCULATE PW HI
140  H = INT(PW/256)
145  REM CALCULATE PW LO
150  L = PW - 256 * H
155  REM SET PULSE WIDTH LO
160  POKE SIDREG + 2, L
165  REM SET PULSE WIDTH HI
170  POKE SIDREG + 3, H
170  NEXT
180  REM TURN OFF PULSE WAVE
190  POKE SIDREG + 4, 0
```

Radiophonics Workshop, found the ominous, robotic voice of those nemeses of Doctor Who, the Daleks.[25]

A form of amplitude modulation, ring modulation takes its name from the ring configuration of diodes that lay at the heart of the analogue circuitry used to achieve the effect.[26] Ring modulation modulates a carrier waveform with a second modulating wave by multiplying the two time-domain waveforms together, generating a new signal

EXAMPLE 3.4. A short program demonstrating the sync wave effect.

```
10 REM WAVE SYNC
20 PRINT CHR$(147)
25 PRINT "WAVE SYNC DEMO"
30 SIDREG = 54272
40 REM INITIALISE SID REGISTERS
50 FOR X = SIDREG TO SIDREG + 24
60 POKE X,0: NEXT
65 REM FREQUENCY RANGE
70 FOR F = 1 TO 255
80 PRINT CHR$(147)
85 PRINT "FREQUENCY VOICE 1: "; F;
90 REM SET VOLUME TO MAX
95 POKE SIDREG + 24, 15
100 REM SET VOICE 1 FREQUENCY
105 POKE SIDREG + 1, F
110 REM SET VOICE 3 FREQUENCY
115 POKE SIDREG + 15, 35
120 REM SET ATTACH/DECAY VOICE 1
125 POKE SIDREG + 5, 84
130 REM SET ATTACK/DECAY VOICE 3
135 POKE SIDREG + 19, 84
140 REM SET SUS/RELEASE VOICE 1
145 POKE SIDREG + 6, 168
150 REM SET SUS/RELEASE VOICE 3
155 POKE SIDREG + 20, 168
160 REM TURN ON SAWTOOTH VOICE 1
165 POKE SIDREG + 4, 35
170 FOR N = 1 TO 25: REM PAUSE
180 NEXT
190 NEXT
200 REM TURN OFF VOICE 1
205 POKE SIDREG + 4, 0
210 REM TURN OFF VOICE 3
215 POKE SIDREG + 18, 0
```

with energy at frequencies corresponding to the sum and difference of the carrier and modulator frequencies.

These upper and lower frequency values are called *sidebands*,[27] since they are the frequency bands that lie on either side of the carrier frequency in a frequency-domain plot of the waveform. If harmonically rich waveforms, such as triangle, sawtooth, or square waves, are substituted for either the carrier or modulator, sidebands are created at each harmonic, making ring modulation very efficient for generating harmonically dense signals and particularly good, when combined with an envelope with a rapid attack and long release, for creating bells, chimes, gongs, and other struck metallic sounds.

Varying the relative amplitudes and frequencies of the two signals generates a range of tones from harmonic through to extremely inharmonic. Although the new frequency content is always mathematically related to the signals, it's not always related in a musically pleasing way.

The TEST bit, when activated, works a bit like a 'panic mode', resetting all of the voice parameters to 0 and creating a potential trap for the unwary.

The three waveform bits respectively activate a triangle, sawtooth, or pulse wave. At least one of these, or the noise signal, must be activated to have any kind of sound output. If more than one waveform is activated simultaneously, the output is the logical sum of the waves, which is another way to increase the sound palette of the SID.

The final toggle in this register, the NOISE bit, toggles a noise generator for that voice. The noise generator uses a 23-bit LFSR, giving a noise signal that is an impressive 8,388,607 bits in length. The frequency of the oscillator determines the rate at which these bits are sent to the digital-to-analogue converter. As with the other waveforms, the noise signal can be combined with the other outputs, but this can quickly lead to a 'feature' of the SID, which forces the states of the LFSR to 0, outputting silence. When this happens, flipping the TEST bit resets the shift register, and so reinitializes the noise signal.

The noise signal can be triggered alongside the pitched waveforms to create a percussive effect, giving a sound like the mechanical key-click on a tonewheel organ, which can be heard in the opening sawtooth line of Rob Hubbard's *International Karate*.

The next two rows of the register map relate to the envelope generator.

The SID's envelope generator is made up of four distinct stages. The first, which takes the signal from silence to peak amplitude, is called the *attack portion* of the sound. The next, the *decay portion*, sees the loudness drop rapidly from this peak to a more steady state, the *sustain portion*. The final portion, the *release portion*, sees the sound fade back to silence. This particular contour, known as a four-stage ADSR envelope, became so commonplace during the golden age of analogue synthesis in the 1970s that many players referred to all envelope generators as ADSRs whether they created ADSR-type envelopes or not.[28]

Typically, we define an ADSR using four parameters. The *attack time*, normally measured in milliseconds, is the amount of time it takes for the sound to ramp up from silence to peak amplitude. The *decay time* is the time taken to fade down to the sustain portion of the sound, which is specified not as a time but as a level, either an absolute value or, more commonly, a percentage of the maximum volume.

On a keyboard instrument like the piano, after the initial attack and decay, the instrument will sustain while the key is depressed. On the C64, the SID will sustain a tone whenever the gate bit is set to 1. Finally, the *release time* specifies the amount of time it takes for the sound to decay to silence. This could be the time between releasing a piano key and the dampers muting the strings or the portion of the envelope that is triggered by setting the SID's gate bit to 0.

The SID uses two registers, 54277 and 54278, to control its envelope generator. Each register is split into two 4-bit nibbles. The most significant nibble of register 54277 gives 16 possible attack times, while the other gives 16 possible decay rates. When the gate bit is set high, the envelope goes into its attack cycle and then decays to the sustain level. The sustain level is set using the four most significant bits of register 54278 and is specified as a portion of the peak level, with 16 levels of control, while the other four bits determine the release time. As soon as the gate bit is set low, the envelope, regardless of where it is in the attack/decay/sustain cycle, advances to the release stage.

These controls are duplicated across the other two voices, allowing for fully independent control over each voice's timbre, pitch, and amplitude envelope and some control and modulation functions, the only provisos being that the sync bit on Voice 2 locks it to Voice 1, and the ring modulation bit substitutes the triangle waveform for the ring modulated combination of Voice 1 and Voice 2. Similarly, the sync bit on Voice 3 locks it to Voice 2, and the ring modulation bit replaces its triangle wave with the ring modulated combination of Voice 3 and Voice 2.

The SID chip also contains a single multimode resonant filter, which can act on any of the voices in isolation or in combination and is accessed using the next bank of memory registers (see table 3.2).

Although, in principle, the filter lends the SID enormous flexibility, hardware idiosyncrasies made filtering on the C64 something of a hit-and-miss affair.

The SID offers three different filter types: a low-pass filter, which attenuates signals above a cut-off frequency; a high-pass filter, which is essentially the reverse of the low-pass filter, letting through frequencies above the cut-off and attenuating those below it, and a bandpass filter, which allows signals in a narrow passband, specified by the filter's Q setting, to pass through unaltered while attenuating those above and below.

The filter in the SID is analogue, but it is controlled digitally. It uses a classic multimode voltage-controlled filter design, using field-effect transistors (FETs) as voltage-controlled resistors to control the cut-off frequency. Two registers on the SID chip, 54293 and 54294, form an 11-bit number and together generate the control voltage for the FETs via a 12-bit digital-to-analogue converter; the least significant bit on the converter had no audible effect on the filter's output, so Yannes discarded it. This, in turn, controls the cut-off or centre frequency, depending on the filter mode selected, and gives a range from around 30 Hz to 12 kHz.

The resistance of those FETs, hence the behaviour of the filter cut-off, varied considerably across the lifespan of the SID, so different batches of SID chips ended up sounding very different. '[It] was the last thing that was worked on', Yannes recollects. 'I ran out of time. The computer simulation said, "This will not work very well"—and it

TABLE 3.2. The control registers for the SID's filter.

Memory location	Data								Description
54293						FC_2	FC_1	FC_0	FC LO
54294	FC_{10}	FC_9	FC_8	FC_7	FC_6	FC_5	FC_4	FC_3	FC HI
54295	RES_3	RES_2	RES_1	RES_0	FLTEX	FLT_2	FLT_1	FLT_0	Resonance/filter
54296	3OFF	HP	BP	LP	VOL_3	VOL_2	VOL_1	VOL_0	Mode/volume

didn't. I knew it wouldn't work very well, but it was better than nothing and I didn't have time to make it better'.[29]

To compound matters, the equations describing the operation of the filters in the technical documentation were wrong, so most early developers either ignored them completely or incorporated features by trial and error. Not so Commodore's Japanese developers. 'The Japanese are so obsessed with technical specifications that they had written their code according to a SID spec sheet, which I had written before SID proto-types even existed', Yannes says. 'Needless to say, the specs were not accurate. Rather than correct the obvious errors in their code, they produced games with out-of-tune sounds and filter settings that produced only quiet, muffled sound at the output. As far as they were concerned, it didn't matter that their code sounded all wrong, they had written their code correctly according to the spec and that was all that mattered!'[30]

Commodore issued a technical note quite early on in the C64's life to say that be-cause of these variations, it was not advisable to include filter settings in commercial software, since it might result in unintentional sounds or even sounds which couldn't be heard on some machines; so filtering on the C64 became a process of trial and error.

'Well, you had to just play around with it', Ben Daglish says;

There was something dodgy about the build quality of the SID chip. I mean, you were never really quite sure how it was going to sound, especially using filters. The only thing that you ever did, really, was the filter sweep, because you were pretty sure that at least you were going to get the sweeping effect, even if you weren't quite sure exactly what frequencies you were sweeping. But yeah, the idea was just that you would throw as much as you could at it and try and make it sound as good as possible on your machine, and then hope for the best.[31]

A later revision of the SID, the 8580, was designed and manufactured to the orig-inal technical specification with linear control over the cut-off frequency and, thanks to better separation between the analogue and digital circuits, better noise and distortion characteristics. Nevertheless, most chip musicians prefer the original 6581 chip, precisely because of the quirks of its filter and the grit imparted by its noise and distortion. That quirky filtered sound, with all of its glitches, was an important part of the SID sound.

The next register is divided into two 4-bit words which determine the signal routing and the filter's resonance setting. The first four bits route four possible sound sources through the filter. The first three bits correspond to the three internal voices of the SID, while the fourth allows an external audio signal to be filtered. The most signifi-cant bits control the filter resonance, offering 16 levels, which can be heard as a prom-inent 'chime' as it increases.

The register at 54296 is divided into two parts, governing the filter mode and the overall volume. The first four bits control the global volume of the SID's output, like a master fader on a mixing desk. Set to full, the C64 will output two-volt peak AC at a DC

TABLE 3.3. The SID's read-only registers.

Memory location	Data								Description
54297	PX_7	PX_6	PX_5	PX_4	PX_3	PX_{02}	PX_1	PX_0	Potentiometer X
54298	PY_7	PY_6	PY_5	PY_4	PY_3	PY_2	PY_1	PY_0	Potentiometer Y
54299	OSC_7	OSC_6	OSC_5	OSC_4	OSC_3	OSC_2	OSC_1	OSC_0	Oscillator 3
54300	ENV_7	ENV_6	ENV_5	ENV_4	ENV_3	ENV_2	ENV_1	ENV_0	Envelope 3

level of six volts, making it perfectly possible to hook up the machine to a hi-fi or amplifier. The fifth, sixth, and seventh bits of the register control the filter mode, swapping its operation between low pass, bandpass, and high pass. These bits could work additively and so could be combined to activate combinations of filters. Activating the high pass and low pass filters in combination, for example, would create a notch, or band reject filter, which let through high- and low-frequency sounds but filtered out those in a band of frequencies in the middle of the spectrum. The last bit disconnects Voice 3 from the audio output, which is usually required when the voice is being used as a modulation source for the other voices.

The final bank of registers (see table 3.3), are read-only and provide a set of additional control functions that can be mapped across to the other registers to create dynamic effects.

Registers 54297 and 54298 contain values that describe the position of the potentiometers when a paddle or other continuous controller is plugged into one of the two game ports at the back of the machine. These ports are connected to pins 23 and 24 of the SID chip, and the analogue signals are sampled at 8-bit resolution to feed the registers.

The final two registers are used to carry information about the state of Voice 3 or the pseudorandom number generator used to provide the white noise signal. Register 54299 provides the instantaneous level of the oscillator and updates at the frequency set by the high-frequency and low-frequency registers for Voice 3, so if Voice 3 is being used as a low-frequency oscillator to modulate one or more dimensions of either of the other two voices, PEEKing in this register provides the time-varying signal that allows that to happen. Using the noise setting produces a continuous stream of random bits in this register.

Register 54300 performs much the same function as its neighbour except that it is filled by a number representing the instantaneous envelope level of Voice 3, which allows for the creation of some interesting pitch and filter enveloping effects.

Lazy Jones

The SID, then, was complex, and it took developers quite some time to explore its intricacies and idiosyncrasies. In the earliest games on the C64, the SID was used as little more than a tone generator, a little digital synthesizer that triggered simple preset waveforms.

David Whittaker was one of the most prolific video game composers of that period and worked across multiple platforms, penning around 800 video game themes. 'David was always the mercenary one of the bunch', recalls the SID music historian and netlabel owner Chris Abbott. 'He was fairly unapologetic in that respect. He did it for the money. He just churned them out, and he's always admitted that quite freely'.[32]

His approach to composition was as slick and as mechanized as any production line. He developed a music driver on the Tatung Einstein, a Taiwanese computer system that was designed and built in the north of England and adopted by many software houses as a game development platform before game code was ported to the final retail machines. Whittaker would work out his musical ideas on a Yamaha CX5 or Roland Juno 6 keyboard before coding the tracks directly into his assembly-level driver on the Einstein, using his system to arrange the musical phrases into subroutines and patterns of code.[33]

Musically, Whittaker was a New Romantic, part of the pop scene that emerged in the UK post punk. Before getting into video game music, he used to gig with his club band, Beau Leisure, who were, he notes wryly, 'quite well known in Altrincham'.[34] The New Romantics, in contrast to the aggressive austerity of the punk sound that preceded theirs, gave pop a synthetic sound that was, initially, quite eerie and sterile, in part a consequence of the musicians exploring the sonic territory afforded by the programmable digital synths that were entering the market in the early 1980s. Over time, dance-infused rhythms and arpeggiated synth sequences were incorporated into the music, and by the mid-1980s, the British synth-pop that had grown out of New Romanticism had a warmer, punchier sound. This was the sound that Whittaker adopted for his best-known soundtrack, *Lazy Jones* (see fig. 3.3).

The game sees the player guide Lazy Jones, a feckless hotel caretaker, through 18 rooms to play a series of minigames. Each of the rooms in the game has its own four-bar fragmentary musical segment that is triggered whenever the player enters and which then transitions seamlessly back into the main game loop when the player leaves, creating a soundtrack that evolves continually in relation to gameplay and uses its musical motifs to create an additional layer of game narrative to help the player navigate through the game environment.

Each of the subtunes uses only two voices of the SID chip—Whittaker reserved the third channel for sound effects in the subgames—which, along with tempo- and key-matching each of the tunes, simplifies the process of transitioning between loops to create a real sense of musical continuity as the soundtrack evolves with the gameplay.

The bassline plays the root in broken octaves throughout (see fig. 3.4) and provides a sense of continuity and a dynamic movement to what might otherwise be quite a static, synthetic track. That bouncing bassline, already a staple of 1980s synth-pop—think New Order's *Blue Monday*[35]—became one of the key characteristics not just of C64 music but of the 8-bit video game sound in general.

Scattered across the levels of Lazy Jones are a number of little musical references and gags. Koenig's *Post Horn Galop* appears in the level *The Turk*, in which Jones must spear

FIGURE 3.3 David Whittaker's Lazy Jones.

FIGURE 3.4 The Stardust Theme from Lazy Jones. The bassline in broken octaves drew its inspiration from 1980s synth-pop and became a staple of the video game music sound.

cooked turkeys with a fork. Visage's *Fade to Grey* features in a shoot-'em-up subgame,[36] and so does Gene Page's disco mix of *Theme from Close Encounters of the Third Kind*.[37] The most blatant of these musical gags is the level 99 Red Balloons, which features, of course, Nena's 1980s Europop sensation *99 Luftballons*.[38]

With musical appropriation providing some of the in-game music for Lazy Jones, it's interesting to note that the music for the *Stardust* subgame was itself appropriated by the German techno outfit Zombie Nation, who, in 1999, built their track *Kernkraft 400* around it. The track became an underground sensation, reaching number 2 in the UK charts,[39] and crossing over from the club scene into the strange world of sports-arena music, serving as the theme song for dozens of teams, including the Seattle Mariners, the Los Angeles Dodgers, and the Welsh national football team, rivalling, perhaps, Baha Men's *Who Let the Dogs Out* for exposure amongst sports fans. In a curiously meta turn of events, that track also ended up back in a sports sim as the *Stadium Chant Mix*, which features in the soundtrack of the 2012 video game *NHL 13*.

That exposure didn't go unnoticed.

Chris Abbott explains:

David contacted the guy [Florian Senfter], who wrote back and said, 'Well, it's only been a hit in Belgium, and so there's no more money to be got from it'. What we didn't know was that at the time, Zombie Nation was just about to sign a deal with Ministry of Sound.

Zombie Nation came up with some sort of deal, which gave [David], I think, 9,000 Deutsch Marks, about £3,000, but the agreement had no jurisdiction, no end date … Basically, it was a complete buyout of his piece. It was a contract that said, 'We own everything … please sign!' At the time, Dave counted that as a win, because as he said in an interview with the BBC, 'I got more for that than I got for writing the game', which, while true, sort of misses the point. Zombie Nation became a millionaire off that track.

Fast forward, now, to 2008, and the guy who did the *Crazy Frog* album comes knocking at my door because he wants to secure the rights to release Lazy Jones. So we went to court in Germany to try to get the rights back, but it failed. Then the action moved to America, but the only thing that we could base [our case] on was deception, because [Senfter] hadn't mentioned the Ministry of Sound contract before David signed the agreement. The problem was, all of the facts showed that David would have signed that contract anyway. Added to that the difficulty of getting the timeline from inside Ministry of Sound, and a $500,000 bill just to get the lawsuit started, and it just stopped. You've no idea how many enquiries I've had [to release Lazy Jones] since then, and I've had to turn them all away saying, 'look, unless you're prepared to start another court case again to get it back, nothing's going to happen here'.[40]

Abbott's frustration about the situation is clear, but it's not unique to this particular case. Abbott has been involved in numerous court cases over video game music rights, almost all of which stem from the fact that in those early days, nobody really gave much thought to the value that was present in the intellectual property of the game. Video game music wasn't something that was imagined to have a life that was separate from the games that housed it.

'[When I was putting together the first Back in Time album], I didn't realize at the time that [Gremlin Graphics] didn't actually have the rights to the *Thing on a Spring* music because of a lack of written contracts', he says. 'And then I went to Ocean and I said, "Look, who owns Martin [Galway's] stuff?" And they said, "Mate, we don't have a clue, we've lost all the paperwork!" That's the thing; there's no one now who's got enough paperwork to go back and prove who owns what'.[41]

Hard Drivin'

Whittaker's music in Lazy Jones was simple but effective. Getting the SID to produce anything more than simple beeps required a complex music driver, a section of code that handled the initialization and manipulation of the SID's registers, all synced to the machine's hardware interrupts to provide the musical pulse. Because music playback, and more precisely, the vibrato, portamento, and PWM effects that would animate it, required a very high degree of precision, typically, music routines had to be written in efficient 6502 assembly language and required a musical mindset that combined both technical and musical creativity.

Thirty years on from its heyday, and despite not having coded a line of 6502 assembly for at least two-thirds of that time, Ben Daglish is still recognized by fans of the C64. Angular and animated, he is a natural showman; charismatic, effervescent, and all the time bubbling over with creative energy. He says:

> It's amazing, yes, that people are still listening to my stuff, still giving me recognition thirty years on. It still blows me away! That job, programmer-musician, was, after all, quite a niche one, and it had a very limited time period. I mean there was me, Rob [Hubbard], Martin [Galway], and Dave Whittaker, and that was it. We were the four full-time Commodore guys in the country. We invented the job of computer musician, which is something I'm still proud of. In total, it lasted maybe 15 or 20 years, if that. But it was a unique crossover where you had to know quite a lot about both the creative and technical aspects. It wasn't just writing music, it was programming it as well.[42]

Daglish certainly had the musical credentials. His parents ran a folk club in London, and from an early age he was dandled on the knees of such luminaries as Martin Carthy and Dave Swarbrick. By the age of four, he was playing penny whistle and harmonica, and he now boasts proficiency on over 200 instruments. His transition from woodwind to coding came courtesy of the BBC Computer Literacy Project. He explains:

> When I was at school, I won a BBC Micro for the place. The BBC ran this competition to write an essay about how computers could be used in your school. I mean, I'm sure it was a fix. I'm sure they just wanted to push a thousand computers or something, and so everybody who bothered to write an essay won a computer! But I won this computer for the school, and so I ended up being one of the few people that were allowed to go into the library and use it, the 'school computer'.
>
> That was the thing that gave me the chance to really push my music knowledge; the fact that you could do music as numbers, that was the thing. All I'd ever done before was make music by ear, so I could always hear the stuff, but I still hadn't

sussed the fact that *Twinkle Twinkle*, for example, goes 1, 1, 5, 5, 6, 6, 5 … 4, 4, 3, 3, 2, 2, 1. That's it, you know? And it moves … the keys and what letter names that you've decided to give the notes makes no difference at all, it's all to do with the intervals, and so yes … That thing of automatically beginning to think in terms of the semitones, think in terms of it all just being numbers and it all relating to each other, that was the breakthrough that the BBC gave me, and suddenly I realized that if you can do that with the notes, you can do that with the rhythm as well. So I figured that you must be able to treat all this purely on a kind of mathematical basis. It wasn't just about making the sounds, you see, it was about making the sounds and being able to program a whole piece and sequence it up and stuff like that. It was an amazingly enabling and creative time.

That was also how I met Tony [Crowther]. He had had a VIC-20 and then he got a 64 and started writing games and stuff…. The second or third game he wrote, he needed it to play Chopin's *Funeral March* at the end when you died. That was it. No music throughout the game or anything, but he just wanted this little tune. He came to me one day and said, 'Hey, you do music, don't you? How do I do the Death March?' I wrote out the notes for him on a sheet of paper and he took that home and typed it into the player that was in the back of the Commodore 64 manual, the one that showed you how to do music in BASIC.

A few weeks later he said, 'I'm writing another game and I want to have *Equinoxe 5* in it'. So I gave Equinoxe 5 a listen and I thought, 'Well, that's all right … This is easy'. So I transcribed that, went round to his house in the evening, and did it that night, typing in the notes myself because it was faster than writing it all down on a piece of paper and giving it to him to do it.

At that point, I was kind of hooked…. And so we spent the next two or three years just developing our player; loads of sessions of me going round to his house, and us working through the night knocking up tracks. That was how we did the first W.E.M.U.S.I.C. demo, and we were doing covers of all sorts of things. You know, we did *Stairway to Heaven*, and loads more Jean Michel Jarre.

After we'd been doing it for about six months, a year, something like that, I heard my first bit of Rob [Hubbard] and suddenly went 'Bloody hell! Can we do that? Oh, bloody hell, of course!' And so instantly, as soon as I heard that, the player that Tony and I had been slowly working on suddenly improved. That was the first time we had heard what a real musician could sound like on the Commodore.

Ostensibly, sound drivers all do exactly the same thing. They take musical data and use it to manipulate the SID's registers to make music. But, just as the touch of different musicians can sculpt very different performances from the same instrument, the code of different computer musicians could impart very different sounds from the same hardware.

'The SID was just a chip', says Chris Abbott. 'It's the way you program it that makes it sound unique. Take vibrato; there's the delay between the note, the vibrato onset, the vibrato depth.... Everybody did it differently. You can tell a Matt Gray tune because the vibrato sounds the way Matt Gray did it, and it's a Galway tune if the effect sounds like Martin did it. These stylistic signatures are very important'.[43]

'Yes, there's an art to it', Daglish adds. 'You can definitely appreciate beautiful code. You know, I often talk about the "the art of programming". I love to look at and hear the effects of beautiful code. That's a big part of it'.

The sound drivers, then, became at least as important as the music itself. Musicians invested a lot of development time and effort in creating efficient code and developing the little stylistic tricks that contributed to their signature sound. Naturally, with their code so intimately entwined with their livelihood, many became fiercely protective of their drivers.

Daglish says:

When we did *Auf Wiedersehen Monty* together, Rob came down to the Gremlin offices and we just spent a couple of days holed up in my office playing keyboard and guitar and just having a good time writing the piece and scoring it out, but when it actually came time to put it into the machine, Rob sent me out. He wouldn't let anybody look at his player because he obviously had loads of little secret tricks, and his player was more evolved and more efficient than the routine that I was using. So although we composed it together, Rob typed in everything himself.

Bigger Than the Beatles?

Everyone sought to emulate Rob Hubbard's routines, although few could make code sing in quite the same way.

For all the influence he has had on video game sound and music across a career spanning 30 years on both sides of the Atlantic, Hubbard is a man you could easily pass by in the street without giving him a second glance. He is quiet, reserved even, but he has music coursing through his veins.

'I hate that term, 'chiptunes', he tells me, very matter-of-factly, moments after we meet for the first time in a restaurant on the outskirts of Hull. 'I mean, what the hell is that stuff about? Where the hell did it come from?'[44]

A professional life spent wrestling with the limitations of video game sound hardware has left him fatigued by the sound and bemused by the notion that others might still listen to the music he created, let alone try to replicate the sound in new compositions. He adds:

I just don't get it. Back in the eighties, when people asked me, 'What do you do?' I used to just say, 'Oh, I program computers'. I knew that if I said, 'Oh I write music for video games', they'd say, 'Oh! You're that guy responsible for those horrible fucking beeps!' Well, I'd be so embarrassed about that that I wouldn't bloody tell them what I did! Do you know what I mean?

I suppose what's strange for me about this whole thing is why, when you've got like, y'know, Kontakt libraries that occupy gigabytes and gigabytes of space and give you, like, a gazillion different instruments at your disposal . . you've got all this stuff and somebody chooses, 'Oh! I'm gonna try and make some sounds with a bloody Gameboy!'

It is a sentiment that is etched across his furrowed brow, but no sooner does the conversation drift to his musical heroes, Chick Corea and Professor Longhair, than his face lights up.

'Years ago', he says, 'I used to give piano lessons. There was this guy, he was a professor at Newcastle University, and all he was interested in was Professor Longhair. He made me flaming well transcribe all this *Tipitina* stuff and try and teach him it. That stuff is really bloody hard to play; getting the groove and the feel is so bloody hard!'

In the early 1980s, however, that was the lot of a jobbing musician, giving lessons and backing cabaret acts in clubs to make ends meet. Sensing the opportunity that the home computer revolution would bring, Hubbard bought himself a Commodore 64 and taught himself to program. He says:

I had a 4-track Teac and I was trying to do recording stuff with that. A friend of mine, he had a Revox, a [Sequential Circuits] Pro One synth, and a [Roland] TR-808. I had the [Roland] TB-303, and we would hook all this stuff up, put a sync track up on tape, you know, and hope that it stayed there. We'd hook all these things up, and we'd take the trigger from this and hook it up to the filter on the Pro One, you know what I mean?

I was reading lots of electronics magazines. 'Well, if you are a musician, you have to learn BASIC', they said. I didn't even have a computer, but as soon as they came out, I just had to pick a 64. It was marketed as a machine with a synth at its heart and it had an elephant's memory. I thought that's the one for me!

Initially, he started out by developing some music education software, hoping to make his fortune, before learning the hard way what we all now know: the home computer as a tool for education is but a myth peddled by children so that their parents will buy the hardware that allows them to play games. Sadly, it was always thus.

Hubbard shifted to game programming, writing his own graphics routines, and in the process getting to know the machine's hardware intimately. Although he didn't have much success with his own games, his publisher was impressed with his music, and he landed his first major professional game music commission with Gremlin's *Thing on a Spring*.

From the outset, Hubbard recognized that creative coding was the key to effective music on the Commodore. His approach was to change the way he thought about music. He coded his own 6502 assembly-level music routine to ensure that his music would run as efficiently as it could, and to squeeze every last drop of performance from the machine, he customised it for each composition, adding and removing features as needed.

He began to think procedurally about musical structure and considered how he could abstract and nest levels of musical detail, allowing whole compositions to be encoded and generated procedurally as a series of functions rather than as a linear data stream. It was a fairly ground-breaking approach, a fractal-style compression that condensed and distilled the musical essence of his works to a concentrated form that could be diluted and replayed later.

At a time when the industry was still professionalizing, Hubbard brought the work ethic of a jobbing club musician. He was, perhaps, the first video game composer—with the possible exception of Koji Kondo—to really elevate the form, creating dynamic, melodic tracks, something he considers the defining characteristic of his music: good tunes, arranged well and with a strong, driving percussion and bass.

I suggested to him, tongue firmly in cheek, that in some respects his career was like that of The Beatles. Both had a conservative period at the start, when they produced safe crowd-pleasers as they found and established their own voices; a confident middle period, adventurous but aware of their limitations and boundaries; and then a transgressive period, the *White Album*, very experimental and not always successful. He laughed self-deprecatingly and agreed.

> That period was unique in the sense that there were absolutely no rules. You had complete freedom to do whatever you wanted, and it was the software aspect of it to me that was really, really exciting. Once you'd got assembly-level machine code programming on the 6502, it opened up so many possibilities: LDA immediate mode 64; store this in location D404, or whatever it was; do a loop here; branch to the loop; check this bit after you have rotated it to sequence on the carry flag, and, if so, branch down there, and all this stuff. And once you got the idea, with your vertical blank interrupt and your faster nonmaskable interrupts, once you got it all running, it kind of opened up the floodgates as to what you could start to do, you know?

Hubbard's earliest work used little of the power of the SID. Mastertronic's *Action Biker*, for example, features a Joplinesque ragtime drag as the title sequence, a piece he describes as 'a real simple little video game kiddy tune'. But before long he was creating provocative electronic compositions that worked the SID dynamically. His soundtrack to the arcade conversion *Commando*, a reworking of the original arcade score, is legendary both as a piece of music and as a model of industrial practice at the time.

He recalls:

The guys at Elite called me up at like twelve or one o'clock one afternoon and asked if I could do a soundtrack for them. 'Get a train down to Birmingham', they said. 'OK', I said, 'I think I can get the train at two o'clock.' So I get the train down to Birmingham, and got there at about five o'clock. We spent most of the night in the pub, and then we went back to the office. Of course, they all buggered off home and I was left in the office all night. So it got to about five o'clock in the morning, and I thought, 'I'd better do a high score tune!' I did that in about 10 minutes, then I knocked out some sound effects and by half past seven or eight o'clock it was all done, and I was back on the train to Newcastle, cheque in hand, by ten o'clock.

Of course, that was far from the routine, but Hubbard and his contemporaries were working at a time when video game music was often added as something of an afterthought. Developers knew they should probably have it but didn't necessarily know what they wanted or how to use it. Hubbard often took jobs on spec over the telephone and was left very much to his own devices to get the music done. He built his reputation on being someone who could deliver, and deliver on time.

I approached everything from a professional musician's background. You know, if you do gigs, right, there's none of this bullshit, 'Oh, you know, sorry I'm late chaps. Have you already started playing, have you? I'll just join in'. There's none of that rubbish. You do it professionally. For a rehearsal at seven o'clock, you're bloody there at seven o'clock. So as a musician, you have that attitude, don't you? It's like you've got discipline, and its drummed into you all the time. In order for me to do this piece I'm gonna have to play this thing slow and I'm gonna have to knuckle down and put the hours in.

So to me, that was the mindset that I had when I was doing it. They say they want it by Tuesday morning? They'll have it by bloody Tuesday morning. I basically approach it like that, with, like, 120 percent effort, so to speak. And the other thing was this was the first time that I was actually earning any bloody money, you know? Back then, I was earning like, 50 quid a gig. When I went to Mastertronic, they asked, 'How much are you charging?' I said, 'About 100 quid'. 'You're not earning enough,' they said. 'We'll put that up to 250 quid'. Suddenly, I went from earning about £5,000 a year to earning something like 26 or 27 grand a year!

It wasn't just his music or his professional attitude that elevated Hubbard to the big league. He brought a technical performativity that allowed him to innovate and push the capabilities of the SID.

I developed a patch system that applied ADSR and vibrato settings. Then I wrote a vibrato routine, a waveform routine, and a few other things. My driver developed as my ideas grew around it, but I could play it all. I used to set, say, two bars—bass and drums and melody or whatever—get that sequence done in the driver and then on the machine code monitor I could get the bytes from the screen for the patches as it's playing, and then tweak the ADSR, you know, to the nth degree to get it to do what I wanted.

It's like playing an arpeggio on an analogue synth and tweaking the knobs. But then also, I could change the music data as well. So I could tweak a D to an E . . . Something like that, you know? I would tend to work on very small two-bar or four-bar phrases and then develop that.

Writing was always part composition and part performance, and partly a puzzle, a Sudoku, maybe. You would have to keep reworking sections to make everything fit together properly. I mean, I did all that stuff with multiplexing voices, so each voice would play maybe three different musical elements. I used to score things on full-sized orchestral score paper and, because I was working that fast, it would be full of sketches and a few notes, and lots and lots of hexadecimal numbers relating to patches and addresses and other kinds of things like that.

Hubbard's musical code wasn't just a series of bytes that related to note sequences, as you might find in a MIDI file. Instead, he encoded his music using a nested modular data structure, creating short phrases that could be sequenced, looped, and pieced together. He would work initially at a Casio keyboard, jotting down phrases on manuscript paper, as shown in figure 3.5. Once the composition had begun to take shape, he would chunk and annotate sections of the music that could be repeated or transposed later to save on memory. These sections would be translated into hex code, along with code that could piece the components back together again to create the full composition.

At the most fundamental level is the pattern, a sequence of notes defined by a variable-length array grouped together in two-, three-, or four-byte chunks. The data structure Hubbard used was very flexible, combining control flags and note data so that each byte of data potentially served multiple functions simultaneously and allowing him to dynamically toggle effects, patches, and musical notes.

At the next level is the track, corresponding to one of the SID's sound channels and made up of a list of pattern numbers in the order in which they are to be played. Above tracks are songs, which are composed of three tracks. The address of each track is stored as two bytes, high and low, so the definition of each song requires just six bytes. This nested approach to musical packing was remarkably efficient; including the driver, Hubbard managed to squeeze the five minutes of music from *Master of Magic* into just 3 kB of memory.

As he described his workflow, Hubbard began tapping out rhythms, using them to illustrate how he would package up his ideas as efficiently as possible, dividing up individual parts and using dynamic patch changes from his driver to interleave multiple lines, using the rests of one part as an opportunity to trigger the notes of another, both

FIGURE 3.5 Rob Hubbard's autograph manuscript from Elite's Commando. Always methodical, Hubbard started from basic chord charts, which can be seen noted in pencil, and worked three staves at a time, one for each of the three SID channels. The letters on the bottom staff on the second page relate to the section annotation Hubbard used when reusing musical phrases, while control bits and parametric calculations are notated in red ink. Images courtesy of Rob Hubbard.

FIGURE 3.5 Continued.

FIGURE 3.5 Continued.

FIGURE 3.5 Continued.

saving space and squeezing an implied four or five virtual channels into the SID's three physical channels.

'OK ... ,' he says, tapping the table with his fingers,

what else is there? Right, I've got this rhythm [taps out a rhythm]. OK, so I need a tune that goes like this [taps out another rhythm]. OK, so that fits there, do you see what I mean? So I would say, 'OK, I've got these rests here, and I've got, like, two other rests there, and that one's a quaver and that one's a quaver. OK ... I can do something to beef up the snare drum there because that happens to be on beat 2, that one there, just before the semiquaver, before the third beat [taps out a rhythm], and I've got a bit of space here'.

Working with just three channels like that, you've got to have a strong melody and bass. It's all about melody and bass. The harmony could be implicit and it would still work, but you have to have a good bassline to give a strong sense of direction. But I couldn't have that using up too many bytes; I'd just have one instance of it and then I would call that up when I needed it. Later on I added in a routine to say how many times it would repeat, which saved space again. You can hear that idea on *Delta*, that Philip Glass thing I did. That plays its theme something like 36 times. I just did a gradual filter change and you get this evolving track.

I guess that, in a sense, there was always that kind of element of minimalism to what I was doing, although I wasn't actually aware of the minimalist movement. You know, Terry Riley, Philip Glass ... I wasn't actually really listening to a lot of that stuff. But that element was obviously there.

Loaders

Around the same time that Rob Hubbard was making the transition from gigging musician to video game composer, a young programmer from Belfast was carving his own path into the industry.

Martin Galway had always dreamed of working in a recording studio, a common enough dream for kids in the 1970s but one that was, in his case, achievable. His father, George, was a musician with the Kings Showband, and his uncle is the flautist Sir James Galway.

'When I got into computers,' he recalls, 'I never thought that music or audio would be involved, it was a very mathematical sort of thing. However, once I noticed you could do that stuff, I gravitated towards it faster than anyone else around me, simply due to my musical background'.[45]

In 1983, Galway, along with some of his classmates, was offered a six-week summer job at Optima Software, the newly created programming division of Database

Publications, who published a range of popular computer magazines. Working on a BBC Micro, Galway and his friend Kevin Edwards developed Optima Software's first game, a Pac-Man clone called *Atomic Protector*.

The following year, while Edwards went on to take up an editorial position at two of Database's magazines, The Micro User and Electron User, Galway found himself working on the music and sound effects for another Pac-Man clone that another friend was writing. Since his friend was too shy to try to sell it, Galway stepped in and acted as agent on his behalf. They found an ad for Manchester-based Ocean Software inside the back cover of that week's Personal Computer Weekly, and Galway gave them a call.

His chutzpah paid off. He struck a deal for the game, and, as any good salesperson would do, offered a sweetener: his own music. He played the team at Ocean his music on a BBC in the office, but David Collier, Ocean's lead games developer, said in his thick Lancashire accent, 'There's no market for t' BBC 'round 'ere lad, what d'yer know about the Commodore 64?'[46] Galway left Ocean's offices with the loan of a complete C64 assembly language development system and the source code for their existing music driver, written by David Dunn, which Galway describes simply as 'dreadful'.[47]

In February 1985, Galway signed a contract as a programmer at Ocean and, using Dunn's driver, wrote his first Ocean score, *Daley Thompson's Decathlon*, a cover of Yellow Magic Orchestra's *Rydeen*.[48]

The game was the first to feature Ocean's new loader system, the Freeload Mastering System.[49] For those used to the few frustrating seconds that it takes today's apps and video games to fire into life, the idea of staring at a blank screen for anything up to 30 minutes while a game loads from tape must seem utterly interminable. Paul Hughes, a young programmer from Wigan, thought he could do better.

Hughes decided to take a look at the C64's ROM file routines and was amazed to find a belt-and-braces system that stored more than four times the data it needed. Every byte required 20 pulses on tape, two for each bit sent, plus a couple of parity bits and a couple of bits to mark the byte end, with all of the data stored again for verification. Hughes realized that he could streamline the whole process using nonmaskable interrupts to keep the timing of his loader system tightly controlled. He successfully shortened the pulse lengths required to store data on tape and freed up the processor to do other tasks while the loading continued in the background. Galway had mentioned to Ocean's software manager, Gary Bracey, that Hughes had written a few loaders, and Hughes was brought in to create the loading routines for every Ocean title from then on.

The loader worked beautifully. After a few seconds, Galway's music bursts into life as a pixellated image of Daley Thompson—one of the United Kingdom's most recognizable athletes at the time—explodes out of the starting blocks behind a set of Olympic rings. The Ocean loaders became one of the most recognizable features of cassette-based games on the Commodore and provided a platform for Galway and others to feature music for its own sake and celebrate the SID.

In fact, the loaders became so efficient that it was possible to co-opt the C64 to run diverting little programs while the main game continued to load. Richard Alpin's Invade-a-Load, for example, which featured on a number of Mastertronic's titles,[50] allowed the player to indulge in a few quick rounds of Space Invaders while the main feature loaded, all the while accompanied by the sonic delights of Rob Hubbard's soundtrack to *One Man and His Droid*. More adventurous still was Mix-E-Load, a fastloader routine created for Thalamus's Delta, which allowed players to remix Rob Hubbard's loading music in real time as the main program loaded in the background. 'That was really the first game where I started to think about having more interactivity with the music', Hubbard says. 'You could change the patches and chord progressions, and do some pitch bends with the joystick'.[51]

Loaders were largely a UK phenomenon, the US market having moved to the faster-loading floppy disks, but they were hugely popular, and even today they retain a dedicated fan base. It wasn't uncommon for fans of Hubbard, Galway, or Daglish to buy a game just because they'd written a new piece of music for a loader. 'That happened all the time', says James Newman, a professor at Bath Spa University, who specializes in the Commodore 64. 'You could go out and buy a budget game from Mastertronic for £1.99. That compared pretty well to the cost of a single, and you could be pretty sure that you'd be getting a few really top-notch tracks from your favourite composer. If the game was playable, that was just a bonus!'[52]

Meanwhile, Galway was working away at his own music driver, which debuted with *Kong Strikes Back!*, conceptually something of a mash-up between Donkey Kong and *Mr. Do's Wild Ride*. The soundtrack to the game (see fig. 3.6) was a Joplinesque rag, which introduced a new technique to the SID's armoury.

FIGURE 3.6 An excerpt from Martin Galway's in-game music from Kong Strikes Back! The chords in this section are encoded as repeated cycles of single notes played back so quickly that they fuse to create the impression of a tremolo chord. The effect is similar to the block chord solos and 'squabble' style of jazz organ playing popularized by Wild Bill Davis and Jimmy Smith.

Galway had been experimenting with his driver to find ways of squeezing more polyphony from the SID's three voices. He had been listening to a lot of Jean Michel Jarre and loved the way Jarre used arpeggiators to take a series of notes played as chords and create synchronized evolving melodic note patterns from them. If that could work as an evolving textural effect on stage, why not in a video game soundtrack? In his music routine, Galway created an arpeggiated chord and cycled through the notes repeatedly and very, very fast on a single SID channel—much faster than the tempo-synced patterns on a hardware arpeggiator. Played fast enough, the notes merged together to give a chordal effect, complete with what Galway describes as 'kind of a wibbly-wobbly, phasey weirdness to the sound'.[53]

From that point on, the arpeggiated chord became one of the key features of chip music. Galway used the technique again and again in his subsequent compositions, and arpeggiated chords were quickly incorporated into the compositional vocabulary of the other composers who were active at the time. Similar arpeggiated chords and filtered noise percussion can be heard opening Rob Hubbard's soundtrack to System 3's *International Karate* and providing the triangle wave accompaniment to Ben Daglish's melody in *Cobra*.

The effect was later incorporated into soundtrackers, a class of pattern-based music sequencing programs which developed as one of the main tools for composing chiptunes. The inclusion of note level commands to arpeggiate chords cemented the technique. As chiptune began to depart from video game music as a form of musical expression in its own right, the sound of arpeggiated chords became one of its most defining features. It is also a sound that has transcended chip music completely to become a staple of contemporary electronic music in general. Alongside the monotonic drone chant of Kraftwerk's *Vitamin* can be heard the bright chirp of chip-style arpeggiated synth chords.

A Hidden Voice

Ever since the problems with its filter became public, the SID chip had developed something of a reputation for having a number of related 'undocumented features'. By combining the control bits of some of the registers, it was possible to coax a fourth sample channel from the SID, 'a strange new waveform', as Rob Hubbard describes it:

> I expanded it to try to use it musically. That was quite a challenge because with it being a nonmaskable interrupt, there was only a certain short range that you could do with it to change the actual pitch of what you were getting out of it.
>
> Towards the end, I had some crude Jean Michel Jarre samples in there that I got from a friend of mine that had an Akai sampler. I was using a few vocal samples, I had a few drum samples, and I had some guitar; rock guitar samples that were on that crazy *Arcade Classics* thing. I remember, I rang the guy who

wrote that and asked him, 'What do you want on this thing?' He was stoned out of his skull and he said 'Just gimme some fucking Hendrix, man!' Hendrix? On a 64? OK, well there's a challenge!

So I got that guitar sample working, and then I needed to tune it. So I ended up working out the fastest interrupt that I could use to keep everything going before the whole machine crashed. So I worked out that I could pitch it up to D or whatever, and down as far as a G. So I would be finding the pitches I could use, and I'd get this pitch and this pitch, and I'd incorporate them into a tune. You know what I mean? It's almost like the technology itself writing the music.[54]

Around 1986, Martin Galway had become intrigued by that same idea and was toying with the possibility of getting the SID to play back short sound samples in his soundtracks. He hacked a drum synthesizer package called *Digidrums* and discovered that by modulating the volume register thousands of times a second, he could also harness that fourth sound channel to play back sample data. He manually created his own simple set of drum samples, which featured in Ocean's port of *Arkanoid* and which Galway describes as a 'series of farts and burps'.[55]

Together with Paul Hughes, he refined the technique, using the C64's nonmaskable interrupts, and refined the sound by using better sample data, so that by *Game Over* in 1987, the SID was dancing to the beat of fairly realistic 4-bit samples in a soundtrack that began with a much harder, Eurohouse sound before mellowing to an Emerson, Lake and Palmer–style outro. Those samples made it possible to capture something of the impactful sound of house in a way that just hadn't been possible with the percussive shaped noise of old.

As with PWM music and samples on the Spectrum, sample playback on the C64 was very processor intensive, so that fourth channel was generally only used on title screens. It also marked an end point in the journey of the C64. 'All the time', Hubbard explains, 'you're always trying to think of something different and something new that you could do, something that you could add that hadn't been done before. But eventually, you know, you just kind of run out. You hit a complete brick wall, and there ain't anything else you can do'.[56]

Digital samples changed the character of C64 music, but change was necessary for the platform to keep up with the changing expectations of its users. By 1986, a new wave of 16-bit machines was beginning to hit the home gaming market, and the arrival of the NES effectively ended sales of the C64 in the United States; the 7 million NES sales in 1988 following its US launch equalled the C64's global sales in its first five years.[57] By the end of 1990, 30 million Nintendos had found homes.[58]

The C64 was still selling strongly in Europe, but developers were beginning to sound the death knell. David Shannon Morse, the CEO of Epyx, warned that 'there are no new 64 buyers, or very few. It's a consistent group that's not growing; … it's going to shrink as part of our business'.[59]

In 1990, a redesigned C64, which repositioned the machine's cartridge port to orient it vertically, was released as the C64 Games System to compete with NES.[60] It sold poorly and was never released outside Europe; its failure contributed to the decision to shelve a planned successor to the C64, the Commodore 65.[61]

In the end, though, it wasn't lack of demand that killed the C64 but the cost of manufacturing its peripherals; the 1541 disk drive ended up costing more than the machine itself, and in March 1994, at CeBIT in Hannover, Commodore announced that the C64 would finally be discontinued. By then, the C64, in all of its various guises, had been in production for more than 10 years and was a testament to an engineering-led period of computing history that already lay in the past.

The Commodore 64 was the result of an autonomous design team who had the freedom to design the machine they wanted from parts they had designed. Without that freedom the VIC Commandos could never have made the technical advances they did. 'If you let marketing get involved with product definition, you'll never get it done quickly', says Bob Yannes, 'and you squander the ability to make something unique, because marketing always wants a product compatible with something else'.[62]

'I knew the Commodore 64 was technically as good and as low-cost as any product that could be made at the time', Al Charpentier adds. 'The freedom that allowed us to do the C64 project will probably never exist again'.[63]

4

Nintendo's NES

A Shop of Strange and Wonderful Things

In the immediate aftermath of the video game crash of 1983, times were tough, in the United States at any rate. As the dust settled in the New Mexico landfill and it looked like there was no future in game consoles, Coleco and Mattel moved back to toys, in the process unleashing on an unsuspecting world the phenomenon that was the Cabbage Patch Kids. Atari, which only a few short months earlier had seemed like an unstoppable behemoth, was broke. Warner, keen to get rid of the albatross around its neck that Atari had become, essentially gave it away on the promise of stock options to Jack Tramiel in the hope that he might make something out of its dusty remains.[1]

In Europe and Japan, that seismic shock barely even registered. Home computers had always been the machine of choice in the United Kingdom and mainland Europe, and Japan, whose domestic video game market was more stable, saw continued growth. There, the video game crash was known simply as Atari Shock.[2]

Nintendo, like Mattel in the United States, was a company that was rooted in tactile play. It began life in 1894 as Nintendo Koppai, having been founded by Fusajiro Yamauchi as a manufacturer of *hanafuda*,[3] handcrafted playing cards painted on mulberry tree bark. In the early 1950s, Hiroshi Yamauchi, who had taken over as president of the company in 1949, travelled to America and met with Walt Disney executives to discuss licensing its characters for Nintendo's cards.[4] Yamauchi realized, as he sat surrounded by icons, that in an age of global entertainment, no matter how successful a family-owned Japanese playing card manufacturer might be, it was a world apart from the big players.

In a bid to diversify and grow, Yamauchi experimented with other businesses, setting up a chain of love hotels, a TV network, and a food company that sold instant rice and noodles.[5] None of them helped Nintendo to break through as a global brand.

That would come from the unlikeliest of products: a retractable plastic grabber called Ultra Hand.

Gunpei Yokoi, who worked as an engineer on the Nintendo assembly line, had created this novelty toy as a pet project, bringing it to the line while he worked. One morning, Yamauchi saw Yokoi with the hand and summoned him to his office. Yokoi was certain he would be fired, but instead Yamauchi explained that he wanted to manufacture and market Yokoi's creation.[6]. It was a smash hit, the first Nintendo product to sell more than 1 million units, and set the company more concretely in a new direction: that of gaming and play.

Under Yokoi's guidance, a range of novelty toys followed. The Ultra Machine and the Ultra Scope, both toys very different from the Ultra Hand, nevertheless built on the success of the original, while N&B Blocks rather shamelessly 'improved' on Lego by introducing curved blocks,[7] an innovation that led to a lawsuit from the Danish company. The Love Tester, a 1969 novelty toy consisting of two metal orbs connected to a control unit that displays a couple's 'love score' when they hold hands,[8] became the first Nintendo product to use electronic components and one of the first to be sold outside Japan. It was the first step along a path that would lead to Nintendo dominating the home gaming market for the next two decades.

In the early 1970s, Nintendo entered into a relationship with Magnavox to produce optoelectronic gun controllers for Magnavox's Odyssey console.[9] After reading an article about automatic ball trap shooting, Yamauchi asked Yokoi if the gun could be adapted for use in an arcade-style shooting simulator. In response, Yokoi created the Laser Clay Shooting System, an arcade game that used overhead projectors to display simulated targets over a forest landscape and optoelectronic reflectors to detect gunshots. Each machine was hugely expensive, costing around ¥4 million to install, mostly in deserted bowling alleys,[10] that particular Japanese craze having largely been displaced by a new one, karaoke.

The Laser Clay Shooting System was a success but also turned out to be a financial millstone, particularly as the economic downturn that followed the oil crisis in 1973 began to bite. Nintendo, finding itself in debt to the tune of ¥5 billion, began to develop a smaller, cheaper arcade cabinet version, the Mini Laser Clay,[11] which launched with *Wild Gunman*, a first-person shooter. It would define the approach of later light-gun arcade cabinets like *Crossbow* and *Operation Wolf*, as well as domestic games like Nintendo's own *Duck Hunt*.

In 1974, Nintendo secured the rights to distribute the Magnavox Odyssey video game console in Japan,[12] but it was a temporary measure. With its growing expertise in video game development, the company decided to go into business for itself. Nintendo would go on to have further arcade success with the Space Invader clones *Radar Scope* and *Space Firebirds*, and, of course, Donkey Kong, the game that introduced the world's most famous moustachioed Italian plumber, known originally as Jumpman.

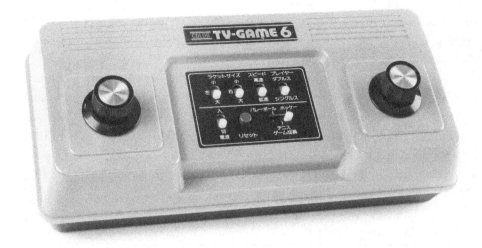

FIGURE 4.1 The Color TV Game 6 was an early Nintendo Pong clone that established the company as a manufacturer of video game systems.

In 1977 Nintendo released the Color TV Game 6 (fig. 4.1),[13] a popular but unremarkable Pong clone, the 6 referring to the number of game variants on the console: one each of volleyball, hockey, and tennis, each of which could be played in either singles or doubles mode. Several variants of this game would follow, each of which increased the complexity and variety of the gameplay. Still more important, though, was Nintendo's hiring of Shigeru Miyamoto, a shaggy-haired apprentice product planner, who, under the watchful eye of Yokoi, went on to propel Nintendo to the very top of the video gaming league.

Very Big Deal in America

Nintendo's move to the American video game market began in 1980. Minoru 'Mino' Arakawa, the husband of Yamauchi's daughter, Yoko, had been selected by Yamauchi to promote the company's arcade games stateside. To break the market, Nintendo manufactured 3,000 Radar Scope cabinets and shipped them from Kyoto to a warehouse in New Jersey. Arakawa's job was simple: sell them all and establish Nintendo's position as an arcade giant.[14]

What neither Yamauchi nor Arakawa had banked on, however, was that the American market simply didn't want another Space Invaders knock-off and certainly not one by an unknown Japanese company. Arakawa worked tirelessly, but in the end only about 1,000 Radar Scope cabinets found homes.

And then Arakawa conceived a master stroke. He realized that he was never going to shift the unsold stock of Radar Scope cabinets. He needed something new to sell, and he would do it not by creating a completely new game but by reprovisioning those un-sold Radar Scope cabinets. The sales on Radar Scope had already covered the cost of the existing hardware; converting the cabinets would save Nintendo the time and cost of manufacturing and shipping 2,000 more.

Miyamoto and Yokoi were drafted in to develop the new game, and immediately contracted with Ikegami Tsushinki, the company that had built Radar Scope, to advise them on what its components could support.[15] Yamauchi wanted the new game to be based on *Popeye*. Back when Nintendo was making instant noodles it had run a line of Popeye ramen, and a Robin Williams movie featuring the character was in production, but when Yamauchi found out it would take years for Nintendo to acquire the arcade rights, the idea was quietly dropped.

Leaving the characters of Popeye, Bluto, and Olive Oyl to one side, Miyamoto found himself intrigued by the underlying narrative: Popeye's continual quest to defeat Bluto, the gorilla-like villain, and save the girl. In Miyamoto's mind, that gorilla-like villain translated quite literally into a gorilla-like villain, a huge King Kong–style antag-onist who captured the heroine and held her hostage at the top of the screen. Miyamoto scrambled for the perfect name. He wanted an English phrase that captured the sense of his 'stubborn gorilla'. 'Stubborn' translated as 'Donkey' and 'gorilla' as 'Kong'.[16]

Miyamoto, a music lover, composed a short score to accompany the game, a huge improvement on the annoying beeps that had accompanied Radar Scope. The music worked in tandem with an animated cut-screen story that played out between levels: Donkey Kong, captive in hand, would climb to the top of the construction site and stamp his feet, tilting the girders, and snatch away the girl once more just as Jumpman got close to rescuing her.

Like a classic Hollywood score, Miyamoto's music supports the action; an over-blown dramatic intro emphasizes the high stakes and makes it clear who the bad guy is, while a chirpy level sting and a bluesy love theme provide contrast to a background music track that becomes more insistent the higher Jumpman climbs. At a time when shooters were at the height of popularity, few games put the focus on characters and story. Donkey Kong, by contrast, created a self-contained narrative with cute, likeable characters that allowed players to act out an age-old quest.

Donkey Kong was a smash hit, and Yamauchi approached Masayuki Uemura, head of Nintendo's hardware-focused Research & Development 2 division, to ask him to investigate the feasibility of a low-cost cartridge-based console.[17] Like Atari, Nintendo wanted a system that could build on its growing reputation for arcade games by allowing consumers to play them at home. Uemura and his team concluded that they could build a machine, codenamed GAMECOM,[18] by packaging up the Donkey Kong components as an integrated circuit and using this as a base. When Uemura told his wife about the project, she said, 'If it's a domestic computer that's neither a home computer nor a per-sonal computer, perhaps you could say that it's a family computer? In Japanese, 'personal computer' is shortened to 'pasokon', so why don't you nickname it the 'Famicom'?'[19]

The Famicom (fig. 4.2) launched in Japan on July 13, 1983, at a price of just ¥14,800, around $60. Housed in a cream and burgundy case, it shipped with three games, all ports of Nintendo's arcade hits—Donkey Kong; *Donkey Kong Jr.*, and *Popeye*—and two controllers that were hardwired to the console.

Rather than Zilog's Z80, which had provided the processor power for Nintendo's earlier arcade games, the Famicom was based around a Ricoh chip, the 2A03, a modified version of the MOS 6502 that was engineered to handle controller inputs and generate both sounds and sprites. Integrating these functions directly on the main processor reduced size and cost but posed a problem for Uemura's engineers, who had neither the experience nor the development tools to work with the new chip. That meant they had to reconstruct their arcade games for the new console from scratch, something that required 'a lot of patience, including tasks such as watching the game screen and measuring the timing of animations with a stopwatch'.[20]

With the Famicom on the shelves, Yamauchi again turned his sights to America. In April 1983, he sat down with Atari executives who had travelled to Kyoto to see a demo of the new hardware and offered them a deal: Nintendo would make Famicoms, and Atari would sell them outside Japan, branded as an Atari product.[21] Negotiations were already dragging out when the crash happened, and the deal fell apart not least because Atari itself fell apart. Nintendo were left without an American partner, but in retrospect it was, perhaps, a blessing; had the deal gone through, the Famicom could have been swallowed up, just one more casualty of Atari Shock.

Instead, Yamauchi decided that Nintendo would break through into the market alone. Arakawa was dispatched to US electronics trade shows with a supply of

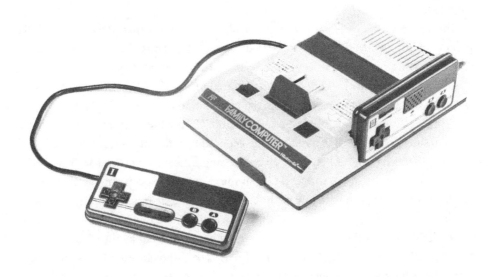

FIGURE 4.2 Nintendo's Famicom.

demo consoles that had acquired a new American-friendly name, the Advanced Video System.[22]

Nobody was interested. The market, still reeling from the aftershocks of the crash, couldn't see the logic, or any future, in trying to launch a new game console.

Yamauchi was undeterred. If America wasn't ready for a new game console, he would sell it as a toy. The Advanced Video System was renamed the Nintendo Entertainment System (NES) and bundled with a foot-tall robot, the Robotic Operating Buddy, or R.O.B., which was designed to work with two specially written games, *Gyromite* and *Stack-Up*, in the hope that toy retailers rather than electronics stores would stock the device.[23] They didn't. Even when it was sold to them as a sophisticated electronic novelty, US retailers wouldn't countenance another game console.

In a last-ditch effort to gain a toehold in the United States, Yamauchi shipped 100,000 consoles to Nintendo America's warehouse in New Jersey. Arakawa and his team worked round the clock to sell direct to as many toy shops, electronics outlets, and department stores as they could, all backed by a cast-iron guarantee: any unsold consoles could be returned for a full refund.[24]

In the run-up to Christmas, Arakawa managed to shift half of the consoles, quite an achievement in such a hostile environment. He continued to push for sales, first targeting Los Angeles, then Chicago, and finally San Francisco. The effort gave Nintendo the toehold it needed, and by the middle of 1986 the NES was ready to launch nationally.

The Audio Processing Unit

The NES departed from the sleek, futuristic lines and livery of the Famicom. Instead, its conservative grey plastic case adopted the more familiar form factor of an early 1980s VCR (see fig. 4.3).

Inside the plastic case was the same Ricoh RP2A03 CPU that powered the NES's Japanese sibling, while those consoles that were destined for the European market shipped with the equivalent RP2A07 (fig. 4.4), which was functionally identical to the RP2A03 but clocked slower—1.66 MHz as opposed to the 1.79 MHz clock in the NTSC system—to compensate for the 50 Hz refresh rate used in PAL video displays.

The RPA203 was something of a hybrid chip. Unlike the Commodore 64, whose dedicated sound chip, the SID, handled tone generation and synthesis, Ricoh integrated an audio processing unit (APU) directly onto a single die of the processor. In terms of computer architecture, then, the NES was similar to the ZX Spectrum, which handled all of its sound commands directly on its Z80 core. As far as programming the device went, however, the APU was treated as a discrete entity and could be issued commands independently of any other processes that were being carried out by the CPU.

The APU offers five channels of sound playback, although each has its own particular characteristics and constraints. There are two pulse wave channels, each with four settings for the duty cycle: 12.5 percent, 25 percent, 50 percent, and 75 percent,

FIGURE 4.3 Nintendo's NES.

FIGURE 4.4 The Ricoh 2A07 chip is the PAL version of the 2A03 that had powered the Famicom. It is functionally identical to the 2A03, save for a slower clock speed to compensate for the different vertical refresh rate used in PAL displays.

although the 25 percent and 75 percent are sonically indistinguishable, since each is a phase-shifted copy of the same basic waveshape. That gave composers three different timbres that could be shifted dynamically, although without the precision or continuous control offered by the SID, to create some tonal variation.

With a limited timbral palette to draw on, Nintendo video game composers often referenced Western prog rock ideas about synthetic orchestration in their games. The square wave, a 50 percent pulse, for example, was traditionally used as a lead instrument—an eerie Minimoog square wave carries Keith Emerson's melody in Emerson, Lake and Palmer's *Lucky Man*[25]—and the NES continued that tradition. The pulse channels were used frequently to carry the melody lines. Just listen to the exposed opening theme of Koji Kondo's *Legend of Zelda* as an example.

The duty cycle, however, could be modulated during play to sculpt new, more complex timbres, effectively bandlimiting the signal as the waveform shifted. The arpeggiated guzheng-type instrument in the soundtrack to Sunsoft's *Gremlins 2: The New Batch*, for example, demonstrates the effect well. Combined with a decaying amplitude envelope, the effect is a more than passable plucked sound that mimics the natural overtone structure of a real plucked string, with a noisy, harmonically dense attack portion that quickly decays as the sound sustains. The effect isn't dissimilar to the simulated plucked string tones created by the Karplus-Strong synthesis method,[26] which applies a low-pass filter to a tapped delay line to create a similar time-varying harmonic structure.

Pushed further, modulating the duty cycle continually could create a warbling effect that was similar to that of the arpeggiated chords that Martin Galway introduced to the C64. At its most extreme, composers could cycle through each of the duty cycles in turn, modulating with every vertical blank of the display. It's an effect that is particular to the NES and can be heard on Data East's 1989 game *Bad Dudes*.

Applying these effects was an intricate process that required a thorough knowledge of the APU's memory registers,[27] which begin at $4000 for pulse channel 1—the dollar sign indicating a hexadecimal address—and $4004 for pulse channel 2, as illustrated in table 4.1.

Each pulse channel has its own length counter, a hardware clock that counts down from a predetermined value and automatically silences the channel, and an envelope generator, a simple affair that offers two options: a decreasing sawtooth envelope, which is enabled by setting the appropriate flag low in the port at $4000, or a constant volume contour that's controlled by the four volume bits. For music programming, both the length counter and the hardware envelope were often disabled and the settings for duration and volume manipulated in software by changing the volume registers on each frame to give more control over note timings and create more sophisticated envelope shapes.

The port at $4001 controls a sweep unit, a time-varying control signal that allows the frequency of the pulse waves to be swept at a rate determined by the sweep period, in a direction, up or down, that is controlled by the negate flag, and with an effect depth specified by the three shift bits. That sweep effect was most often used for sound effects,

TABLE 4.1. The memory control registers for the pulse channels of the NES APU.

Memory location (channel 1/2)	Data								Description
$4000/ $4004	DC_1	DC_0	LCF	ENV	VOL_3	VOL_2	VOL_1	VOL_0	Duty cycle/ length counter flag/ envelope flag/ volume
$4001/ $4005	SWF	SWP_2	SWP_1	SWP_0	NF	$SHFT_2$	$SHFT_1$	$SHFT_0$	Sweep flag/ sweep period/ negate flag/ shift
$4002/ $4006	$FREQ_7$	$FREQ_6$	$FREQ_5$	$FREQ_4$	$FREQ_3$	$FREQ_2$	$FREQ_1$	$FREQ_0$	Freq LO
$4003/ $4007	LC_4	LC_3	LC_2	LC_1	LC_0	$FREQ_0$	$FREQ_0$	$FREQ_0$	Length counter/ freq HI

TABLE 4.2. The memory control registers for the triangle channel of the NES APU, running from $4008 to $400B. The registers at port $4009 are not used.

Memory location	Data								Description
$4008	LCF	RLD_6	RLD_5	RLD_4	RLD_3	RLD_2	RLD_1	RLD_0	Length counter flag/ reload value
$4009									Unused
$400A	$FREQ_7$	$FREQ_6$	$FREQ_5$	$FREQ_4$	$FREQ_3$	$FREQ_2$	$FREQ_1$	$FREQ_0$	Freq LO
$400B	LC_4	LC_3	LC_2	LC_1	LC_0	$FREQ_{10}$	$FREQ_9$	$FREQ_8$	Length counter/ freq HI

but it did crop up in music tracks from time to time. Tim Follin's prog rock–inspired soundtrack for *Silver Surfer* uses the sweep unit to create smooth portamento effects, for example, while the *Identify Believer* theme from *Gimmick!* uses it to create pitch slides at the end of phrases, an effect similar to a guitarist rounding off phrases by finger-sliding down the neck at the end of a line.

The 11 frequency bits across ports $4002 and $4003 are used to set the frequency of the note using a frequency divider that is clocked to the master clock speed, 21.477272 MHz for NTSC systems and 26.601712 MHz in the PAL variant. In fact, these values relate to wave periods rather than frequencies and control a counter that is used to determine the period of the waveform, and so the lower the note in hertz, the higher the value specified across those 11 bits.

The final five bits at $4003 set the length counter, which is used to set the duration of the note if the length counter flag is enabled at $4000.

The next channel (table 4.2) provides a 4-bit triangle wave, a softer-sounding waveform that was sometimes used as a lead line—listen to the flute-like lead of the *Overland* theme from *Dragon Warrior*, for example—but was more commonly used to provide basslines, largely because the triangle channel offers no volume or tone-shaping controls, a feature that can work reasonably well to provide a consistent bass level throughout.

The port at $4008 controls a linear counter, which provides an accurate duration counter for the triangle wave. This is toggled using the control flag and controlled using the reload value. As with the two pulse channels, the frequency of the triangle channel is determined by an 11-bit value formed from port $400A and the least significant three bits of $400B, while the remaining five bits of port $400B provide the length counter value. Unlike the pulse channels, which are clocked to the APU, the counter that controls the triangle wave is synced to the CPU clock, resulting in a different set of frequency relationships and pitching the triangle an octave lower than the pulse channels for the same set of timer control values.

The noise channel (table 4.3) occupies the next set of registers from port $400C and uses a 15-stage LFSR to output a pseudorandom noise signal. By default, the LFSR is initialized, or *seeded*, with the initial value of 0x0001 on startup with taps at registers 0 and 1, generating a maximal length sequence some 32,767 bits long. However, it can also be placed in an alternate mode, *short mode*, which taps registers 0 and 6 to generate either a 31- or 93-bit output sequence, depending on the initial values of the registers. The effect is a metallic buzz and can be heard in the *Quick Man* level of *Mega Man 2*.

The port at $400C controls the volume of the noise channel, with flags to enable the length counter and envelope control, just as on the pulse channels. The frequency control for the noise channel is limited to a 4-bit word, giving just 16 different tones from which to choose, although with the two modes, selected using the flag bit on port $400E, and two different cycle lengths in short mode, this gives 48 different noise tones, which could be combined sequentially to create a huge range of dynamic effects.

Finally, the port at $4000F defines five length counter bits, which, provided the length counter flag is enabled, provides automatic duration control over the channel.

The noise channel provides a straightforward way of generating percussion sounds, using different frequency settings and envelopes to simulate kicks, snares, and hi-hats. A low-frequency, high-volume long-mode noise burst with either a linear or exponential

TABLE 4.3. The memory control registers for the noise channel of the NES APU, running from $400C to $400F. The registers at port $400D are not used.

Memory location	Data							Description
$400C		LCF	ENV	VOL_3	VOL_2	VOL_1	VOL_0	Length counter flag/ envelope flag/ volume
$400D								Unused
$400E	SMF			$FREQ_3$	$FREQ_2$	$FREQ_1$	$FREQ_0$	Short mode flag/ frequency
$400F	LC_4	LC_2	LC_1	LC_0				Length counter

decay envelope, for example, provides a kick drum, while a similar midrange tone works as a snare. Lots of NES games used exactly this kind of drum synthesis exclusively. *The Guardian Legend*, for example, uses only two drum sounds created in exactly this way to provide snare variations as drum rudiments are drilled out beneath soaring lead lines.

The NES APU has one other trick up its sleeve. The fifth channel, the delta modulation channel (DMC) (table 4.4) can automatically handle 1-bit delta-encoded samples, allowing for sample playback without tying up the CPU as sample playback did on other platforms.

In a delta modulation scheme,[28] the only data that are stored relate to whether the sampled signal has increased, corresponding to a one, or decreased, corresponding to a zero, since the previous data point. These values are then used to continually modulate the duty cycle of a pulse wave. It's a system that works reasonably well, but, as I showed on the Spectrum, it introduces noise: delta modulation can only track the original signal by one delta value per sample and so can miss out the high-frequency detail of a very fast-changing signal; and with only two options—higher or lower—it can't accurately deal with static signals, instead fluctuating above and below the true level.

As an alternative, programmers could use the DMC's Direct Load port at $4011. Sending a succession of 7-bit numbers to this port at a defined rate allowed programmers to create custom **pulse-code modulation** (PCM) samples at custom rates, albeit with the same cost as before: the data-throughput and processing tied up the CPU to such an extent that its use was limited to nongameplay situations and title screens. The effect can be heard on *Bart vs. the Space Mutants*.

The limiting factor for sampled sounds on the NES was cartridge memory. Linear PCM sound samples, even at relatively low-bit resolutions, can chew through memory remarkably quickly, and, without bank switching, the APU allowed for only 16 kB of sample data. Consequently, the DMC was used mainly for percussion sounds—the soundtrack to *Super Mario Bros. 3* is a fine example of this—or very short samples of speech.

'For sampling, the resolution of the sound was very low—it sounded cheap', says Hidenori Maezawa, who composed many NES soundtracks for Konami in the

TABLE 4.4. **The memory control registers for the delta modulation channel of the NES APU, running from $4010 to $4015. The registers at port $4014 are not used.**

Memory location	Data								Description
$4010	IRQ	LPF			$PFREQ_3$	$PFREQ_2$	$PFREQ_1$	$PFREQ_0$	IRQ flag/ loop flag/ playback freq
$4011		DLD_6	DLD_5	DLD_4	DLD_3	DLD_2	DLD_1	DLD_0	Direct load
$4012	SA_7	SA_6	SA_5	SA_4	SA_3	SA_2	SA_1	SA_0	Sample address
$4013	SL_0	SL_0	SL_0	SL_0	SL_0	SL_0	SL_0	SL_0	Sample length

mid-1980s. 'Normally, when you sample, your software will interpolate the whole scale. With the Famicom, though, we had to sample every single note. But of course, doing that eats up memory space. So really, it was terribly limited—I had to decide which notes we were going to use, and which ones I should sample. It was all very complicated and difficult'.[29]

The most significant two bits of port $4010 control one of three DMC playback modes, either playing the sample until the length counter reaches zero, with or without sending the CPU an interrupt request, or looping the sample continuously, while the least significant four bits specify the sample playback frequency.

It's important to note that in terms of sample playback, what determines the frequency is this playback speed relative to the speed at which the data were originally sampled. If, for example, a sample was recorded at 2 kHz and the sample data read at 4 kHz, twice as quickly as they were laid down, then the data will be used up twice as quickly; the period will therefore be halved and the frequency correspondingly doubled.

The DMC frequency control bits, then, configure a series of timer values, outlined in table 4.5, that determine how long the channel waits before it reads the next data byte from memory. The timer is decremented at the frequency of the CPU and fetches the next sample byte when the count reaches 0 and then resets. This process repeats until either the channel is disabled or the length counter has reached 0, depending on the playback mode.

TABLE 4.5. Playback frequency values and timer settings for the NTSC NES delta modulation channel.

Playback frequency	CPU clock count	Playback frequency ratio	Equivalent playback pitch	Pitch discrepancy (cents)
0000	428	1	C8	0
0001	380	1.13	D8	−5.94
0010	340	1.26	E8	1.51
0011	320	1.34	F8	−3.45
0100	286	1.5	G8	2.08
0101	254	1.69	A8	−3.34
0110	286	1.89	B8	−5.55
0111	214	2	C9	0
1000	190	2.25	D9	−5.94
1001	160	2.68	F9	−3.45
1010	142	3.01	G9	−10.06
1011	128	3.34	A9	10.24
1100	106	4.04	C10	−16.26
1101	84	5.1	E10	−18.98
1110	72	5.94	G10	14.15
1111	54	7.93	C11	16.1

The absolute frequency at which the sample data are read is calculated by dividing the CPU speed by the clock count, and so a frequency setting of 0000, corresponding to a CPU clock count of 428, corresponds to a frequency of 4,181.71 Hz. If we take this as the unity playback frequency, that is, if we assume that reading the sample data at this rate corresponds to the sample being replayed at the same pitch at which it was recorded, we can calculate the different pitches at which the sample can be replayed and the corresponding discrepancy in cents from the equivalent equally tempered pitch.

We can see that the first eight frequency settings correspond to successive notes of the diatonic scale, and, although all but the C8 and C9 pitches are out of tune, it is only by a few cents. Pushing the tuning into the second octave and higher results in samples that are far enough out of tune to limit their use. Very few games, then, used pitched samples, and those that did—and Sunsoft more than any other played with sound-track samples—tended to use them in basslines, using a combination of short pitched multisamples in semitones to provide the most consistent sound quality across a usable chromatic range.

The ports at $4012 and $4013 specify a sample address and sample length, which are used by the automatic sample playback routine. When a sample is started, the APU reads the sample address, sets the number of bytes remaining to the sample length, and continues to work through the sample data without any further intervention until the sample data are exhausted.

One consequence of using the DMC was that, because of the nonlinear mixing used by the APU, increasing the values of the registers in port $4011 reduced the volume of the triangle and noise channels, and by the time the maximum value, $01111111, was fed to the DMC's PCM control register, the level of the noise and triangle channels dropped to around half that of normal, an effect that was sometimes used to apply limited volume control to the triangle channel and can be heard in *Ice Climber; Clu Clu Land*, and *Super Mario Bros.*

Mario time!

The NES, as a console, wasn't really set up to allow the easy development of software by the end user. In fact, for a significant portion of its lifespan, there was no official NES development kit at all; developers had to create their own development tools and software drivers from scratch. Nintendo did, however, release *Famicom BASIC*,[30] a software cartridge that was bundled with a computer keyboard and textbook and allowed users to program their consoles and save the programs to cassette tape. The instruction manual included a section that described how to program Japanese popular music. It was written by a new recruit at Nintendo, Koji Kondo.

Kondo was born in Nagoya in 1961 and cut his musical teeth when he was just five years old on a Yamaha Electone electronic organ. By the time he was in his teens, he was gigging regularly with a band, turning out covers of the artists he loved most: Deep

Purple, Yes, and ELO. As he grew, so did his musical tastes, taking in Cassiopeia, Chick Corea, and Herbie Hancock. 'I [wanted] to be a keyboard player', Kondo recalls, 'but just a little! But not so much becoming a famous on-stage performer—more like a studio musician, playing with lots of different kinds of music'.[31]

That chance came in his senior year at university. Kondo came across an advert from Nintendo on a college noticeboard. They were looking to recruit people to develop music and sound effects for a new home video game console. 'I graduated from university in 1984', he recalls. 'I found my way to Nintendo by looking at the school's job placement board. You're supposed to apply to many different companies, but I saw the Nintendo ad, and had a love of making synthesizers, and loved games, and thought—that's the place for me. I interviewed with one company, Nintendo, and that's where I've been ever since'.[32]

Kondo joined Nintendo alongside Hirokazu 'Hip' Tanaka, who would later go on to score the music for Game Boy *Tetris*, and Yukio Kaneoka. All three were assigned to work on creating scores and sound effects for Nintendo's games.

Kondo's first work with Nintendo was to create the sound effects and musical stings for the arcade boxing game, *Punch-Out!!* 'I really learned everything about programming from Mr. Kaneoka', he says. 'It's thanks to him that I was able to learn how to program sound effects, and all the basics of sound engineering. The whole engine behind creating sounds via programming, I learned from Mr. Kaneoka'.[33]

His music was good: arcade style but infused with Western jazz; just listen to the main theme from *Devil World*, a cute platformer whose soundtrack includes a *Nut Rocker*–inspired sting.

Devil World also paired Kondo with Shigeru Miyamoto, who recalls:

Back then I was doing all the design work myself, so it was a big help just to have another designer [in Takashi Tezuka]. When [he and Koji Kondo] joined [the team], I was part way through Devil World, so I had them help me with that.

Around the time of Donkey Kong we didn't have anyone but Tanaka-san who could write music, so I was often talking about how we'd be in trouble if we didn't get any sound specialists. And I said that in the coming years we would definitely need not just musicians, but designers as well.[34]

Kondo says:

Mr. Tanaka and Mr. Kaneoka were both graduates in electrical engineering. Mr. Tanaka had been in a band as a hobby and Mr. Kaneoka had a lot of interest in music, but neither of them had an educational background in music, per se. [Their] focus was mostly on sound effects and how to create unique and original sounds in that arena. Mr. Kaneoka was very interested in that and really enjoyed doing it—occasionally, they would add some fanfares and things like that, but that was really the extent of their musical incorporation into games.

Meanwhile, other companies in the video game landscape had started paying more attention to music, and adding more music to games. That pushed Nintendo to re-examine their own method of dealing with music and start bringing in more music in addition to just the sound effects.[35]

Miyamoto loved Kondo's work and his attitude, and they both loved the same bands. Their take on video game music was driven by that shared passion, and it bubbled over in some unusual ways.

'[We] made a song for Devil World's bonus screen', Miyamoto says. 'Kondo-san thought up the tune, and Tezuka-san wrote some lyrics. I thought, "They're nice, so let's put them in the instruction booklet!" Writing words for video game music and including the notation and lyrics in the instruction booklet wasn't something anyone was doing back then, so I was all for it'.[36]

A friendship forged, Miyamoto and Kondo began working on a new project, Super Mario Bros. Miyamoto and his team pooled their expertise, fashioned from work on other games. The characters and the gameplay mechanic would come from Mario Bros., a game that resurrected Miyamoto's hero from Donkey Kong and united him with his younger brother, Luigi, who had followed him into the family plumbing business. Miyamoto liked the way Mario Bros. played, particularly the enemy attacks and power-ups, but he wanted to include scrolling, a colourful background, and bigger characters moving around. In the mazes of Devil World, they had already managed to move characters twice as big as those in previous games, so they knew that it could be done. Add to that the scrolling technology and level warps from Excitebike; Donkey Kong's sloping platforms, lifts, and conveyor belts; and Donkey Kong Jr.'s ropes, logs, and springs and the heritage of Super Mario Bros. is clear. It was the culmination of everything Miyamoto had done until that point.

All he needed now was a narrative, and that came in the form of an epic quest: Mario Mario, the plumber, not exactly a classic hero, would be a stranger in a strange land, the Mushroom Kingdom. Littered throughout were all manner of classic archetypes: Bowser, the pantomime villain, and Princess Toadstool, née Peach, the classic damsel in distress. Split across four stages in each of eight worlds, Super Mario Bros. was a game that had both depth and longevity. It was exactly what was needed to revive the US interest in video games.

From the outset, Kondo knew that the score would have to be different. With its range of characters, each with their own personalities, and evolving plotline, Super Mario Bros. needed music that would work with the game on a fundamental level, not just sit alongside it.

'I wanted to create something that had never been heard before', Kondo says. '[Something] where you'd think: "This isn't like game music at all, [is] it?" … First off, it had to fit the game the best, enhance the gameplay and make it more enjoyable. Not just sit there and be something that plays while you play the game, but is actually a part of the game. As I'd create a piece of music, I'd set it aside and start working on another one, and then notice that something didn't fit, so I'd go back and fix it. And so all of my rewriting and recomposing was self-motivated'.[37]

With Super Mario Bros., the team were able to use a newly developed 256-kilobit cartridge. At the time it was a luxury, but even then, 32 kB of memory wasn't a lot of space into which to squeeze 32 levels of gameplay, graphics, sound, and music.

Toshihiko Nakago, who coded the game, recalls:

Back then, we scrambled around for open memory. For example, 1 block [of graphics] was 3 bytes, maybe 2, so if there were 20 bytes open, you could put in 10 blocks. Miyamoto-san would say, 'I want to put in 10 more blocks', and throw them in. You'd rapidly run out of memory that way. Then, Kondo-san was about to compose the ending music, so I asked: 'How many bytes do you need?' He said he could loop a song with 40 bytes. And 20 bytes were left over, so Miyamoto-san said: 'Let's make a crown!'[38]

Like a 1960s Hanna-Barbera cartoon, looping a wraparound background behind Yogi and Boo Boo, Miyamoto and his team reused those chunks of memory mercilessly. Clouds and bushes are the same sprites, coloured differently, while many of the sound effects are used multiple times throughout the game. Kondo's soundtrack, no more than three minutes of original score, was also played repeatedly. His genius was in writing three minutes of music that not only functioned as music to enhance the gameplay but also could be heard over and over again without driving the player to distraction. This was, perhaps, the first true video game underscore.

Kondo began work with the *Underwater Theme*, a lilting ragtime-style waltz that captured something of the grace with which Mario swam among the Bloopers and Cheep Cheeps. It seemed to Kondo that this movement was the easiest to imagine and capture musically, and the waltz, with its flowing triple-time feel, seemed the perfect way to do it.

Kondo worked hard to capture the feel of the level and the gameplay, synchronizing the tempo with some of the on-screen movement; the Cheep Cheeps flick their tails in time with the music, and the gold coin counter at the top of the screen shimmers along to the tempo.[39] It was this integration of the different elements of the game perhaps more than anything that made the music to Super Mario Bros. different from all the game music that had come before it. On the C64, game music had similar, catchy melodies, but few were integrated with the gameplay in the way Kondo envisioned. 'With Mario', he recalls, 'the music is inspired by the game controls, and its purpose is to heighten the feeling of how the game controls'.[40]

The Underwater Theme (transcribed in fig. 4.5), like all the other tracks in the game, loops to conserve valuable memory. It begins with a short introduction, which Kondo includes as part of the loop, with those extra few bars squeezing as much variety from the music as possible.

FIGURE 4.5 The Underwater Theme from Super Mario Bros. is just 32 bars long but captures a flowing sense of character movement appropriate to the setting. The inclusion of the introduction as part of the loop breaks the direct repetition of the main waltz itself and adds variety, aiding the 'lastability' of the track.

Undoubtedly, however, the jewel in Kondo's soundtrack is the *Overworld Theme*, a syncopated jazz calypso that has transcended its gaming roots. Its sound is instantly evocative of the NES, a sound shaped by the constraints of the APU and the NES's meagre memory. 'When we were working with limited notes', Kondo recalls, 'the challenge really was what can you add to the music within that limited note structure to make it sound robust and more full'.[41]

Kondo drew on his love of jazz. With only three pitched voices to play with, he used shell voicings, stripped-back arrangements of the sort favoured by, among others, Bud Powell and Bill Evans.[42] These arrangements reduce complex extended chords to their fundamental parts, normally a root, third, and seventh, retaining their essential character and, from that and the musical context, implying their rich tonal colour.

The intro to the Overworld Theme (fig. 4.6) begins with a D9. The triangle channel and Pulse 1 channel emphasize the root and third of the chord, respectively, while Pulse 2 carries the melody, switching between the ninth and flattened seventh, creating a clear sense of tonality and providing a strong pull towards the resolution of the G major chord in the next bar, which is again voiced with just the root and the third. This, in turn, pulls towards the main melody, which begins with a C major chord, meaning the whole introduction functions as a modified ii-V-I progression, a common substitution, particularly in jazz-blues turnarounds, and perhaps the single sequence that provides the primary harmonic motivating force in jazz.

This approach stands in fairly stark contrast to the arpeggiated chords of the C64.

Neil Baldwin, who composed the soundtracks for several PAL-format NES releases, says:

> There weren't that many European composers working on the NES. I was never really a fan of that Japanese style.... Don't get me wrong, the tunes and arrangements by some of the Japanese guys were incredible but they just never seemed to be rendered properly.

FIGURE 4.6 The introduction to Koji Kondo's Overworld Theme from Super Mario Bros. functions as a modified II-V-I progression, providing a strong sense of musical motivation. Note the shell voicing in the opening bars.

The Japanese guys were probably using the NES in the way it was designed to be used! I've had my style described as 'European' because of the judicious use of fast arpeggios to mimic chords. It did tend to be European guys that did that and I've read that Japanese people found the sound of those arpeggios a bit ugly.[43]

Rather than pushing the hardware beyond its capabilities, Kondo's approach was to work to its strengths, stripping harmony in particular back to its fundamentals and focusing on getting the most out of just two or three channels, looking instead to the rhythm to create complexity.

Syncopation, shifting the emphasis of the beat from the strong up- and downbeats of the musical pulse to the weaker beats between, has long been a way of creating musical interest. It can be heard predominantly in music that has its roots in Africa—everything from Scott Joplin's piano rags through to the polyrhythmic funk of Parliament and Funkadelic, whose dense rhythmic textures derive from the interplay between different layers of simple lines, some emphasizing the straight downbeat while others focus on the spaces in between.[44]

Kondo creates a similar interplay between the tone channels, which move together in straight time, with a swing percussion line (fig. 4.7). This interplay between the duple-time melody and bass and the triple-time percussion creates a shifting rhythmic emphasis, similar to the effect created by Debussy in his first *Arabesque*, which layers a flowing, dreamy melody in quavers over an arpeggiated triplet accompaniment.

In a 2010 panel discussion to celebrate the twenty-fifth anniversary of the game, Kondo spoke of the importance of the rhythm to Iwata, the president and CEO of Nintendo, along with two other Nintendo composers, Nagamatsu and Yokota.

Kondo: [My original Overworld Theme] got canned. I realized that an easy-going sound wouldn't match Mario's running speed and the way he jumps. I remade

FIGURE 4.7 The opening four bars of section A of Super Mario's Overworld Theme shows how rhythmic complexity is created from the interplay between the tone channels, which are mainly in duple time, and the noise channel, in triple time.

the song so it would match the rhythm of his movements, and that became the Ground Theme.... There's a noise in there like triplets. Tee tee-tee ... tee tee-tump ... I took that from the first song I made. I was going to remake the whole thing, but when I wrote the new melody and listened to it, I decided to try out that noise, and it just seemed to fit. It had a groove that suggested moving forward, so I kept it just as it was.

Nagamatsu: Musically, that's really unusual. It goes tee tee-tee tee ... So usually you would have to change the melody to fit it.

Yokota: If you had composed it normally, the melody would have adopted a swing too, too.

Kondo: Yeah.

Nagamatsu: It seems like they aren't a perfect fit, but somehow I think that matches the game. I think it formed a striking characteristic of the music.[45]

As with the underwater theme, Kondo worked with the limitations of memory and the structure of the music to create an extended soundtrack by looping shorter sections, playing with the listeners' expectations by repeating sections outside the anticipated sequence (see fig. 4.8) so as to strike a delightful balance between the familiar and the unexpected, while within each phrase, individual bars and phrases were reused to conserve on memory. It is a nested, pattern-based approach to composition and is both memory and time efficient.

By committing to tying the music of Super Mario Bros. so tightly to the gameplay, Kondo had to make it work with all of the other aspects of the game. Remember, the 2A03 had only five channels of sound playback in total; four channels were used for the soundtrack and, with memory already at a premium, there was no space available to make use of sample playback. Note stealing was a necessity, and without any dedicated hardware to handle prioritization, it all had to be done as part of the game logic.

Musically, it meant that Kondo had to write in such a way that elements of the music could drop out to trigger effects without the integrity of the music being compromised. All of the effects, from collecting coins to Mario jumping and shooting fireballs, were split between the two pulse channels. In sections where the soundtrack was playing in rhythmic unison, elements could be dropped from one or both channels without much impact, while in others the melody or harmony lines would noticeably drop out, leaving it to the aural memory of the player to fill in the familiar gaps, although in the most extreme situation, Mario repeatedly headbutting the underside of a multicoin block, the repeated chime of the coin effect tended to drown out the music completely.

FIGURE 4.8 By assigning a letter to each distinct section of the Overworld Theme, we can see how Kondo created an irregular musical structure, playing with the listener's expectations to get the most value from a limited stock of material.

These cue-driven effects, however, still had to fit with the music, something made even more challenging because they could occur at virtually any point in the gameplay. All of the effects, from the jump sound to the sting that is played when Mario gains an extra life after he collects his hundredth gold coin, are designed carefully so that they complement the underlying harmonic structure of the music, and because of Kondo's uncluttered arrangement, they sit comfortably with the music, maintaining the continuity of the score.

Periodically, Mario is presented with a *super star*, a power-up that bestows a short period of invincibility. At this point, the music switches, changing in character to a double-time two-chord stomp, the *Starman Theme* (transcribed in fig. 4.9), a familiar blues format that can be heard on tracks like Little Walter's *Evan's Shuffle* or *Groovin' for Mr. G* by Richard 'Groove' Holmes.

That shift in tempo, coupled with an arpeggiated, almost Latin-style bass, beautifully complements a finely balanced shift in gameplay, but it's an effect that poses a real creative challenge. As with the cue-driven effects, the collection of a super star can happen at virtually any point in the soundtrack. When it happens, the music transitions immediately to the new theme, a technique known as *horizontal resequencing*[46]—imagine the timeline of the game as a horizontal line and the underscore being resequenced along that line as different gameplay events occur. It's far from a straightforward task to write two contrasting pieces of music that can be interchanged at any point without creating abrupt disjoins, but that's exactly what Kondo achieves; his light, open arrangements are as much a function of the need to create a score that tightly integrated with the gameplay as of his love of jazz fusion or the technical constraints of the hardware.

Kondo's real innovation, then, wasn't so much with form or timbre. It was in defining the formal grammar and style of a new form of media music, the interactive game underscore. Like the music of the SID, it was dynamic and tuneful, although the more restrictive NES APU meant that the arrangements were more limited. This, in turn, meant that composers like Kondo couldn't rely on creating stand-alone tracks that aped the sound of Jarre or Yellow Magic Orchestra. Instead, the limitations of the APU

FIGURE 4.9 The Starman Theme from Super Mario Bros., a double-time, two-chord stomp.

forced them to think about how the music could function within the constraints of the hardware yet still add new dimensions to the gameplay.

Nintendo retained tight control over game titles for the NES; only those that met its high quality standards received the Nintendo 'Seal of Quality'. As such, that Nintendo sound became an integral part of the Nintendo house style. So while new generations of console and the PC took up the mantle of home gaming, bringing with them much more sophisticated multichannel digital audio and a more cinematic style of video game soundtrack, Nintendo continued with its signature sound, at least for those game franchises that were at the very core of its brand.

The SNES, or Super Famicom as it was known in its native Japan, for example, combined an 8-bit Sony coprocessor and a powerful DSP capable of mixing eight simultaneous voices in 16-bit stereo and at a sample rate of 32 kHz.[47] But while some soundtracks conformed to the new gaming conventions of the time—*F-Zero*, for example, has an unremarkable rock soundtrack made up of exactly the sort of sound samples that were becoming ubiquitous, courtesy of General MIDI and Creative's SoundBlaster series of soundcards—Nintendo's big-ticket titles retained the characteristic sound and charm of the SNES's elder sibling. In *Super Mario All-Stars*, for example, the sound is richer and more polished, with little melodic flourishes dotted here and there, but the additional sonic power is used to fill out Kondo's original shell voicings and add harmonic colour. It is a Kondo remix rather than an overhaul.

This approach continued through successive generations of Nintendo console. The GameCube, Wii, and WiiU continued the trend and kept those key stylistic elements of that original chip sound alive, albeit in a more polished form, for new generations of gamers and provided a direct link back to those classic 8-bit game sounds.

The Ultimate Soundtracker?

When you think of Australia and its principal exports, mineral ores and backpacking baristas perhaps spring to mind more readily than do digital synthesizers, but in the mid-1970s, Australia gave the world a ground-breaking electronic music workstation that would shape the look and feel of music technology for decades to come.

Two friends, Peter Vogel and Kim Ryrie, fresh out of high school, set up a music technology business, Fairlight Instruments, in December 1975.[1] They took the name from the hydrofoil that served Sydney Harbour,[2] a service whose route passed in front of Ryrie's grandmother's house on the waterfront, below which he had a small workshop.

Ryrie, like countless other teenagers in the 1970s, had discovered *Switched on Bach;*[3] he had found himself transfixed not just by the fusion of old and new sounds but by the very notion that each component of every sound was the result of a painstaking configuration of the hundreds of patch cables, knobs, switches, and sliders that were the Moog's livery. Unlike most teenagers, however, Ryrie knew synthesizers inside out; a few years earlier, he had developed the ETI 4600 analogue synth with engineer Trevor Marshall for the DIY enthusiasts' magazine Electronics Today International.[4] And so, with the unshakeable confidence of youth, he set about trying to improve on Bob Moog's design.

Working in Ryrie's basement workshop, Vogel and Ryrie struggled to make much headway until, early in 1976, they met Tony Furse, a Motorola consultant who was working with the Canberra School of Electronic Music to build his own cutting-edge digital synth, the Quasar M8,[5] an eight-voice polyphonic synthesizer built around two 8-bit Motorola 6800 processors wired together in parallel.

The M8 used additive synthesis and allowed users to input and edit wave data directly on a monochrome video display using a light pen. It was all controlled by a four-octave piano-style keyboard and an on-board sequencer, Furse's MUSEQ 8 sequence playing system.

Vogel and Ryrie were intrigued by the M8 and licensed the technology from Furse. They reworked the machine around a redesigned version of the dual 6800 processor layout and a new operating system, adding a more responsive six-octave keyboard alongside the M8's light pen, to create the Fairlight Quasar M8 CMI.

At first, they tried to synthesize tones from scratch, creating dynamic timbres by computing the complex transients and temporal shifts of harmonic spectra in real time, but the hardware just couldn't keep pace with their ideas, and the results were disappointing. As a last resort, they decided to speed things up by using short snippets of digitally recorded real-world sounds as a starting point. Ryrie remembers that by-passing the synthesis stage to get a quick fix felt like cheating: 'We felt it was unaccept-able behaviour, but it was fun'.[6] A redesign of the M8 CMI added digital recording to the machine's repertoire, and the legendary Fairlight CMI was born.

Initially, the interest in the machine was as much about its technical capabilities as it was its creative potential. The BBC's popular science programme, *Tomorrow's World*, for example, showcased the Fairlight in 1980,[7] and, in the best tradition of British light entertainment, presenter Kieran Prendiville made it bark like a dog, using a novelty ar-rangement of *How Much Is That Doggie in the Window* to introduce sound sampling to the Great British public.

The Fairlight, however, was much more than just a novelty. Those sampled sounds could be triggered by an on-board sequencer that was capable of storing up to 50,000 notes. It was already a useful tool in the first-generation CMI, but when Fairlight re-leased the Series II in 1982, the sequencer was revised and renamed Page R: The Real-Time Composer.[8]

Page R, a typical session of which is illustrated in figure 5.1, is an eight-track, pattern-based graphical sequencer that displays each note in a music sequence along a horizontal timeline. Up to 255 patterns could be combined in 26 phrases, allowing com-plex compositions to be constructed relatively easily from modular chunks. Although se-quencers had been around for a number of years—the analogue Moog 960,[9] for example, had become a regular part of the electronic rigs of both Tangerine Dream and Michael Hoenig in the 1970s—the Real-Time Composer offered possibilities and a form of graph-ical interface that simply had not been available before. All of a sudden, the role of music programmer, which had always been a technical role, was elevated to the rank of the cre-ative, ushering in a new style of tech-pop typified by Peter Gabriel and The Art of Noise.

Stephen Paine, a cousin of Gabriel, with whom he set up Syco Systems to distribute the Fairlight in the United Kingdom, notes: 'Nowadays all sequencers work in a similar way to Page R, but at the time, it was a phenomenally original idea, and people just went nuts over it. There were people who bought the Fairlight from us purely because of that facility'.[10]

The Fairlight was revolutionary, but that musical flexibility came at a price. At a time when the average UK home cost £25,000,[11] the Fairlight Series II retailed at £30,000.[12]

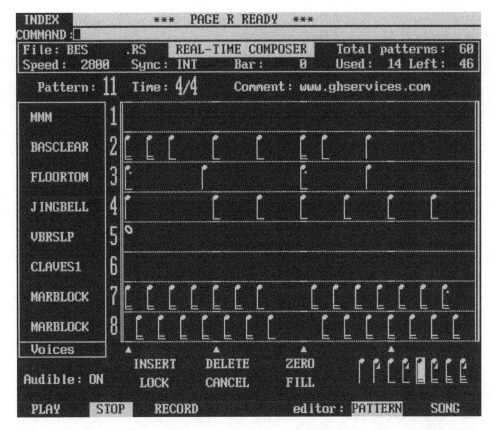

FIGURE 5.1 The Fairlight CMI's Real-Time Composer introduced multitrack graphical editing of music sequences, coupled to high-quality sample playback. Image of Fairlight Page R courtesy of GH Services.

Switching on Bach … Again

This was the backdrop against which the Commodore 64 launched in 1982. Although it had been conceived as the ultimate gaming machine, the C64 was marketed not just for play but as a versatile and powerful creative tool. Commodore chose Bach's Two-Part Invention no. 13 in A Minor as the soundtrack for the early C64 television commercials,[13] and it very quickly became the machine's signature tune.

Bach's invention lent the C64 a touch of class. It was the continuation of an image Commodore had worked hard to cultivate since the launch of the VIC-20, which had been promoted by no less stellar a figure than Captain James Tiberius Kirk.

'Why buy just a video game?' Shatner asked viewers directly as he posed casually in front of a scrolling starfield. Why, indeed? When viewed as a synthesizer, the C64's £399 price tag was a veritable bargain, and with a £70 add-on cartridge from SFX, it could do sound sampling and graphical editing just like the Fairlight.

The complexities of programming the SID, however, stood in the way of most home users making music with their Commodores. Almost inevitably, third-party music applications began to appear, their principal aim being to put the SID chip into the hands of the home musician.

Synthy 64 was one of the first. An enhanced version of Piper, a BASIC-like music programming language for the VIC-20, it gave access to the SID's capabilities but greatly simplified its programming. It encodes musical data as a series of text mnemonics and simplifies coding by basing programming keywords on text modifiers like # and % to encode sharps and flats. Other commands define envelopes, repeats, tied and dotted notes, key signatures, tempo, and volume, and the package could also handle simple user input, making it possible to run simple rule-based and algorithmic music.

The Synthy 64 code in example 5.1, for example, plays a major scale from C5 using quarter notes (/4) at a tempo of 120 bpm, condensing all of the low-level register manipulation required by Commodore BASIC into just a few lines of code that express musical ideas in an abstracted form that is very close to the way music is normally annotated.

Synthy 64 was a beautifully thought-out and easy-to-use package, but for all of its simplicity, there were two fundamental issues that limited its appeal. First, its command-line interface dictated that music making was a very considered and drawn-out affair, and while that suited the workflow of some musicians, it was a far cry from the immediacy of most 'real-world' musical interfaces. Perhaps more important from a platform perspective, however, Synthy 64 offered no facility to compile the code or dump it into pure Commodore BASIC. Without a mechanism to include music in other programs, musicians who wanted their music to appear in games or demos had to look elsewhere.

Commodore set out to address the first of these issues with its own Music Composer. Released in 1983, it was a cartridge-based system that borrowed some of the ideas introduced in Fairlight's Page R, combining real-time synthesis with a traditional score-based graphical display. On loading, the software presents the user with three musical staves, corresponding to the three voices of the SID chip, to which can be written note sequences for one of nine preset instruments.

Pressing 2 turns the C64 keyboard into a makeshift music keyboard controller, allowing music to be sequenced using the keys from 'G' (low C) to '=' (middle C) as the white keys and using the keys in the row above as the black keys. It's a reasonable compromise, but it's not terribly intuitive, and, like learning to play any new musical instrument, it requires some patience and practice to achieve a degree of fluency.

Music Composer was followed a year later by Music Maker, a more performance-oriented package that came bundled with an SFX-branded plastic keyboard overlay (fig. 5.2) that transformed the QWERTY keyboard into a much more familiar style of music controller and allowed for both monophonic and polyphonic playing.

EXAMPLE 5.1. A short Synthy 64 program to play a major scale. Note the simplicity of the code in comparison to the Commodore BASIC in examples 3.1–3.4.

```
1    RUN
10   T120
20   C5/4  D  E  F  G  A6  B  C
30   END
```

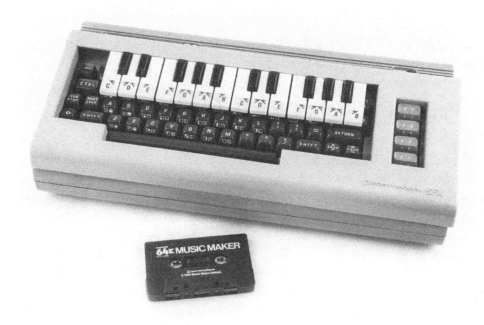

FIGURE 5.2 The Music Maker keyboard overlay.

The Music Maker package came with the keyboard, a set of stickers to mark out the note names, a music book, and several presequenced tunes; 'Including the hit song: "When I'm 64"', a sticker boasted on the front of the box. Music Maker is more of an auto-accompaniment program than a serious synthesis or composition tool, although it does allow for simple note sequencing.

The SFX logo appeared courtesy of a collaboration with the UK music publisher Music Sales Ltd, which published a range of music tuition books and arrangements and transcriptions under its SFX division. In fact, Commodore did not own the copyright to the SFX devices or software, and the tie-in was a cooperative venture between Commodore UK and the publisher to capitalize on the growing public interest in micro music.

At the World of Commodore II show in Toronto in November 1984, John Van Til, the manager of the new media department of Music Sales, was at the Commodore stand showcasing the Music Maker package not far from another stand where an identical device, the Incredible Musical Keyboard, designed and manufactured by Wisconsin-based Sight and Sound Music Software Inc., was being demoed. When he saw the Music Maker keyboard, Sight and Sound's representative, George Staleos, was furious and claimed that Commodore and SFX had stolen its design.[14]

Van Til denied any connection between the products, but Staleos claimed that Van Til, who had worked as the head of European operations for Sight and Sound before moving to Music Sales, had been involved in negotiations to acquire a licensing deal for the Incredible Musical Keyboard and had gone ahead with its manufacture after failing to reach an agreement. In the end, Commodore managed to weather the storm and broker a deal, as both keyboards subsequently went on sale, with the Music Maker package being sold throughout Europe and the United Kingdom and the Incredible Musical Keyboard selling in the United States.

A Step in the Right Direction . . .

Up until this point, most music applications had drawn on traditional notions of music and music making. Their interfaces were based around abstracted forms of traditional musical notation, either condensing full score notation down to a truncated form that encoded notes, rests, and accidentals as a string of alphanumeric characters or combining text entry with a graphical display that presented the user with simplified notes and staves. Neither was particularly user-friendly, and few of the commercial music editors provided the depth or functionality that allowed users to really get at the SID's guts and play with its filter and advanced synthesis. What the C64 needed was a different approach to music notation and editing, one that would allow users to play with the new musical dimensions offered by electronic synthesis. The solution would come from the centre of Germany, the spiritual home of electronica.

Chris Hülsbeck was born in Kassel to a family of music teachers, but despite, or perhaps because of, this auspicious start to his musical life—his grandmother was an old-school disciplinarian who rewarded mistakes with a rap across the knuckles with a ruler—Hülsbeck rejected formal tuition in favour of self-styled experimentation and invention.[15]

Hülsbeck was also an avid gamer. As a youngster, his parents had bought him an Atari VCS in the hope that he wouldn't pump all of his pocket money into the slots of the coin-op machines in his local arcade, but when the Commodore 64 came along, it seemed to offer everything he could ever need, and the teenage Hülsbeck just had to have one. He saved the wages from his paper round for six months until, along with a 100 DM subsidy from his grandmother, he had saved enough to get the machine of his dreams.[16] And, just like every other kid who found themselves with a new C64, Hülsbeck spent the next year playing games.[17]

But the more he played, the more he found his interest piqued. Like an inquisitive child who spends Christmas morning unscrewing the new toys to see what makes them work, Hülsbeck began poking around in Commodore BASIC. He soon discovered that writing games in BASIC was a slow and frustrating experience, and before long he began to dabble with 6502 assembly language. He concluded, quite early on, that he was no game programmer, but he did have a flair for coding music, so when the German magazine 64-er launched a competition to find the very best C64 musicians, Hülsbeck entered.[18] He spent most of his time refining his music driver and didn't even begin working on his track, *Shades*, until the night before the closing date. Starting work late in the evening, he worked through the night, finally completing the track at four o'clock in the morning. The next morning, he handed the disk to his aunt and begged her to drop it off at the post office while he headed, bleary-eyed, to school. Shades won the competition, and transformed Hülsbeck the schoolboy into Hülsbeck the fledgling music professional.

When Hülsbeck wrote Shades, he was still writing music by entering note data as hexadecimal values directly into a machine code monitor, a piece of software that allows users to view and modify the data stored in computer memory. It was a perfectly workable approach, but only because Hülsbeck knew exactly what values to write to which memory locations. For anyone else, it was completely opaque. Hülsbeck knew that the process could be improved, and started working on a dedicated music editor. He worked throughout the summer of 1986 and submitted the result, *SoundMonitor*, to 64-er, who published the code as their listing of the month.[19]

SoundMonitor is, to all intents and purposes, a prototracker, and many of the elements that would come to typify the tracker experience can be seen in its interface. Figure 5.3 illustrates the interface: three vertically scrolling tracks, one per channel, and dedicated control commands to trigger portamento effects and arpeggiated chords. In terms of user-friendliness, it was a massive improvement over coding music directly or modifying data within a machine code monitor, and it provided a platform for very detailed SID programming for those musicians who understood the basics of the technology.

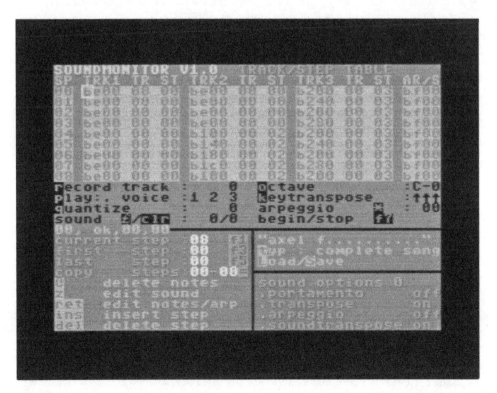

FIGURE 5.3 Chris Hülsbeck's SoundMonitor for C64.

It also had one crucial advantage over the other music packages: with SoundMonitor, music created in the system could be exported and packaged as a stand-alone track using a piece of code called the *Music Master*, a variant of the driver Hülsbeck had written for Shades a few months earlier.

SoundMonitor provided an avenue into C64 music for many musicians and a platform for development for other coders, particularly in Hülsbeck's native Germany. Thomas Detert, a noted C64 video game composer in his own right, started using SoundMonitor soon after, scoring demos for the Omega 8 group. But the more he tried to push it, the more he found that the CPU load needed by the driver routine was just too great;[20] the music he was writing in SoundMonitor was pulling resources that the group needed for the graphics routines.

To improve things, Detert turned to his friends at X-Ample Architectures, another German demo group. Together, they combined the core of SoundMonitor with a new driver written by Markus Schneider and a front-end interface by Joachim Fraeder to create the X-Ample Music Player, a music system that was customized specifically for the needs of the group and introduced automated features that Detert and Schneider used frequently, including an automatic echo routine, for example, which would generate echo effects from a single note and command entry.[21]

This approach, of developing bespoke routines by hacking and adapting the work of others, was fairly commonplace and perhaps goes some way to explain the coherence of the C64 sound. Schneider notes that '90% of the music players were based on Rob Hubbard's techniques.... Most people just optimized it and invented more tricks'.[22]

Hülsbeck's own development of his routine didn't stop with SoundMonitor. Emboldened by the success of his music and code, he made the audacious move of cold-calling the director of Rainbow Arts, one of Germany's biggest developers, and asking him if he needed any music written for his games.[23] Two hours later, having played most of his back catalogue over the phone and with the promise of a brand new Ensoniq ESQ-1 on which to work, Hülsbeck, still in the middle of his twelfth grade, quit school and took up his new post at the company.

As he found himself working on more titles and across different platforms, Hülsbeck began work in 1987 on a new routine, TFM—The Final Musicsystem—adding an ironic X for 'eXtended' as the functions of this final system continued to grow. It greatly extended the functionality of his SoundMonitor, adding features like logarithmic pitch-bends and individual tempos for each track, but it was the system's macro sound programming language that really made it stand out. The moment a note is triggered in TFMX, it also triggers a program script that directly addresses the SID chip, allowing for complex chains of effects and sound manipulation on each step of the music, variants of which can be found today in trackers like Little Sound DJ on the Game Boy.

The system was very flexible, and variants of TFMX formed the basis of many of Hülsbeck's routines for other consoles, including successive generations of Nintendo, where the technology was licensed by the company as their official developer tool, but it was with Commodore's next machine, the Amiga, that Hülsbeck really made his name.

The Commodore Amiga

If one man were to be singled out as the father of Commodore's Amiga, it would be the soft-spoken, bearded engineer Jay Miner, who spearheaded the development of the Atari VCS in the mid-1970s.

A Berkeley graduate, Miner spent most of the 1960s and early 1970s designing microchips for small electronics companies in California until, in 1974, just as the first video game bubble was at its peak, his friend Harold Lee, who was already working as an engineer at Atari, introduced him to Nolan Bushnell.[24] Bushnell, impressed with the young engineer, asked Miner to join the company and design chips for a new home gaming system he had in development.

After the launch of the VCS, Miner went on to design the architecture and chipset of Atari's first home computer, the 400, and a more powerful version, the 800,[25] which was released with a larger case and improved keyboard, the look of which foreshadowed Commodore's own C64. At a time when most of its competitors could display only monochrome or eight-colour graphics and rudimentary sound, Miner's new chips, the Color Television Interface Adaptor (CTIA) and the POKEY, were ground-breaking.

Yet neither the 400 or the 800, despite their merits, were commercial successes. Both were complex and expensive to build, and Atari, carrying over its protectionist strategy from the VCS, fiercely guarded the technical information relating to the operation of its hardware, even going so far as threatening to sue developers who attempted to create software for the platform for infringing Atari's intellectual property rights.[26]

Atari was also keen to avoid placing its new computers in direct competition with the VCS, whose sales had finally started to pick up after a fairly slow start, so it positioned them as 'serious' machines. Unfortunately, this placed them in direct competition with established business models from Commodore and Apple, and that market proved difficult to break.

Nevertheless, thanks to strong VCS and cartridge sales, this period saw Atari netting healthy returns. But this period also saw growing disenfranchisement among Atari's employees. Thanks to some creative accounting, in which all of the development costs of the 400 and 800 were written off in the first year of production, the company's books showed just enough of a profit to not quite trigger the performance bonus payment it had promised to its engineers and programmers. This was the catalyst for the company to implode from an exodus of talent.[27]

Miner moved to ZyMOS, a small medical electronics company, and spent the next three years designing special-purpose computer chips for pacemakers. It was there, in the summer of 1982, that he took a call from his old Atari colleague Larry Kaplan, who had also left Atari in 1979 to cofound rival developer Activision.

'Doug Neubauer and I went to talk to Jay Miner … about doing a new game system', Kaplan recalls. 'I had seen the Nintendo NES at the CES in June '82 and thought we could do better. [Bert Braddock, the] president of the company contacted the owner in Texas and by October we had hired [David Morse,] a President from Tonka Toys and got $6 million in funding'.[28]

They named the company Hi-Toro and set up shop in a small office in Santa Clara. As the venture started to gain a bit of momentum, Braddock asked Kaplan to speak to Nolan Bushnell to see if he would serve as chair of the board of directors. Instead, Bushnell offered Kaplan a job back at Atari, and Kaplan accepted, leaving behind Hi-Toro, its offices, its business plan, and its financing.[29] Hi-Toro had money, premises, and a CEO but no engineer or programmer, so Morse asked Miner to take Kaplan's place. By the end of 1982, almost by accident, Miner found himself vice president of the company.

In truth, it was just the opportunity Miner had been waiting for. Ever since his days at Atari, he had dreamed of designing a computer around Motorola's new 68000 chip,[30] a hybrid processor that shifted data in 16-bit chunks but performed its internal operations at 32-bit resolution. In his previous life, Miner had discovered that Atari's management just wasn't prepared to invest in an untested and expensive new technology while it was still getting so much mileage out of the 8-bit 6502, but at Hi-Toro Miner managed to convince Morse and the financiers that a low-cost 68000-based machine designed for video games was not only viable but could be, so to speak, game-changing.

The initial plan was to build a games console.[31] At the time, sales of personal computers were tiny in comparison, and it made sense to target the bigger console market. Then came the crash; but while the bottom fell out of the console market, sales of personal computers kept growing steadily. Parents, it seemed, could justify paying a little more money for a system that was, on the face of it, at any rate, educational. The Hi-Toro investors asked Miner if it might be possible to convert the new console into a full-blown personal computer. Miner told them that this was what he had been planning all along.

This shift in focus brought with it a change of name. Hi-Toro sounded like the name of a Japanese lawnmower manufacturer, so Amiga Inc.—a name that, conveniently, placed the company ahead of Atari in the telephone directory—was born.[32]

The new machine was codenamed Lorraine after the wife of David Morse. The components of Miner's chipset became Agnus, Denise, and Paula,[33] (see fig. 5.4) the latter shouldering the burden of sound generation, allowing Lorraine to play back four simultaneous monophonic 8-bit digitally sampled waveforms with a maximum sample frequency per channel of just under 29 kHz.

The Amiga's chipset was years ahead of its time. Miner and his team hadn't just provided helper chips, they had developed a sophisticated system of resource management, incorporating direct memory access (DMA) channels and a blitter chip that could perform a range of graphics processing tasks, such as drawing lines and filling polygons, much more efficiently than the main CPU. Collectively, the chipset relieved the main processor of much of its computational load, with Denise handling complex graphics

FIGURE 5.4 Paula, the voice of the Amiga.

operations, Paula taking care of four-channel digital audio, and Agnus managing both direct memory access and the other two chips.

The Lorraine prototype, renamed the Amiga 1000, was demoed at the CES show in January 1984.[34] Amiga Inc. rented a booth in the West Hall with an enclosed space behind the public display to showcase the machine to invited trade guests. The operating system and other software were nowhere near ready to show, so two software engineers, Robert Mical and Dale Luck, worked through the night to create a rolling demo that would showcase the power of the chipset. They created *Boing Ball*, a short animated sequence that displayed a red and white rotating chequered ball that bounced around the screen synchronized to an impactful 'boom' sound that shifted around the stereo field with the movement of the ball. That sound was created by sampling Amiga Inc.'s head of software engineering, Bob Pariseau, hitting a garage door with a foam baseball bat;[35] it gave Amiga Inc. a presence at the show that leaked out far beyond the confines of its booth.

The January show was a roaring success for the Amiga team, but the fledgling company was fast running out of money. Dave Morse tried to get investment from a number of big companies, including Sony, Apple, and Silicon Graphics, but the only one that showed any kind of interest was Atari, by then headed by Jack Tramiel, who had bought the company from Warner Communications in July 1984 following an acrimonious split from Commodore in January that year. Tramiel lent the struggling company $500,000 on the understanding that if the loan wasn't repaid by the end of the following

June then Atari would own all of their technology. 'This was a dumb thing to agree to', Miner recalls, who had already taken a second mortgage out on his house to keep the company going, 'but there was no choice'.[36]

By late 1984, Commodore was itself licking its corporate wounds, having lost a number of key engineering staff to Atari. In an act of corporate hubris, Commodore stepped in and gave Amiga Inc. the $500,000 to pay back Atari,[37] before going all-in and paying $24 million to purchase the entire company. It was an action that was pointedly designed to snub Tramiel and recast Commodore with new engineering talent, but it was a move that would have longer-term repercussions for both companies; business had always been war to Tramiel, but this broadside made it very personal indeed. He went all out to get his revenge on Commodore, and that revenge would come in the form of the Atari ST, which was rushed into production to compete directly against the Amiga.

The Amiga 1000 launched at a lavish event on July 23, 1985, at Lincoln Center in New York.[38] Alongside the Commodore glitterati, all dressed to the nines in tuxedos, Andy Warhol walked onstage with Blondie's Debbie Harry before digitizing and manipulating her image using a prerelease version of the graphics package *Pro Paint*, creating something reminiscent of the most vibrant images from his famous Marilyn Diptych.

From the buzz and hype that surrounded the launch, it seemed as though the Amiga would be a runaway success, but that early momentum was lost. Commodore struggled to get the machine into production, and it wasn't until November that customers could walk out of stores with Amigas under their arms, and no sooner had machines hit stores than Commodore's advertising, which was already pretty lacklustre, disappeared completely. Commodore, in dealing with the launch of a machine orders of magnitude more complex than anything that it had handled before, alongside defending and counter-striking in its protracted battle with Jack Tramiel, had been left teetering precariously on the verge of bankruptcy.[39]

In March 1986, a deal was done that injected a further $135 million of funding to help get Commodore back on an even keel.[40] This deal kept the doors open, certainly, but Commodore was now known far and wide—not least to potential Amiga buyers—as a company on the edge.

As the months passed it became clear that the Amiga wasn't the mass-market sensation Commodore had expected.[41] It had a loyal following among the tech-savvy, who saw the machine for the technological achievement it was, but while Commodore had hoped that it would be compared to higher-end machines like Apple's Macintosh, Commodore's reputation as a low-end, mass-market manufacturer of home gaming computers proved difficult to shake off, and in the press and in the minds of the public, the battle was between the Amiga and Atari's ST.[42]

Part of the problem stemmed from the Amiga's position, or rather lack of it, in the competitive home computer marketplace.[43] Although its design was elegant and full of

FIGURE 5.5 The Amiga 500.

neat little touches, including a slot in the main case into which the keyboard could be docked when not in use, it remained too expensive for most home users and too limited for professionals. In response, Commodore replaced the 1000 with two new models in 1987, moving more mainstream with the domestic 500 (fig. 5.5) and a little more up-market with the PC-like 2000.

The Amiga 500 marked a return to Commodore selling computers aimed at the home gaming market through mass retail outlets, and in that respect at least it was a spiritual successor to the old VIC-20 and C64. It was housed in a compact, though slightly ungainly, beige plastic case. On the left-hand side and behind a trap-door hidden on the bottom of the machine were two expansion ports that enabled users to upgrade the machine's memory, and on the rear were serial and parallel bus ports, two joystick ports, and a proper set of audio connectors, courtesy of a pair of phono sockets. The Amiga 500 didn't particularly extend the capabilities of the original design, but at less than half the price of the Amiga 1000, it was the commercial break Commodore needed, particularly in Europe. By early 1989, more than 1 million Amigas had been sold.[44]

Trackers

The Amiga was a musical dream machine, as a stand-alone device at any rate. Although a number of MIDI sequencers were produced for the machine, including the versatile modular production suite *Music-X*, the Amiga never really established itself as a studio hub in the same way Atari managed to establish its ST. The Atari's internal MIDI ports gave it an edge, as did its software: C-Lab's *Creator*—the proto form of Apple's *Logic*[45]—and Steinberg's *Pro-24*—an updated version of the C64 sequencer *Pro-16* that would later evolve into *Cubase*[46]—both started life on the ST.

The Amiga's biggest strength was its native sample playback. In many respects, the speed at which sampling and sequencing had filtered down from the Fairlight was remarkable. Just five years after the launch of the Series II CMI, the Amiga 500 put dedicated sample packs and graphical sequencers at the fingertips of home users.

Electronic Arts led the way with *Deluxe Music Construction Set* in 1986, a companion application to its popular *Deluxe Paint* series of graphics packages. It was the first full desktop music package for the Amiga and combined sample-playback and sequencing with MIDI functions and notation. Along with its drag-and-drop interface, which mimicked the classical idea of composition, albeit an abstracted version that was more contrived and somewhat slower than actually scribbling dots on staves, Deluxe Music still feels reasonably familiar to users of today's digital audio workstations.

Electronic Arts also experimented with alternative forms of user interface and computer-assisted composition. On the back of Deluxe Music, Electronic Arts released *Instant Music*, a side-scrolling pattern-based sequencer that allowed the user to improvise by moving the mouse up and down to shape a macro-level melodic contour, while a simple algorithm applies chord-based pitch quantizing to make sure that the user-generated notes make some sort of musical sense against accompaniment tracks that loop in the background. While it wasn't a runaway success, Instant Music was a very warmly received diversion. Amiga World described it as 'the most fun you can have with your Amiga and your ears',[47] while Bruce Webster at Byte said that the software had to be simply outstanding if it allowed an untalented hack like himself to make music.[48]

And then, in 1987, Karsten Obarski, a programmer and musician with the German software house EAS, was asked by his friend, Guido Bartels, to produce a C64-style soundtrack for an Arkanoid-style game he was developing. Obarski had bought himself an Amiga 1000 a few weeks earlier and had already written some simple sample-triggering music routines. He had also worked with Chris Hülsbeck's SoundMonitor on the C64 and liked its vertical, column-based layout. As figure 5.6 shows, his *Ultimate Soundtracker* combined the two.

Obarski simplified the interface of SoundMonitor, losing some of the complexity of the C64 program by bringing all four of the Amiga's four channels together into a single editable 64-step grid called a *pattern*. Each pattern displays the four channels as vertically scrolling columns of cells, headed *Melody, Accompany, Bass,* and *Percussions,* with a horizontal time bar that stretches across all four tracks to show the current play position. These patterns give a simple overview of the order and structure of the music, something like a musical spreadsheet, and can be sequenced and arranged in different ways to produce a song.

Each cell on the timeline provides a space for the pitch. The tracker is controlled by the Amiga's QWERTY keyboard, which is used—just as the C64 was used to drive

```
POSITION        0000 +|-|    PATTERN       USE PRESET
PATTERN         0111 +|-|     PLAY         SAVE SONG
LENGHT          0119 +|-|     STOP         LOAD SONG
PRESET          0001 +|-|     EDIT         LOAD SAMPLE
SOUND           0001 +|-|
LENGHT          1686 +|-|      THE ULTIMATE
VOLUME          0048 +|-|    SOUNDTRACKER
REPEAT          0012 +|-|
REPLEN          1656 +|-|    1987 by Karsten Obarski   V1.21  PAL
SONGNAME:       CHUBBY-CHIP-CHIP_____
SAMPLENAME:     ˙-˙-˙: MARK KNIGHT ˙-˙-˙:

00      Melody      Accompany      Bass      Percussions
34  G-1  FA0A    C-2  F037    ---  2424    C-3  C000
35  C-2  FA0A    ---  0037    ---  2A0A    D-3  D000
36  C-3  2C40    G-1  AA03    ---  2A09    D-3  D000
37  D#1  FA0A    A#1  AA03    ---  2A08    D-3  B000
38  C-1  FA0A    C-2  AA03    ---  2A07    D-3  D000
39  C-3  2C40    ---  0A03    ---  2A08    D-3  D000
40  C-1  FA0A    C-2  0A03    ---  2A09    D-3  D000
41  D#1  FA0A    C-2  AA03    ---  2A0A    D-3  D000
42  G-1  FA0A    C-2  F037    ---  2424    C-3  C000
43  C-2  FA0A    ---  0037    ---  2A0C    D-3  D000
44  G-1  FA0A    D-2  AA03    ---  2A0D    D-3  D000
45  C-3  2C40    ---  0A03    ---  2A0E    D-3  D000
46  C-1  FA0A    D#2  AA03    C-3  1A0F    D-3  B000
47  C-3  1C40    ---  0A03    ---  1A0E    D-3  D000
48  D#1  FA0A    D#2  AA03    ---  1A0D    D-3  B000
```

FIGURE 5.6 Karsten Obarski's Ultimate Soundtracker. Note the dense packing of musical notes, with multiple channels interleaved to create virtual tracks, and effects commands at every step in the grid. This squeezed the maximum performance from a limited system.

Commodore's Music Composer—as a two-manual short-compass keyboard, with the cursor and function keys providing a simple means of navigating quickly around the grid. Next to each cell, a four-digit control value is used to specify patch and control changes that modify the way the sample is treated by the playback routine, allowing the user to recreate many of the musical effects that characterised C64 video game music, including arpeggios, portamenti, and modulations.

This no-nonsense interface removed graphical metaphors altogether, instead focusing on a concise textual representation that gave a complete overview of the musical 'source code'. That move made it fairly straightforward to learn the screen layout and simplified the process of reading and editing music for those who weren't fluent in traditional score notation. The software's simplified layout and the keystroke interface turned the process of composition into something that more closely resembled musical touch-typing.

'You worked with a tracker by feel', as Mark Knight describes it; Knight is a game audio professional who now travels the world recording Formula 1 and rally cars for Codemasters, but in the late 1980s he composed tracker music under the pseudonym TDK. 'When you were sat there, writing music on an Amiga, you became almost like a drummer with the patterns. You wouldn't even be looking at the screen half the time. You'd be doing something else, but you'd be doing the right thing because you'd be feeling it. You can't do that on an iPad, and you can't do that in something like Cubase either'.[49]

Although the stark aesthetic of the tracker interface, then, might initially be off-putting, it seemed to hit a sweet spot, providing just the right balance between the accessible presentation of information and useability, something that created a sense of *flow*, with the user, the software, and the hardware working together in productive harmony.[50]

'Beginners often find that they can make simple edits that can be quickly and easily auditioned', explains Dr Chris Nash, a Bristol-based academic who specializes in performativity in digital music systems:

> This has several consequences. Firstly, it means there is little or no literacy barrier to writing music; users can experiment with the notation and use playback to understand the syntax and elements of music, taking an iterative, evolutionary approach to building melodies, harmonies, and whole pieces. Moreover, such rapid edit-audition cycles foster a focused, high-energy workflow, where the user is literally immersed in the sound of the music. This delicate balance of challenge and ability gives rise to 'flow' experiences, supporting intrinsic motivation and creativity in a way sometimes lacking in other music user interfaces. Moreover, this process becomes even faster when users develop motor skill with the keyboard and program, something that is often reflected in the name of the programs themselves—FastTracker, for example, Scream Tracker, or Impulse Tracker.[51]

Trackers didn't just change workflow, they changed the way users conceptualized the music they wrote; the modular, pattern-based structure favoured a progressive, developmental style.

'I think trackers are one of the best ways to write music', says Gareth Morris, a chip musician who performs as gwEm and who developed his own tracker, *maxYMiser*, for the Atari ST:

> That it runs vertically is very interesting because most other ways of representing music, they all run horizontally, which I find a bit counterintuitive. I don't know, but it seems to me that vertical is more like a mixing desk layout, which feels a bit more natural for electronic music, especially when you're working with tracks. Also, you've got the best elements of a drum machine, where you can string patterns together, and you can see the position of the drums and things relative to each other in time, and then you can fit your melody around that. So it's kind of like all of the advantages of a drum machine with the advantages of something like a classical notation. It also relates very closely to the hardware, so you know

there's really nothing separating you from your instrument and you feel you're really getting the best out of it as well.[52]

That sense of direct connection to the sound source is fundamental to the practice of writing electronic music. Unlike the traditional model of compositional practice, in which the musical score provides a platform for interpretation by performers and their instruments, electronic composition allows artists to have complete control over all aspects of the music and its ultimate realization. The manipulation of timbre in particular, from the selection and modulation of raw electronic waveforms through to the chaining of filters and other time- and frequency-based effects, has come to form a central dimension of the aesthetic of all electronic music. So, whereas traditional sequencers and their workflows draw on traditional music theory and practice to construct the metaphors around which their interfaces are built, trackers provide a low-level way of controlling and manipulating raw sounds. They are digital tools for the creation of digital music.

Realising that Ultimate Soundtracker had all of the elements that might make it a saleable music application, EAS bundled the software with the now infamous ST-01 sample pack, which Obarski had sampled from his Yamaha DX21 FM synth, and released it to the public in December 1987.

It bombed.

As a piece of software it was somewhat illogical and temperamental, but as any cult movie aficionado knows, all it takes for something quirky and characterful to really find its feet is time and a small band of dedicated followers who love it, despite—or perhaps because of—its flaws. And those who loved Ultimate Soundtracker really loved it.

Mark Knight explains:

In terms of writing music that other people heard, it all started with [Ultimate] Soundtracker on the Amiga. It's no exaggeration to say it transformed my musical life. I did my GCSE music homework on the Commodore 64, but the only person who got to hear that was my music teacher. There were some really good music packages for the Commie: I tried using SoundMonitor, of course, and Ubik's Music, but I just couldn't get my head around them. They were too complex. I just wasn't a programmer at all. I had a piece of software called Electrosound, which was a bit more musical. It was a step sequencer, and it made [writing music] easy. The problem for me was that it didn't deal with [arpeggiated] chords, so I was never going to get a Rob Hubbard sound. Tracking was when it all started to make sense. It was just more accessible for idiots like me.[53]

Before long, a band of hardcore technical fans, beginning with the Dutch coder Exterminator, had disassembled Obarski's original code, keeping the core intact, while addressing its shortcomings, and redistributed it in the public domain. Updated release followed updated release, and each modification spawned a new title and added new features. Swedish developers Mahoney and Kaktus released *NoiseTracker 2.0*, which added keyboard shortcuts for frequently used functions, improving the flow of the software and making it feel much more pleasant to use, while in 1990 *ProTracker* by the Amiga Freelancers was released along with a very useable sample editor. This was the point when the tracker really became the sequencer of choice on the Amiga.

The Anatomy of a MOD File

Once a piece of music had been tracked, it could be exported from a tracker as a MOD file, a custom format that packaged up the note data and the associated samples in an 8-bit PCM format. By embedding the sounds directly within the distributable MOD file, composers could be certain that their music would be replayed exactly as intended on another machine, something that couldn't always be guaranteed with other music file formats. For example, MIDI files encode only performance data, decoupling the music from the sound source, and rely on the onboard voices of a host synth to give the music voice. That particular synthesizer's soundset might differ wildly from the one used to compose the music originally, and the playback synth might interpret control information very differently, so the same MIDI file can sound completely different on two different synths.

Linear PCM sample streams on the other hand capture the sound of a particular performance, which can then be distributed and replayed precisely and without any loss of quality, but this too comes at a cost: information about the detail of performance is not recorded, so subsequent editing is limited to manipulating blocks of audio rather than performance detail and is very, very resource heavy. By virtue of using only very small, memory-efficient samples, MOD files were more compact and more editable than a PCM sample stream yet were much more editable and offered a similar level of reproducibility. They were a low-bandwidth solution to the problem of high-fidelity music sharing.

To be fair, the idea was not new. The Fairlight, after all, worked in exactly the same way, sequencing short snippets of digitally recorded sound and bundling together sequencer data and samples on disk, but this was the first time that such a simple editor with such scope had been so widely accessible.

When opened, a MOD lays bare its musical patterns, allowing end users, if they so desire, to see how their favourite tracks were created and to become creators themselves, adapting and incorporating sounds and sequences in their own tracks. It is akin to a record company releasing the individual stems and mix automation of their back catalogue so that anyone might remix or mash up classic hits. It was a collectivist approach that allowed for the rapid promulgation of that 8-bit sound.

'I think there was always quite a lot of plagiarism', laughs Mark Knight, as he describes the long days he used to spend poring over other people's MODs to figure out how they worked:

If you go and talk to Ben [Daglish] or whomever, they were always ripping off whole pieces of music. You've got Rob Hubbard, half of his repertoire is by a bloke called Larry Fast, you know, and Ben did quite a lot of Jean Michel Jarre.

With trackers, I think we all tended to plagiarise techniques rather than pieces. I'm pretty sure that it was Matt Simmonds who discovered that you could track a sequence and trigger a note, then change the sample number as you're scrolling down and it will switch to a new waveform but not retrigger. That's how he got that movement in his tracks, almost like a PWM-type effect, with the chip sounds. I remember looking at it and thinking, 'I could use that!' So I nicked it! Everybody was ripping off everybody else.[54]

Matt Simmonds, also known by his musical alter-ego 4mat and now also a video game composer and sound designer, was also taking his first tentative steps in Amiga music in the early 1990s. He began writing in Master Soundtracker 1.0, progressing onto NoiseTracker before finally settling on ProTracker 1.3b, which he still uses to compose; his 2010 album *Decades* was tracked with the same software he had been using for 20 years.

Simmonds had, like many others who were tracking at the time, grown up with the video game sound, and the focus of his early tracks was on trying to capture that same sound on the Amiga. 'I was playing in a band at the time', he recalls, 'so my 'real music' ideas were focused on that. My chip stuff was about trying to make the same sort of sounds and file sizes that the custom players like [Metin Seven's] *SidMon* had. First it was, 'How can I make chip sounds in Soundtracker?', then it was, 'How can I do this chip effect in a tracker?' and so on. I got quite into that back in the day'.[55]

Simmonds experimented with short, looping samples, often only a few complete cycles in length, to recreate the classic sounds of the previous generation of computers and video game consoles. The Amiga didn't have any in-built real-time effects in hardware that might help recreate the chip effects he wanted, but that didn't matter. Using a few sequencing tricks, it was possible to add dynamic movement to a track in just the same way that the C64 composers had done with their custom assembly-level music routines.

As he experimented with sequencing tricks and effects, Simmonds shared the results. Others scrutinized his music and adapted or incorporated the neat ideas and custom samples that they liked into new works. The MOD files were like an evolutionary microcosm: the best ideas would survive to feature strongly in future music, while the rest would simply fade away, the forgotten relics of musical Darwinism.

Those sequencing effects became the musical vocabulary through which composers could show off their tracking prowess, but the effects needed track space to work. Each was the result of a sequence of commands, each of which in turn occupied a track line in the pattern, and on the Amiga, with its four playback channels, track space was at a premium. The competition to outtrack everyone else turned composition into a packing problem: How much music could you cram into a four-channel, 64-step grid?

Mark Knight, says, wryly:

> I think the whole point of chip music was that you had to fill every single fucking
> pattern in your song. That's it—it's got to be busy! I remember a guy called Brett
> Paterson, who is the guy behind [the interactive sound system] FMOD. He wrote
> most of it while he was working with me at Electronic Arts. He was the audio
> programmer while I was there, and he used to use one of my chiptunes, *Orgasmic
> Chip*, to test it. It was a 6k MOD, but it was apparently the most processor-
> intensive MOD that he could find, because every slot in the sequence was filled
> with something; arpeggios, volume changes, slides, and whatever, and he used
> that to test his module player to make sure it wouldn't fall over.[56]

The Modscene

For that competition to take hold, however, musicians needed a way of distributing their
music and getting it heard. In the days before the ubiquity of the Internet, file sharing
was nowhere near as straightforward as it is now. Music files were often shared on individual bulletin board systems (BBSs), remote computer servers that hosted software and
services. By the mid-1980s, Fidonet, a global network that connects together different
BBSs, had begun to emerge, making it a little easier to post and swap MODs.[57]

That online sharing took place mainly in North America and western Europe, and
from it emerged an active community of practitioners—not just musicians but coders
and graphics artists—who developed custom fonts and graphics for *musicdisks* and
packdisks, packaged distributable collections of music that were like digital concept
albums. Gareth Morris's *Phatt Demo*, for example, is described in the accompanying
notes as a hardcore rave album for Atari ST and was written using his own tracker,
maxYMiser. It presents an evolving visual narrative told in combination through the
stylized graphics of the digital artist Colin Perry and Morris's own hard-edged electronic music. It was a concept that evolved through a coming together of two people
with something to say and a shared interest in technology.

Morris explains:

> In the beginning I just wanted to showcase my latest tracker. I kind of wanted to
> show off, I guess, but that's also part of the demoscene tradition, right? You know,
> you're demonstrating what you can do, right? So, yeah, I was happy about the
> tracker, so I made a bunch of songs and played them to a friend of mine who is an
> artist. He studied art quite formally and was nothing to do with the demoscene
> at all, and he said, well, I can see a concept that I can wrap around this. So
> I changed the songs a little bit and he put together this story, and we presented it
> more like an art piece in the end. So it became a concept.[58]

Like many other 'virtual' communities, the modscene was virtual only in the sense that it was distributed and mediated by technology. After all, at the front end were still real people logging on via telephone lines, forming real friendships and participating in community activities. For some, it was exactly the sort of safe and inclusive space the real world couldn't provide.

Mark Knight says:

As somebody who was pretty socially inept back then, the whole modscene and demoscene was probably my saving grace. I had something that I could really get involved with, and it was great.

I got really into MODs when I was doing my A-levels at sixth-form college. My mum would go to work, and I'd go to the park, wait until she'd gone, and then I'd go back home to work on my Amiga. In the end, the college phoned up and said, 'Mark's not been to college in two weeks, is he okay?' Mum had no idea that I was skipping back home.

Most of the half-decent chiptunes that I wrote back then were from bunking off college. I just used to write and write and write, put it out there online, and people would get hold of it. Some of it would get used and some of it wouldn't. It was great. It's probably one of the only long-term things where I've felt part of a community. I ended up working with a group called Melon Dezign, and they were always after stuff. I would get phone calls from the guys in Copenhagen saying 'We've got another crack coming out, we need some music for it,' and I'd write them something.

My original plan had always been to go to college or university and study music, but there were only two courses in the UK at the time. There was the Tonmeister course at Surrey, and Salford did a music technology degree. That was it. Tonmeister was out because I wasn't doing maths and physics at A-level, but I got an interview at Salford. You had to do a performance as part of the interview, and so I took my violin with a piezo pickup on it, and I borrowed some foot pedals from Future Music, a shop in Brighton. When I got there, they had nothing for me to plug into, and so I said that I could still play some violin. They refused. I did the tests and whatever, but the feedback that I got was that they didn't think that a classically-trained musician would be able to deal with music technology. So in a way, being part of the scene was a big fuck you to the system.[59]

Mark Knight and Matt Simmonds both began to collaborate with digital collectives. For Knight it was the Scandinavian group Melon Dezign, while Simmonds started working with the UK group Anarchy. Their music, video game–style tracks, began to trickle through onto the scene. As more and more of these sound chip–style musicdisks were circulated, MOD fans found themselves in need of a term to differentiate them from other forms of tracked music. The Amiga, of course, could sound like a PSG, but it could also sound like a rock band or an orchestra. By 1990, *chip* had started to appear as a stylistic designator in MOD filenames, and in 1991 the term *chiptune*, meaning a piece of chip music, appeared as a title on Nuke's *mod.chiptune-12k* on an Anarchy packdisk.[60]

'Yeah, the phrase chiptune came on the Amiga from the chiptune scene back in the early 90s', Mark Knight says. 'On the Commodore 64 ... Well, of course, all music was chiptune on the 64, it was all that it could do, but on the Amiga, we needed a name to describe a particular sound and technique. That's what it was. It was single-waveform samples to make tiny little tunes for cracks or whatever, and, because they were written to sound like the stuff we were writing on the old sound chips, they were called chiptunes'.[61]

What Kind of Justice Is This?

By the early 1990s, trackers were sufficiently well established to have become a development platform in their own right. While most trackers evolved along the lines of efficiency, with successive variants introducing playback routines that consumed as little of the processor time as possible and interfaces that encouraged users to think in terms of packing as much music as they could into a fixed space, Teijo Kinnunen's *Music EDitor*, aka *MED*, was aimed much more directly at creative musicians and bridging the gap between the tracker interface and the traditional score-based music editor.

MED offered patterns of arbitrary length and a more complicated compositional structure. It incorporated external MIDI controls and so allowed users to hook up to a new breed of low-cost, high-quality General MIDI modules, like Roland's Sound Canvas series, alongside the Amiga's samples, and, with the release of an enhanced version in 1991, OctaMED could run eight discrete channels internally, using software mixing to increase the channel count with only a small degradation in sound quality albeit with a sixfold increase in the processor load.

That combination of tracker interface and musical flexibility was intriguing. OctaMED was shareware, but it also cropped up regularly as legitimate bundleware on magazine coverdisks throughout its life. Accessible, powerful, and relatively easy to use, OctaMED found its way into the performance rigs of several DJs and electronic musicians.

Urban Shakedown was a musical duo that consisted of Claudio Guissani, who was a lover of old skool hip-hop, and Gavin King, better known now as the producer Aphrodite, who was into the harder end of Chicago house. The pair met at the University of Coventry at the height of the acid house craze of the late 1980s, and after King bought a set of cheap decks they began DJ'ing in local clubs. One afternoon, a fellow student showed them an Amiga demo that featured music sampled from Bomb the Bass and Snap's *The Power*.[62]

'We just couldn't believe that this computer was making these sounds', Guissani recalls. 'We thought that they used loads of keyboards and stuff. A couple of months later, Gavin bought himself an Amiga, and I got one pretty soon after'.[63]

King and Guissani started collating samples from vinyl and tracking them in MED. To get around MED's four-track limit, the duo worked across their two Amigas, syncing them together in the simplest way possible: King would set up a four-bar click track at the start of the song, while Guissani would put a similar three-bar click at the start of the sequence on his machine. The first machine would give a one-bar count-in, prompting Guissani to start the second. Synchronization was then just a matter of adjusting the tempo until the two machines ran perfectly in sync.

There is something endearing about that low-tech approach. It links back to the DIY ethos both of punk and the early days of home computing, something that would resurface again as chip music reemerged in the early 2000s. Urban Shakedown's sound, described as being 'distinct, intelligent and eminently danceable',[64] was at the heart of their early 1990s jungle hit *Some Justice*, a track that was awarded Melody Maker's coveted single of the week and helped to shape the sound of early 1990s hardcore and drum 'n' bass.[65]

Emulation Nation

By the mid-1990s, as more musicians embraced what trackers had to offer, tracking software started to emerge on other platforms, eventually coming full circle and returning to the PSGs that the Amiga's Paula chip had broken away from a decade earlier.

The first trackers for the Amiga's great rival, the Atari ST, appeared in 1990 with Equinox's *ST Soundtracker*, and by 1994 *Octalyser* was giving Atari musicians the same opportunity to track in eight channels that OctaMED had given Amiga users. *SoundTracker 1.1*, by Jarek 'Bzyk' Burczynski, brought the tracker experience to the ZX Spectrum 128. Combining the native square waves and envelopes of the Spectrum's AY chip with a sample playback routine, SoundTracker offered up to 31 patterns of 64 notes, along with a real-time spectrum analyzer and a compiler that exported songs as machine code. Even the humble ZX81 got in on the act with a tracker that could be used to play back chip music using an external AY peripheral.[66]

In 1998, Michael Iwaniec, known as Bananmos, took the tracker interface and ported it to MS-DOS; the result was *Nerdtracker ii*, a PC tracker that was designed to capture the spirit and sound of Nintendo's NES. It couldn't run natively on the NES, of course, it was an MS-DOS program after all, and by the same token the PC couldn't natively sound like the console. Instead, Iwaniec added a custom software sound engine that ran behind the tracker and emulated the NES's 2A03 chip, offering two independent square waves, a triangle wave, a noise source, and a PCM channel.

That first iteration didn't sound identical to the 2A03 but was by no means bad. Certainly, it was good enough to audition tracks, and Nerdtracker allowed users to package up its sound playback routine and music data as 6502 NES code. With a bit of patience, an **erasable/programmable read-only memory** (EPROM) burner, and some technical know-how, that music code could be burned onto a custom NES ROM and replayed authentically on original NES system hardware.

Now it's worth stopping at this point and considering the notion of authenticity. It's an important commodity in the chip music community, and it crops up frequently, particularly in the context of emulation, but it's a notion that is difficult to unpack.

On the face of it, it seems like a fairly straightforward concept; after all, using original hardware to replay NES music is, in some sense, more authentic than playing it using a software simulation of that same hardware. The problem arises when 'authentic' is used as a label to ascribe value: who gets to define what is and isn't authentic, and who gets to apply the definition? After all, authenticity isn't really a property of music, it's something we impose on it, and it's something that depends on the social and cultural perspectives we bring to it.[67]

Marilou Polymeropoulou, a scholar from the University of Oxford, describes the response she received from an unnamed representative of a netlabel when she asked about its quality control policy. 'I was told that they release anything that is "good" chipmusic', she says. 'They explained . . . 'good' qualifies as anything that is composed on the original computers and not on sound chip emulators'.[68]

The focus on that one particular aspect of chip music making is understandable; the sound chips were what gave voice to the music originally, and moving from them to software or hardware imitations might well change the characteristics of that voice. But it's also perplexing: the Amiga, after all, uses sound samples as its source; there isn't a genuine sound chip in sight. Do we discard its contribution to chip music simply because it doesn't conform to one particular perspective on hardware?

In any case, while it's true that that an emulated sound chip and a hardware sound chip might generate sound in different ways, it is possible to emulate PSGs with a remarkable degree of accuracy, and certainly to within the manufacturing tolerances that were present between different generations of the original hardware. Alongside software models like those built into Nerdtracker, hardware emulators, like the SwinSID chip, a direct pin-correct replacement for the original SID, and Papilio, a type of user-programmable integrated circuit that offers hardware modelling on a gate-by-gate basis of a range of classic PSGs, provide a range of options that take emulated sounds astonishingly close to those of the original chips.[69]

If it's possible to create emulators that sound indistinguishable from the original, does it matter if the sound waves are generated in silico or in software? When pressed, many musicians will admit that emulation feels to them like a poor substitute. Some will go further still and admit that emulation makes them feel uneasy, almost as if the hardware has some kind of totemic quality, an ineffable spirit that could never be captured in any other way.

'Yeah, totally', says Michael Cox, who performs as The Comptroller:

The hardware can become fetishized. You know, a lot of people who make this kind of music have the sort of personality that means that they pay very high attention to detail, and I think that can come out in this way. I think there's always this sense that you might be missing a trick with an emulator. Even though you have this perfect emulation, there's still this thing that you can't quite put your finger on that means you have to go back to hardware to make sure that it's definitely there.

I do it myself. The NES can be almost perfectly emulated. The Game Boy, though, is a bit more finicky, particularly if you're pushing it to its limits or intentionally creating glitch effects. I think that if you're really going to explore what a Game Boy can do, you need to make use of what makes it unique in the first place. It's like a mysterious organic beast, so I think you're cheating yourself if you just use emulation. There's a kind of wonder about it.[70]

In his book *Supersense*, Bruce Hood illustrates exactly that sense of wonder by describing a stunt he often pulls at the start of a lecture.[71] He will begin by handing out a black fountain pen dating from the 1930s that once belonged to Albert Einstein. There is invariably a clamour as the audience, overcome with reverence and awe, scramble to touch it. Hood then asks if anyone would be willing to wear a shabby, well-worn cardigan he has brought along, even offering a prize for those willing to pull it on. There are always puzzled looks as the audience try to figure out the catch, but almost everybody is willing to give it a go. It is only when Hood tells them that the cardigan belonged to the serial killer Fred West that the volunteers disappear in a ripple of nervous laughter.

Neither the pen nor the cardigan really have the provenance Hood claims. He is using them to illustrate the irrational emotional power that objects' histories can have over us, and how, by association, we imbue them with human qualities. As strange as it may seem, those 8-bit sound chips exert a similarly powerful emotional pull.

Mark Knight admits:

The truth is that on my last album, *Reawakening*, the only bit of genuine Commodore 64 that you can hear is the background noise, which I added for a bit of authenticity. Not a single Commodore 64 was harmed in the making of that album. Everything is emulated soft-synth in Cubase. I mean, I was still using exactly the same sort of techniques that I would have used had I been sitting in front of ProTracker with my four Amiga channels, and I worked with the same restrictions: if I wanted a delay, I could only have it if I had spare slots in other channels and that sort of thing. I think as long as you're sticking to the roots, it's fine. That's authentic. The roots of chip music for me are limitations, and

I can fake the limitations. Then it's just all about the melody, really. Good chord sequences and good melodies, that's what makes an enjoyable piece of music.

The thing is, though, if anybody asked me, I lied and said, 'Yeah, it's all authentic, and it's all done on a Commodore 64'. Even the album notes said that I used Commodore 64s. I knew that to a lot of people, that stuff really matters, and when I started doing it, I think it really mattered to me too because I was coming back into a scene I'd been away from for a few years. I was desperate to be a part of it, but I knew that there was a risk that I probably wouldn't be taken seriously, so in my head, at least, I decided I had to do everything properly, and be a purist.[72]

But there is a difficulty in reducing authenticity down to the single dimension of sound. After all, the process of using Nerdtracker on the PC to burn custom carts that can be replayed on an NES console might provide some sort of hardware authenticity, but the same can't be said for the process of writing music. Composing on a PC using a sound tracker is a very different experience from coding Nintendo 6502 assembly language, and those original NES composers, remember, had to balance compositional flourish against the need for the music to run alongside gameplay. Without a game to hog resource, and free from the worry of sound effects note-stealing from the melody, all of the meagre power of the NES can be unleashed to give voice to the music. It can afford to be busier and more complex than it would be otherwise.

'People do appreciate authenticity', Gareth Morris explains, 'although I think they don't really need it. The most important thing is that the music itself is good. I can see why you'd want to use [an emulator]. It's a lot more convenient and you don't need to buy an old computer, but you know, if you really want to be 8-bit, part of that is the interface that you have to work with to produce the sounds. The way you work is definitely part of it'.[73]

Sleepers awake

Nerdtracker was followed by *FamiTracker* in 2005, which picked up the NES music baton after development on Nerdtracker was discontinued in the early 2000s. While FamiTracker adopted the same look and feel as previous tracker software, its interface was somewhat slicker, and the emulation of the NES hardware had become very sophisticated, allowing the direct exporting of high-quality digital audio files, although, of course, the option to output NES-executable code was there for those who insisted on only the most accurate playback.

Lasse Öörni's *GoatTracker*, a cross-platform tracker, brought emulated SID sounds to the PC and Mac while offering the option of exporting SID files and C64 code to be executed on original hardware, and *SIDTracker 64* brought together sound emulation and tracking with a touchscreen interface and external MIDI control to create a complete chiptune production package for the iPad. It's convenient and accessible, but the move to touchscreen changes something about the tracker workflow; paradoxically, losing something of the tactility of the interface.

'It's not quite satisfying', explains Oliver Wittchow, the designer of Nanoloop, one of the first independent Game Boy music systems,

> because moving the interface to the iPad just doesn't have the same immersive character. I'm not sure why, but I think it's the discrete control. On a tracker, you only move in digital steps in a grid. When you have analogue control, like on a touchscreen, you can get a bit lost, and it feels different. I tried to implement this more digital control when I ported Nanoloop to iPad, but it's just not there. The touchscreen can't give you that digital feel, and with the iPad you don't have such a good view of what you're doing because your fingers get in the way.[74]

The evolution of the tracker interface, from its roots in video game music to multi-faceted and self-contained music production systems on multiple hardware platforms, is surely a sign of health. In the same way that language must evolve both in its grammar and vocabulary if it is to remain current and useful as a way of describing the world and our experience within it, so too the tracker has adapted to meet the changing needs and preferences of a growing and diverse user base.

Chris Nash has done more than anyone to understand the peculiarities of the tracker interface and its role, alongside other music technology devices, as an alternative form of notating and playing with music. In pursuit of the perfect tracker, he has incorporated all manner of design touches drawn not just from tracking but also from music production and performance and from coding. His tracker, *reViSiT*, runs as a VST plug-in on a host sequencer and fuses the tracker with some of the advanced features of digital audio workstations and a unique, high-level encoding of musical form and structure, which allows the composer to play around with rule-based composition and procedural music, reuniting music composition with performative computer programming.

Nash explains:

> 'reViSiT was initially driven by the desire to integrate tracking and sequencing practices. As a composer with experience of both approaches, I recognized the relative strengths and weaknesses of each and was looking for a way to combine them. This came at a time when established tracker programs, such as FastTracker and Impulse Tracker, were becoming obsolete; as DOS programs, they were difficult to run on modern systems, and couldn't avail themselves of the advantages that DAWs had begun to offer, notably software effects and synthesizer plug-ins. Since using trackers involves developing skills and knowledge of the program, designing a new program has to be done in sympathy with existing approaches and technologies, so that users do not have to relearn their technique.

Broadly, there are two lineages in trackers, the FastTracker lineage, inspired by the Amiga's ProTracker, today exemplified by the *Renoise* tracker, and the Impulse Tracker lineage, inspired by *Scream Tracker*, and the initial basis for my program. Hence, the blueprint for the initial version of reViSiT was a clone of Impulse Tracker 2, faithful to the keyboard shortcuts and the notational syntax of the original DOS program.

reViSiT has evolved significantly since then, based on feedback from users and research. Much of this is about pruning the eccentricities of the older tracker technologies, and facilitating faster workflows. The research, especially, has been extremely helpful in identifying the factors that support the immediacy of the user experience, making it easier to preserve this key aspect of the program. Like other trackers, the design is significantly informed by the suggestions and needs of users, especially those active in the community, as much as it is by the new opportunities afforded by advances in technology, though it is often difficult to balance legacy with progress; new working methods risk alienating experienced users, but some tracking conventions are not ideal for attracting new users.

The next iteration of the software will represent a significant streamlining and update of the user interface, and though efforts will be made to support long-standing working methods, it will probably be presented as a next-generation alternative rather than simply a new version.[75]

As the tracker interface continues to evolve, the work of Nash and others keeps it at the forefront of musical innovation. Tracking has been a constant part of the electronic music scene since the late 1980s; not mainstream, perhaps, but the interface of choice for those who just want to create without fuss or drama, a Q-car or sleeper whose drab exterior belies a powerful engine beneath. The tracker is here to stay.

Going Underground

Early in 1975, Steve Dompier boarded a flight to Albuquerque to pick up a computer kit. The machine in question was an Altair 8800; Dompier, like hundreds of other computer hobbyists who had seen the machine on the cover of the January 1975 issue of Popular Electronics, was desperate to get his hands on one. Micro Instrumentation Telemetry Systems (MITS), who manufactured the Altair, had expected to sell a few hundred kits. In fact, they struggled to keep up as thousands of orders flooded in.[1]

Dompier had first seen the Altair at a meeting of the Homebrew Computer Club,[2] an informal group of DIY computer enthusiasts in California who met in the garage of Gordon French, one of the founders of the group. The club's initial response to the Altair was a little underwhelming. 'There was nothing to it but switches and lights', Lee Felsenstein recalls. But as he and 30 or so others huddled around the machine, there was a sense that they were witnessing something revolutionary: 'That may have been the moment at which the personal computer became a convivial technology',[3] he recalls.

Thirty hours after returning home with the kit he had travelled across states to secure, Dompier's Altair was up and running. He faced a conundrum, however: What do you do with a machine that has no software, no I/O boards, and no peripherals? Simple. You hack some together.

Hacking

The term *hack* has its roots in the slang of MIT's Tech Model Railroad Club. Its members had a permanent track layout in their clubroom, but while the track itself was impressive—a sprawling vista of meticulously crafted engines and buildings—it was nothing compared to the immaculately engineered matrix of relays and wires that lay beneath. The circuitry was the very embodiment of a hack, a project undertaken not solely to fulfil some constructive goal but for the sheer pleasure of the task itself.[4]

Dompier powered on his machine. As he began to hack around with different sort routines, he noticed that the long-wave radio he had on in the background began making strange noises when he hit the run switch on the computer. Each time the Altair sorted a list of numbers, the radio started going 'ZZIIIPP! ZZIIIPP! ZZIIIPP!!!'—it was picking up the computer's switching noise. After experimenting with different sections of code and timer loops, Dompier drew up a table of pitch values and wrote a short assembly program that used a series of counter loops to replay music entered as a list of numeric values. To test his new routine, Dompier grabbed the closest piece of sheet music he could find, a copy of The Beatles' *The Fool on the Hill*, and set about translating it into code.[5]

At the next club meeting, Dompier set up his Altair and played his music demo for the crowd. Even in its very earliest days, creating intriguing computer demos, short programs that showcased the capabilities of a system and its programmer, was central to home computing.

The audience demanded an encore. In an act of digital showmanship, the Altair broke into its own rendition of *Daisy Bell*, a moment Dompier described as 'genetically inherited'[6]—a reference to the IBM 704's performance of the song at Bell Labs in 1961,[7] which was, in turn, the inspiration for HAL's eerie rendition at the end of Stanley Kubrick's *2001: A Space Odyssey*.[8]

Dompier's demo caught the attention of a young associate of MITS, one Bill Gates, who had visited the Homebrew Computer Club as a part of a nationwide 'Altair on the Road' tour in the MITS Mobile, a converted Dodge camper van that drove around the country 'bringing the message of low-cost computing to thousands of people'[9]. His write-up of Dompier's program appeared in the Altair company newsletter, Computer Notes:

> The best demo programs I've seen for the Altair are the ones that control the signals on the bus to give musical output. Steven Dompier has an article about the musical program that he wrote for the Altair in the People's Computer Company publication. The article gives a listing of his program and the musical data for 'The Fool on the Hill' and 'Daisy'. All that is required is an AM radio that sits near your Altair. His article gives an explanation of how to output different notes, spaces and rests. He doesn't explain why it works and I don't see why. Does anyone know?[10]

Gates, it seems, was genuinely intrigued and perplexed by Dompier's program. His own interest in the Altair was as a platform for the BASIC interpreter that he had developed with Paul Allen. Dompier's code, however, was written in assembly and was really a case of music-by-accident rather than by design, using the 'undocumented feature' of the Altair's unshielded electrical components to achieve its ends. By hacking around with the Altair, Dompier was able to move beyond the capabilities of the system and work laterally with the technology, an act of creative transgression that granted a new perspective on the hardware, allowing it to be applied, along with the transistor radio, in a way that seemed—to Gates, at any rate—like magic.

Inventive coding like that was a talking point at club meetings. It helped to sell hardware, and hardware sales meant royalties for Gates, at least in principle. Gates was about to be thrown into a fractious dispute with the Homebrew Computing Club that would characterize the difference in mindsets between the hobbyists, who believed passionately that software should be free, and the increasingly corporate approach of Microsoft.

An Open Letter to Hobbyists

At one time, computer software was not something that was bought or leased separately from hardware. As prototype computing hardware became commercialized and trickled out from research labs in the early 1950s, most end users wrote programs themselves, largely because none of the hardware manufacturers provided any. IBM's first production computer, for example, the 701, came with little more than a user manual: 'The vendor delivered ... a number of copies of Principles of Operation (IBM Form 24-6042-1) of 103 pages (including four pages of octal-decimal conversion tables), a primitive assembler and some utility programs (such as a one-card bootstrap loader, a one-card bootstrap clear memory, and the like). That was it'.[11]

Developing large-scale applications was a major undertaking that required specialist support. Even relatively mundane programs might require thousands of lines of code. They were difficult to debug and needed continual modification and improvement in response to the demands of a changing business environment,[12] and so, alongside hardware, most companies maintained a team of programmers to service a single mainframe machine.

IBM, which even in the 1950s was an old and well-established company,[13] recognized the value of providing user support and training; by developing their own bespoke programming tools and applications, IBM's customer base was essentially reinventing the wheel with each new mainframe installation. R. Blair Smith, a sales manager in IBM's Santa Monica office, became increasingly worried that the cost of programming would rise to the point where users would have difficulty in justifying the total cost of computing.[14] He formed a cooperative user group to better support IBM's customers: the Digital Computer Association.

The group met for the first time at the Santa Ynez Inn in California in November 1952. 'We had dinner [at the meetings]', Smith recalls. 'All they had to do was just talk over dinner about, "Well, I'm trying to do this, and he's trying to do that, and my goodness! Let's get together and share it." In fact, the later user group was called SHARE for that very reason'.[15]

The group's new name represented its key mission: to share information and programs, thereby reducing the overall cost of computing and making IBM's machines a more cost-effective and better-supported option than the competition. That collaborative approach to development also had the effect of concretizing and standard-izing notions of operational computing that continue to the present day; operating sys-tems, for example, emerged as a stable concept from the group, as did the notion of what a basic suite of programs should include.[16] So too did the idea that software could—and should—be something that was freely distributable, as something whose main value was in making the leasing of hardware more attractive rather than something that had value in its own right. When IBM started to develop its own software packages, it continued in this tradition and bundled them free with its machines.

By the late 1960s, IBM had become the dominant player in mainframe systems. Much as Microsoft would do with its operating systems throughout the 1980s and 1990s, IBM, by power of ubiquity, had created a de facto standard and by bundling its services was able to provide users with a group of co-dependent products. That pre-sented a problem.

That level of integration gave IBM a significant advantage over its competitors. When the choice presented to customers was to go with an IBM system, complete with training and support, or to try and bring together several applications from different suppliers that had not been proven to work together and might receive uncoordinated updates and fixes from their individual manufacturers, most customers didn't consider it a choice at all.

In 1967, the Antitrust Division of the US Department of Justice began an investi-gation of IBM,[17] citing bundling as evidence of the company's anticompetitive practice. IBM executives met with senior Department of Justice officials, and in a move designed to preempt a Department of Justice suit, IBM announced that it would unbundle its services and charge separately for the five elements previously included for free: sys-tems engineering, education and training, field engineering, programming services, and software packages.

But while the courts had established the principle that software should be a sep-arate chargeable commodity, the growing body of computer users around the country still believed very firmly in the idea that software should be free. And it was just one such body of users, largely from the Homebrew Club, that Bill Gates met when the MITS Mobile stopped at a packed Hyatt Rickey's Hotel in Palo Alto early in June 1975 to demo the Altair running Gates's and Allen's BASIC.[18]

Many club members had already built an Altair and were waiting with growing impatience for BASIC to be released, so when they saw that the machines on display were all running it off a punched paper tape, someone decided to take matters into their own hands. Dan Sokol, a club member who worked for a semiconductor firm, recalls that one unnamed member 'borrowed' the paper tape and handed it to him, asking if he had any way of making copies. Sokol took the tape and used the DEC PDP-11 at his office to run off a few copies.

At the next Homebrew meeting, there was a cardboard box filled with dozens of BASIC tapes for members to take, with just one condition: you had to make a couple of copies for each one you took.[19] The tapes were snapped up and shared, not just within the Homebrew Club but among other clubs across the country; as a result of that sharing Altair BASIC had a huge user base, even before it was officially released.

Gates was furious. He and Allen had sold their BASIC to MITS on the basis that they would earn royalties for every copy sold, but who would buy Altair BASIC when they could pick up a copy for free from a cardboard box at their local computer club? The one saving grace was that the copy that was doing the rounds was full of bugs that Gates was in the process of ironing out. He imagined that people would buy the full de-bugged version when it was finally released, but it became clear quite quickly afterward that it wasn't selling in quite the numbers he had hoped; either people were putting up with the bugs or, more likely, they were having a whale of a time debugging the code themselves.

With all the tact and decorum of an idealistic 19-year-old burning with righteous indignation, Gates wrote an emotionally charged open letter that set both the tone and the agenda of the debate around software rights that has raged ever since.

'Will quality software be written for the hobby market?' Gates asked. He estimated that the value of the computer time that was used developing and debugging BASIC ran to more than $40,000 and calculated that the effect of the unauthorized copying valued that time at less than $2 per hour. Why, he pondered, would any professional invest the time, money, and effort required to write, test, and debug software if the returns were likely to be so poor? The implication was clear. Unauthorized copying was likely to kill software development stone dead. Without the incentive of remuneration, why would anyone bother to create professional software?

To drive the point home, Gates laid the blame squarely at the feet of the hobbyists themselves:

> As the majority of hobbyists must be aware, most of you steal your software. Hardware must be paid for, but software is something to share. Who cares if the people who worked on it get paid? Is this fair? ... One thing you do do is prevent good software from being written. Who can afford to do professional work for nothing? What hobbyist can put 3-man years into programming, finding all bugs, documenting his product and distribute for free? The fact is, no one besides us has invested a lot of money in hobby software.... Most directly, the thing you do is theft.[20]

Bootleggers, Pirates, and Thieves

Devoid of tact it may well have been, but Gates's letter marks the beginning of a drive towards increasingly tight control of the intellectual property around computer software, itself part of the broader neoliberal drive towards commoditization and free trade.[21]

The free ethic of the hacker stands as a counterpoint to this enterprise-driven process of making intellectual property out of everything, from sound recordings to software.

The issue became more pressing as the hobby market grew and the home computer became a platform for entertainment software and video games rather than the focus of entertainment:[22] a means to an end rather than an end in itself.

As sales grew, the infrastructure to support this emerging tech subculture grew with it. Popular computing magazines hit the newsstands, providing gaming news and reviews and pages of type-in programs, which introduced hundreds of thousands of readers to programming. Bedroom coders, a semiprofessional band of developers, began burning the candle at both ends, balancing the demands of school or a day job with the furtive, nocturnal work of designing, coding, duplicating, and distributing games.

With car boots full of self-recorded C15 cassette tapes, each with its own scruffy black-and-white photocopied inlay, bedroom coders travelled from computer show to computer show to hawk their wares, extending their reach by placing adverts in the backs of magazines. Some, whether by luck, persistence, or—in some cases—spite, made it big enough to set up as development houses and in turn recruit the next wave of talent. The 'industry' part of the computer games industry began to grow, and grow quickly.[23]

Computer games, too, made the transition from being cheap novelties made by enthusiasts for enthusiasts to commercial products that were slickly produced and heavily marketed. With that came the need to maximize sales and minimize unauthorized duplication and distribution. With consoles it was easy; games came on cartridges, and few people had a pressing plant at home. Those early computer games, however, typically came on tape or floppy disk, which could be copied quite easily. Just as the home computer professionalized hobby programmers, so too it criminalized a generation of schoolkids.

The earliest forms of copy protection for video games arrived on the Apple II. Personal Software's *Microchess*, for example, used a two-stage loader to deter casual copying. The software first copied a small loading routine into memory, which displayed a message to the user that loading was in progress before carrying out some novel housekeeping that would simultaneously obscure and load the code required for the game to run. By using a system of modifying counters and XORing the game code into memory, the two-stage loader provided a means of confounding those who might wish to load only the game code into memory: trying to load the second stage directly resulted in nothing but unreadable junk.

Of course, as a means of preventing casual copies, the method was quite easy to circumvent—users could simply copy both stages to a new tape. However, for some, the challenge of understanding how the loader encoded the game data proved to be a more interesting and stimulating puzzle than the game of chess it enabled. This was the beginning of an arms race, a game of technical cat and mouse that pitched the ingenuity and commercial interests of software publishers against the free ethic of the hacker.

Hackers hated the idea that copy-protected disks obscured the game code. According to the hacking ethic, software should be free, not just in the commercial sense but in the sense that it should be accessible, readable, and modifiable.[24] A well-crafted algorithm was something of elegant beauty. Hackers wanted to admire it, learn from it, and improve on it, but copy protection took that code and locked it away. As a matter of principle, then, it became a duty of the hacker to crack copy-protected software, and hackers did just that. As soon as a new form of copy protection came along, software crackers would deconstruct it and set the software free.

Of course, for any cracker smart enough to beat a copy protection system, the temptation was, like a cat burglar, to leave a calling card. Initially, these took the form of simple *crack screens*, little more than a text message that flashed the crackers' *handles* or *aliases* along with call-outs and notes of thanks into screen memory as the game loaded.

Many of those handles were expressed in *leet*, the informal language of hacking culture that substitutes combinations of numbers and letters to form alternate expressions of words and phrases.[25] Like a gang colour, those leet handles were part of a shared code that signalled to other users that one was on the inside, a part of the community. Learning that communal tongue was the first step towards initiation into the scene, although as a newcomer, or *noob*, you would also often have to demonstrate your worth by completing coding tasks set by the elite or run the risk of being branded a *lamer*.

Choosing the right handle was crucial. Given the overlap with video gaming in the early days of the crackscene, many were three-letter tags, a hangover from the hi-score tables on arcade cabinets, which, if chosen carefully, could imbue a certain credibility and enigmatic mystique. Handles were deeply personal and personalised and often referenced other elements of teenage fan culture, particularly sci-fi and fantasy.

Mark Knight explains:

I have at least two alter egos, but the one I'm probably most recognized for in the chipscene is TDK. When I was 15 or 16 I suppose it was, I was getting active in the scene, writing music for cracktros and the like, and me and my mates were talking about handles. I thought, 'I'm going to call myself Warlock. Warlock sounds cool!' That didn't last very long, though. It was a bit tacky.

Then someone said to me 'Why don't you call yourself The Dark Knight?' Believe it or not, I didn't know back then that the Dark Knight was Batman. I had no idea! So I was like, 'Yeah, okay ... Mark Knight, the Dark Knight ...' And then I figured that you could shorten that to TDK, which was also the brand of cassettes that I used to record all of my Commodore 64 music and my Amiga music onto. So it kind of worked on two levels.[26]

I'm Spinning Around

As the crackers cracked, publishers responded with more complex copy protection routines, often hiring hackers who had cut their teeth breaking other companies' routines as their security experts; they were poachers-turned-gamekeepers who knew intimately both the weak points of protection routines and the methods used to crack them. Mark Duchaineau was one.

Duchaineau had supported himself through college by working at a computer store, the Byte Shop, in Hayward, California.[27] A natural hacker, he thought nothing of cracking copy protection just for the challenge; he rarely had any need or desire for the programs themselves. One day, as he was exploring the disk control routines of Apple's operating system, Duchaineau figured out a new way to store data on disk.

The routine involved arranging data in spiralling paths on the surface of the disk so that the code couldn't be accessed concentrically, like a stylus following the groove on a record. As an additional layer of security, it collected system information while the game booted and carried out periodic rechecks. If the computer gained or lost peripherals along the way, the game guessed that it was being hacked and terminated. For a while, at any rate, Spiradisc confounded crackers.

It wasn't, however, impervious. In an article for Computist, a magazine devoted to the practice of software cracking, the contributor M. McFadden as he is listed in the publication describes how he cracked the Spiradisc routine on Sierra Online's *Frogger* using a Super Saver ROM chip to examine the game code in memory, before reorganizing and removing the problematic system checks and bespoke disk operating system to convert the game to a regular file that could be saved and distributed on any floppy. He rounded off his article by noting: 'An extremely complex copy protection scheme [has been] shot down in flames by changing four bytes. I guess they'll never learn'.[28]

That sign-off marks an important development in cracking culture. No longer was it enough to leave a modest calling card; it was also necessary to deride the creator of the software or the copy protection routine as being beneath contempt, as can be seen in figure 6.1—a shift in tone that could be found quite regularly in the pages of Computist. 'The copy protection is really quite minimal', noted Gary Kowalski of Anaheim, California, in issue 25 of Hardcore Computist. 'By booting Dos 3.3 from a normal disk, [Sierra Online's] *Mickey's Space Adventure* can be CATALOGed. (Which is only the beginning of the simple-mindedness of their protection.)'[29]

The traditional crack screen might be read, then, as an opportunity for the cracker to mark territory and stake a claim to the achievement of the crack, the digital equivalent, perhaps, of planting a flag in frontier territory. The stark tonal shift from braggadocio to contempt in later crack screens, however, showed that cracking culture was not just about an interaction with computers and code; cracking was a form of social networking that brought with it a definite hierarchy. Crackers would reach out to others who were on—and at—their level while deriding those they felt were beneath them. Far

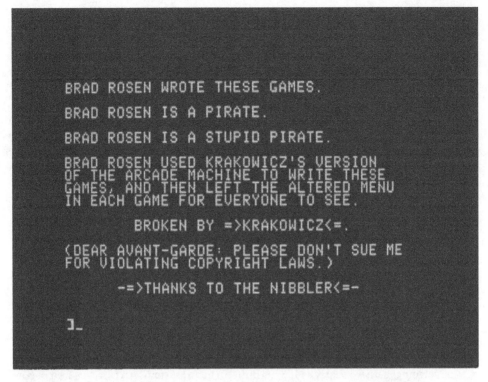

BRAD ROSEN WROTE THESE GAMES.

BRAD ROSEN IS A PIRATE.

BRAD ROSEN IS A STUPID PIRATE.

BRAD ROSEN USED KRAKOWICZ'S VERSION
OF THE ARCADE MACHINE TO WRITE THESE
GAMES, AND THEN LEFT THE ALTERED MENU
IN EACH GAME FOR EVERYONE TO SEE.

    BROKEN BY =>KRAKOWICZ<=.

(DEAR AVANT-GARDE: PLEASE DON'T SUE ME
FOR VIOLATING COPYRIGHT LAWS.)

    -=>THANKS TO THE NIBBLER<=-

]_

FIGURE 6.1 The crack screen taken from Avant Garde's 1983 title *Arcade Insanity* directs a character assassination towards the game's author, Brad Rosen. This shift towards an edgier tone mimics that of *trolling*, which also grew out of discussion groups and BBSs around this time. It also demonstrates the value placed by the extended hacking community in originality: Rosen is called a lame pirate because he adapted someone else's code.

from the public image of the hacker as a socially stunted, lonely geek, a cracker had to have well-honed social skills to establish and hold position in a distributed peer group.

'It's just a pissing contest', the cracker FreOn noted. 'We're all thrill seekers. All crackers want to crack the hardcore games before anyone else can. You can almost taste the respect and prestige you get from releasing a respected crack.... I get really annoyed when coders write shoddy protection programs that take five minutes to break. It's not fun. I mean, why bother? I like busting out my ninja skills and cracking the stuff no one else can'.[30]

This attitude also began to spill over to being directed at other crackers. Like two heavyweight boxers raising the stakes by verbally sparring at the weigh-in, crack screens became a platform not just for poking fun at one's adversaries in the copy protection battle but also for hurling insults at others in the cracking community.

This shift towards a much edgier tone shares much in common with the phenomenon of *trolling*, which also grew out of the bulletin boards and UseNet groups around this time,[31] as the anonymity of the screens and cracking handles gave license to the sort of vitriol that might not otherwise be vented.

As the personal stakes were raised, crackers tried to outdo one another, showing off their coding skills not just through the removal of copy protection routines but by creating more and more elaborate crackscreens. These digital graffiti, vibrant illicit tags in communal game space, raised a defiant middle finger to authority and further distanced the elite crackers from 'ordinary' computer users. *Cracking crews* began to coalesce, bringing together individual specialisms, including those of tech artists and musicians, who, together, worked on developing sophisticated animated crack intro sequences, or *cracktros*, with colourful graphics and music.

The release of a crack, within the scene at any rate, became an event. Crews weren't just releasing games, they were creating audiovisual showpieces, works of digital art that showcased their talent and attitude. The actual game was almost irrelevant. What was important was the crack and the cracktro that announced it, something that quickly became embedded in an informal code of distribution; the game itself could be freely distributed, but the original cracktro was not to be removed or changed. Just as in graffiti culture, cracktros and their visual style were a key part of the identity of a crew. Copying cracker handles and logos and 'painting over' another crew's digital tags was an act of disrespect that could trigger a sustained electronic war of words.

The Demoscene

Commodore's C64 attracted crackers from the very beginning, with organized cracking groups getting together as early as 1982.[32] Bulletin board systems gave C64 users a means of swapping games and contacting other users, and exchange networks and crack crews for pirate software sprang up all over Europe and the United States.

One of the first European groups, JEDI 2001, took its name from the initials of its members, Oliver Joppich, Oliver Eikemer, and Oliver-Thomas Dietz. Dietz recalls about the reference to 2001 that it seemed 'to be some date from far into the future. We were thinking of a name that more represented our identical names—O3 or Ozone—but the force was with us, and it still is'.[33]

The JEDI 2001 group really rose to prominence with their crack of the Epyx title *Summer Games*. They modified the code to convert the game from NTSC to PAL format, so successfully that Epyx went on to release the modified game officially throughout Europe. The line between the illicit and the legitimate, the corporate and the amateur, was always fuzzy.

Many of those in the crackscene lived a dual existence. The three Olivers, for example, continued to work on commercial games and software tools while active as JEDI 2001, while Andreas Arens, the lead cracker of the group Antiram, was behind the Turboplus tool cartridge for the Aachen-based developer Kingsoft. For others, the crackscene was a platform for launching their own legitimate careers in game development; it was how Mark Knight landed his first major job, scoring the *Wing Commander* soundtrack in 1992.

Without an established tradition to draw on, the audiovisual language of cracktros developed by referencing the gaming media from which it had grown. Music was frequently ripped directly from games, and groups would often leave tags and messages hidden in hi-score tables or strewn around the game landscape, like a speechwriter cheekily playing with the audience by dropping song lyrics into an oration. JEDI 2001's crack of *Pole Position* on the C64, for example, dispensed with an intro entirely, embedding a knowing wink directly within the game by trailing the group's logo behind a blimp as the player lined up on the grid and prepared to race.

Even the notion of play itself was incorporated into the form and structure of the cracktro. The Dutch group ABC Crackings, for example, presented an interactive intro on their cracks of *Carry on Laughing, Hyper Circuit, Jouste,* and *Shoot the Rapids,* posing this conundrum to the user: 'Who cracked this program?' and prompting the user to use the cursor keys to choose from seven options. Only the correct answer, a knowingly self-referential pat on the back, would start the game; the other responses triggered an affectionate chide.

The look and feel of those C64 cracktros was also shaped by the machine's hardware architecture. Colour bars, sprites, and scrolling text, all easily achievable using the C64's chipset, featured from around 1984 onwards. ABC's crack of Ocean's *Hunchback II,* for example, combined multiple side-scrolling logos placed on rainbow-coloured horizontal colour bars. The German crew GCS began to incorporate the flag of the Bundesrepublik as the backdrop to their vertical-scrolling logo.

The trend continued as Commodore's Amiga picked up the C64's baton in the latter half of the 1980s; its custom chipset allowed for the development of the visual effects that would come to define the look and sound of cracktros.

Alongside the now common scrolling text, the Amiga made it possible to ripple and wave the text as it scrolled, while coders, by dynamically shifting colours, could create plasma effects as light shows that pulsed in time to the music. Without dedicated hardware support, 3D graphics required some coding ingenuity, but with some clever programming, raster bars could be stacked to create the illusion of 3D shapes, an effect often termed *Kefrens bars,* after the Amiga demo group who popularized them.[34]

Driven partly by advances in hardware and partly by coders and artists pushing against the constraints of that hardware, intros became ever more advanced; the graphics and animation grew slicker, while the music—soundtracked samples that referenced techno, acid house, and rave, the sound of the electronic underground of the late 1980s and early 1990s—acquired an edge that distanced it from its video gaming roots. Static's *Humantarget,* for example, which featured on the Melon Dezign demo of the same name, moves away from the melodic video game style of the Amiga and C64 and adopts a more progressive structure that is built around sampled stabs and hits.

As the audiovisual elements pulled more focus, slowly the scene began to split, and cracktros drifted away from their illegal roots to become *demos:*

A gradual shift occurred, from people cracking games to writing graphic/sound demonstrations that showed off the computer they had just learned to program.

> Sure, cracking games was still popular, but some people decided that learning
> about the machine and using it as a tool for creativity was 'cooler' than cracking
> one dime-store game after another.[35]

That split also broke the link between demo teams and the commercial world. Cracking depended on a constant stream of commercial software and so was fundamentally bound up with the video game industry, whereas the demoscene, which was focused primarily on digital artistic expression, was self-contained and self-perpetuating, a celebration of hardware and ingenious code. In that respect it was closer to the culture of the first generation of hackers, although there were some important differences; sharing code, for example, something that was at the very core of hacking, was rare in the demoscene. Here the culture was one of secrecy, and coding tricks were kept a closely guarded secret.[36]

As the nascent demoscene established its own identity, it distanced itself further from video games. Demos were rarely interactive; unlike games, they were meant to be watched, not played. *Diskmags*, electronic fanzines full of articles, music, and code that had once been awash with game reviews, hints, and tips, began to drop gaming articles completely and to publish articles that described gamers as *lamerz*.

Parties, informal gatherings where sceners could meet and swap and distribute demos, were organized and coordinated like any community meeting; hand-printed paper invitations (see fig. 6.2) or text files were distributed physically and on BBSs to reach as many interested attendees as possible.

Håvar Hojem, who was a teenager in Norway at the time, recalls his first tentative steps in the scene:

> I got into the demoscene through collecting and swapping games. I'd really
> enjoyed the first few demos I'd seen [and] I wanted to become a coder and code
> my own. I was very into heavy metal music at the time, though I also listened
> to synth and electronic music, which was a weird combination for the time,
> certainly where I grew up, so when I chose my handle [Zero The Hour], I was able
> to take inspiration from heavy metal music.
>
> First, I was a member of Foxx, writing small demos in BASIC and machine
> code and often borrowing ideas from more seasoned programmers. It was a time
> in which I learned many valuable things about how machines worked and how
> demos were made. In the summer of 1987, some local friends and I decided to
> form a group of our own, and The Hidden Forces (THF) was born. It was Power
> [Norwegian Geir Reitan] and myself who were the leaders of the group, though
> three or four other local members were also involved.
>
> We traded with people all over Europe and I also had one US contact. Some
> weeks, Power would get eight to ten parcels every weekday. He was a little

```
Instructions:

Ædelse , drikkelse og soveposer skal selv medbringes.(madrasser
findes i hytten)
Sodavand kan købes for 3 slanter pr stk.

Hvis vi skal følges to party-hytten,skal i troppe op med fuld
oppakning ved  HERSTEDØSTER BUSSTOPPESTED imellem 13. og 14.
For at komme til busstoppestedet skal i med en susende fart finde
en super-tog til GLOSTRUP eller ALBERSLUND STATION.Derefter
skal i løøøøøøøøøøbe(løbe , spurte , vralte)ind i bus nr.143
eller nr.149. Hop,spring eller JMP$C000 af ved HERSTEDØSTER
BUSSTOPPESTED (eller der.hvor der står en masse andre computer
freaks!!!!!!)

          HVIS DU KOMMER FOR SENT SKAL DU:

jump´e fra $c000 til E000 og JSR$etellerandet dernede

               ELLER:

henvend til til  Peter strand (cruncher charlie)
               Espensstræde 4
   i BYEN HERSTEDØSTER!!!!!!!
```

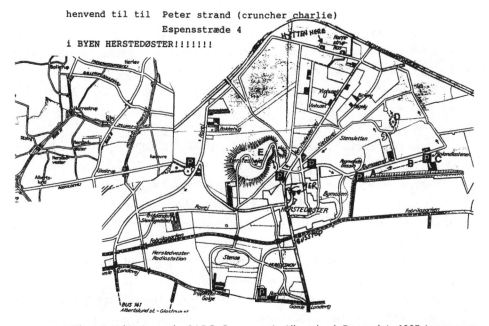

FIGURE 6.2 The printed invite to the S.I.P.C. Copyparty in Albertslund, Denmark in 1987. Image courtesy of Carsten Jensen and Microtop, and archived at http://www.retro-commodore.eu.

older than me, so he went to represent us at the Silents Party in Sweden, just before Christmas in 1987. I couldn't go with him because my mother forbade it. I had only just turned 16 and was still at the mercy of my parents. At the party, Power met up with some of our Swedish contacts and strengthened the bonds between us.

[That summer] we travelled to Denmark for the Danish Gold party. We had plans to finish a huge demo at the party. We all took the night train to Oslo, where we met up with Rocky and others, including Sauron and people from the group Compufix. [We] took the train from Oslo in Norway to Gothenburg in Sweden, then a ferry to Copenhagen in Denmark. We then boarded another train for the final leg to Odense, where the party was being held.

The party has since gone down in C64 scene history. A lot of famous groups, hackers, programmers, crackers, and traders were there, as well as game designers. The first party venue had to be abandoned on the first night as it was too small and didn't have enough electricity, so we relocated to a bigger place the next day. It ended in carnage—total mayhem.[37]

The parties were exactly as you would imagine gatherings of—mostly—teenage males to be. Alongside demo making and copying software, partygoers would get very little sleep, sustaining themselves with Coke and hot dogs. When the pressures of coding and junk food grew too great, attendees could escape to a movie room.

'This was a side project a lot of sceners were involved in', Hojem continues; 'getting the newest and most violent movies of the day. Back then, Norway had a government agency censoring films before they ran in cinemas or on video rental. Horror movies were cut the worst. You could not buy original films back then, so we copied them using 2 VHS machines. There were always people sitting and watching the movies while they copied; a break from the computer screen, watching video on the TV screen instead'.

In those early days, demo meets felt like house parties, gatherings of perhaps a few dozen, mostly local or regional participants, but from the early 1990s the size and scope of parties grew; by 1997 The Gathering, for example, a huge demoparty that is still held around Easter each year at the Vikingskipet Olympic Arena in Hamar, Norway, was attracting around 5,000 participants each year.[38] The scale of the operation is breathtaking and the logistics a challenge; a behind-the-scenes crew of around 500 unpaid volunteers work around the clock to keep the event running, between handling event planning, budgeting, advertising, sponsorship, and entertainment.

Kebu, an electronic musician from Finland, closed The Gathering in 2016 in a spectacular concert that fused the classic sounds of analogue synthesis with the real-time approach of the demoscene.

As a musician who embraces the challenge of playing analogue technology live and having to react to all of its unpredictable quirks and idiosyncrasies, Kebu's sets have an organic and improvisatory feel to them, despite the amount of preparation that goes into each one. His approach is all about testing the limits and the possibilities of the classic synths he uses, the musical embodiment of the ethos of the scene itself.

As the event came to a close, Kebu performed surrounded on all sides by banks of keyboards and modules as a projected light show danced behind him. The event had the feel of a festival gig, the glow of the thousands of computer monitors around the arena substituting for the waving of butane lighters or the screens of mobile phones.

Compos

One of the key features of demoparties is competition, something that has always been a core component of the scene. 'It's all about being able to outgeek the other guys and prove that you're the alpha geek', Ben Daglish explains. 'It's always been a thing. It's not just been a case of "Oh! I've got to do as good as that ..." it's "Oh! I've got to beat that!" you know? Geeks love being able to prove that they're geekier than anybody else'.[39]

Competitions, or compos, evolved for different disciplines, allowing programmers to compete with programmers, musicians with musicians, and artists with artists. Each discipline was constrained by a set of prescriptive rules and conventions, most commonly imposing artificial size restrictions on the work to force makers to work within the same limitations and constraints as had existed in the days of 8-bit hardware. Typically, competition intros were size-limited to 64 kB or 4 kB, although other categories existed that squeezed the memory restrictions as low as 64 bytes.

Those size restrictions were crucial for keeping the chip music aesthetic alive. While in the commercial world game developers like LucasArts harnessed the more realistic wavetable sounds of PC soundcards to give video game soundtracks a more cinematic feel and Sony used the CD-ROM streaming of its new PlayStation console to cross-promote some of the electronic music artists it held in its back catalogues, the demoscene kept that raw, lo-fi electronic sound alive and gave it an edge. It was the sound of techno-counterculture, of geek rebellion.

Alongside the most common platforms and compos, executable music and *oldskool* music events for the C64, Amiga, and PC, today there are events to cater for every possible musical niche, from ZX Spectrum beeper music written entirely in BASIC through to events that celebrate specific trackers and hardware.

To celebrate the launch of his ST tracker, maxYMiser, for example, Gareth Morris organized an online competition in 2006. He was closely beaten to the winning spot by his collaborator and friend Nils Feske. When I suggested to him that the experience had echoes of Charlie Chaplin coming third in a Chaplin lookalike contest, Morris laughed. 'No, no!' he protested, 'it's not like that at all. Firstly you can't win your own competition, so I was absolutely delighted not to win, and Nils inspired a lot of the stuff on maxYMiser. He's a really great musician'.[40]

Freestyle music compos and wild compos relax the constraints of competition, allowing for the inclusion of additional elements—vocal samples or external hardware, for example—which encourages a healthy and inventive diversity of sound. Linus Åkesson's *LFT Variation 18,* for example, his entry in the Wild Compo at Revision 2015, fuses together live performance and a video narrative, which begins with a floppy disk being loaded into a Commodore 1541 disk drive.[41] Åkesson sits at the piano and plays a sensitive rendition of Rachmaninoff's Rhapsody on a Theme of Paganini before the screen splits to reveal his orchestra, a bank of three time-synchronized C64s, which are in turn augmented by more C64s. The effect is dramatic and surprisingly emotive, a real fusion of acoustic and electronic performance and a reminder that coding, something that on the face of it may look like a very isolating activity, can be performative and creative and a way of connecting with others.

Growing Pains

Today, the demoscene is bigger and has a greater following than ever before, but while that growth has given the scene a sense of currency and vibrancy, it has also brought a degree of tension. Like a cottage industry struggling to hold onto its unique indie charm as its growing popularity forces it to scale up and corporatize, the early days of ad hoc meets wherever sceners could find space are very different from the slick, sponsored events of the scene today, full-on festivals of geek culture that bring together gaming, coding, cosplay, and music. But the scene is, after all, the embodiment of the passions of those who populate it, and inevitably it changes over time. Change isn't always easy to deal with.

Mark Knight says:

> I think at some point I just grew out of all of that underground countercultural shit. The atmosphere in the early days was great; just really fun and really geeky. I remember being at a party, in about 1990, I think it was, and this kid comes up to me, gets down on his knees and starts bowing down in front of me, saying, 'Oh wow! You're TDK!'
>
> But that all changed. It got edgier, nastier, maybe. I went to the Melon Dezign Birthday Party in Copenhagen round about 1993. I did a TDK concert. The guys took us out for a meal the night before the demoparty, and at this place you had the restaurant on the top floor, you had the exit on the middle floor and then the cloakroom was on the bottom floor. We had the meal, and then they just ran out of the restaurant without paying for the food that we'd had. I was like, 'What do I do?' I didn't have any money. So I ended up running out after them and chasing them, but I was really not happy about it.
>
> And for the actual demoparty, they had got these Dutch neo-nazis for security. You know, big guys, bald heads, baseball bats.... I was very, very uncomfortable. So that was what made me leave the scene. I thought, 'I've had enough of this. This is what it's turned into now'. I'd already been in games for about a year at that point, and I wasn't finding the time to write any music in my spare time. I just thought, 'Now is the time to let the kids get on with it'.

But then I did a gig at the Revision demoparty back in 2014. I mean, it was a big demoparty. There were over a thousand people there, all programming on their Amigas and their Ataris and their Commodores and whatever, and it made me really want to get involved with the scene again. And I would love to do it … I would love to … But you just don't find the time for it now, you know?

But then, I suppose I am still involved. I've been asked to do some chiptune music for a new demo project, so I'm still writing, and although I'm maybe not at events, because, you know, that's for the kids, really, the mindset of the demoscene is still with me. It's always been about a special sort of creativity, all about the limitations. That's the really fascinating bit. All the other stuff, all of the demoscene stuff, all of the music culture stuff, it's a kind of interesting by-product of that.[42]

The Game Boy
A Handheld Revolution

Looking back at Nintendo's Game Boy today, more than a quarter century on from its launch, it's easy to look at its chunky, brick-like design and forget just how profoundly it revolutionized handheld gaming. It wasn't the first handheld console, but it brought handheld gaming to the masses; in 1989, the Game Boy was everywhere.

Ten years later, when its already antiquated hardware was beginning to look positively prehistoric, the Game Boy reached the end of its production life, but its story doesn't end there. It found a new lease of life as a musical instrument and turned chip music into something new; something live, something performative.

Of course, the Game Boy didn't arrive ex nihilo. Its DNA is woven through the grey plastic and printed circuit track lines of all the portable gaming devices that came before it, and those track lines lead back to Mattel's *Auto Race*.

A New Dawn

In the wake of the first wave of home video gaming in the mid-1970s, the toy giant Mattel, which had made its name in the 1950s and 1960s with tactile toys like Barbie and Hot Wheels, had been eyeing the video games market keenly from the sidelines, convinced that its experience in tactile play could bring a new dimension to home gaming.

George J. Klose, a product development engineer at the company, had become fascinated by the idea that electronics could support play after seeing an electronic roulette wheel, which used LEDs to represent the spinning balls of a roulette table,[1] and a calculator that processed stored chess-playing algorithms.[2] He began working on a game concept that would repurpose the LED display of a handheld electronic calculator to display simple graphics formed from its display segments that could be moved around the screen to create a field of play for an electronic game.[3] The trouble was, Mattel didn't have any expertise in game development—few people did back then—so they looked for a partner. Mattel's choice was the US defence contractor Rockwell Industries.

Now, of course, Rockwell didn't have any experience in game design either, but they did at least know how to manufacture microprocessors and electronic components. They also had Mark Lesser, a product design engineer, who jumped at the chance to work on the project.

The mood elsewhere at Rockwell was a little more ambivalent. As the project was a back burner, Lesser had to do all the circuit design and programming himself, and although he was confident with the componentry, he had never written a program before. Because of the cost involved in designing a new single-chip computer, he had no option but to turn to one of the calculator chips he had to hand. It had limited I/O, next-to-no ROM or RAM, and a clock that ran so slowly it could almost be measured in geological time. Lesser's challenge was to take this and turn it into something playable.

It's difficult, I think, to find words that adequately convey that combined sense of excitement and terror that is felt when you find yourself working at a frontier like this, but that's exactly what Mark Lesser described to me. Remember, he was working at a time before high-level programming languages. The now ubiquitous programming language C, for example, had only just been invented at Bell Labs, and video game development was still largely hardware-based and in its infancy. He was using the processor and the display from a pocket calculator to handle gameplay, and he had to fit the whole thing into just 511 bytes—not K—bytes of memory.

'[It] was an exciting time indeed', Lesser recalls, 'as the early stages of any endeavour might be. Back then, I was excited by the problem at hand, and had no idea that Auto Race would be interesting to someone forty years hence. Not to wax too philosophical, I think the total absorption in creative work is, in itself, the most valuable part; more valuable, perhaps, than the product of that work. What is most memorable to me was the sense of not-knowing whether anything of any value could be created within the severe technical limitations. There was no path to follow'.[4]

The finished game was housed in an off-ivory plastic casing (see fig. 7.1) and powered by a single nine-volt battery. The gameplay was simple. The player car, represented by a vertical display segment at the bottom of the display—a simple calculator-style segmented LCD rotated through 90 degrees and mounted vertically—moved up towards the top of the screen, and the player used the thumb controller to avoid the nonplayer cars that worked their way down from the top. The payoff, when the player made it to the top of the screen after completing four laps, was 'the beeping sound of victory,'[5] a simple auditory reward that mimicked the chimes and bells that accompanied multiballs and bonus games in pinball.

Auto Race was a definite risk for Mattel. Lesser was breaking new ground with the product. Nobody really knew if it would work, let alone whether it would be a marketable product, but of course it did, and it was.

FIGURE 7.1 Mattel's Auto Race.

Mattel followed with variations on the theme, most notably with *Football* in 1977, which shared a similar gameplay mechanic—the rules and methods that determine how the player interacts with and experiences the game—and was mated with a horizontal LED display.

The following year, the Milton Bradley Company launched *Simon*, a sound- and colour-based eidetic memory game, which was inspired by an old Atari coin-op called *Touch Me*.

An electronic version of the children's game Simon Says, Touch Me was an unusual misstep from Atari. The game was built into a short-body cabinet and did away with a display screen altogether, instead using a row of four illuminated dark red buttons mounted horizontally across the top. Once a quarter had been deposited, the player had to watch and listen to a sequence of flashing lights and tones and repeat them in the same order.

By the time Ralph Baer discovered the game at the Music Operators of America trade show in 1976, Touch Me was already two years old. Baer was less than impressed by what he saw but was particularly scathing about the 'terrible execution [and] … miserable, rasping sounds'.[6] Yet there was something in the gameplay that he felt he could make work. He built a mock-up and pitched it to Marvin Glass & Associates, an independent toy design firm he had worked with in the past, who then licensed the design to Milton Bradley. Careful to address the shortcomings of the Atari coin-op, Baer revised the interface, which evolved into the familiar disk-shaped case (see fig. 7.2), with four illuminated buttons arranged in quadrants around it. This clever innovation not only looked better but also made it possible to play Simon as a collaborative multiplayer game, with players facing one another around the device.

The game was released in a blaze of publicity at a midnight party at Studio 54, one of New York's hippest night spots. That high-profile launch, helped along in no small part by the climactic game of intergalactic Simon that played out at the end of that year's movie blockbuster, Steven Spielberg's *Close Encounters of the Third Kind*, made Simon a pop culture phenomenon, in the process cementing the link between music and electronic play.[7]

FIGURE 7.2 Milton-Bradley's Simon.

Buoyed by the success of Simon, Milton Bradley launched Microvision in November 1979. Microvision (see fig. 7.3) was the first true handheld console system, in the sense that it provided a base unit on which different game cartridges could be played. Unlike almost every other cartridge-based system before or since, however, the Microvision body was little more than a housing for the 16- by 16-pixel monochrome LCD display, a small speaker, and the game controls. The game code and the CPU required to execute them were housed in the cartridge itself and connected directly to the console body via copper pins, leaving the low-voltage cartridge circuit vulnerable to electrostatic discharge. It was, perhaps, a system ahead of its time, and technical problems, along with a lack of game cartridges, eventually led to its demise in 1981.

As the 1980s dawned, the cost of LCDs had fallen to a point where it had become feasible to use that technology to replace the more common LED displays in handheld games. LCDs allowed the display of custom objects and shapes, giving finer detail and greater resolution, but their flexibility was still limited. On an LCD screen, all graphic objects needed to be preformed and configured at a particular point in the display field, so every possible location and state of the game objects had to be preset. Although this

FIGURE 7.3 Milton-Bradley's Microvision Console and Blockbuster cartridge.

restricted the nature and visual complexity of the gameplay, it focused the designers on creating visually simple but engaging games.

Gunpei Yokoi, whose Ultra Hand had helped recast Nintendo some years earlier, bought into the idea completely. He practiced a design philosophy that he called *lateral thinking with withered technology*;[8] he would take cheap, well-established and well-understood technologies and apply them in novel and innovative ways. One morning as he sat on the train to work, he watched another passenger idly pass the time by playing around with the buttons on a pocket calculator. He realized that if he reshaped the display segments, he could create a graphical interface that would give his fellow passenger something more engaging to play with than just numbers.[9]

The result was Ball (fig. 7.4), the first in Nintendo's Game & Watch series.[10] Designed by Yokoi around commoditized components and stripped of any superfluity, it was a simple game at low cost, but one that had very little compromise in terms of engaging gameplay and playability.

Ball was a simple juggling game that needed only simple controls—a left and right button—but Yokoi wanted more. He wanted to recreate the gaming experience of some of Nintendo's most popular coin-ops: games like Donkey Kong (fig. 7.5). Yokoi realized, however, that he couldn't just drop a joystick onto the top of a pocket game—that would hurt its 'pocketability'—so he developed a flat alternative, what we now call the directional pad or D-pad controller.[11]

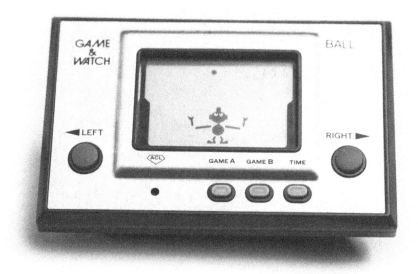

FIGURE 7.4 Nintendo's Ball, the first in its popular Game & Watch series.

FIGURE 7.5 Nintendo's split-screen Game & Watch release of Donkey Kong marked the first appearance of the D-pad, which would go on to become a universal controller for both portable and home consoles.

The Game Boy

The Game Boy brought together all of these components into a single package. It was the embodiment of Yokoi's philosophy. It had a form-factor and colour scheme similar to those of Mattel's Auto Race; it used the same D-Pad controller as Donkey Kong; and it took the idea of swappable cartridges introduced on the Microvision and made them all work in perfectly judged harmony.

In terms of its technology, the Game Boy was only ever adequate. At its heart was a custom 8-bit Sharp LR35902 operating at 4.19 MHz, a variant of the same Z80 processor that had powered Sinclair's ZX Spectrum at the beginning of the decade. Although it lacked a dedicated sound chip, the core CPU was designed to support integrated sound generation, giving the Game Boy native sound capabilities that were similar to the NES

FIGURE 7.6 Nintendo's Game Boy and Tetris. It was a combination that gave handheld gaming a universality it had never had before.

and greatly superior to those of other handhelds, which until that point had used simple beepers.

Its LCD screen had four shades of greyscale, although greenscale is, perhaps, a more accurate description, because it lent all of the graphics a pretty sickly pallor. It wasn't as high-res as the colour LCD in Atari's Lynx, but then nor did the Game Boy chew through batteries the way a teething puppy does the living room furniture.

'After we released the Game Boy', Yokoi recalled, 'one of my staff came to me with a grim expression on his face: "There's a new handheld on the market similar to ours ..." The first thing I asked was: "Is it a colour screen, or monochrome?" He told me it was colour, and I reassured him. "Then we're fine".[12]

Yokoi's design philosophy led him to the realization that hardware design was not just about making the most powerful device possible; by considering hardware, software, and user requirements together, he was able to create a device that was accessible and cheap, both to buy and to play. And so it was that the less technically able Game Boy (fig. 7.6) put video gaming in the pockets of the people.

Tetris

Few games have defined a platform as completely as Tetris did the Game Boy, and part of Nintendo's marketing genius was to bundle the machine with what was undoubtedly its killer app. The straight edges of the tetriminos work perfectly on the Game Boy's low-res screen, and with shape and orientation driving the gameplay, the screen's motion blur and limited tonal range just didn't matter. It was the perfect blend of simplicity and challenge, a game whose appeal transcends age, gender, and even skill.

Game Boy Tetris features three music tracks, all arranged or written by Hirokazu Tanaka, who had joined Nintendo in 1980 as a sound designer and had provided Jump Man's footsteps and leaps for 1981's Donkey Kong.[13] The default track, Theme A, was an arrangement of an old Russian folk tune, *Korobeiniki*.

The tune first appeared in Spectrum Holobyte's version of the game for the Apple IIGS and Mac in 1987. That arrangement, written by Ed Bogas, the media composer hired by Atari to score Snoopy and the Red Baron, is more complex than the one on the Game Boy, featuring a harmonic riff and a tuba-like bass to accompany a series of repeated melody notes designed to simulate the rhythmic style of a balalaika, but it suffers, perhaps, from being slightly too ambitious. In trying to emulate the sound of the balalaika, Bogas accentuated the artifice of the arrangement. Arguably, chiptunes are at their very best when the composer works to make a feature of the hardware, the polyphony, and the raw waveforms. When he ported it to the Game Boy, stripping 'Korobeiniki' back to a simple harmonized melody, with a bassline in broken octaves and the chirp of filtered noise providing a percussive backbeat, Tanaka created the perfect accompaniment to the game.

Theme A would have been one of the first pieces of music that players heard when they turned on the Game Boy for the first time, and they would have heard it over and over and over again. Little wonder, then, that both the game and the music quickly became very deeply ingrained in the public consciousness, something the game's creator, Alexey Pajitnov has mixed feelings about: 'When kids of the world hear these pieces of music', he opines, 'they start screaming, "Tetris! Tetris!" That's not very good for Russian culture!'[14]

And then, as if to undermine Russian culture that bit more, two singles were released that took the music of Tetris and gave it mass appeal. In 1991, an Italian house duo, Eugenio Passalacqua and Andrea Prezioso, released a dance version of Theme A as the Game Boys. It was little more than a sample of the original Game Boy soundtrack with a four-on-the-floor beat behind it, but it became an underground sensation and spawned a series of remixes. It was a collision of club culture and video game culture and showed that video game music could be something more than just functional media music: it could be popular music in its own right.

If that was a message that needed driving home then it was driven home with some force the following year, when Doctor Spin released a Eurodance cover of Tetris (fig. 7.7) that got to number 6 in the UK charts.[15]

Doctor Spin, was little more than a front end for British composer and theatre impresario Andrew Lloyd Webber and his collaborator, producer Nigel Wright. The single highlights Lloyd Webber's ability to read the shifting sands of popular taste, and with

FIGURE 7.7 Tetris by Doctor Spin, a manufactured front for theatre composer Andrew Lloyd Webber. The single brought together club culture and gaming culture and demonstrated that video game music could have a reach beyond games.

both gaming and Eurodance in their ascendancy at the time, Tetris brought the two together head-on.[16]

The Game Boy Camera

Following the launch of the Game Boy, a range of accessories designed to make the console run longer or play better found their way to market. Nuby's Game Light, for example, provided a battery-powered night light that improved screen visibility and contrast, while Sunsoft's Soundboy, released in July 1991, provided an external battery-powered stereo amplifier that connected to the Game Boy's headphone socket.

When Nintendo released the *Game Boy Camera* in 1998, they realized its limitations as a photographic tool and instead marketed it as a novelty device, the 'world's smallest digital camera'.[17] The cart shipped with a suite of applications and minigames, including a variant of Ball, which replaced the juggler's head with the player's Game Face, an early precursor of the Mii avatars that would later feature on Nintendo's Wii console.

Alongside Ball and a fun Space Invaders–style minigame, *Space Fever II*, the Game Boy Camera offered another unusual creative 'game', *Trippy-H*, a customizable step-sequencer with a traditional keyboard layout, whose design apes that of Roland's classic TB-303 bass synth (see fig. 7.8).

Three tabbed edit screens provide a user-friendly way of accessing the core sound functions of the Game Boy. Sound I offers a pulse wave with variable duty cycle, to which a variable amplitude envelope and an independent gate can be applied, providing some fairly complex sound shaping. The inclusion of a secondary LFO modulator with variable depth and rate and a choice of sine, square, and random modulation sources

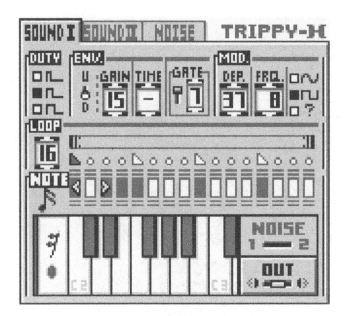

FIGURE 7.8 Trippy-H, a multichannel 16-step sequencer that put the lo-fi Game Boy waveforms in the hands of players.

lifts Trippy-H from just an interesting novelty to a well-featured music application. The Sound II channel broadens the tonal palette, providing a sample channel at the expense of some of the amplitude and frequency modulation options, and the Noise channel uses enveloped noise to generate percussion tones.

Moving out of Edit mode takes the player to the play screen (see fig. 7.9), where a virtual DJ with the player's Game Face spins tracks on a set of low-res graphical decks and keyboards. Using the D-pad and buttons, players can mix their tracks in real time, play with the tempo, and scrub the audio backwards and forwards.

Although the step sequencer of Trippy-H was too limited to produce anything more than simple loops, it did, perhaps, show that gaming controls could work quite effectively as an electronic music interface.

Nanoloop

In 1997 Oliver Wittchow, a design student at the University of Fine Arts in Hamburg, came to the same conclusion. As an undergraduate project, he decided to try and hack the Game Boy and turn it into a handheld synthesizer.[18]

The idea had been running around his head since as a teenager he had plugged his brother's Game Boy into his father's stereo and for the first time really listened to the Super Mario sound. It wasn't like the techno he normally listened to, but there was something about its primitive waveforms, a roughness that he describes as 'the analogue end of digital', that spoke to him. The more he thought about it, the more he realized

FIGURE 7.9 Trippy-H's Play mode.

that the Game Boy, beneath its plastic case, was just a computer. It might have a small screen and no keyboard, but it had a processor and ran programs from cartridges; surely it should be possible to program it?

Developing on the Game Boy wasn't actually all that difficult. Initially, he wrote to Nintendo to ask for support; perhaps unsurprisingly given Nintendo's closed development model, he never received a reply. Instead, Wittchow turned to the unofficial development community online and to Jeff Frohwein, who had developed a Nintendo BASIC interpreter and documented almost every aspect of Game Boy development.

Wittchow began coding directly on the Game Boy in BASIC. To say it was clumsy would be an understatement: his code was entered using the D-controller and the A and B buttons a single character at a time, much like sending SMS messages on an early mobile phone. His first programs were unstable and very slow, but already he was hooked.

He started attending programming classes at university, switching to C, and, as his coding became better, his Game Boy synth became slicker and more capable. He entered an early prototype of his creation, *Nanoloop*, in a lo-fi music contest at the club

nanoloop 1.0

music created on the nintendo
game boy™ with nanoloop::::::::
:::
:: vladislav delay⁄antye greie
fuchs ::dat politics ::merzbow
::pita ::hrvatski ::blectum from
blechdom ::ascii ::felix kubin::
::pyrolator ::stock, hausen &
walkman ::scratch pet land :::

FIGURE 7.10 Nanoloop 1.0, a multiartist compilation that showcases the range of approaches to music making that were emerging on the Game Boy.

Liquid Sky in Cologne in the spring of 1998. He was nursing a heavy cold, and he remembers the software glitching almost to the point of collapse, but the crowd loved it. They loved the sound, and they loved seeing a familiar toy reimagined as a musical device. Spiritually, Wittchow was applying Yokoi's philosophy and breathing new life into a tired old platform.

Wittchow's prize was a record deal. He released a seven-inch single titled simply *Nanoloop* on the XXC3 label the following year. It was, of course, an important release—the first chiptune explicitly written and produced for a commercial pressing—but by entering into a commercial contract, Wittchow had to cede some editorial control of his music. The label had a certain idea of how electronic music should sound, and it wasn't the same raw, minimal sound that Wittchow had worked hard to create. XXC3 took the master tracks, added some effects in postproduction, and then mastered them, changing their character in the process.

The single was followed in 2002 by a CD, *Nanoloop 1.0* (see fig. 7.10). Wittchow remembers the experience of producing the CD as being much more relaxed and musically satisfying. The label contacted other artists from its catalogue to ask if they would collaborate on the project and sent out Nanoloop cartridges to those they wanted to feature on the release, including the Aphex Twin, Richard James, who produced some initial material, which, sadly, wasn't included in the final master.

The tracks on the CD present a showcase of that early Game Boy chip sound across a diverse group of electronic musicians and show how far the Nintendo had moved from its video game roots. Wittchow and his collaborators were, after all, electronic musicians first and foremost, so a Game Boy running Nanoloop was primarily a lo-fi handheld synthesizer, not a gaming console.

Some tracks, like *burbanked* by blectum from blechdom, present the raw sound of the device in all of its glory. Others, like ostinato's *gameboy girl*, add vocals and process the tracks further using production software, principally Emagic's Logic and Pluggo's *Flange-o-Tron*. Two of the tracks, hrvatski's *cy twombly* and the improvised *401k*, by asciii, were performed and recorded live direct from Game Boy, giving listeners the closest sense of what it might have been like to experience Wittchow's original performance in Cologne. Together, the tracks cover quite a bit of musical territory, and the flavour is very much that of the hard, contemporary electronic sound of the turn of the millennium, ranging from the glitchy electronic *pillion passenger* by Stock, Hausen & Walkman and the noise art of pita's *nloopcbn* through to the house-style sound of *nanodance*, a very accomplished electronic dance track from pyrolator, which really showcases Nanoloop's capabilities.

The key to Nanoloop's appeal is its interface (fig. 7.11), a step sequencer arranged as a four-by-four grid and controlled using the D-Pad and the A and B buttons. It's a game-inspired interface that encourages a playful, improvisatory approach to composition and lends itself well to performance. The approach came from Wittchow's experience of working with FastTracker on the PC.

He explains:

> We didn't really make tracker music; it was more minimal techno house stuff, sampling from a record, a jazz record usually, and playing loops. We mainly used the tracker for playing loops and adding minimal beats. [My friend] also had some drum machines, some cheap Yamaha practice machines, and we played with those. We often sat around just leaving the loop running, then from time to time, we would transpose it by a semitone and listen to it again for half an hour, so it was very minimal stuff; evolutionary, and more about loops. At that time, I was going to the early techno parties, and for me, I liked the aspect of techno being not 'musical' at that time. It was almost like an antimusic, like punk rock. It was not melodic, it was only beats and samples—noises—and we tried to implement this kind of music in trackers.

Nanoloop moved into commercial production in 1999, selling initially in Wittchow's native Germany before becoming available worldwide in 2000. The early cartridges were manufactured in China, and to protect his intellectual property,

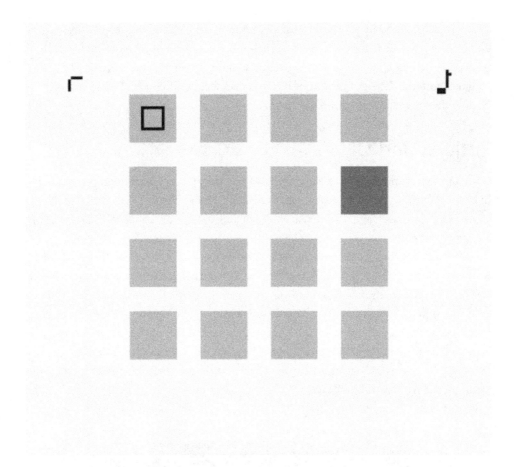

FIGURE 7.11 Nanoloop's main step sequencer is arranged as a four-by-four grid. Combined with the Game Boy's D-Pad and buttons, it encourages a playful, improvisatory approach to music making.

Wittchow opened every cartridge and bent some pins so that the circuit couldn't easily be copied. But as sales increased, the linguistic and cultural barriers that arose from doing business across continents became more and more tiresome to deal with, and in 2005 he started to design his own printed circuit boards and manufactured them in his native Germany, giving him much more control over the evolution of his product.

Wittchow's approach to product design mimics his approach to music itself. The feature set of his software has expanded and contracted as he has continued to play with his designs, using the software to reflect on his own music-making practice. Always, he is trying to find that sweet spot between accessibility and control, and he draws on inspiration across engineering and contemporary electronic composition. The latest Nanoloop versions offer complex pattern manipulation options, allowing the user to run sequences of different lengths simultaneously and to create polyrhythmic and polytextural layers—complex sounds that emerge from simple structures.

While that complexity is important, Wittchow feels strongly that it should not be imposed by design but should emerge in a bottom-up way through musical experimentation and play. 'The control system is so simple that you really know what's going on', he explains. 'It's not some random button you push or dice you throw … [but] it does get complex and maybe unexpected … so that you get interference and rather complex patterns. It's very primitive, but it makes such a difference. It fits very well the Nanoloop approach: very minimal control'.

Little Sound DJ

Nanoloop was fundamental in transforming the Game Boy from a handheld console into a portable musical instrument, and as more and more people discovered its capabilities as an expressive device, they also explored alternative approaches to music making and performance.

While Nanoloop focused on the idea of improvising and playing with sound, Johan Kotlinski's *Little Sound DJ* (LSDJ), released in 2000, introduced a tracker-style interface (see fig. 7.12) to give its users total top-down control over the Game Boy sound system.

Kotlinski joined the computer music scene in the early 1990s. As a teen, he learned piano and dreamed of having a studio of his own packed full of the sort of music hardware that he read about in the liner notes of his favourite albums, but as was the reality for most, he just couldn't afford to make music this way. Instead, he turned to the Commodore Amiga and ProTracker.[19]

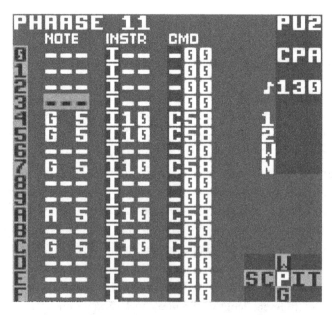

FIGURE 7.12 The phrase-level display of Little Sound DJ allows editing of note- and command-level detail. This essentially gives the same level of control over the music as the tracks on something like Ultimate Soundtracker; but by nesting layers of detail, Little Sound DJ makes the most of the limited display space of the Game Boy and allows for a flexible, modular approach to composition.

As it turned out, Kotlinski preferred both the sound and the interface of the Amiga. He loved the freedom and the creative possibilities offered by sampling, and the way that tracker interfaces unlocked the hardware of the Amiga to give full voice to his musical ideas, unconstrained by instrumental ability. The music flowed, and Kotlinski started to release music as part of the demo group Hack n' Trade.

Following the release of the Gameboy Color, in 1998, some members of the group bought consoles and development kits and started to experiment with little pieces of music software. Kotlinski realized that with the right software, the Game Boy could be used as a complete portable music production suite, and he became interested in pushing the Game Boy to its musical limits.

Even then, the idea of a portable music workstation wasn't new. Yamaha had entered the market in the early 1990s with the QY series of 'walkstation' devices,[20] which combined sample-based General MIDI synths with on-board sequencers and miniature rubber keys set out as a single-octave keyboard. The Game Boy, of course, had a similar form factor but already had a much larger user base than these much more expensive dedicated synths. Kotlinski also liked the glitchy, characterful sound.

He explains:

The sound is pretty special. It has four different channels, and each channel has some special characteristic, like, one by one they sound pretty crappy but together they are still OK enough to be used musically. I think I like the most that I've been able to make a music program that's customized for me, and it doesn't have a lot of buttons or stuff to fiddle around with—it's just a few buttons—it's not too hard to keep track of everything you're doing, so you can keep everything simple and finish your songs pretty fast, that's what I like the most.[21]

That flow, the speed with which musical ideas can be laid down, arranged, and edited, is certainly effective, but it comes with experience. The Game Boy's small display means that only a limited amount of data can be presented to the user at any given time, making the process of composition feel a little like playing a memory-puzzle game.

Little Sound DJ takes many of its ideas and features from classic trackers and tweaks the way they relate to one another and interact to better suit the Game Boy. As with most trackers, the timeline reads from top to bottom, and each column represents a single sound channel, labelled by timbre: two pulse channels, a sample channel, and the noise channel.

The two-digit hexadecimal entries on the song screen represent *chains*, deeper-level nested patterns that can be triggered at each step in the sequence. Chains, in turn, are built from *phrases*, each of which is a 16-step note sequence. The number of phrases in each chain can vary between one and sixteen. Together, this gives quite a degree of structural control over the music, but it also necessitates a more complex conceptual model than Nanoloop, which creates a different workflow; while you code music in LSDJ, you play with it in Nanoloop.

Moving between these different layers is straightforward. Navigation is handled by the D-controller and a graphical mnemonic in the lower right of the screen, which shows the user's position in the song hierarchy. With a little practice, manoeuvring between different layers becomes very fast indeed, and those structural elements, the chains and phrases, become editable and manipulable musical fragments in their own right.

This is where the real power of LSDJ lies. In addressing the issues of interface on the Game Boy, LSDJ encourages users to approach music composition from multiple perspectives. In the same way that a fugue is ultimately just a collection of notes, to think of it as such ignores all of the metalevel structural detail: how those notes form phrases; how those phrases are transposed, inverted, and augmented; and how those developments work across time to provide the musical momentum that drives the piece forward. In LSDJ, the notes of each phrase provide a musical building block that can similarly be transposed and rearranged in the chain, allowing for the creation of complex pieces of music in a very time- and space-efficient way.

At the most detailed level, LSDJ uses the familiar note-level commands to trigger arpeggios, portamentos, pitch bend, and volume but goes further, introducing *tables*. Tables in LSDJ are, to borrow a gaming analogy, similar to the combo sequences in beat-'em-ups. They allow the user to create sequences of transpositions, commands, and amplitude changes, which can be executed at any speed and applied to any channel. They can be linked to an instrument or applied arbitrarily at any point in a phrase. They can either be synced to the LSDJ's musical clock or be automated, with each command or set of commands executed line by line with each new note. The Tables function is extremely powerful, similar in function to a modulation matrix on a classic analogue synth, and is a refinement of Chris Hülsbeck's program scripts in TFMX, providing a way to add tonal dynamism to the Game Boy's flat synthetic tones and an opportunity to experiment and explore new musical territory.

Although LSDJ's feature set isn't unique, its combination of game-derived navigation, flexibility, and the nested modular implementation of its feature set make for a very distinctive music-making experience, particularly when combined with the Game Boy itself; tracking with a device in your hand as you sit on a park bench or bust a groove on stage is very different to tracking on a desktop computer in a study. It forces you to be more reactive, both to the process and to your environment. Little wonder that the software went on to become the cart of choice for many Game Boy musicians.

Game Boy Live!

On July 18, 2008, musician Nickolas Walthew took his instrument into the streets of Seattle. As he prepared to play on the corner of East John Street and Broadway East, passersby wandered past, paying little attention to the busker.

There is nothing particularly unusual about this scene. It is one echoed across the globe, in fact, as street musicians ply their trade on everything from the great highland bagpipes to stripped-down acoustic pianos. What made this different was that Walthew, better known as Fighter X, a member of the guerilla collective Lo-Tek Resistance, was hooking up his Game Boy to a couple of speakers powered by a car battery. As the familiar Game Boy start-up tone chimed, Walthew, seated on the speakers and, hunched over his console, launched into a high-powered lo-fi electronic track.

'I was pretty shy up there losing my Lo-Tek Resistance virginity', he said immediately after he had finished playing. 'I was nervous. More nervous than I usually am at a regular show. Apparently, I was just staring at my Gameboy the whole time. I didn't even want to look up at the crowd. I'm just sitting there.... Yeah, pretty much with every Lo-Tek event, there can be a lot of confused pedestrians. A lot of people think that we're just playing Mario or Tetris or something. They don't think that we're making music or playing music that we made ourselves'.[22]

There is a definite ambiguity about playing music on a video game console, an ambiguity that is perhaps best expressed by a gag that does the rounds in the discussion groups that surround the scene: 'How do you play a Game Boy live?' asks a noob. 'You just hit the start button and dance', replies an old hack.

It's an affectionate and fairly droll quip, but it highlights a fundamental truth about electronic music performance, a blurring of the boundary between what is and what isn't a moment of spontaneous musical creation that doesn't always translate into a visual focus for the audience.

Josh Davis performs Game Boy music as Bit Shifter and well remembers having to decide on just how to present his act live:

> I think I had a show booked. I thought it would be cool to do, but I didn't have any idea what I was going to do. So I emailed Jeremiah [Johnson; Nullsleep], sort-of out of the blue; we didn't know each other at all at that point. I just asked him for advice, like, 'Hey, what do you do when you play live? How do you translate this into a live performance?' His advice was just, you know, like, change parameters on the Game Boy, like tempo, and wave your fist around. That's pretty much what I've been doing ever since.[23]

The issue of how you make electronic music a performance event is not something that is unique to the Game Boy; musicians who gig with laptops, modular synths, or even—as I once witnessed at an avant-garde electroacoustic performance—the amplified squeaky hinge of a set of stepladders, have to address the idea of performativity when music making is recast on unconventional instruments using unconventional musical gestures. It is, however, something that the Game Boy's size and video gaming heritage amplifies.

On an acoustic instrument, performance has traditionally brought together musical intentionality and production in a single moment that is made explicit for the audience. When I sit at a piano or strum a banjolele, there is a direct and very observable moment of musical creation, one that is tactile and physical. My audience can see, appreciate, and understand the craft and skill of performance, even if they don't themselves play. The concentration and expressivity is etched on my face and in my posture. They can draw on centuries of tradition to appreciate what is happening before them; it is all there in the psychophysical cues that tell of the years of training, the fine motor skills and muscle memory that are required to coax the full expressive range from my instrument at that precise moment in time.[24]

Electronic instruments, and particularly digital musical instruments, isolate the back-end tone generation of the instrument from the front-end control interface.[25] They offer musicians much more scope for the creative manipulation of sound in performance, but in accommodating multiple layers of control and automation, these instruments obfuscate and distend the moment of creation, making it more difficult for audiences to connect what they see on stage with what they hear.

This physical independence means that the gestures of musical control are essentially unconstrained:[26] anything that can be digitally captured and encoded, from the thumb-strokes of a Game Boy's D-pad to the performer's instantaneous heart rate and blood pressure,[27] can be used to generate control signals. With no direct physical connection between the player's gestures and the sound produced, the player has an almost limitless flexibility in approaching performance, but each layer of abstraction masks the performer's agency and requires more input in the way of preparation ahead of performance.[28] This is not to say that virtuosity and spontaneity aren't still a part of electronic performance—of course they are—but that virtuosity manifests in different ways and at different points in the process.

However, arguably, that has always been the case. Take the classic example of musical spontaneity: the jazz solo. No matter how much it feels 'in-the-moment', it is the cumulative result of many thousands of hours of practice and experimentation, of building an expressive vocabulary and the fluency necessary to combine that fragmentary lexicon into complex and fluid musical expression during performance.[29] That preparatory work is just as real and has just as much impact on the nature of performance as do the physical mutes and other objects that John Cage advises performers to experiment with so that they might shape the sound of the instrument in his works for prepared piano.[30] The only real difference between the two is that with the latter it's much more explicit that the preparation has taken place and its effects are much more visible. In both cases there can still be those 'happy accidents' that result from improvisatory play around the frameworks that have been created by preparatory work, perhaps suggesting that performance is better considered as a process than as an event.

There is also the ambiguity of the performative gestures of gaming. A performer hunched over a tiny LCD screen thumbing a joypad might well be making music but might just as well be ploughing through rows in Tetris. Indeed, one of the reasons that synthesizers have evolved around the traditional piano-keyboard interface is precisely because performers needed to signal to audiences that they were performing.

When he launched his range of modular synths, Bob Moog was keen to look for alternative controllers that didn't limit the machines to discrete tones and traditional ideas of tonality, but in the end he conceded: '[It] looks good if you're playing a keyboard. People understand that then you're making music. You know without it, you could be tuning in Russia! This pose here [acts out the pose of the left arm extended] graphically ties in the music and the technology'.[31] And so, as analogue synthesizers began to find their way into rock and psychedelia acts in the 1960s, they were largely seen and used as extensions of other electromechanical keyboard instruments, finding their way into the rigs of keyboardists. Nevertheless, some musicians, particularly those given to flamboyant showmanship, looked to extend and play on the expressive capabilities of the synth using alternative modes of control. Moog's own ribbon controller, for example, an enhanced version of Léon Theremin's fingerboard theremin, used a resistive strip to create a control voltage that could be used as a controller for a tone module.[32] Keith Emerson famously used one hooked up to his Moog Modular, clamping the two-foot-long device to his groin and grinding like Jimi Hendrix as he improvised soaring synth solos. As a device it afforded more in the way of stagecraft and showmanship than precise musical control, but it did so by substituting one form of familiar musical performance cue, the keyboard, for another, the guitar.

The importance of stagecraft grew steadily throughout the late 1960s and early 1970s, as the camp theatricality of prog and glam rock gave way to the aggressive posturing of punk and then the foppish androgyny and pageantry of New Romanticism.[33] In contrast to the raw spontaneity and live sound of punk, New Romanticism concretized the synthesizer and sequencer. At a stroke, music became more mechanical. With the computer at its heart, music now had a quantized soul, with copy and paste giving it form.

That early British synth-pop sound itself had its roots in Krautrock, the improvisatory minimalist electronic music that originated in Germany in the late 1960s, and right at the heart of that movement was Kraftwerk.

Florian Schneider and Ralf Hütter met as students at the Robert Schumann Hochschule in Düsseldorf in the late 1960s. Early line-ups fluctuated: Hütter and Schneider worked with around a half dozen other musicians during the recording of their first three albums and their sporadic early live appearances. Kraftwerk never set out to be a touring band, but by the release of *Ralf & Florian* in 1973, they had started to cultivate a stage presence that reflected their musical ethos. In those early days, Hütter and Schneider, like many in the German electronic music scene at the time, considered themselves less as part of the rock scene and more as performance artists who were making a musical art statement,[34] and the inside cover of Ralf & Florian shows them seated at their instruments with, on the floor in front of them, the distinctive neon signs and traffic cones that would become part of the visual signature of the band's Gesamtkunstwerke (total works of art).

By the early 1980s, Kraftwerk had developed an approach to performance that made a feature of the mechanistic relationship between performer, technology, and performance, celebrating the fusion of human and machine and showcasing the mundanity and routine of musical interaction.

The Game Boy sits just at that point where the top-down control of electronica collides with the raw self-expression of punk. It is cheap, accessible, and ubiquitous and—when loaded with a Nanoloop or LSDJ cart—can be subverted to function as an all-in-one lo-fi electronic music production system. Its form factor and interface dictates an intimate, one-on-one relationship between user and device, offering little in the way of opportunity to make performance a spectacle.

The Polish ensemble Mikro Orchestra, who have also performed as the Gameboyzz Orchestra Project, tap into that tradition of mundane performance; on stage the band remain static, their concentration focused completely on the Game Boy screen, contrasting sharply with the pacey electronic tracks they play. Their sets make a feature of the accessible low-tech hardware in a world increasingly dominated by polished and produced electronic acts. That is a low-tech punk ethos; it was a sentiment that was echoed by the alternative music impresario and fashionista Malcolm McLaren.

McLaren had found himself intrigued by the chip music scene in 2003, just as the Game Boy's popularity surged and in an article for Wired he declared the genre to be 'the new punk', embracing the retro–futurist benefits of using Game Boys to make music, calling it 'the Velvet Underground of the 21st century. The next step in the evolution of rock and roll'.[35]

For McLaren, the intrigue was in the accessibility of the music and its honesty: 'Chip musicians plunder corporate technology and find unlikely uses for it. They make old sounds new again—without frills, a recording studio, or a major record label. It would be facile to describe the result as amateurish; it's underproduced because it feels better that way. The nature of the sound, and the equipment used to create it, is cheap. This is not music as a commodity but music as an idea. It's the Nintendo generation sampling its youth'.

McLaren's intention may have been to throw his weight behind a new and exciting music scene to create a buzz and hype, but his article angered many of those in the chiptune community who doubted his motives: he had a history of co-opting cool new acts to cross-promote his fashion lines, and his plans to use 8-bit punk as the theme for his Fashion Beast party in 2004 did little to dispel this idea. The community responded with an angry open letter from Gareth Morris,[36] at the time an active member of the micromusic.net community.

Morris derided McLaren's understanding of the genre's history and corrected his assumptions about the way the music was made. He recalls:

Yeah, it was very controversial. We saw that McLaren was hanging around the scene. I was playing this party in Paris when I was with this record label called Relaxed Beat, and as I was on my way down to the party on the Eurostar, I ended up sitting on the same table as this Guardian journalist. Later I met this same journalist at the party, and he's like 'Oh, you should come and talk to Malcolm McLaren, he's a mate of mine, and actually the reason that I'm here is to write about his [Fashion Beast] party for the Guardian'.

I was really excited. Well, who wouldn't be, you know? But I was kind of talking to him [McLaren] about 8-bit and he really just didn't get it at all, you know? He was really just thinking about how he could use it to promote his clothes. He had this Japanese girl punk band called the Wild Strawberries or something and he wanted to use 8-bit to push that and some of the clothes that he was doing, so I could tell straightaway that he didn't really understand what was going on. I'm all for 8-bit crossing over and becoming more mainstream, you know, and I think that's brilliant, but I don't really think that Malcolm McLaren was the guy to do it.

Micromusic.net asked me to prepare this letter, which was meant originally for a book that they were writing about 8-bit, and it was meant to be a kind of general message from the whole community. The next week it gets put on the web with my name at the bottom, and it's sent out to every Micromusic member by email and there was kind of a real backlash about it. Yeah, I got a lot of heat from that letter. A lot of people thought that I was being ungrateful, you know? That this guy is a music industry figure, he's interested and he's ... They maybe didn't quite know his history. Sure, it's a good thing that he's there, but I just thought: 'Well, he's not the guy', you know?

So I'm pleased that I wrote the letter, but I don't think that McLaren ever read it, and even if he did, I don't think that he really cared. I did meet him again later at a fashion show in Berlin. He didn't recognize me at all, and didn't really seem to care. I got the impression that it was just kind of a cool culture that he could use ... an aesthetic he could tack on to make himself look cooler.[37]

Beyond Handheld

The Game Boy may not have kickstarted 8-bit punk in quite the way McLaren might have hoped, but it has become one of the most visible icons of the chipscene.

Oliver Wittchow says:

I think that Game Boy music or chip tune music will last. Just like nowadays people still play on the theremin: there is a great renaissance in theremin, and I think that this will continue with Game Boy. Game Boy stands for a whole era, and, yeah, I think it will be a musical instrument like a piano or something. If I was Nintendo, I would have capitalized on that and rereleased the Game Boy for its twenty-fifth anniversary. With today's technology you could make a really nice, flat, e-paper device with a month of battery life, but they didn't do it. I think they don't get it, and it's sad. I have some hope they are moving in this direction and appreciate what we—the chipscene—are doing for them, because in German we say *unbezahlbar*, like you can't do the marketing. People are gigging and partying with Game Boys. They're having fun and praising Nintendo. That sort of goodwill money can't buy.[38]

That is the dimension that gaming brings. It's not that chiptuners are making video game music—they're not—but that this music, the sound and the vibe, is loaded with positive association: of childhood, of carefree play and fun. Performing on a Game Boy draws on these very powerful emotional bonds. Game Boy Gabba musician DJ Scotch Egg, for example, opened his set at the Boiler Room in Berlin in May 2014 dressed in a floral apron and broke off from performance to flip pancakes. Sonic Death Rabbit, a chip fusion two-piece that combines chiptune with death metal and breakcore, use Game Boys alongside toy guitars, turntables, and screaming death metal guitar to construct a performance that relies as much on the audience's understanding of the cultural weight of the toys and games they use as on the sounds they create.

Peter Berkman, lead guitarist with chip-rockers Anamanaguchi, explains:

We're using the 8-bit sounds as a piece of the picture instead of the whole thing. It was definitely a deliberate decision, but not one that I made thinking I'd be able to 'get more fans' or something. It all stems from having a really musical background, I think. In electronic music there are always artists who strive to be more technical than musical, and we're definitely the other way round.

I grew up playing video games as much as the next Generation 2K-bro, but I view it as something that's separate from my music. I think it's also important to make the distinction that we aren't writing video game music—I'm thinking way more about [the Beach Boys'] Brian Wilson and old Rivers Cuomo [of Weezer] than Hip Tanaka—who rules, though—when I'm composing. [Other chip artists] sound literally nothing like video game music and no doubt get frustrated when people don't get past that.[39]

The emergence of nu-rave in the mid-2000s was undoubtedly an influence on Game Boy music and may have helped the reception of the Game Boy as a musical instrument as audiences and artists became reattuned to seeing synths on stage and hearing a fast-paced, digital, dancey sound. That hardcore rave sound is one of the things that most clearly distinguishes this wave of live-oriented chip music from that which grew out of the demoscene in the late 1980s. It is an altogether harder and more aggressive sound that fully decouples the devices from gaming. For the new wave, the Game Boy is a lo-fi instrument first and foremost, not a gaming device. It's a form of self-expression, with a sound that embodies affiliation not to a retro gaming culture or an ethos of pushing hardware to its limits but to a sound, to an aesthetic, and to a lifestyle.

Accompanying that sound, the physical moves of the rave scene have also worked their way into performance. Niamh Houston, who gigs as Chipzel, a London-based Game Boy musician, describes the appeal of chiptunes as 'being a weird form of dance music for the younger generation',[40] and she busts moves to work the crowd as her Game Boy grooves, just as Bez, from the Happy Mondays, did 20 years earlier when indie rock was at its height.

Mark Knight says:

Niamh's great. She's one of my favourites, because she's just such fun. You get people on the scene who don't have any sense of performance, no idea that they should be doing something in front of the crowd. Niamh's really good at that. She's really good at getting the crowd going, jumping up and down and bringing them in. I mean, they already know what the music's going to be like. They've heard it before. What the Game Boy does is give you quite a bit of freedom to be seen. You're not hiding behind gear. The challenge is to figure out how to make what you do worth watching.[41]

That challenge, of making chip music performative, has inspired many responses. Michael Cox, The Comptroller, is part of the post–Game Boy generation and came to chiptune via punk.[42] He says:

I started off playing guitar in a succession of weird experimental garage punk bands in the late nineties. Around that time I dug out my old NES from my parents' house. They had found it in a cupboard and gave it to me, bricked. I was like, 'Oh, I'll go online and find a way to repair this,' so I went online and chanced upon NESDev forums and found out that not only were people fixing these things, but they were writing new software for them and writing new music for them, and that kind of opened up my mind to this whole world of chiptune. I found a YouTube clip of Nullsleep playing a gig on a Game Boy with a keyboard attached to it in some random basement club venue somewhere in Europe, and I was just like 'Christ! There are actually people out there who are taking this stuff out live!', you know?

Cox experimented with MIDINES, a cartridge that adds MIDI ports to the NES console, allowing its 2A03 chip to be controlled from an external controller,[43] but he switched to working on the Game Boy, largely because of the practicalities of taking a NES onstage. One evening in 2006, he found himself standing in front of an audience with just a Game Boy in front of him. Even for a seasoned performer, it was nerve-wracking.

I got up on stage and there was just me and a table and two Game Boys, and I did this thing where I was like … I felt it would just be like cheating if I were to go up and just press Start, so I intentionally juggled up the structure of the songs and started DJ'ing, just so that I would be doing something to force the songs to happen.

It was weird. I was terrified before the show, even though I'd played a couple of hundred gigs with other bands by that point. With this one I was really nervous, I remember, because I had no idea what I was doing or how it was going to go down. I didn't mind so much that the audience didn't know what to expect, because the band I'd been playing with previously had been a two-piece, and we'd both wear suits and balaclavas onstage, so I was used to being confrontational. Actually, I quite liked that the audience might not like it, it was more the idea that I just didn't know what I was going to be doing while I was up there. That's what bothered me.

There is, though, a tacit expectation that live music will involve an element of performance. The discomfort Cox felt arose because he understood that expectation and felt the pressure to deliver ... something. He explains:

By necessity, when you're taking that stuff on stage, you have to do something to fill in the performance gap. I come from that background of aggressive, confrontational punk music, so when I was up onstage with the guitar, that was always something that you could just thrash at and the audience would respond to it. With Game Boys and the like, there's just none of that, and you have to find different ways to fill the space.

Honestly, though, a lot of my live set is about me frantically trying to get the next machine set up for the next song. So probably if you were to look at me playing live, the song starts, and then straightaway I'm pulling wires out, and turning this on, and changing cartridges ... There's spectacle in that, I guess, but it's not just for show, I genuinely am working hard to keep everything going. I have a set list that tells me that this cartridge needs to go in there now, and this needs to be preloaded ... And sometimes there are weird glitches, so I'll have a note that says that I need to play the first two bars of this track before I play it live because it's got a weird jump that only occurs the first time you play it through. It's almost like firefighting on stage.

When things are running smoothly, I stand, staring at the audience or I make these bizarre arm movements, so I kind of do these ridiculous dance moves on stage and pull weird, po-faced, and threatening gestures. I don't really know I'm doing them. I guess you could say that they've become part of my stage persona, but not really consciously. The more that it's gone on, though, the more I get the sense that there's this 'comptroller identity' that I can play up to.

That idea of having an alter ego, a stage presence that can imbue you with confidence and dramatic license, is quite common on the scene.

Gareth Morris says:

A lot of us are very shy guys and girls; gwEm is certainly a bit more outgoing than me. I think he puts me in touch with a part of my life that I don't ever get to show every day. You know, I'm dreaming of a better world and that's what I want to try to create on stage, so it's kind of my chance to do that. Honestly, there's nothing better than ripping out a guitar solo, but it's not something that I normally get to do, so yeah my persona is like an alter ego, and it lets a part of me live that I just can't address otherwise.[44]

Like Michael Cox, Morris's approach to playing chiptune live has been informed by years of playing heavy metal and drum and bass. He explains:

I've got two live sets. One is the DJ thing, where I use the [Atari] ST like I would decks, and then there's the guitar show with a heavy metal, punk influence going on. When I first heard metal I really liked it, but then, I also really liked it when I first heard the Prodigy or drum and bass, and I kind of wanted to put them together, but that wasn't really possible until I discovered chiptune: with chiptune you can really do anything.

So for my live show, well I wanted it to be, you know, a bit like the Ramones, and a bit like Iron Maiden, and I wanted it to be a bit like a rave, really involve the audience, you know? I always think people have paid good money to see you— well … maybe not for an 8-bit show, although they might have travelled a long way— so you want to try and figure out what they like and try and put on a show for them.

So the guitar is there for the show; it's quite a powerful look. When I was a teenager, that Flying V was *the* guitar wasn't it? Kirk Hammett from Metallica, he played a Flying V; Judas Priest and Scorpion, who I didn't know so much about then, they all played Flying Vs. I just thought 'If I'm ever going to play a guitar, I'm going to play a Flying V'. I had this idea for a punk song, *Fuck You Management Wanker*, and I wanted to have a guitar on it, but I couldn't play, so I went to the local music store and there was a secondhand one and I just thought, 'Yeah, that's perfect!'

So that's how I came to the V. I think it's the most iconic guitar. I mean, the BC Rich Warlock and the Les Paul are great shapes too, but I think that if you go on stage with a Flying V, you kind of know what to expect. OK that's true with a Warlock as well, but the great thing about a Les Paul is that you can literally play jazz or balls-out metal and that's appropriate to the guitar. With the Flying V you know you're going to get rock, they're not going to be messing around. That's all the things I wanted to project.

My drummer once said that it's a good thing that I play a V because it just looks like I'm a great guitarist who's having an off night, and I think that's true.

Now I'm a bit older and I've got a few more grey hairs I sometimes play a Strat, which I really like, but I feel like I have to work a bit harder. I mean, if the V's there, then it's already doing some of the show for you without you having to do anything.

While My gAtari Gently Beeps

As more musicians started to use the Game Boy as a performance instrument, they started to adapt its hardware to better suit their needs. Among the most common modifications were the Pro-Sound mod, which involved replacing the on-board 3.5-millimeter headphone jack with a better-quality quarter-inch stereo TRS socket or breakout XLR connectors, and mods that allowed the player to hook up an external footswitch to trigger the start button remotely. Modding instructions were freely traded online, encouraging novice electricians to open their consoles and poke about.

Morris, who has a PhD in electronic engineering, explains:

There's this thing called circuit bending that overlaps with 8-bit, where people are more interested in asking 'What will happen if we solder these wires? What will happen if we break this line?' To me, that just seems like … Well, why would you do that? It's not been designed in that way! But the truth is, that if you don't know what you're doing, then you're doing experimentation and could come up with some amazing things.

A lot of that circuit bending of 8-bit stuff is sort of brilliant and I'd never have come up with it. And then those circuit benders learn more about how electronics works and develop more of their own stuff. So there's loads of homebrew electronics now. A lot of the designs are available for free, or at least for cost price. I think it's brilliant, actually, and I see this attitude being absorbed into the larger DIY synth community, because there's quite a few synths that you can buy and put together yourself.[45]

That was precisely the trajectory Oliver Wittchow took with Nanoloop. 'The Game Boy BASIC stuff was the first code that I ever wrote', he recalls,

and so I really learned from the ground up. By 2005 or so I had designed my own circuit and, of course, nowadays you have flash memory and so on, and so I began to do my own circuit design in flash. That was a lot to learn. I mean they were really simple circuits, but I never did a circuit before, and I needed to learn the circuit layout, the design program, solder prototypes, and so on. And now, with rapid prototyping, you can have your own PCB [printed circuit board] designed and have it printed and it's industry quality; there's no difference between the prototype and the mass product, [they have] the same technology and the same quality.[46]

As Wittchow's confidence in circuit design grew, he released a MIDI connector for Nanoloop,[47] a dongle that connects the Game Boy link port to USB, allowing it to be triggered directly via MIDI using the mGB software extension that can be loaded onto a Nanoloop cart as extra ROM. It works in a very similar way to the open-source Arduinoboy,[48] a DIY Arduino-based hack that hijacks the microcontroller's serial controller to provide an external MIDI interface.

'I don't quite get what that's good for actually', Wittchow says. 'I don't understand the desire for it, because if you only want the Game Boy sound, well the sound is so generic that you can do it just with square waves. You can easily do that with any audio program, you just open a patch and go. But then, of course, there are certain glitches that may be difficult to reproduce. I think people want to play the Game Boy because it's a Game Boy and not because of the qualities of the sound'.

With the Game Boy showing how a gaming device could be retrofitted with MIDI and integrated into an existing live music rig, chip musicians started experimenting with tabletop consoles.

On the Commodore 64 the MSSIAH (see fig. 7.13) cartridge combined a MIDI interface with five different music applications, adding a sequencer, drum machine,

FIGURE 7.13 Mark Knight's C64, modified to provide external filter controls, and the MSSIAH, CYNTHCART, and PROPHET 64 music cartridges, which added professional synthesis capabilities to the machine.

synths, and a sampler, all sync'able via MIDI.[49] With the addition of a display, ideally a vintage portable television set for that old-skool vibe, the SID, which had always been conceived as a performance synth, could finally be taken onstage and played.

The ZX Spectrum Orchestra, the brainchild of Mike Johnston and Brian Duffy, has been performing since the early 2000s, combining glitchy lo-fi sounds and blocky projected imagery in its live sets. Duffy says:

> We first started because we'd been going to lots of [car-boot sales], and seeing these beautifully designed computers and wondering about them. I bought a manual for them for 10 pence, and inside it, it said there was the BEEP command, and my imagination was taken by the notion of BEEP, and I wanted to know what the BEEP sounded like.
>
> So we concocted this idea that maybe it's possible to have multiple Spectrums onstage and started pursuing that. And only when we were booked to do our first gig did we realize what an absolute nightmare it is! It's like having a gang of naughty schoolchildren onstage that could just do anything they want to do at any moment. It's not like using modern technology at all.
>
> But the way it works live is that you can't sync the computers together, so that's one of the big differences between Spectrums and modern equipment that has MIDI—most musical instruments nowadays can communicate with each other, so they can keep in time with each other. Whereas with the Spectrums you just can't do that, you just have to rely on the maths of it. A lot of ZX programmers attempt to program everything into one machine—the drums, the melodies, everything. We tend to divide it between machines and not worry about the fact that they don't sync.[50]

Further down the road, however, Matt Wescott, a web developer and demoscener, showed that Spectrums could, in fact, talk to one another by tackling one of the problems posed by the same user manual that had fired Brian Duffy's imagination at the car-boot sale.

Chapter 19 of the ZX Spectrum manual (partially reproduced in fig. 7.14) included a program called Frere Gustav, a few simple lines of basic that translated the brooding melody of Mahler's funeral march from his Symphony no. 1 into BEEP commands. The chapter ended with a challenge exercise: 'Program the computer so that it plays not only the funeral march, but also the rest of Mahler's first symphony'.[51]

'I actually missed out on that chapter the first time round', Westcott says.

> The Spectrum I grew up with was the Spectrum+, which came with a different, more cut-down manual. It was probably only in the late 90s that I learned about it, when I joined the first wave of Speccy retro communities on the Internet. At that point, the BEEP chapter with its Mahler references had taken on a kind

FIGURE 7.14 Chapter 19 of the ZX Spectrum manual challenged users to write a program that would play all of Mahler's Symphony no. 1. It was a challenge that would take more than thirty years to complete.

of semi-legendary status; I guess it captures the spirit of what learning BASIC programming as an 80s child was really like. It wasn't just plodding through a dry textbook, it had its own cheeky sense of humour that really engaged its readers. And there was a very real sense that you could make the computer do anything—all the way up to playing a full symphony—if you just knew the right commands to give it.[52]

The idea of putting together an orchestra of Spectrums was something that formed gradually. Westcott had spent an evening writing a program to convert MIDI files to Spectrum BASIC BEEP statements for a single machine and, naturally, was curious about what kind of results he might get from trying to play more than one at the same time. He had explored the idea before, having gigged live with Spectrums, which had given him some idea of the technical challenges of keeping the machines in sync.

The final impetus came from his friend Dylan Smith, the creator of the Spectranet network interface, which plugs into the back of the machine and allows it to network.[53] Smith had created a few demos of his interface, including multiplayer gaming and posting to Twitter, and the two wondered what else could be done with networked Spectrums. It struck Westcott that there was an obvious candidate, one that nodded back to Spectrum history.

Westcott linked together 12 ZX Spectrums (see fig. 7.15), all coordinated by a single Raspberry PI acting as timekeeper and conductor, at Geek Out,[54] an event hosted at the

FIGURE 7.15 The Spectrum Mahler Project connected 12 ZX Spectrums using the Spectranet Ethernet interface and made them all dance to the same (chip)tune. Photo by Dylan Smith.

Oxford Museum of the History of Science in 2014, and made good the challenge posed in the user manual 30 years earlier.

'It was certainly nerve-wracking!' laughs Westcott.

> I had very little idea of how it was going to turn out. We did a dry run with four machines the night before, and that was as close as I got to hearing a preview of it. The beginning of the music itself added to the drama; the piece starts with one instrument playing two alternating notes in solo, before the other instruments join in. That solo seemed to last an eternity, and then at the moment when the second Spectrum joined in, it turned from panic to relief and actually being able to enjoy the music.
>
> The atmosphere was really magical. The slight imperfections in the timing and tuning meant that there was a real organic quality to the sound, not just coming from an automaton, and the audience was hanging on every note.[55]

Even the old Atari VCS has found a new lease of life as part of the live chipscene. Paul Slocum's *Synthcart* turns the machine into a basic but characterful synth, complete with an arpeggiator and preset rhythm patterns. It's designed to be used without a display, making the VCS much more viable as a performance instrument, something that was seized on by the Australian chip artist, Chris Mylrea, or cTrix, whose live setup shoehorns a vintage Atari running custom sequencing software based on Slocum's original code into an oversized guitar body complete with a fretboard packed with Boss stompboxes. The gAtari is perhaps the ultimate fusion of console and performative controller, a retro-future instrument that has seen Mylrea shredding chip sounds at festivals around the world.

'The gAtari was my excuse to do something a little silly after I discovered that the Atari 2600 was more limiting than I realized!' says Mylrea. 'I needed an EQ which could take a high voltage and drop it down to line level, the Boss bass EQ, plus a way to hold loops between tracks and parts, the Boss delay. So rather than have a DJ-style config, I thought I'd make something a little more creative'.[56]

Jeri Ellsworth took that idea in a different direction with her Commodore 64 bass keytar.[57] She took a bandsaw to the body of a bass guitar and mated its neck and strings to a vintage breadbin model C64. The keytar uses a field-programmable gate array chip to perform a frequency count on each string, before the guitar signal is resampled on the SID chip, meaning Ellsworth can adjust the sound on the fly by pressing the function keys, while the keyboard itself doubles as a synth controller, triggering SID waveforms in real time. All of this is amplified by a small, portable amplifier that she wears on her belt. The only downside, Ellsworth admits, is its power consumption: the keytar eats through 18 AA batteries every eight hours. With typical flair, Ellsworth displayed the instrument at the 2012 Bay Area Maker Faire, thumping out the rocking bass of *Sunshine of Your Love* while rolling around the auditorium on skates.

But the ultimate in chiptune performance instruments must surely be Linus Åkesson's Chipophone,[58] a homemade 8-bit synthesizer built into the case of an old Holmsjö electronic organ. The Chipophone project began when Åkesson was gifted the organ by his friend, Håkan, who had bought it in a thrift shop, only to have it languish, unloved, in his cellar. Åkesson gave the organ a new home on the understanding that he could indulge in a spot of Frankenchip-style experimentation.

He ripped out the organ's innards and connected the key contacts, pedals, knobs, and switches to an ATmega88 microcontroller, which transforms the controller signals from the keyboard into MIDI data. The hack threw up a few oddities. The volume pedal, for example, was not based around a straightforward potentiometer but a small light bulb that shone through an opening whose width would vary as the pedal was operated, in turn varying the amount of light that fell onto a photoresistor on the other side of the opening. All of this adds to the Chipophone's retro character and unique charm.

Åkesson then added a second ATmega88, running custom code to synthesize typical chiptune sounds: eight independent waveform generators capable of generating pulse waves, lo-fi 4-bit triangle waves, and white noise, as well as some SID-like features, like ring modulation and variable pulse widths, all in glorious 12-bit mono, using an intelligent algorithm to allocate voices and arpeggiate chords dynamically as keys are pressed.

The organ interface lends itself beautifully to chip performance. There are three parts, played via the upper and lower manuals and the pedals. Watching Åkesson play is a visual treat. His fingers dance over the keys, and his feet kick pedals as he blasts out the theme from *Megaman 2*, a real one-man chip-band.

Such inventive recycling of hardware is a refreshing counterpoint to the relentless drive of technological progress. Users might drift to new machines that boast more memory, faster processors, and better sound, yet by looking at these machines through the creative eyes of a hacker, by poking around in the darkest recesses of their hardware and code, we can recast them and breathe new life into them. There is, indeed, life in the old dog yet.

Netlabels and Real-World Festivals

As more and more musicians began playing with vintage gaming hardware and using it expressively, the world of chip music was evolving into something approaching a protoscene. Eight-bit and early 16-bit hardware had given musicians a production platform and a technically driven aesthetic, if not a concrete style. From these grew the core philosophy of the scene, the idea that technology is only as useful as we make it; that the pursuit of the shiny and new might blind us to the untapped potential of the obsolete.

The growing sophistication of digital communications, beginning with those early bulletin boards and developing with the World Wide Web, allowed that philosophy to spread and helped to create and grow communities of practice: on the one hand the demosceners, rooted in the traditions of hacking and interested in taking systems to their limits, and on the other a new generation of performance musicians who embraced the sound of the machines and were more concerned with using them as instruments to find their own expressive voices.

Participation and output was growing. The nascent chipscene needed a platform for expression, something that would connect the music and the musicians to audiences. It needed, if not an industry—and the chipscene's roots in hacking and its culture of free naturally inclined it away from commercial exploitation—then at least something approaching that kind of infrastructure.

Major Business

These days, the term 'music industry' tends to be used almost synonymously with the recording industry, although looking back through history, it was not always so. From the eighteenth century right up until the 1920s, when shellac recordings began to sell in numbers, music publishing was perhaps the dominant form of commercial music,[1] and, of course, troubadours and minstrels had been plying their trade as live performers for quite some time before that.[2]

The arrival of recording, however, was transformative. The printed score had offered a tangible means for people to enjoy their favourite music over and over again, but it was the arrival of 'talking machines' in the early part of the twentieth century that really provided listeners at home with an accessible and reproducible means of consuming music.[3] Music performance became commoditized, and its capitalization was driven largely by the engineering technology that supported its reproduction.

When recording companies began to exploit the popular songs and singers of the day, however, they were forced to negotiate with those other areas of the music industry to secure rights from music publishers for the use of their songs and to contract with musicians under the terms and conditions of their union agreements. While it may have started as a branch of engineering, the recording industry was shaped by its relationship with its older siblings: live performance and publishing.

The barriers to entering the industry were high. Manufacturing costs for shellac discs were immense, and the fragility of the discs made it costly to build and maintain distribution networks. This prevented small independent companies and individual artists from entering the marketplace, so a small number of powerful companies, the majors, wielded disproportionate control of the market.[4]

As their power and market dominance grew, economies of scale further tipped the balance in their favour. They could be more efficient in terms of the manufacture, distribution, and promotion of their records, all of which gave them a significant competitive advantage, while the brand recognition that went along with that profile served as a form of tacit quality control in the minds of the record-buying public. All of this limited new entries into the market and further bolstered the power of the majors.

Those on the inside maintained their position in part through the implicit knowledge associated with artist management and record production. It was an arcane knowledge that was difficult to formalize or challenge. As a result, with no standardized professional qualifications, the induction of new personnel into the industry tended to happen on an informal basis, often through patronage, further perpetuating an exclusive community of practice that was difficult for an outsider either to comprehend or to become a part of.

It was the early 1960s before that started to change. That decade saw the rise of youth culture and the mainstream emergence of the teenager.[5] In response, a music press grew up that aimed to satisfy the needs and capture the disposable income of those new teen audiences.[6] Music magazines presented intimate perspectives on the stars behind the music, and the stars, as their exposure grew, sought control over how they were presented and portrayed, something that had previously been the domain of managers and producers.

Artists like The Beatles and Bob Dylan stopped performing material that had been written for them by professional songwriters and began writing their own songs,[7] rejecting established convention in favour of a freer, more improvisatory approach; think of the trajectory of The Beatles as they developed from a skiffle and rock 'n' roll band through the confident experimentation of *Revolver* to the psychedelia of *Sgt. Pepper's Lonely Hearts Club Band* and *Magical Mystery Tour*. Approaching songwriting obliquely, musicians relied on instinct to create, feeling their way spontaneously and expressively rather than subscribing to tried-and-tested formulae. It was the first stage in the democratization of popular music.

While artists were wresting control of the creative process away from the recording industry, the other barriers to entry into the commercial music arena remained high. The different facets of the industry were interdependent, and a recording artist's success was linked to his or her success as a live performer and as a songwriter. Only the industry had the financial clout to launch new artists and give them the exposure they needed to become commercially successful. For artists even to get the stage where they could innovate with their music, they had first to make it past the industry gate-keepers: A & R people, producers, and engineers.

It was the arrival of punk in the late 1970s that dragged music, kicking and screaming, further down the road of democratization. Built around an ideology of self-expression and self-actualization, all legitimized with a healthy dose of authenticity, punk brought with it a DIY ethos and aesthetic that promoted individual freedom, free thought, and rage against authority.[8] This was all infused with an aggressive and confrontational style, most spectacularly expressed by artists spitting and pissing on their fans at gigs and audiences storming the stages and responding in kind.

Punk flattened the distinction between the audience and the performer;[9] its brutally austere and elementary sound showed that there was no barrier to participation. Anyone, regardless of musical ability, could be a part of punk, a sentiment that extended into the very means of production. The records were often ragged and rough-sounding, eschewing the complex and costly technology of professional recording studios in favour of cheaper and more accessible multitrack tape machines.

Established labels, of course, were not interested in marketing and promoting DIY tracks, so DIY labels grew up to promote and distribute the music.[10] Punk labels bypassed mainstream distribution channels completely, instead creating their own informal independent networks. Building these was difficult and costly, but they allowed labels to make their own, autonomous decisions,[11] and in punk, turning a profit, covering costs even, was not as important as authentic self–expression and an independent voice.

Diskmags and Archives

The home computer, soundtrackers, and sampling had a similar democratizing effect on computer music. All it took to become a producer was a computer and some public domain software. Bulletin board systems offered informal distribution networks, and in the late 1980s the first *diskmags*—electronic floppy disk–based fanzines featuring digital art and music, news and stories from the scene, and best and worst lists of everything from music to BBS services—started to appear. They served as distribution channels and popular press combined: services for the community by the community.

By the early 1990s, the World Wide Web was gaining traction with home users,[12] allowing for cheap and easy international distribution of content. What the web offered was virtual real estate; websites could provide an online repository for the music, photos, and information that diskmags offered but were not constrained to just the few artists and tracks that would fit on a single floppy disk. MOD files, by then the de facto standard for chip music, made the transition from musicdisks and diskmags to the web.

Alongside original MOD music tracks grew a demand for the specific sound of classic 1980s video game music in its original form.

'When I … bought my Amiga 500, I missed the old good times I had with my C64', Per Håkan Sundell explains. 'Since then I have tried my very best to make all the old programs work on my new machines. One of my first attempts was to resurrect the old C64 music, the famous SID chip. In 1990 I and Ron Birk released a demo called "*100 most remembered C64 tunes*", which was very popular, and in 1991 we released the very first tool for Amiga called *PlaySID* which later inspired a lot of similar programs on other platforms'.[13]

Both the demo and PlaySID replayed SID music data using a custom software emulator that mimicked portions of the C64's core CPU and, of course, the SID itself. In the process, Sundell and Birk introduced a music file format, PSID, that has since become the standard for distributing music made on the C64.

PSID packages up not just a list of note data and instruments—the actual music— but also a dedicated play routine for the code and a header chunk that describes the file's contents and structure. It is remarkably space-efficient; each track occupies no more than a few kilobytes of memory, a huge saving on the roughly 10 MB per minute for uncompressed CD-quality PCM samples.[14]

The trouble was, extracting the music data from those classic video games was far from a trivial task. Each track was buried deep within the game code and was indistinguishable from it; finding the music data and the player routines to replay them required a good bit of detective work, a task made all the more difficult because of the very different programming styles and sound drivers the original composers used.

For those music fans who were so minded, however, the game code could be loaded into a machine code monitor and scanned for the telltale signs of a music routine. Since one of the things a music driver would do most frequently was to change the volume registers, a sensible place to begin would be to search for the recurring value 8D 18 D4, the hexadecimal form of the 6502 code that would instruct the C64 to change the value of the volume register located at $D418.

With a possible hit identified, the code in memory would then be disassembled and inspected so that the machine instructions could be reverse-engineered and deconstructed into the player and the music data, a process that, while it got easier the more one did it, was never routine.

Collections of community-ripped SID files began to crop up on the Internet very soon after the release of PlaySID, but these were often incomplete or buggy. In sheer frustration, David Greiman, an American scener known as The Shark, set about combining all of these resources into one exhaustive, fully catalogued, and definitive collection, the High Voltage SID Collection (HVSC).

The task was not as straightforward as simply pooling together all of the SID files that were already circulating; often tiny errors in the ripping process would cause tunes to glitch or drift out of sync, rendering many of the existing rips unusable, while others whose music routines and data had been excised carelessly would be truncated or might include code that didn't relate to the music.[15] The HVSC sought to standardize the collection by using only 'clean' rips, those that contained only the player and the music data, thus stripping down the file size to the minimum possible while playing exactly as they did in the original source.

As the HVSC grew, the archive pointed to holes in the collection; many well-known SIDs were missing, leading to a mass community effort to source and rip music from the C64 software archives. It caused the collection to balloon at an amazing rate.[16]

In addition to missing files, the HVSC crew noticed that there were inconsistencies and misattributions, a detail they were determined to address: 'One sure way of solving these mysteries was to contact the original composers. Over time we gradually tracked several of them down and received a tremendous amount of information. As you may have figured out, we are SID archaeologists patiently piecing together SID history with only fragments of information'.[17]

The care and scrupulous attention to detail is a consequence of the level of affection in which the music is held by its fans, coupled with a desire to reach out and share their passion with others. 'A lot of my drive for this', explains Chris Abbott, one of the current HVSC crew, 'is probably coming from trying to prove to people that SID music is music, because my mum certainly never believed it. She used to hear *Monty on the Run* played on the television and go "What is that racket?" "It's not a racket!" I would say, "It's the best thing in the entire world, ever!" I always knew that musically it was something special'.[18]

That desire to accumulate and collect completely is a common feature in most fan communities,[19] and the dedication with which the HVSC crew and the site's contributors have amassed not just a repository of music but a carefully researched cultural archive, complete with composer notes, background detail, and trivia sourced from contemporary sources, is amazing: a staggering example of affirmative community action. The sheer scale of the operation is difficult to comprehend. The most recent release takes the collection to more than 48,000 tracks. To think that all of that effort and the quality of the work stemmed from a community enterprise fuelled by nothing more than goodwill and affection makes it truly remarkable. The HVSC is a ludomusicologist's dream.

Nor was the C64 the only object of such affection. In the mid-1990s, hacker Kevin Horton developed a hardware NES music player, a combination of a field-programmable gate array, which handled the I/O, timers, memory bank-switching, and most of the logic; an EPROM running his custom music player routine; and an NES APU.[20]

Horton's HardNES was a pared-back system, using only the necessary and sufficient components and software to replay music. Just as with the SID, however, NES music files were buried deep inside the code on game cartridges and had to be surgically removed and transplanted to a host file, in this case, a Nintendo Entertainment System Music file, or NSF.

Ripping NES tracks is broadly similar to ripping C64 tracks, although the specific tricks and techniques used to try and identify music data are quite distinct. Just as happened with the Commodore, however, the combination of a standardized file format, a passionate community of fans dedicated to the task of ripping every single Famicom and NES game, and a growing assortment of NSF players and emulators on just about every conceivable platform saw an explosion of online collections of NES music. Akumu's NSF Archive,[21] for example, contains around 1,400 commercial NES soundtracks.

While the original intention of both SID and NSF was to preserve classic video game music, both formats have since become popular with chiptuners. GoatTracker, one of the most popular SID trackers, outputs directly to SID files, as well as to a native C64 ROM format that can be executed on original hardware, while FamiTracker, the ever-popular NES tracker, does likewise for the Nintendo.

Micromusic

Late in 1998, an online hub emerged to serve the growing 8-bit music community. Micromusic.net describes itself as 'an underground sound community [and] a digital lifestyle platform'.[22] It was always about more than just the music. Users were encouraged to be active members of the community, to promote local and regional *microeventz*, and to work as a distributed but close-knit group of creatives.

Emma Davidson, also known as lektrogirl and part of the micromusic board, recalls the communitarian aspect fondly. Years before Facebook, the site served as an online and offline meeting point, providing a social and cultural backdrop for the musical activity that served as the glue that held the community together. Davidson says:

> There is a really strong social scene. When they organize festivals in different cities, you know, people fly over from Germany to come to London for our events, and other people come from America to go to the ones in Germany, you know? … I always find it's a bit like a village fete or something, do you know what I mean? Someone'll want to make a banner, and someone'll want to make posters, and someone'll want to make a birthday cake, and it'll be someone's friend's birthday for real, and so we'll have a party for that.

When we organize an event in London, everybody that performs at the event pays for their own travel, they play for no fee, and everybody kind of pitches in to help, so it's always got that friendly kind of atmosphere. And it's nice reading the reviews on other people's blogs and websites, that have come to the event, and said, 'I went there to the micromusic festival at 93 Feet East, and it was like going to a family Christmas'. It's not like a gig where everyone's trying to be big stars or something.[23]

Gareth Morris adds:

Yeah, it was completely about that. I mean sometimes you used to meet anyway and just hang out and stuff. It was really nice. It had its own problems as well, you know, like keeping everyone on board. Everyone had different ideas about it, but I think that these community projects often come across those things....

It's not quite the same now, but there is still something of a community in the scene. It's just so wide now. I mean there's thousands of chip musicians now. Back then I knew every single chip musician personally, you know? Everyone on the site, everyone I played at parties with, I knew them all personally. I met them and they were friends of mine. And now ... there's chip musicians, hundreds of them that I've never even heard of, in almost every country of the world.[24]

Micromusic.net didn't prescribe, it just advised that users 'suck and see! It doesn't matter how you make it—or what instruments you use—but after tasting a few tracks you will soon work it out'.[25] But neither was micromusic.net completely open. A *microboard*, consisting of a rolling membership of community leaders, approved uploads, providing a sense of quality control and a corresponding sense of achievement if self-uploaded tracks made it into the new release list and into the charts. Even ground-up collectives seem to spontaneously create gatekeepers because of the need to help artists and listeners connect in a vast and varied ocean of possibilities.

Morris recalls:

It was completely musically tolerant. You could do nearly anything.... You could do some quite challenging stuff. I think that the 8-bit scene was broad at the beginning, and I think it's kept that broadness now. If anything, the micromusic website kind of blew the doors open because ... people who weren't part of the demoscene became exposed to the sound and just did whatever they wanted with it. They started putting on their own parties, which wasn't necessarily happening in that way in the demoscene, and this kind of fine element came in and it became something different.[26]

Micromusic distanced itself from the demoscene in other ways, too, most significantly ditching the MOD format in favour of MP3s.

Dragan Espenschied, known in the micromusic community as DRX, and a member of the band Bodenständig 2000, explains:

> The speciality about micromusic.net is that it breaks with some ideas that computer freaks and Internet idealists have or had. The trick is a combination of knowledge and styles from the computer kid culture and pop music culture. Everybody knows computer kids are stylish, but sometimes they stick to traditions which are simply not working anymore, for example MOD files. They rule but most people cannot listen to them. So micromusic is an MP3 label which not only makes it better accessible, but also really asks for a crossover of home computer music with different styles.[27]

That combination of inclusivity, diversity, and accessibility made micromusic.net an attractive prospect for artists. Publishing was as easy as uploading tracks via the 'up-/downloadz' link. Coarse filtering allowed listeners to access only the most recent tracks ('latest micromusic releases') or the most popular ('download_chartz') or the highest-ranked according to the site's 'pointz' system, leading to a 'hall of fame!!' featuring the top 50 ranked tracks on the site.

Of course, when artists' music is distributed for free, the netlabel brings in no royalties, so the system of rewards on micromusic.net was built on status and prestige, which has currency only within the community itself. For the artist, releasing music through a netlabel can be seen as a form of peer validation and recognition. It offers something concrete in terms of exposure and a degree of prestige in seeing one's releases alongside other respected artists from the community. The use of voting is an extension of that, bestowing prestige through informal democracy on those whom the community itself decides are the most deserving of it.

The look and feel of the website contributed to that sense of the homegrown, with a quirky and colourful DIY design that relies on large swathes of primary-coloured text and animated gifs. The website's structure made explicit the many different cultural forms that had by that point grown up around the community: music, clothing, and hardware were all available in the 'microshop', software tools were found in the 'microwarez' section, 'microradio' continuously streamed user-contributed material, and 'microhype' hosted video content.

Micromusic was an important step in the maturation of the chipscene, but as it expanded and took the music into new territory, it struggled to pull along the community as a whole.

'The openness in the community's gone a bit', Gareth Morris says. 'At the beginning it was more about like, "Oh, everyone's a star" or "No one's a star" or "Everyone's equal", and now it feels a bit like the 8-bit scene promotes this silly sort of hero worship thing that I don't really like to see. As the scene's grown, people's egos have been boosted, but in reality, it's still quite a small scene, but it has lost some of the more charming elements'.[28]

Venues and Festivals

The earliest chip gigs grew from online communities like micromusic.net. For those chip musicians who were stepping out on their own to explore a new and uncertain cultural space, they offered an important sense of validation.

Michael Cox says:

When I started doing this, I was completely isolated. I didn't know anyone else who liked this stuff or that I could talk to about it. All my friends were listening to more mainstream music, and I would occasionally lose confidence in the validity of my interest, you know? I felt that it was a little bit ridiculous and more than once I almost went, 'Well, fuck this', and just like ... sold the Game Boy or something.

So I started to put feelers out and this guy contacted me. He wasn't a chip musician, he was a laptop musician who made breakcore, but we hung out, had a few drinks, socialized a bit, and started to organize our own shows. We started to try and find more people who made chip music in the UK and beyond, and things really just took off from there. We gigged, we hung out. Meeting those guys was quite remarkable, because I was able to just talk about these really obscure musicians or bits of software and they knew exactly what I was talking about. That was really cool. It was just a really successful time. Nobody knew what they were seeing. Nobody came down looking for a chip show. There was a sense that we could do anything.[29]

Across the pond in New York, that process of coalescence was focused around the Tank, a creative collective that spans comedy, theatre, music, dance, and storytelling.

'I started the Tank with a group of friends in late 2001, early 2002', says Mike Rosenthal.

We started up as a very small, very sort-of seat-of-your-pants kind of scrappy, nonprofit arts space. Actually, the very first night that we ever had any show at the Tank, our big opening-night party, I had put out just a random open call on Craigslist for electronic musicians to come and play the show, and one of the people that responded was this guy Bit Shifter. He just rocked the Tank. I'd never heard anything like it. Even with all the experimental music that I was familiar with, this was really someone who was taking something that was very nerdy and code-oriented and making something really fun and really energetic out of it.

Our relationship with the chiptune scene has been really awesome over the years, despite billing Bit Shifter that first night as Bitch Shitter because of a misunderstanding, a communication problem. He forgave us for that. So yeah, so every time someone was coming in from out of town or something, he would ask if there was some availability in the Tank and it just became this thing where a lot of chiptune people became familiar with going to the Tank to see shows.[30]

New York was the perfect incubator for chip music; it's a city that is full of venues and has a population that is constantly on the lookout for a new and exciting cultural fix. Electroclash, for example—a mash-up of 1980s new wave, synth-pop, and 1990s rave—really took off there following the Electroclash festival in Washington, New York in 2001,[31] and New York City was home to a vibrant circuit-bending community.[32] There was a sense that the New York chip music scene could tap into that and provide a focal point. That focal point arrived in 2006 with Pulsewave, a monthly event dedicated to the sights and sounds of chip music.

Peter Swimm, the organizer of the event, recalls:

Josh Davis and I, still flush after the success of a massive chip show at The Tank the previous October, discussed how we could capture that same momentum at other chip shows throughout the city. The half-baked suggestion of a monthly residency was lost in the conversation that followed, but, a few days later, I got an e-mail from Mike Rosenthal who was acting on Josh's suggestion.

The first few months of shows were rocky, but exuded great potential. We put on amazing line-ups for crowds, sometimes so few in number that it hardly seemed worth the effort. Over time, however, things began to change. [It was something] that people wanted to be a part of.[33]

Pulsewave showed there was demand, and it triggered a desire to do something bigger.

The New York–based chip music collective and netlabel 8bitpeoples had launched back in 1999, the brainchild of Jeremiah Johnson, known better as Nullsleep. 'The first 8bitpeoples website was hosted on a desktop computer that was sitting in my dorm room when I was a freshman at Columbia University', Johnson says. 'It came out of an idea that my friend Mike Hanlon had for an artist collective. The name was his suggestion as well. It sounded great to me—I'd just started writing music and it was a way for me to get it out there and meet other people doing interesting things'.[34]

Early in 2006, Johnson and Josh Davis—Bit Shifter—embarked on a self-financed world tour.[35] The International Chiptune Resistance tour circumnavigated the planet, and the pair played 20 venues across Europe and Japan. They returned invigorated by what they had seen and heard and were more convinced than ever that the community could support a full-blown music festival. Blip took place over four days at the tail end of November and early December 2006.

In some respects, Blip was just like any other electronic music event; artists stood on stage behind a table of gear as VJs projected blocky light shows onto a segmented screen behind them.[36] Alongside the New York crew—8-bit rockers Anamanaguchi, the classically trained pianist and experimental musician Bubblyfish, and 1-bit composer Tristan Perich—was an eclectic group of international chip musicians, who showed just how broad chip music had become. Coova, from Japan, for example, played a complex and evolving folk-infused set, while Jeroen Tel, the Dutch composer of countless C64 video game classics, laid down fast and heavy electronic dance grooves. The Japanese two-piece KPLECRAFT combined chip sounds with saxophone and percussion, playing an abstract but funky improvised groove—think *Bitches Brew* meets Tangerine Dream— while Bud Melvin combined Game Boy, banjo, and voice to perform quirky country and western–style bitpop.

It was charged and it was fun. In an article for Wired, Joel Johnson described how he 'came away from [the] show with a Luigi-like spring in my step. It was—and I am really not using this word lightly—joyous'.[37]

A second festival followed in New York in 2007, and then Blip went global, visiting Aalborg, Denmark, in 2009, Tokyo in 2010, and Melbourne, Australia, in 2014. Each show had a very different character that reflected the sound of the host city; while Blip NY was multifarious and at times abstract, the European event had a heavier, more consistently Eurodance sound, while Blip Tokyo (see fig. 8.1), a city that was culturally far

FIGURE 8.1 Gareth Morris (gwEm) playing Blip Tokyo in 2010. Photo by Chiptography.

removed from anywhere in North America or Europe, was much more focused on video game sounds.

Gareth Morris says:

> Every musician wants to play in Japan, right? So when Blip Tokyo happened, I asked if I could play, and [Josh and Jeremiah] said, 'Yeah, right. Of course!' Tokyo is a bit more video games centric because video game soundtracks have always been a big thing in Japan. It was a bit weird playing there, because I couldn't interact linguistically, but in many ways, they were just another chip audience; really enthusiastic, really knowledgeable, really up for it. I played a couple of songs in Japanese which they really liked, but then, you make up for the language thing with a bit more energy and enthusiasm, so yeah, it was a good experience.[38]

Hot on the heels of Blip came other community-grown events. Eindbaas,[39] for example, started in Utrecht in 2009, pulling hundreds of fans and musicians from around the globe to the centre of the Netherlands. In the United Kingdom, Superbyte has grown year-on-year to become not just a music event but a global collective, an international platform for networking and the sharing of ideas and skills.

Wi' Jammin'

In many ways, netlabels like 8bitpeoples and micromusic.net function like traditional record labels. Using the Internet as a mechanism for distribution to a committed but specialist audience, they offer cost-option MP3 downloads, CDs, and DVDs alongside no-cost MP3 tracks. In 2004, the German netlabel Jahtari emerged to target an even more specialist group: fans of 8-bit-style dub and reggae.

On the face of it, reggae and chiptune are unlikely bedfellows, but scratch beneath the surface and some remarkable similarities begin to emerge.

Reggae grew from the amalgam of cultural influences that bore down on Jamaican communities in the late nineteenth and early twentieth centuries.[40] Most of the inhabitants of the Caribbean were the descendants of slaves brought originally from Africa by colonialists as labour to work the sugar plantations. Their indigenous music and culture survived through myth and memory, its diversity fusing to create a creole that came to define the sound of *nyabinghi*, a style of drumming whose rhythms went on to provide the foundation of ska, rocksteady, and reggae.[41]

Just as the call-and-response form work songs of the cotton plantations in the southern states of America combined with the folk music of European settlers, the rhythmic vamp of railroad carriages and the diminished wail of their horns to shape the sound of the early blues,[42] *mento*, the early sound of Jamaican folk music, was shaped by the sounds and the music of the islands—European rhythms, quadrilles, and mazurkas—to create a uniquely Jamaican sound.[43]

In the beginning, the music would have been played on improvised instruments, fashioned from whatever materials could be found. Rhumba boxes, for example, improvised idiophones on which players would sit as they beat out rhythms and plucked out basslines on their metal tines, were fashioned from discarded packing crates and scrap metal.[44]

With the electrification of music in the 1950s, however, a sudden demand for imported records arose. Yard dances grew up where locals could hear the latest US records played on mobile—and often improvised—sound systems. Competition, both to import the newest sounds and to have the biggest and loudest sound system, was fierce,[45] creating a DIY culture of rivalry and technical innovation.

With the demand for local music running sky high, some entrepreneurial sound system operators took the next logical step and began to record and produce their own music.[46] Using imported tape machines and vinyl lathes, recording studios sprang up, mainly in Kingston, and over the next decade Jamaica's indigenous music industry took off.

It became the norm to release vinyl singles with a full mix of a song on the A-side and an instrumental 'dub' on the B-side. DJs would use these dubs as backing material, *toasting* over the top,[47] rhythmically rapping or chanting in the style of the classic West African griot. The instrumental dubs provided both the democratizing means for sharing the underlying musical ideas and a platform for reworking and building on them.

As a consequence, reggae has always been in a state of flux, but that has ensured that it has remained current and relevant, and those who embrace it bring to it a very rich set of musical perspectives and take it in some quite unexpected directions.

Jahtari, its very name a mash-up of Rastafari and video game iconography, continues that tradition, creating a new creole, digital laptop reggae, which fuses classic dubstep and reggae with an 8-bit aesthetic.[48] There are no hang-ups about the authenticity of the hardware; the driving force is to keep the sound fresh.

'We always try to do stuff to reggae that hasn't properly been done before', says Jan Gleichmar, also known as disrupt. 'To achieve this it wouldn't make much sense to use the same technology that, for instance, Lee Perry used. He got all out of his gear that's possible, and it's no use to do that very same stuff over again, so we have to look for ways to dub things up in a way that wasn't an option back then'.[49]

With that idea at its core, the underlying technology is almost immaterial, a sentiment Gleichmar expounds quite openly:

A lot of things happened since 2005 music- and technology-wise.... You can produce tracks on your bloody telephone now. Nothing [has] changed with the way we approach Dub and Reggae, [we] always try to throw something new in there, [but no] matter how many great virtual instruments there are around nowadays, the main drawback remains: you can't really lay your hands onto any of them. When exploring something as complex as a synthesizer just with your mouse you are bound to stay on the surface of it. This actually very creative process feels not very different from writing an email or ordering some books online: click, click, click. A *real* synth is another matter; you dig much deeper.

That's when we (re-)discovered using hardware gear again. Machines that are built for one purpose only: to make sounds. You just switch them on and they work flawlessly. In the last [few] years, a lot of amazing Do-It-Yourself projects came about via the net, so anybody who can hold a soldering iron and follow some basic instructions can build their own music machines.

So now we're forcing ourselves to use the computer as little as possible. The idea behind this is to get out of the laptop comfort zone and learn all about making Dub music with new tools, and to make the machines interact in a way a computer can't.... It is about re-learning those skills that ... somehow got lost in the last decade while holding a mouse in our hands. Most likely the result ... will sound a little different and more alive. One thing is for sure: it's a lot more fun. In the end it doesn't matter with what tools music is being made, all that counts is a good idea. But having fun while doing it is the crucial motivator, and that is where the machines come into play.[50]

The Jahtari front end embodies that idea of playful fun; the site uses an 8-bit style interface that leads into a themed storefront offering both free net releases, digital mixtapes, and commercially pressed vinyl.

Why that emphasis on physical product? Set against the collapse of the physical re-cording industry and the distributed digital nature of the musical infrastructure around chiptunes, it might seem incongruous to make the switch back to high-cost physical media, but in contrast to music services like Spotify, which offer only intangible and transient musical experiences, many netlabels and a growing number of physical labels have arrived at the same realization: music consumption has never just been about the music.

Popular music has always signified different things to different groups, and people invest in music in different ways. For some, it is a form of self-regulation. For others, it is a disposable commodity, a soundtrack to life. Yet others build up a relationship with it. For them, music and the cultural artefacts that come with it are bound up with their sense of identity; it is how they present to the world.

In the classic days of vinyl, when consumers bought an album, they were buying, in addition to the music, cultural affiliation. They were buying into the style, attitude, and appearance of musicians and their music, and the physical presence of an album, the imagery, the touch of it, its weight, and the smell of the cardboard sleeve, were all ways of sharing that sense of connectedness with others.

Indeed, it is possible to enjoy popular music entirely on the basis of the look and the feel. Jordan Katende, for example, is just one of a growing rank of vinyl consumers who buy for no other reason than to make a style statement. Katende doesn't even have access to a turntable: 'I literally do it based on how it looks or if I feel like I have a connection with the artist. I'll just go and get it. So if I think it'll look good on my wall then so be it.... It kind of gives me the old-school vibe.... Once I get it I'll go back, look at the cover, look at the songs, look at the featured artist and ... listen to it online'.[51]

Whereas in the past it was enough for a record label just to create and release tracks and find a way of getting them to market, to get people to pay for content in an age where the expectation is that it will be free, the focus has to be on something other than just access. Labels must create and market meaning. There is also value in scarcity. Digital files have neither. A limited vinyl pressing on the other hand can come loaded with both.

Jamie Crook, founder of the all-vinyl video game soundtrack label Data Discs, was drawn to the video game music sound through a love of experimental electronic and electroacoustic music. 'The technological constraints inspired a certain level of ingenuity and creativity that is fascinating, particularly when removed from the context of the games themselves', he says. 'Vinyl has been my preferred format since my early teens ... and I love everything about it. It's not a 'retro' format—it's always been relevant and always will be. I think it's very misleading when people discuss a 'vinyl renaissance', since it has never really gone away'.[52]

Data Disc's first release, the soundtrack to Sega's 1991's beat-'em-up *Streets of Rage*, highlights the care these boutique labels take to add value to their products. Their vinyls are beautiful physical products with high-quality sleeves and original artwork. Many are limited edition pressings, lending them rarity value. They have the look and feel of collectables.

This approach, of building connections with a fan base and selling meaning rather than music, is part of a growing trend. On October 8, 2007, for example, Trent Reznor, the frontman of the industrial rock band Nine-Inch Nails, announced that the band had fulfilled its contractual commitments to Interscope Records and was now free to proceed as a 'totally free agent, free of any recording contract with any label'.[53]

Reznor had grown increasingly disillusioned with the marketing and pricing strategy Interscope had imposed on the Nails.[54] As someone who understood the shift in consumption that peer-to-peer sites like Napster had catalyzed, he looked to see how he could leverage that disruptive technology to get his music directly to fans.

The result was Ghosts I-IV, an improvised instrumental collection that was recorded over a 10-week period in the autumn of 2007. The only rules were that there should be 'no clear agenda, no overthinking, everything driven by impulse. Whatever happens during that time gets released as ... something'.[55]

He uploaded the first nine tracks, Ghosts I, onto BitTorrent under a Creative Commons Attribution Non-Commercial Share Alike licence, knowing that the moment he did so the music would be out there, being shared freely; that was, after all, the point. The album was available to buy digitally on the Nine-Inch Nails website for $5 alongside a $10 two-CD set, a $75 deluxe edition CD set, and a $300 ultradeluxe CD set.

Only 2,500 copies of the ultradeluxe edition were printed. Each was numbered and signed by Reznor, offering a tangible mark of authenticity and a sense of accessibility to the man himself. While limited editions and collectors' editions existed in the pre-Internet age, Reznor used the Internet, the very thing that was undermining physical sales, to start the process of distribution. By putting his music on peer-to-peer, he accepted that most people would listen to it for free, but he knew that those who heard it and liked it would visit his website. Once there, they were presented with the opportunity to support the artist directly and-for only $300-to become a member of an exclusive set of superfans. The ultradeluxe collectors' edition sold out in just 30 hours.[56]

Nevertheless, there is a tension here. Chiptunes emerged from an open culture of sharing, and around it has grown a hierarchy based on esteem. That reputation is very easily dented if those amongst your network of peers begin to see you as a sellout.

Mark Knight says:

> After I brought out [Reawakening], and I put it on pay-as-you-like ... I started getting the stats through on Bandcamp. After about three months or so, and I'm probably interpreting this in my way, which is always that the glass is half empty rather than half full, I had made the realization that 87 percent of people who downloaded my music thought that it was worthless. That's how I interpreted it, which is a pretty bad way to look at it, of course, because it's not worthless. But hey, look at the numbers! Eighty-seven percent of people thought that it was worthless, that it wasn't worth paying for. That's where I have my struggle. But then you put a price on it, and it doesn't sell anything, which is even worse.
>
> The thing is, right, I completely understand it, but it is frustrating, you know, to have people complaining [that you're asking for money] when you release an album for 3 quid. I think that if you've got something that is of value, then you should get something for it.

But with access to technology now so cheap, and with so many artists who are willing and happy to gig just for the experience, musicians like Knight are fighting a strong tide of market forces. Organizers of events often put on sets with the idea that the artists will be happy only with the exposure that they receive from performing. Some organizers go further still and charge performers an up-front fee for the use of the venue and its facilities, an operational model known as pay-to-play. It remains a contentious issue.

Knight continues:

> You know, they're like, 'We'll pay the security guards, and we'll pay the bar staff and we'll pay the sound engineer and the lighting engineer, we just won't pay the people who are going on stage and actually performing'.

But I don't need fucking exposure! I want money, you know? I mean, I've had lessons, I buy equipment, I buy strings and this, that, and the other. CDs cost money to make. I spent nearly £1,000 in software and hardware making my album, and it'd be nice to be able to make some of that back.

I'm probably one of the few [chip artists] who has that kind of philosophy. I don't do pay-to-play, for example. If I'm going to do a gig I don't see why I should be out of pocket. That's another reason why I think that TDK doesn't get many bookings. The chipscene doesn't get a lot of coverage. It doesn't get a lot of people going to see gigs. Superbyte is probably the exception in the UK, but at a lot of them, there might only be 10, 20, 30, 40 people going, in which case there isn't a lot of money to go around. But on the flip side of that, I'm of the philosophy—and this isn't just to do with chip music—that if you can't afford to put on a music festival and pay the artists, then you shouldn't be doing it.[57]

Nevertheless, live events and netlabels brought the chipscene exposure and the capacity for growth. They brought together both a passionate but dispersed community of practice and the systems of distribution and appreciation that helped the 8-bit sound to gain real traction, as well as recognition and validation as a pop-culture phenomenon. This was the point at which loosely aligned chip music activity really became the interconnected chipscene.

9

Fakebit, Fans, and 8-Bit Covers

One hot and sticky day in June 2007, a three-piece jazz combo took to the stage in the Hannah Maclure Centre, a compact performance space at the top of a student union in Dundee, to round off the exhibition of video game art and animation that was due to close the Six Cities Design Festival. Hugh Hancock, an Edinburgh-based virtual filmmaker and cofounder of Strange Company, had introduced the audience to the world of machinima.[1] He had shown a collection of animated films created using hacked graphics engines and cannibalized soundtracks. As the jazz trio climbed behind their instruments—an acoustic Gretsch kit, a Jackson electric guitar, and a Hammond B3 and Leslie 122—only a laptop perched on top of the organ, waiting to livestream classic 8-bit gameplay to a cinema screen behind them, even hinted at the retro gaming theme that had linked together the day's events.

A few moments later, the opening notes of Koji Kondo's Super Mario theme rang out as the band launched into a video game music set, covering the familiar tunes with a bebop edge. Funk, Latin, and acid-ska covers followed, courtesy of the in-game music from Paperboy, Outrun's *Magical Sound Shower*, and of course Tetris Theme A. Fifty-five minutes later, the audience demanded encores and were rewarded with a little more Mario and the mellow tones of Jimmy Smith and Reuben Wilson.

'I loved it', said one audient, as she filed out of the auditorium at the end of the show. 'Where did you get the idea?'

I looked up from behind my Hammond and smiled. 'Mr. Bungle', I replied.

Nintendocore

These days, Mike Patton is best known as the singer of Faith No More, but in the mid-1980s in Eureka, California, he was the frontman of a band he formed with his high-school friends: bassist Trevor Dunn, drummer Danny Heifetz, alto saxophonist Theo Lengyel, tenor saxophonist and clarinettist Clinton McKinnon, and guitarist Trey

Spruance. They took their name, Mr. Bungle, from the obnoxious puppet star of a 1959 children's educational film,[2] and they mixed a thrashy, death metal sound with jazzy funk and ska to create a weird and eclectic collision of sound and style. It was 'the sound of a bunch of insanely talented young men with a lot of ideas and no real strategy of what to do with them',[3] but it worked, and it worked beautifully.

When they played live, Mr. Bungle would turn out unusual and often tongue-in-cheek set lists, everything from Ennio Morricone's *Metti, Una Sera a Cena* to a hardcore electro version of John Williams's *Cantina Band Theme* from *Star Wars*.[4] It was just one small step from movie soundtrack covers to video games, and on December 27, 1989, Patton, a lifelong lover of all things Nintendo, performed a dense rock medley of music from Super Mario, Kid Icarus, and Bases Loaded as an encore at the River Theatre in Guernville, California.[5]

In recontextualizing the music of the NES, Patton was tapping into a rich tradition. Liszt, for example, invested much of his time in transcribing the work of other composers for solo piano, often condensing entire symphonic works, and all of the subtlety of musical dynamism and expression that they contained, into a distilled form that still conveyed the essence of the original.[6] His piano transcription of Saint-Saëns's *Danse Macabre*, for instance, couldn't hope to recreate the tonal variation the original tone poem uses to suggest character and action, but by restricting himself to working within the constraints of the piano as a solo instrument, Liszt forced himself down an avenue of musical invention that arguably introduces elements of expositional narrative detail that are more complex than in the original composition.

In Guernville, Mr. Bungle played a radically altered interpretation that took the original material and recast it in a manner more commonly associated with jazz fusion, using the source material as a framework for interpretation and improvisation, a result, perhaps, of the jazz origins of the band and their producer, John Zorn.

That Mr. Bungle found a receptive audience suggests something more than just musical reinvention, however; it suggests a willingness on the part of the fan base to rediscover the familiar sound of the music they loved through a process of transgressive musical experimentation. The performance was a coming-together of the original source material and an inventive fresh perspective that offered listeners a new insight into the musical detail of Kondo's music outside the context of the game.

Back in Sacramento, California, drummer Spencer Seim had come to a conclusion similar to Patton's. He had seen Nick Rogers and Forrest Harding performing live video game music at a talent show in Nevada City and realized that there was mileage in exploring video game music from the perspective of live performance. The three got together and The Advantage was formed, specifically to play rocked-up covers of music from old NES games,[7] a style that came to be known as Nintendocore.[8] They weren't alone. Minibosses in Arizona evolved from the Jenova Project, a group of dorm-room buddies at the University of Massachusetts at Amherst who would get together after class and play video game covers.[9] Guitarist Aaron Burke and drummer Matt Wood recruited bassist Ben Baraldi to form the Minibosses early in 2000,[10] and they have been playing Nintendo covers ever since, even opening the 2004 tour for the Eagles of Death Metal.[11]

When the band played Shotfest 2, a music event at the Yucca Tap Room in Tempe, Arizona, that had only one rule—everybody drops a shot before each song— local journalist Jonathan McNamara described the experience: 'As the Minibosses came on stage, the crowd immediately began yelling "Ninja Gaiden", "Mega Man" and other video game titles toward the stage. The bosses hit the ground running and played like they had infinite continues. As their chords reverberated down Southern Ave., they seemed to be sending out a message that at least for this shot-filled night, 8-bit music rules'.[12]

It's Not Where You Take Things From, It's Where You Take Them To

The expression of the video game sound in popular music has a history that stretches back almost to the very beginning of video gaming itself.

In 1981, Jerry Buckner and Gary Garcia were living in Atlanta, eking out a living writing radio jingles.[13] As they watched the video game craze unfold around them, they decided to record a musical tribute, *Pac-Man Fever*, and took it to the major labels. When the labels didn't bite, Buckner and Garcia released the song themselves, and it flew.

CBS Records stepped in and offered a contract in return for a full album, and the pair set about immersing themselves in the sounds and sensations of arcade culture and tried to capture it in song.[14] The album and the single were a runaway success, selling over 2 million copies,[15] and accounted for most of CBS's profits that quarter.[16] Sadly, however, having invested so much of their energy in shaking off their Pac-Man Fever, few people were keen to *Do the Donkey Kong* when it was released as a single the following year.

Although Bruckner and Garcia's songs affectionately referenced video games and their soundtracks—most of the album's video game sound effects were recorded directly from the machines in video arcades[17]—they weren't so much covers as novelty songs about games. Yellow Magic Orchestra on the other hand bought into gaming wholesale and built their entire sound around it. The opening track on their debut 1978 album, *Computer Game: Theme from the Circus*, combines the sounds and stings of Exidy's 1977 coin-op to create a textural weave, like musique concrète, from which a steady rhythm and Japanese synth-pop sounds emerge. The band's three members, Ryuichi Sakamoto, Haruomi Hosono, and Yukihiro Takahashi, tapped into the spirit of video games and their hardware to create tightly structured sequenced compositions that removed the unpredictable variances of human performance, just as Kraftwerk, human and machine working as one, had done before them.

Just as Yellow Magic Orchestra drew on the sounds of video gaming for their inspiration, the next generation of game composers would find inspiration in their work. Martin Galway, for example, featured a cover of Yellow Magic Orchestra's Rydeen as the theme for his first commercial title, Ocean's Daley Thompson's Decathlon on the C64, and it was a track he would later revisit for the soundtrack to *Stryker's Run*. While the C64 wasn't the first of the home video game systems to feature musical covers in its soundtracks, the scope and musical capabilities of the SID chip elevated these from pale imitations of the original tracks to computer synth-pop covers that in some cases surpassed the source material on which they were based.

Imagine's port of Konami's button-bashing arcade classic *Hyper Sports*, for example, features a very credible cover of the theme to *Chariots of Fire*. In his review for Zzap!64, Gary Penn noted that 'the loading screen is brilliant with some outstanding music (64 music really is reaching a stunning peak)',[18] and it's hard to disagree. Galway uses almost every technique possible to create a beautifully evocative and texturally dynamic track, beginning with a pitch-swept sawtooth that cross-fades with an enveloped drone to become the repeating pedal bass. Phasing, vibrato, and arpeggiated chords all contribute to a sense of dynamic musical movement before the enveloped noise of the synth percussion comes in, echoing the synth claps of Vangelis's original track. Counter-melodies and arpeggiated flourishes add to the sense of musical progression throughout the full three minutes of the track, forming one of the most accomplished pieces of title music created for the Commodore. Certainly, it's a much more complete version than that of the game's predecessor, *Track and Field*, which used a fairly flat two-channel version of the same track as its loading theme.

Vangelis, like Jean Michel Jarre and Yellow Magic Orchestra, was an influential figure on the Commodore music scene, and his work found its way, both officially and unofficially, into many video game titles. The most interesting—and bizarre—of these is undoubtedly CRL Group's *Blade Runner*.

Released in 1985 on ZX Spectrum, Commodore 64, and Amstrad, the game was supposed to be a movie tie-in,[19] but negotiations to purchase the video game rights broke down when it proved impossible to get agreement from all the rights holders involved in the production.[20] To be able to go ahead with the game, CRL changed their plan and credited it as a video game interpretation of the film score by Vangelis.

While the C64 game featured a quite passable cover of the movie theme, the concept of the game-of-the-soundtrack-to-the-film doesn't quite follow through: this was more of a creative dodge to get around the rights issues than a genuine attempt to be innovative with the gameplay.

In general, music-themed computer games have often proved to be a bad idea; at best an uninspired mishmash of loosely related musical iconography to provide a focus for otherwise unrelated and often quite generic gameplay, and at worst a cynical marketing ploy to shift woeful games to fans. *The Blues Brothers*, for example, is an enjoyable little platform game in the mould of *New Zealand Story*, but aside from passably convincing Jake and Elwood sprites and a soundtrack that murders Henry Mancini's *Peter Gunn*, there's little to connect it to the movie or the music.

But while Blade Runner illustrated how not to make the game-of-the-music-from-the-movie, Denton Designs' *Frankie Goes to Hollywood* showed how, with the right balance of creative interpretation and technical execution, the music-of-the-game-of-the-music could work very well indeed.

Frankie Goes to Hollywood tapped into fan culture, bringing together the social symbolism and the overtly sexual themes that had made the band both notorious and ubiquitous in the summer of 1984. The game begins with an intro screen that features the game's core symbols: sperm, locked together in a yin-yang-like embrace to represent pleasure; a bullet, representing war; a heart for love; and a cross, representing faith. As the game begins, the player is presented with a bland, featureless avatar in the land of the mundane, the objective being to complete tasks and, through experience, develop the different facets of Frankie's personality and help him to become a real person.

Throughout the music is superb, and the composer, Fred Gray, demonstrates how effectively synth-pop could be stripped down to suit the features of the SID's characterful but limited output. The loading screen is accompanied by the band's *Relax*, while the bass riff to *Welcome to the Pleasuredome* drives out insistently throughout the game. Every now and then, Frankie finds himself in a night-time field in the Flower Power minigame. It's oddly calming as one of the most soothing scores ever written for a C64 game takes over, and Frankie finds himself with flowers falling gently from the sky.

The whole experience is unusual, perhaps more of an interactive experience than what most people would call a game, and in that respect similar in concept, although different in execution, to Deus ex Machina. In an article for *Pop Matters*, Kit MacFarlane discusses how the stripped-back riff of Pleasuredome becomes almost transcendent in its execution, contrasting against the free-form gameplay and providing an open platform for experiential exploration.[21] Along with games like *Elite* and Turbo Esprit, Frankie gave a glimpse of the form that would become the sandbox game.

Of course such tie-ins almost demanded chip covers in the soundtrack. Ocean's *Highlander*, for example, features an interesting cover of Queen's *A Kind of Magic*, while the opening music to *Short Circuit* takes *Who's Johnny*, the percussive El DeBarge title song from the movie, and strips it back to a synthetic three-part arpeggiated track, with the bass and accompaniment serving the same function as the drums in the original; by his own admission, synth percussion was never one of Martin Galway's strongest points.

That process of reworking tracks to conform to the constraints of the host hardware was in itself a very creative act that often took the music off in a completely new direction. In 1986, Galway was handed *Miami Vice*, a game that was being developed for Ocean by a third-party team. Originally, he had decided to rework Jan Hammer's *Miami Vice Theme* and *Chase*, but while he was coding the music his SID intervened and forced him to change tack.

'David Collier was sitting in the office with me while I was working on it', Galway recalls,

> but while messing with it while everyone else was at lunch, I came across this cool sound. I added to it and added to it, and when we applied the non-sync'd filter sweep we both flipped out! I decided to abandon the conversion of that tune and simply go with the cool sounds I had stumbled upon. When the guys came back from lunch and listened to it they swore that there was a cassette deck connected somewhere and it wasn't the C64 playing it! Such a sound had not been heard before by any of us out of the C64. So I extended it and turned it into this tripping-out 11-minute piece.[22]

Used carefully, covers could provide a very effective thematic backdrop to a game, leveraging all of the cultural capital brought by the original songs. Datasoft's turn-based strategy war sim *Theatre Europe*, for example, uses a cover of John Lennon's antiwar anthem *Give Peace a Chance* along with a pledge in the instruction manual that the game is dedicated to peace to lend the title a suitably sober atmosphere from the start. As often as not, however, the covers were references to the designers' favourite tracks. *Helikopter JAGD*, for example, released only in Europe under the QuelleSOFT label, features Giorgio Moroder's *Ivory Tower*. Galway had asked Tony Pomfret, the designer and programmer, what music he wanted for the game, to which he had replied very matter-of-factly, 'I want the B-side from the Limahl single *Neverending Story*'.[23]

Given the prominence of Jean Michel Jarre in the mid-1980s, it's perhaps not surprising to find him cropping up again and again in soundtracks on the C64, and as a result he came to shape much of the style of SID music. *Yie-Ar Kung Fu*, for example, features an arrangement of *Magnetic Fields*, while *Magnetic Fields 2* provides Mark Cooksey's soundtrack to *Bomb Jack*. Interestingly, the coin-op version of the game used The Beatles' *Lady Madonna*, but because that track had only been licensed for use in the arcade, not on the home versions of the game, it didn't feature.

The title music to Ocean's *Parallax* also bears more than a passing resemblance to Jarre's *Rendez-vous*. Before starting on this game, Martin Galway had been listening to Jarre almost on rotation, and when he sat down to work on Parallax he found Rendez-vous was unconsciously creeping into the music. He only realized it as he listened to the album again after the game had shipped.[24]

Press Play on Tape

The C64, then, was perhaps different from other gaming platforms. Its SID had the capabilities of a multitimbral digital synth, and it was used as such. Its music was shaped by the sound of European electronic pop and experimental Krautrock, and it was more musically complete than the rawer, lo-fi sound of the Nintendo. In time, that sound would come full circle, and musicians, rather than referencing popular music tracks to encode on the SID, would use the music of the Commodore as a starting point and re-interpret it once more.

Press Play on Tape proudly self-identify as the world's geekiest group, and with good reason. The band formed in 1999 when six friends, all studying computer science at university in Copenhagen, were drawn together by a nostalgic love of Commodore 64 music. 'Back then', explains Theo Engell-Nielsen, a keyboard player with the band, 'we played games and listened to these songs hundreds of times. It was part of our child-hood. While our parents heard the melodies as something terrible … blip-blip … we heard them as big bands and rock music'.[25]

'We'd all been toying around with computer music since we were kids', drummer Søren Trautner Madsen continues. 'One day, we just thought: "Hey, shouldn't we just form a band and play these old game tunes? No-one plays these game tunes, and they're awesome". So that's pretty much what we did'.[26]

The band first took to the stage alongside the Danish Eurodance musician Das Saint and the Dutch house artist C-Jay at Party 2000: Back to the Roots, a demo meet that was held at the Messecenteret in Aars, Denmark, at the end of December. The band's set kicked off with Rob Hubbard's Commando and moved through Thing on a Spring, Krakout, and Auf Wiedersehen Monty before finishing with a flourish on Sega's arcade classic *Out Run*, with *Warhawk* as an encore.

'In the beginning', Madsen says, 'we just took the songs and did them strictly as they were, but it's actually more fun, we learned over the years, just to be free to work with the arrangements and make them into songs that work when you perform them. So it's all about making these songs work in a live context. We really wanted to listen to these tunes as rock music, with distorted guitars and bass and real drums'.[27]

This reinterpretation is a common feature of fandom and sits alongside fan fiction and cosplay as markers of the level of affection and ownership fans feel for the source material. As such, it marked an important step in the development of the culture of 8-bit music; it was a move towards its reification, as new live and studio versions of classic in-game tracks offered a concrete point of departure from the definitive and perfectly reproducible originals in code. As Press Play on Tape discovered when they started playing these tracks live, a straight cover of a classic video game track is a difficult thing to pull off, not least because the six players on stage increase hugely the capacity for polyphony and timbre and take the performance away from its original sound. When that sound is so intimately tied up with constraints and limitations, casually stepping beyond them changes the nature and meaning of the music.

This in itself doesn't necessarily impact the ways bands might approach covers, but as I have shown, the constraints of those chips forced composers to look for novel ways to introduce dynamic movement and musical interest. Often that involved harnessing the power of the computer itself: 'Half the point of writing some of the music that I did',

Ben Daglish recalls, 'was that it meant that I could use notes that were never actually meant to be played by human beings. I could do really fast runs, scales, and arpeggios'.[28]

It was more than just extreme scales and arpeggios, however. The way a composer coded vibrato or applied the filter was an important part of a video game music track, mediated through code and realized on the hardware. Any cover that sought to emulate the notes and the sound of the original tracks would necessarily have to be technically mediated and would present real challenges to the liveness of performance.

Press Play on Tape's approach was largely to preserve the intent of the original tracks, staying close to their structure and sound but recasting them to make them work as live performances with all of the spectacle that brings.

'We recreate the music as a regular rock music that we are able to play live', Engell-Nielsen says. 'We sit down and listen to the music and get some thinking going on about how we can interpret the six instruments'.[29]

'Everybody has a different opinion on what to do', Madsen adds. 'I make a first idea of who is going to play what, and then I come up with a suggestion of you play the solo, you play second harmony, and you play whatever, and that turns out pretty well, because through the years we've worked out who will be better at playing all the different parts so it actually works out'.[30]

Back in Time

Press Play on Tape were not the only ones with a fondness and ambition for the C64 sound. Chris Abbott is, by his own admission, about as stubborn an individual as you are likely to meet, but in his case stubbornness is most definitely a virtue because it has made him one of the driving forces in the C64 music scene, perhaps the closest thing it has to an impresario.

'I make things happen', he says. 'I'm not particularly creative, but I know lots of people who are, and by shifting things around from person to person I can make things happen. All the way through, there have been people who have said, "Who are you? Why are you doing this?" I just reply, "Well, someone's got to"'.[31]

Abbott is driven, passionate, protective of the music he loves, and very knowledgeable.

He continues:

> I really, really wanted to be a games musician, and although I did a demo disk
> on the Commodore 64 using Ubik's Music, when I sent it off to software houses
> I got the usual set of rejection letters. But I just loved the SID and its music. You
> have all this musical quality to the chip, and it comes out in the music; all these
> composers have had a life outside of the chip, which means that there were lots
> and lots of different musical influences coming in, and that was all put into those
> wonderful tunes, and the people who were inspired by those tunes were *only*
> inspired by those tunes.

In many ways, the SID has always been an underground to the underground, really. It's not chip music as many people would understand it because it can do so much more than square waves. But with that, you've got a scene that becomes progressively less and less varied until you end up with just a one standard sound, and that's a shame. It's just as true on the SID; people reusing the same driver so that everything sounds like Maniacs of Noise. It's a bit like having a great cake and people fetishizing the icing.

But that was where the *Back in Time* album came from. It was a project borne out of necessity. Part of it was trying to prove to the world that this was music that was worthy of the name, part of it was injecting a bit of variety, partly it was historical preservation because we didn't know that emulation would become so good, and part of it was because there were people who were talking about releasing the ultimate album of C64 music, but then, of course, nothing ever happening with it.

So I just started sequencing. I was using [the software tool] SID2MIDI to get the notes right, and, of course, there were some things, like vibrato, that you could *only* really capture with SID2MIDI, those coded elements that convey the spirit of the original composer. I was working on a couple of Yamaha modules, an MU80 and a VL70m, and I was using some sound fonts on [a Creative Labs] AWE32. I didn't have the disk space to multitrack with WAVs, so everything was sequenced live and recorded directly to DAT'.

Abbott's first *Back in Time* album was released in 1997 and marketed through his own netlabel, c64audio.com.

'That was created for the Back in Time album', he explains. 'Before that, I was releasing my MIDI-remixes on the Internet. Back then I was doing web design at City University in London, and I had the wonderfully catchy URL of www.city.ac.uk/killthexa325, [which no longer exists] so I needed my own domain'.

Back in Time sold well enough to spawn a second album, *Back in Time 2*, in 1999, and that provided an excuse for Abbott to expand his recording setup. He augmented his Yamaha sound modules with a Roland JV2080, a Korg Z1, and a Novation Supernova, all of which, of course, were orders of magnitude more powerful than the SID itself. With a bit of programming knowhow and a custom database script, Abbott could extract control data from original SID files and use it to drive the Supernova in real time to create a fairly convincing emulation of the original.

As Back in Time and Abbott's label began to gain a little momentum, he found himself, almost by accident, becoming the default A & R person for the Commodore scene.

'People started coming to me with stuff, and my approach, generally, was to say, "Yeah! Why not?" That's pretty much been the theme throughout my entire career. I'm a Why Not? guy', laughs Abbott.

I find that takes you to some interesting places, albeit with some financial consequences. But I think if this—if the whole scene—was done by the numbers, then it would never work. I mean, there have been some albums I've released because they came in and no one else was going to publish them; so even if I didn't particularly like them myself I thought well, somebody probably will, so I'll put them out. Of course, they never did that well financially, but, you know, I'll never know how much of that was just the general trend of sales decreasing in the music industry as a whole, and how much was because of the album. It's very difficult to unpick those two things.

BITLive

Abbott then made the bold move away from publishing remixes and recorded covers to a live event, Back in Time Live (see fig. 9.1), and pulled together what can only be described as a chiptune supergroup, the SID80s.

'Chris decided that he was going to organize a live gig', Ben Daglish recalls.

The first one that we did was down in Brighton. He spoke to Andreas [Wallström], who runs c64.com, and they pulled all of us together. I can't even remember who was in the first incarnation. That was the marvellous thing about the SID80s: every single time we played for the first 10 years or something,

FIGURE 9.1 Rob Hubbard and Ben Daglish play Back in Time Live, Brighton, 2003. Photo by Peter Sanden.

every single gig we did was a different bunch of people. The same rough crowd, of course, Marcel [Donné] came in and did a couple of gigs, there was this guy Pascal [Roggen] who came in and did fiddle before Mark [Knight] did it, and Reyn [Ouwehand]. It's stabilised now around me, Jon [Hare], Jeremy [Longley], Mark, and Andreas, but it's a lovely thing. It's a lovely thing because we never know, until we actually turn up and do it, we're never sure who's going to be playing, or even what instruments we'll be using.[32]

'It has its challenges', adds Mark Knight, who plays fiddle for the band.

When we did BITLive in Brighton in 2015, that was going to be my last gig, because I was just so pissed off with it all. We're so spread out around Europe that we can't rehearse, and it's really difficult to work on arrangements. The band's been going for more than 12 years, and the set is still basically the same as it was when we started, although, as it was pointed out to me, we've only done about six gigs in that time, so I'm not sure that it really matters! So I went down to Brighton, and I hadn't really practiced. I was so not into it. I was half hoping that the Kickstarter didn't fund the event because I just couldn't be arsed. Of course, it was awesome, really good fun. The band were the tightest they've ever been, the arrangements were good, everybody got on with each other, and everybody worked together. You just can't beat that buzz.[33]

'That's right', laughs Ben.

We did a [gig in] Blackpool a few years ago [R3PLAY 2010]. It was really funny. I did bass, because we didn't have anybody to play, and so I turned up and played, and I would have been fine if we hadn't decided to have a rehearsal in the afternoon. This was the first gig where I'd ever had to play bass, and so by the end of the rehearsal I was beginning to get a little bit tingly on the fingers, but I thought I'd be all right for the gig, you know? But then, I started playing the first number at the gig, and by the end of it I had a blister on my finger. So then I started switching and doing a bit of slappy stuff, and about two numbers later I started getting a bit of a blister on my thumb. I kid you not, by the end of the gig I had ended up playing bass with my little finger. I don't know if you've ever played bass with your little finger, but it's the hardest thing in the world! But if we hadn't had a rehearsal throughout the day I would have been absolutely fine! Performing is great. It's rehearsing that buggers you up.[34]

The band's sets are lavish, professional, and well-staged, although not without their problems.

'It's an event that's succeeded despite itself', says Abbott.

> At the last one, I mean, the bands didn't have enough food, the people on stage kept getting electrocuted by the mic, the sound guys were terrible, and we had to stop the event two tracks early because of a curfew at the venue. I had folks in the VIP seats, people who had pledged over £100 a ticket to be there, who couldn't hear anything. Luckily, instead of complaining and demanding their money back, they came down and had a beer at the back of the venue. They were awfully forgiving. But that's the spirit of Back in Time Live.[35]

'It's geeky', Daglish continues. 'incredibly geeky. I quite often tease them. I say, "So are you all here while your girlfriends go shopping? Girlfriends? What girlfriends!" I tease them all the time, but I'm allowed to because I'm alpha geek, you see? Yes, they're geeks, but lovely, all of them. Absolutely lovely'.

And that combination of affection and geekery translates into a very particular type of audience. 'They all know every single note', Daglish adds.

'They know what you're going to do before you do it. Part of the joy in performing is trying to surprise them a little bit, but it's a very interesting experience playing to that sort of superknowledgeable audience who are watching every single thing you're doing. At times, I'm hyperaware of that, but it's also nice, because the affection from the crowd means that they'll let me get away with the occasional fluff because of who I am. We wrote the sound-track to people's childhood, as it were. So there's always going to be that sort of affection'.[36]

Abbott's audiences travel from across Europe and the United States to attend. They are made up largely of thirty- and forty-something males whose children have grown up and who can afford to pick up with their musical icons from where they left off. It's a demographic that has shaped the nature and location of the festival itself.

'I've always tried to hold Back in Times in attractive places', Abbott explains,

> so that guys can pitch it to their wives that they can do some proper shopping the next day, hence Brighton and London. The Manchester events never really worked on that level. It was like, 'Yeah! Let's go to Failsworth—oh, boy!—or Chatterton. I mean they're nice enough places, but it's not what people want. In London, when we were in Soho there was a great buzz around the event, people were looking forward just to being in Soho. Same kind of thing in Brighton, you know? So, there was always an element of trying to make it easy for people to come along and to bring their significant other, and so hopefully they would enjoy some music, too. And they were often surprised.[37]

Part of that surprise comes from the spectacle of the event. Back in Time, avoiding the clichéd performer-on-stage-with-box format, builds the show around original composers and bands playing live covers. The tunes are familiar, but the format and the sound are not.

Video Covers

While live events and netlabels provide a platform for 8-bit covers, the reach of live events is limited. Audiences are, comparatively, very small—it's not unheard of for performers to outnumber audents at some venues—and while this gives the scene a very close-knit, perhaps almost familial feel, it is ultimately self-limiting. 'You don't just go to a chip concert to see something', Abbott explains, 'the 'something' is really an excuse for you to go and have a few drinks and chat with a bunch of people you already know'.[38]

User-generated content platforms, like SoundCloud and YouTube, on the other hand divorce the music from its social context but lay it before a potential audience of millions; they are new and powerful platforms that afford new ways of creating, distributing, and consuming music.

YouTube first appeared as a registered domain name on February 14, 2005, but it wasn't until April 23 that the first video content, a 19-second video titled *Me at the Zoo*, was uploaded by one of the site's cofounders, Jawed Karim.[39] It grew, both in scale and popularity, phenomenally quickly; by mid-2006, 100 million clips were being viewed and 65,000 new ones added daily.[40] At the time of writing, YouTube is the second most visited site after Google.

Just as the phonograph changed the way music was created and consumed, YouTube has changed the relationship between music, musician, and audience: 'Teens evidently don't see computers as technology. It's as if they have developed an innate ability for text-messaging, iPodding, gaming and multitasking on multiple platforms. They can share their life story on Facebook, entertain each other on YouTube, muse philosophically in the blogosphere, contribute to knowledge on Wikipedia, create cutting-edge art on Flickr, and compile archives on Del.icio.us'.[41]

YouTube offers an open, postproduction performance space, allowing users to refine and develop both their work and their skills and get feedback directly from their audience. Video tutorials break down, step by step, how to sequence or perform all sorts of music. They can be viewed exhaustively, allowing users to engage in all sorts of informal learning and over time copying, embellishing, arranging, and ultimately improvising and composing with the music they find there.

Users create and post new videos, cover versions, and fan tributes delivered directly to camera. Like other revolutions in technology, YouTube is a democratizing force that has connected small pockets of geographically dispersed groups who share niche interests and created mutually supportive communities of practitioners and consumers.

In that sense, YouTube is much more than a media-sharing site; it is a social network that happens to use media sharing as its focal point. From a musical perspective, its size counts both for and against it. Now that all people can practice at home and produce and release their own fan media, lots of people do, and as a result YouTube is awash with music, some of it ground-breaking, much of it mediocre, and some of it truly awful. There are reimagined video game themes featuring impossibly fast electronic note runs picked out with remarkable precision on guitar fretboards; 8-bit style covers of classic rock and pop tunes—full albums of chip-style Iron Maiden and Megadeth, for example—that have a charm about them that is a world apart from the heavy, studio-produced sound of the originals; and countless tracks that somehow squeeze the richness of Pachelbel, Beethoven, and Rachmaninoff into just a few channels of geometric sound.

One track more than any other, however, has fuelled this explosion of musical fan fiction. Tetris holds the honour of being the bestselling video game across all platforms,[42] and its music must surely be one of the most covered. In the 25 years since Game Boy Tetris exercised the planet's thumbs, Tetris Theme A, 'Korobeiniki', has been performed by countless artists in almost every style imaginable. Alongside the inevitable dance remixes sit some very interesting alternative takes on the track. American power metal band Powerglove, for example, combine 'Korobeiniki' with Tetris Theme B and a tarantella, linking the different thematic ideas with ease and creating a driving and uplifting take on the music. Californian band Ozma also brought together a range of stylistic influences on their version, which features on their album *The Doubble Donkey Disc*, a double EP that fuses traditional balalaika and flute with driving rock guitars to create a sound that the band describe as 'Russian Coldfusion'.[43] Returning the music to its folk roots, the Blue Collars, an indie ska band from Tulsa, Oklahoma, released a raucous version on their 2001 album *It's Casual*, complete with improvised solos. Sonya Belousova released a very accomplished Lisztian arrangement for solo piano on her album *Player Piano*.

One of the quirkiest arrangements—yet the one that perhaps retains most fully the spirit and characteristic sound of the original Game Boy soundtrack—was released on YouTube in 2013 by Smooth McGroove,[44] the professional soubriquet of American musician Max Gleason. Gleason's musical career began when he was 11 years old and began playing the drums. In college, he began recording some MIDI tracks and posting them on MySpace, before he and some friends started a rock band.[45] In addition to being the drummer, Gleason found himself doing the audio mixing and production. When the band fell apart, he decided he would turn those production skills on himself and began rapping about video games and their music.

Since then, Gleason has recorded music from many popular video game series, including *The Legend of Zelda*, Super Mario, *Sonic the Hedgehog, Final Fantasy, Mega Man*, and *Street Fighter*. His videos garnered millions of views, and he eventually left his job giving private music lessons to focus fully on his videos.[46] What shines through is the quality of his productions and the playfulness of his arrangements. They are true to the sound of the originals; he vocalizes the music, multitracking and producing each layer of sound and tweaking it to get the tone and pitch just right.

His videos have been so successful, at least in part, because they are so wonderfully engaging. He has a warm and friendly on-screen persona and brings a performativity to his recordings that has been shaped by years of playing live. There are cheeky little glances to the camera that bring to mind Oliver Hardy's exasperated appeals to the audience, lending Gleason's videos a humour and personality that enables people to connect both to the music and the musician.

In an environment where everyone is both artist and consumer, Gleason has managed to find an individual voice, a very personal way of channelling the affection he feels for those video game sounds. It's not just the production quality of his music, although this is excellent, or the idea that he has a gimmick that gives his tracks a standout factor that others do not; it's that he has successfully managed to find a way to use the visuals to really add value. He understands the social dynamic and the importance of making a direct and personal connection to the audience.

He is not alone. YouTube is weighted towards the extraordinary, and in their efforts to gain traction, YouTube musicians have come up with ever more inventive ways to distinguish themselves as islands of excellence in a vast sea of mediocrity. Martin Leung, the Video Game Pianist, gained a worldwide following when, as a high school senior at University High School in Irvine, California, a video of him playing the Super Mario theme blindfolded on YouTube went viral.[47] He played to an enthusiastic crowd of 11,000 at the Video Games Live concert at the Hollywood Bowl in 2005,[48] bringing the same passion and emotional intensity to Kondo that he would to Beethoven or Chopin.

As a student at the Cleveland Institute of Music, Leung convinced his tutor, Paul Schenly, of the potential of video game music, showing the very best of it for what it is: catchy and memorable music, arranged simply and played electronically. Rearranging it and performing it live just encourages people to reframe it and experience it on its own terms. 'We did an outreach program for disadvantaged kids', Schenly says, 'and I asked him to play a couple of little selections from video games, and you should've seen how their eyes lit up, which, in a way, is what used to happen when Liszt was performing or Beethoven or Mozart. They would take the most popular tunes from the opera and compose variations on those themes. Martin is just using what people relate to'.[49]

Leung has made it a mission to popularize video game music, using it to bridge the gap between popular and classical music, and who can blame him? After all, Tetris and Super Mario perhaps mean more to most than Stravinsky.

Fakebit

While a new generation of musicians have rediscovered the music of early video games divorced from their consoles and computers, another group has been doing exactly the same with their sound. Rather than explore chip sounds through the original hardware, some musicians began using modern music production environments, synthesizers, and software plug-ins to create music with the same quality of sound but arriving at it from a very different direction.

That step is a natural one to take. The qualities of the 8-bit sound, those simple waveforms and densely packed arrangements, are easy to replicate on modern synths and sequencers. After all, PSGs were themselves little more than basic synthesizers, and music drivers and their associated data were software sequencers, albeit sequencers with an arcane set of controls and user interface.

'At the moment', says Mark Knight,

> I don't really have a hardware chiptune setup because it's all been put away in a cupboard so that I can concentrate on actually making music.
>
> When I first started, I thought, 'Okay, let's do it all properly in a tracker'. So I got a couple of 64s and the MSSIAH Cartridges, and a SidStation, but I don't have time for all of that, not when I have Cubase, and QuadraSID and Chipsounds and whatever. Besides, I hated using the SidStation, because programming it was a nightmare; if you've got this little LED screen and miles and miles of menus, I really can't be bothered.
>
> Basically, I think I'm lazy. Cubase is up there and it works, you know? The way that I work now is completely in-the-box, and to do anything else is a complete pain in the arse. For me to do something on the Amiga or the Atari, well, like I said, they're in a cupboard somewhere. Once they're set out, then I may well become more authentic, but to do that, it needs to be much more straightforward to use; a case of switching it on, and having it up and running. I mean the monitor for the Amiga is behind a door at the moment, because I've got nowhere else to put it. So that's it for me; I don't like things that end up being a hassle, because then it's just not fun.[50]

Fakebit, chip-style music that captures the sound of 8-bit but in whose production the original hardware is ditched in favour of DAWs driving emulators, samplers, software plug-ins, and hardware synths arouses strong emotions on the chipscene. There are those, like Knight, who see it as a perfectly legitimate way of producing music, fusing old and new technologies to free up the composer to focus on the music. Others feel that it is impossible to conceptualize chip music without the hardware.

That tension is due in part to the different perspectives that different generations of chip musicians bring to chip music and its performance. Those who come from the demoscene are perhaps the most purist, in terms of both ideology and approach to music making, particularly the efficiency of the code. Demos, Menotti Gonring states, 'are appraised not only by their plastic beauty, but also by their algorithmic elegance—which can be evaluated by their size in bytes'.[51]

There is a sense, then, that artists who make music on original hardware are 'better' simply because writing music that way is perceived as being more difficult. It requires a level of technical knowledge about the hardware's unique sounds and quirks and the programming languages that can unlock these.

Dan Ariely, James B. Duke Professor of Behavioral Economics at the Fuqua School of Business at Duke University in Durham, North Carolina, has made a career of studying the relationship between effort and perceived value.

'One day, I locked myself out of my house and somebody comes and opens the door, and takes, maybe, a minute and a half, and then he charges me $120', he says,

and as a consequence, we have a discussion about his pricing model, and he tells me this really interesting story. He said that when he was a beginning locksmith, he was just not that good at it; it would take him a really long time to open a door, he would often break the lock, and he would charge people the $120 for his service plus the $25 to the replace the lock, and he said people were really happy and they would give him a tip. Now, he says, it only takes him two minutes, nobody gives him a tip, and everybody argues about the price.

Now, if you think about these two worlds, one in which you wait outside in the heat for 25 minutes for somebody to unlock your door, and one in which you wait two minutes, which one should you be willing to pay more for? Of course, the one that you wait two minutes, but what happens is that we pay, often, not for what we get but for the effort that has gone into that. And if you think about it, we actually are paying for incompetence, but we have a hard time evaluating what we get. So what do we do? We evaluate the effort that goes into it. So effort is a heuristic that we use to evaluate how much something is worth.[52]

Alongside effort, the idea of doing it yourself, a key feature of the demoscene, is still highly prized. 'Generally, it was 'better' to do everything yourself, from scratch. Even if some people used parts of other demoscene works, they ran the risk of being called lame instead of elite. The romantic notion of the isolated author-genius was thus highly present in the demoscene'.[53] There is a sense that *fakebit* dilutes that originality, with artists recycling ideas, using manufactured soundsets in commercially produced software. In some respects, it represents a mainstreaming of the chip ideal, a watering-down of the core identity of the sound to make it more accessible to a wider, less well-informed audience.

'There was this whole scene in London a few years back, the Babycakes scene, all weird, infantilized kids, and the music was very much this saccharine, poppy, dancey chip stuff', Michael Cox says.

It's just this surface-level notion of what chip music is. So when you come across what would be referred to as a typical 'My First LSDJ Track' cropping up from some kid who's just joined chipmusic.org, that's how it will sound, because he's got a surface-level understanding of what the scene is, and he's very excited about the fact that he's managed to string together 45 seconds of track in LSDJ and upload it. I understand that maybe sounds elitist, but I remember my own first steps in getting involved with chip music. I took my time and did my research first before I actually posted anything. I kind of had some sort of level of respect for it, and I was there long term; I remain here, like, a decade on. These guys will crop up and ask ridiculous questions and they'll be gone in a month.[54]

The ease and the speed with which fakebit allows noobs to create convincing-sounding chiptunes has seen an explosion in the number of chip-style MP3s, and platforms like YouTube have laid them bare for all to hear. Many of the negative reactions to fakebit are reactions against what artists and fans see as the dilution of quality through that churn factor: 'I'm so very tired of artists that simply do NES/C64/what-have-you covers and ride off the novelty', says beverage, a user of the reddit chiptunes forum, 'instead of use the exciting medium for something unique'.[55]

For others, however, the reaction is about the means of production, something that is intricately bound up with what chiptune is; the method and the instrumentation shapes the way they conceive of, realize, and consume the music. Ordinarily it would be absurd to conceive of a whole class of musical expression in terms of its technical restrictions, but for a form of music that is so intimately bound up with technology, there is some weight to the view that the way that sound is mediated is everything.

Out of the Living Room, into the Studio

One of the key drivers of fakebit has been the explosion of virtual instruments and software plug-ins that very accurately capture not only the raw sounds of the PSGs but also their interactions and their idiosyncratic quirks.

Plogue Software's *Chipsounds*,[56] for example, is a software synth plug-in that emulates the sound of 15 vintage 8-bit era sound chips, including the NES's 2A03, the Yamaha AY-3-8912 from the ZX Spectrum 128 and Atari ST, the SID and Atari's TIA, as well as some more esoteric PSGs, like the SN76489, which provided service in the ColecoVision and the BBC Micro, and the P8244/P8245 from the Magnavox Odyssey.

What sets Plogue's plug-ins apart from others is the near-obsessive level of detail that has gone into modelling the sound chips, an approach that extends to creating impulse responses of arcade cabinets and CRT televisions and the DACs of vintage consoles, all of which can be applied via a companion plug-in, *Chipcrusher*, to add some of the grit and tonal colour of the original hardware. The process is catalogued in an entertaining and informative technical blog that shows the care and attention to detail lavished by the Plogue team as they created the soundset.[57]

The results are stunning. The sound is, to all intents and purposes, completely indistinguishable from hardware, and Plogue's interface allows users to recreate those Hubbard-style arpeggiated flourishes and wave-sequenced effects.

One of the strengths of the Game Boy as a music-making platform is its portability; LSDJ and Nanoloop turned the pocket console into a pocket synth, a role that tablets and smartphones can now fulfil. SidTracker 64, for example, turns Apple's iPad into a three-channel soundtracker, complete with an accurate emulation of the 8580 SID chip and an arrangement of Rob Hubbard's classic, Commando, that is ripe for remixing. Even Nanoloop, the Game Boy app that kickstarted the live chiptune revolution, has migrated to the iPad, combining Oliver Wittchow's step-sequencer with a synthesizer and sampler but in the process losing some of the tactility of the original interface.

That sense of tactility is just one reason why many musicians still prefer hardware. There is something just as satisfying about feeling the weight of a Game Boy in your hands as you manipulate the D-pad controller as there is tuning the knobs on a Minimoog to dial in a swooping lead patch. It's a niche that has seen the release of a series of boutique synthesizers, designed to allow chip sounds to integrate seamlessly into a full production or live sound rig.

The ATMegatron (fig. 9.2) is just one model in a range of lo-fi chip-inspired hardware synthesizers from Paul Soulsby.[58] The look of the synth, with its wooden end cheeks and a white aluminium top panel, is contemporary, but the sound is unmistakably retro.

Soulsby has had what many sound geeks would consider a dream career. After graduating from the University of York, he spent six months working with BBC Scotland as a broadcast technician in Inverness, followed by a period as a recording

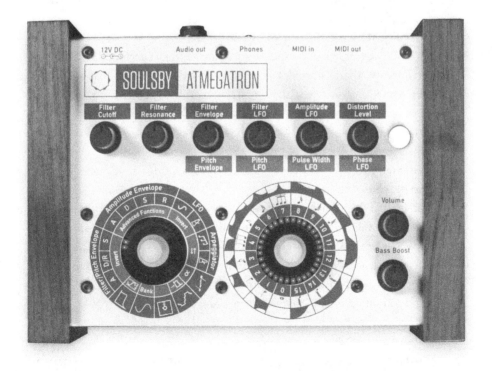

FIGURE 9.2 The Soulsby ATMegatron, a hardware chip synth that brings a lo-fi digital sound to the studio. Image courtesy of Paul Soulsby.

engineer in an independent studio, before he carved out a position as a game show programmer.[59]

'No, it's a thing', he says, as he registers the quizzical expression on my face.

A game show will normally have a computer system behind it. So if you take any game show, you'll see that all the lights and sounds and scores and buzzers and the graphics, they're all synchronized together, and that's because it's one computer driving the entire studio.

About six years back I worked on a game show that involved a computer-controlled conveyor belt with a briefcase on it, and the producers needed to know how to control it. Someone said to me, 'There's this thing called an Arduino, you should use that.' And that was where the idea for the synth started.

I'd been into chiptune for a while at that point, not really making any, but I remember, when I was at the BBC in Inverness, I bought Nanoloop for my Game Boy, and I'd just sit there in every break doing little nanoloops over and over. It used to drive everyone mad!

So I'd been playing about for years with that sort of sound, and when I realized that the Arduino could do it really easily, it just went straight from there really. All of a sudden there was this period of a few days where I suddenly stopped doing any work and just threw myself into developing the synth core, basically an Arduino with a speaker stuck out of it. It was just one of those things where I discovered I could do something cool, and it sounded good. And then, of course, you just keep going and going and going.

Initially, I was allowing the speaker to distort and just sort of filter itself by its physical nature. Then I started reading up on filters and going through different options. I started off with one that I just found off Instructables, it was a passive one, and then I started looking at active designs. I spent a long time with the filter, about six months all in. I was adding features all the time; it's very hard to remember exactly the order, but obviously the wave table oscillator, the filter, the bi-quad filter, envelopes, the arpeggiator, and then, I think it was near the end, I added the phaser and distortion.

I had it all in this prototype box, all off-the-shelf components, and I was like, 'Oh, I suppose I'd better put it in a case,' thinking this would be the simple bit, only to discover that that was going to be a further six months of work. So then it came to manufacture. I made a hundred. This was after two prototypes. Two prototypes, then I made a hundred, and that went on sale in February 2014. So a year and a month it took to manufacture. From nothing.

The Atmegatron's 32 factory waveforms, 15 digital filters, LFO, arpeggiator, and bitcrusher contribute to a deliciously lo-fi sound that bristles with 8-bit attitude, while a dedicated PWM knob and a portamento effect provide a very controllable route to those evocative chip sounds.

Soulsby's move into synthesizer design and manufacture was an extension of his professional life, combining his love of sound production with his passion for code. The boutique approach allows him to have a much more direct and hands-on approach both to design and sales; he secured his first magazine reviews by picking up the phone and calling round editors in the hope of landing a full-page spread.

It's an approach that has brought the chip sound into the recording studio and to a wider audience, and it's been made possible by the arrival of microcontrollers, like the ATMega and the Arduino, rapid prototyping, desktop fabrication, and online independent sales channels. It is part of a growing trend back towards physical computing, that same convivial technology that began with Lee Felsenstein and the members of the Homebrew Computer Club when they first saw the Altair demoed in the 1970s. It's a trend that looks set to revolutionize hardware design and manufacture just as the microcomputer did for software in the 1970s and 1980s.

Together with open-source online code repositories, like the Arduino Playground, the barriers to hardware development have been well and truly broken. It's a definite step towards mainstreaming, bringing together hacking, performance, coding, and music making, generating critical mass and popularity by appealing to distinct though overlapping user groups. Physical computing also legitimizes hardware appropriation by turning ordinary users into hackers. That in itself creates a tension: can subversive hacking really be subversive if everybody is doing it?

'I like the idea of misuse', says Oliver Wittchow.

> With Nintendo, for example, they don't allow any unofficial development; I think it's not illegal, but it's not complying with the rules. So when I developed Nanoloop, the effect was that I was kind of misusing their machine. But if something's meant to be for chiptunes, if it's designed for that, then it doesn't have that subversion. Or, if it's designed for hacking ... That's a very common word nowadays, you know? New devices are advertised as being 'hackable', they are designed to be misused, which is not really possible. You can't provide tools and a means for misuse. That's not misuse! There's a contradiction there, I think. I don't know ... For me it doesn't really work as a concept.[60]

But that in-built hackability has been the very thing that has opened up devices like the ATMegatron to the mainstream. It's designed for lo-fi chip sounds, but at its heart is a microcontroller than can be reprogrammed to give the synth either a slightly different character or a whole new personality. Hackability offers the potential for customization, allowing elements of the chip sound to be incorporated into other styles just as users see fit.

In keeping with the open-source ethos, Soulsby included a programming interface on the back of the device, which enables one of seven different synthesis engines to be uploaded to change the functionality and sound of the synth, and he even provides a synth called the miniATMegatron, a low-cost synth shield kit for the Arduino Uno that is more overtly targeted towards the hobbyist market.

Soulsby's synth is just the latest in a long line of boutique synthesizers that have brought chip sounds to the mainstream of music technology. Elektron's SidStation,[61] for example (fig. 9.3), took that idea and applied it to the SID. It's a fine example of retro-futuristic design, with a smooth brushed aluminium case housing a backlit LED, a set of chunky real-time editing knobs, and a 16-button alphanumeric keypad that looks like it has been lifted straight from Sinclair's old MK-14. The SidStation is every bit the machine that electronic musicians of the 1960s might have imagined we would all be playing in the future.

Although the SidStation is unabashedly a digital machine, its architecture is laid out like that of a classic analogue synth, an approach that bridges the gap between the technical capabilities of the SID chip and its integration into a studio rig. Elektron's master stroke was to build a musician-friendly interface around the SID and complement its core features with MIDI-sync'able arpeggiators, a 32-step wavetable, and additional filters.

The sound is unmistakably SID: its lo-fi digital core tends towards harsh, aggressive, and cutting lead sounds, a feature that has allowed the SidStation to find a home

FIGURE 9.3 Elektron's SidStation, a hardware synth with a genuine SID at its heart.

onstage in some wonderfully diverse crossover acts. Machinae Supremacy, for example, a SIDMetal group from Sweden, use a SidStation alongside screaming metal guitars to create a unique blend of metal and chiptune.[62] Daft Punk, the Prodigy, the YouTube sensation Psy, and Timbaland have all worked the unique, grungy sound of the SID into their music.

The SidStation was limited to a fairly small production run and has become something of a cult classic; secondhand ones regularly crop up for sale at two or three times the original retail price. Interest in the SID sound, however, hasn't diminished, and demand for chiptune hardware that allows musicians to fuse chip sounds with other instruments and other styles of music continues to grow.

The MIDIBox SID is a customisable DIY SID synthesizer project, released in schematic form,[63] that allows for a scalable synth that can be anything from a few simple components soldered together on breadboards to get sound out of the chip to a complete hardware control surface, often built into a modified C64 case, with up to eight SIDs running in parallel. For those who found the complexities of the MIDIBox just a little overwhelming, the SammichSID (fig. 9.4) was released as a 'no excuses' synthesizer kit.[64]

FIGURE 9.4 The SammichSID hardware synthesizer in component form. The system was marketed as a low-cost DIY kit, and it was up to end users to house the components in a suitable case. As a result, as many ended up housed inside stripped-out C64 cases as did in regular project boxes.

Twisted Electron's Therapsid,[65] a spiritual successor to the SIDStation, combines the raw sound and musician-friendly interface of Elektron's synth with much more of a focus on the hands-on control of its parameters. Therapsid is housed inside a wood and metal case similar to that of Soulsby's ATMegatron; the top panel is covered in rotary encoders and buttons, providing an accessible and straightforward way of manipulating and visualizing the SID's registers and providing a very familiar synth-style interface to tweak the tone. Alongside its sibling synth, AY3, which combines two AY3-8912 sound chips in a rugged black anodized aluminium case, and companion apps, which allow direct graphical control over the synth and its 16-step sequencer, Therapsid continues the drive to connect musicians of all flavours with the chip sound.

And that trend isn't just happening at the top end. Teenage Engineering released the first of their Pocket Operators handheld synths at the 2015 NAMM Show in Anaheim, California.[66] Co-founded by an ex-member of the Elektron team, Jesper Kouthoofd, Pocket Operators are all pocket-calculator-sized synths with miniature LCD graphics acting out the sound creation process, like a musical Game & Watch, where the 'game' is to sequence some four-on-the-floor grooves.

The synths are stripped back to the bare bones; devoid even of cases, their exposed PCBs and rubber contact switches are the interface. It's a quirky little design touch, but it suits the approach and the quality of the sound perfectly, particularly the PO-20 Arcade synthesizer, which is tuned for chip music. It's a device that's designed specifically to present you with creative limitations and in the process tease out new ideas.

Chips with Everything

'Everybody's hitting on the 8-bit aesthetic', says Gareth Morris, as we sit in a noisy bar in the shadow of St. Paul's Cathedral in London.

> It's a really good thing, because it means the scene is expanding. People talk about this kind of crossover ... I randomly heard this metal band called Five Finger Death Punch on YouTube recently. Even they had some 8-bit stuff going on. Iron Maiden have done an 8-bit music video. Kylie's done an 8-bit song. You hear it everywhere. Anamanaguchi have done very well, they're playing big venues in America. If you go to Bandcamp, some of the top artists on there, a lot of them are chiptunes. Chipzel's done really well there for example. You know, maybe it's ... maybe it is becoming mainstream.[1]

It's hard to deny. That chip sound has cropped up in mainstream contemporary music more and more over the last few years. La Roux's *Bulletproof* from 2009 and 2010's *Famalam* by Jme both drop chip sounds into contemporary mainstream tracks, while Grandaddy's *A.M. 180*, an indie rock track from way back in 1997, begins with a chip-style blip synth intro. Beck's *Girl* begins with a syncopated chiptune intro whose melody is picked up by the vocals and acoustic guitar as the song develops, while Kesha fuses chiptune hooks and video game sound effects to create a video game beat in the intro to *TiK ToK*.

That *bitpop* sound, one that fuses the lo-fi electronic sound of chiptune with electric guitars and vocals, is distinct from what might be described as pure chiptune and different again from fakebit. It's a fusion that blends elements of the sound of 8-bit with that of contemporary pop, and it hints at the mainstreaming of the sound.

Anamanaguchi, an American four-piece group, draw on chiptune as a component of their sound, but it is part of a very rich palette that ranges from classic rock like Weezer and the Beach Boys to J-Pop acts like Perfume via TV sitcom themes.

'You have the Bee Gees and The Ramones', says guitarist Peter Berkman,

and you have these lush production techniques with crazy strings and stuff
and then you have that phased down to the base level of just a distorted guitar.
There's nothing dirtier than that. What we're doing is literally taking the simplest
electronic waves and trying to make them sound good. How do you make a
distorted guitar sound good? You make it simple.

There are a million different ways to use [that 8-bit technology]. You can make
pop music with it. You can make rock music with it. You can make hip-hop with
it, and people do. And that's why it's interesting. There's so much variety in such
a limited palette. When you're using something like a Game Boy or Nintendo,
you're using a very, very limited sound set, and the sheer variety that comes out
of a bunch of different artists has always impressed me. Which is why I want
to associate with the kind of other people that do this kind of thing, but also
realizing that we play a different style of music than a lot of them. So we can kind
of branch out and play rock party music'.[2]

Anamanaguchi's rock party sound was the perfect soundtrack to *Scott Pilgrim vs.
the World: The Game*.[3] 'The music alone is worth the price', notes Hilary Goldstein in a
review for IGN. 'Seriously, this has got to be one of the best game soundtracks I've ever
heard. It fits so perfectly, but stands strong on its own. You'll love it. And if you don't,
frankly, you don't deserve this game'.[4]

What is striking about the entire Scott Pilgrim franchise is the care and the attention to detail that all of those involved lavish on translating the comic book to the big
and the interactive screens. The video game references and iconography become a core
part of the movie, while the game is an enjoyable play in its own right. The affection that
is shared by the production team for Pilgrim's universe shines through.

Music is central to the Pilgrim story. In the original graphic novel, he plays bass
and wails backing vocals in a garage punk trio, Sex Bob-Omb, a feature that draws on
the experience of his creator—Brian Lee O'Malley's—past as an indie rock musician in
Toronto.[5] 'Music was always going to play a huge part in making the movie', says Edgar
Wright, who directed the film. 'It's about bands and indie rock and young people … so
it was never, ever going to be an afterthought'.[6]

Wright looked to the indie rock scene to give voice to the fictional bands in the
movie: Beck for Sex Bob-Omb, Broken Social Scene for Crash and the Boys, and Metric
for The Clash at Demonhead. 'There was talk of Sex Bob-Omb being Black Lips, or
Times New Viking', Wright says, 'but we sent the books to Beck and he understood
what we were going for'.[7]

It was an inspired move. The sound of the album has an authentic underground
indie feel that will be instantly recognizable to anyone who has ever stood at a kerbside
outside a club handing out photocopied flyers.

Throughout the movie, there are 8-bit stings and throwbacks. It opens to a stylized chiptune version of Jerry Goldsmith's Universal logo music before the intro sting from *The Legend of Zelda: A Link to the Past* segues to the opening scene in the kitchen. Later, a dream sequence features *Great Fairy Fountain* from the Zelda series as Scott Pilgrim dreams of Ramona Flowers, a track performed by two members of Supergrass that was signed off by Nintendo after Wright wrote to the video game giant describing the music of Zelda as 'nursery rhymes to a generation'.[8] Sound effects from Sonic the Hedgehog, Street Fighter, and The Legend of Zelda all punctuate the action, and Pilgrim picks out a bassline from Final Fantasy IV during his band rehearsal.

The effect is to create a layered set of 8-bit references that work on multiple levels. Like the music of Anamanaguchi, the movie can stand alone, but taking the time to unpick the threads from which it is constructed reveals a complex weave that has been very carefully crafted and that brings together a range of mainstream and niche elements and handles them with genuine affection and understanding.

Video Games in the Museum

Tristan Perich is a New York–based composer and artist who works with low-level electronics. 'I'm from the same generation as chip tune artists', he explains. 'The aesthetic of the sound itself, the buzz and tone is something I find to be really beautiful. Lately I have tried to take it more toward mathematics and the limits of logic rather than chiptunes, but then it's all microchip music so I am part of that world'.[9]

Perich's *1-Bit Music*, a self-described circuit album, houses an electronic music–generating circuit with a headphone jack inside a transparent CD case that plays back 11 preprogrammed 1-bit tracks. 'There's something very different about having the chip synthesize the music live, rather than listening to something that is pre-recorded', he says. 'What's important to me is simplicity, whittling down. I don't really think of it as a limitation … I think of it more as writing for simple voices. As you go down the sampling bit rate, when you get down to one bit, every value is either zero or one. There is no volume control, there is no timbral adjustment, it's a really raw, beautiful electronic tone'.[10]

On February 29, 2008, Perich performed a concert as part of the celebrations for the Whitney Museum of American Art Biennial, combining classical composition and 1-bit electronic music across three movements. The concert kicked off a busy year of events, including a performance at the South by Southwest festival in Texas and a residency at the Issue Project Room in New York.

The work of Perich, and others, suggests a growing acceptance of chip music, alongside 8-bit video game art and animation, as a legitimate form of cultural and artistic expression, an idea that has been validated by two very big-ticket cultural events.

In 2009, the National Museum of Computing hosted a performance of *Obsolete?*, a specially commissioned piece of music by chip musician Matthew Applegate, also known as Pixelh8. The Museum is at Bletchley Park, once home to the Allied code-breaking teams during World War II, and houses an eclectic collection of antique hardware that spans objects from mechanical calculating machines to bedroom micros.

Applegate was commissioned to explore the Museum through sound, using the chip sounds and electromechanical noise of its machines to make music out of hardware that most would consider utterly obsolete.

The commission came on the back of the Museum's reconstruction of the Colossus Mark 2 computer,[11] which was used for code-breaking in World War II. Originally developed by a post office engineer, Colossus was built using components from the standard telephone exchange. The clicking of its relays as they flip-flop between states, the grinding of the uniselectors, and the ethereal ambient hum of its tape relays embody the spirit of a bygone time and place.

'Each computer room has a unique sound', Applegate says.

> There was so much there that could be expressed musically. One morning, as I passed Colossus ... it was making a different sound. It usually has a set rhythm and a set sound, but that day it was running a different algorithm and some of the panels for the relays had been removed, and the sound was very different. I quickly set up my recording equipment and was delighted with the new sounds that I captured. . . . If you listen to it for quite a while, you get quite taken away by it. I've taken all these different sounds and sequenced them to create different rhythms.[12]

Applegate used 10 of the machines from the collection, including an Elliot 803, a Bunsviga adding machine, a BBC Micro, an Atari 800XL, a Dragon 32, and an Amstrad CPC464. The percussion came courtesy of an IBM 029 punchcard machine. 'It's probably the most unlikely drum kit you'll ever hear in a piece of music', Applegate says,

> but it has various kinds of clicks and spinny things. . . . Most of the rhythm in the Obsolete? piece is actually based on the sounds that come out of this machine. . . . It's [been] really nice to drag these [machines] into more mainstream culture, taking these industrial, quite specific machines into music and making them more accessible. It's been a huge learning curve for me, because I come from the home market of computers, and then to come here and learn about all the histories of all these machines, it's been a wonderful experience.[13]

The music certainly captures something of the experience of Bletchley. In its production, Applegate applied no pitch alteration and no effects. The sounds were presented as he had experienced them so as to create a true sonic perspective of the space, putting visitors in touch with the experience of computing in the past; it's easy to forget just how noisy, how physical, computing used to be.

In 2012, the Smithsonian American Art Museum hosted an exhibition charting the evolution of art within the video game medium over its 40-year history.[14] Its curator, Chris Melissinos, founder of PastPixels, an organization dedicated to the long-term preservation of video games, and chief gaming officer for Sun Microsystems, conceived the exhibition to challenge the notion, using the cultural lens of an art museum, of games as just a form entertainment.

'Video games are literally the collision of technology and art', Melissinos says.[15] 'The goal of the exhibition isn't to determine once and for all whether video games are art, but us 'bit-babies'—those of us who were born in the 1970s and first appropriated these technologies into our lives—we've always viewed them as art, as something bigger than ourselves'.[16]

Certainly, the exhibition was popular, attracting nearly 700,000 visitors over its six-month run. Other museums seem to be following suit. The Victoria and Albert Museum in London, for example, appointed Sophia George as its first game-designer-in-residence in 2013,[17] leading to a unique art game, *The Strawberry Thief*, inspired by the William Morris pattern of the same name.

The question, perhaps, is not so much whether video games or their component media can be art as what that discussion means for the form. The very fact that it is being platformed at all suggests that there is a valuable discussion to be had, and that there is a real currency to these issues. The fact that Anamanaguchi and others command an international profile and handle mainstream commissions, while international festivals like Blip and Superbyte have become topics for serious exploration by documentary filmmakers in *Reformat the Planet* and *Europe in 8 Bits*, all point a growing appetite for chips with everything.

The Dark Side of the Mainstream

That may not, however, be where the chipscene wants to go. Dan Majors gives voice to one unnamed blogger in an article in the Pittsburgh Post Gazette: 'Hoping to god this genre never goes mainstream. It's too [expletive] brilliant to get run over by the masses'.[18]

Much of the unique charm of the chipscene comes from it being a fringe activity. It's definitely not 'popular music' in the sense that we would normally use that term. For many on the inside, that is a big part of why they are involved. In colliding with the mainstream, the risk is that chiptune will lose its authentically representative voice, and once that voice exists more in the imagination of audiences than in the practice of musicians, it is lost, and the scene with it.

Nowhere is that more visible, perhaps, than with punk. Once it was 'the dementia of a nihilistic generation'.[19] Now John Lydon, once one of the most outrageous and volatile performers on the planet, is a nod away from being a national treasure and advertises butter,[20] although in truth, this self-referential act of subversion may be the most punk thing he's ever done.

Much of the criticism Lydon faced following his appearance in those adverts came from fans crying 'sellout', reusing the old arguments levelled at indie punk acts and record labels who became commercially successful. Lydon, though, used the proceeds from his appearances to fund his Public Image Limited tour in 2009,[21] recognizing a commercial reality faced by all creatives: we all want to make great work, but the popular stuff often pays much better.

'Am I waiting to sell out?' Mark Knight asked himself contemplatively as we shared a coffee.

> Yeah, of course! We all are. I mean I get why some people on the scene think differently. I totally get it. Most of them are considerably younger than me, they're at uni or college and they just want to go out and party and play, and they've grown up with the economy of free, so they're like, yeah, that's how it is. But you know, eventually, you have to be out and working otherwise you can't afford to live, and that steals time and creativity. If I could, I would totally sell out, then I could afford to take the time to do some really fucking great stuff.[22]

But for a scene founded on the culture of free, the idea of commercializing its music is, for many, anathema, and something the scene is not at all well positioned to respond to.

One of the most melancholic examples of chip music is surely the theme from Ocean's Game Boy port of *RoboCop*.[23] Written by Jonathan Dunn, it's a slow, trance-like synth-pop track, with arpeggiated minor chords riffing over the top of an introspective bass-y melody line. It was an unusual accompaniment to a platform-based shoot-'em-up, but the perfect fit, seemingly, for a washing machine commercial. In 1992, Ariston, a subsidiary of the Italian white goods manufacturer Indesit, advertised their appliances in the United Kingdom with a TV ad that ran that same Game Boy track over a looping backdrop of a young family whose lives revolve around Ariston products dotted around some Escherian architecture as the slogan 'Ariston ... and on ... and on ...' is chanted in a Kraftwerkian drone and scrolled continually across the bottom of the screen. It is a surreal—and wonderful—moment of TV advertising. With Ocean's approval, the soundtrack was recorded directly from the headphone socket of a classic Game Boy and mixed with the chant to provide the finished soundtrack. Jon Dunn didn't receive a penny for his efforts.[24]

That, though, is part of mainstreaming. As that 8-bit sound has grown in popularity, and others have recognized the value and recognition factor that comes with it, there are those who will move in to exploit it.

The spat that arose in response to Zombie Nation's use of Dave Whittaker's score to Lazy Jones is another early example, but even that is not unique. In 2007, the American producer Timothy Z. Mosley, better known as Timbaland, was drawn into a protracted and quite hostile Internet campaign that began on Internet forums and escalated to the law courts. It all started with a YouTube clip,[25] which pointed out similarities between *Acidjazzed Evening*,[26] a track by the Finnish demoscene artist Janne Suni, and *Do It*, a single Mosley had produced for Nelly Furtado.

Suni had originally published his track in Vandalism News, an Australian diskmag that covered C64 and Amiga demos, and from there it had filtered through onto the scene, where Mosley picked it up and reworked it. Although he acknowledged Suni's track as his source material, Mosley reacted strongly to the escalating situation and responded with a full-on attack that served only to inflame the situation.

In a radio interview for WWDC-FM's Elliot in the Morning, host Elliott Segal raised the issue on air, asking Mosley flat out if he had ever ripped anybody else off. 'I haven't ripped nobody else off', he replied, 'but have I sampled? Hell, yeah. I don't have to [steal], I'm too good'.

When pressed by Segal about 'those guys from Finland who say you stole their stuff', Mosley continued:

> that mess is so ridiculous. I can't really talk about it because I'm in legal discussions and whatever, but I'm gonna tell you, [what] the hell wrong with them? That's all I can tell you. It's from a video game, idiot! Freaking jerk.
>
> My whole thing is … sample, and stole are two different things. Stole is like I walked in your house, watch you make that beat, took your Pro Tools and went to my place and gave it to Nells and said, 'Hey, I got this great song'. Is he crazy? I live in America. I don't even stay in Finland. I ain't gonna get into it.
>
> Then sample is like, you heard it somewhere, and you just sample it. But you didn't know, maybe you didn't know who it was by because it don't have the credits listed. So you just use it. Hey, I don't know, I like it, but I'm gonna use it. Maybe somebody, you know, might well put a sample claim in, or, I don't know. You know what I'm saying, but … I don't have no researchin'—time is coming up when I got to turn a record in. So, that's what sampling is. That's not stealing, 'cause everybody samples from everybody every day.[27]

On June 11, 2009, Kernel Records Oy, which had acquired the rights to Suni's track in 2007, filed a lawsuit in the Miami-Dade Division of the United States District Court for the Southern District of Florida claiming that Mosley and Furtado had used the 'original and central identifying melodic, harmonic and rhythmic components' of the track.[28] Kernel Records, however, had not registered its copyright prior to bringing suit in the United States, and Mosley pressed for summary judgment, arguing that by making the track available for download from an Internet site, the work was simultaneously published in every country and so was subject to the US registration requirement. In 2011, the District Court agreed, and granted the motion. Kernel appealed.

The appeal hearing rejected the District Court's analysis and basis for the summary judgment, stating:

The district court ... confounded 'the Internet' and 'online' with 'World Wide Web' and 'website'. Because of the strict temporal and geographic requirements contained in the statutory definition of 'United States work', conflating these terms had a profound impact on the district court's evidentiary analysis. By confounding 'Internet' with 'website', the district court erroneously assumed that all 'Internet publication' must occur on the 'World Wide Web' or a 'website'. The district court then erroneously assumed all 'Internet publication' results in simultaneous, worldwide distribution. [A] proper separation of the terms yields a very different analysis.[29]

The court ultimately held that Mosley had failed to meet his factual burden in establishing the exact nature of the online posting of the song and its intended scope of distribution to support summary judgement in Mosley's favour. However, the court went on to rule alternately that summary judgement was still warranted because 'the record reveals a lack of sufficiently probative evidence to determine that Acidjazzed Evening is a foreign work'.[30]

It was hardly a resounding moral victory, but it highlights two very different perspectives on the business of music. On the one hand is an economy built on trust, honour, and goodwill; on the other an economy driven by cold, hard cash and egos, in which the creative producer is only the front end of a vast and well-resourced corporate machine that can pursue and defend its interests. From a music industry perspective, the case was pretty small beer, but the human interest angle was a David and Goliath story, and it caught the attention of the mainstream media, featuring in the New Musical Express, Rolling Stone, and Wired and on MTV and VH-1. For both sides, perhaps, the whole affair demonstrated the old adage that no publicity is bad publicity.

Chipping the Future

So what next? Everyone I spoke to as I developed the text of this book was optimistic about the future of chiptune, although almost everyone had a different vision of what it might look like. While most artists acknowledged with a degree of discomfort the gradual creep towards the mainstream, they recognized the benefits it brings, not least the opportunity to play live to more diverse audiences who would understand what they were trying to do.

'The chip music form is so accepted now', Gareth Morris says.

You can speak to people and they know what 8-bit is, they know exactly what you're doing, they might even have been to a few parties, and know some of the artists. It's much bigger than before. I mean, I've played ... I don't know how many shows in New York, Tokyo, all over Europe, and wherever else, and the reality is that the amount of money I make from my music is like beer money, really, and no one recognizes me when I walk down the street. But it's absolutely brilliant to be able to do it. I mean, I dreamed of being able to do this kind of thing. It's quite perfect, really.

My original prediction a few years back was that 8-bit was going to join up with the Electroclash movement, which was happening at that time. But it didn't go that way at all. Hopefully the scene will still have a place with me on it. But there are so many of these kids doing really amazing stuff. You've got to be as good as those guys to play. Being a bit older doesn't help because I've got a bit less free time and I'm very much aware that I've kind of got to earn unfortunately, and so maybe that's the way it should be. We'll see. I don't know if my kind of 8-bit has a place on the scene any more; a lot of my ideas about 8-bit are already old-fashioned. All I really want to do, though, is keep playing.[31]

But mass market is not the only possible future for chiptune. As Chris Abbott has shown with his netlabel and SID music festivals, it's perfectly possible to sustain events and products, even for very niche audiences; crowdfunding and the Internet allow geographically dispersed groups to come together and celebrate a shared interest.

'I spent a lot of time between 2008 and 2014 really not being very enthusiastic about any of this', he says.

There was that period, between about 1990 and 2007, when I was busy with the music all the time. Back in Time happened, I did Back in Time Live, but then at that point, it started to look as if the scene didn't need me anymore. Besides, I had a day job doing something else entirely, so I took a back seat for a while. And then Kickstarter happened.

That was what got me back in. In 2014, a French guy came to me and said, 'Look, we've got this orchestra wants to play C64 music'. Now I'd first looked into that back in 2000. I even went as far as getting some quotes from the Royal Festival Orchestra, but I couldn't make it work back then, because you were shouldering all the risk and you'd no idea whether or not you'd make enough back to cover all the expenses you'd have to shell out up front to get things off the ground.

Kickstarter flips that idea on itself. It's like selling people the concept first, and getting advanced sales, so you know that it will pay for itself, and all I have to do then, is pull it all together. That's what I'm good at!

It's basically like saying, 'I'm going to do this nice thing for people; I'm going to do this nice thing for people, and I'm going to do this nice thing for people. So it's like you put together all these lovely things that you know people will like … well, hopefully they'll like them! That's the fun bit, of course. The less fun bit is when, three days after you've launched the Kickstarter when the funding starts going, you begin to wonder, did I get this massively wrong?

Part of the problem with that, though, is that a lot of my projects end up being these really complex, niche things. That makes them very hard to describe to people. Take BITLive; it's chip music, but it isn't—it's live performance of chip music that been arranged for a rock band that has no chips in it and is performed by the original composers. I think it's far too many levels of abstraction to be easy for people to buy into. I mean, a book about Commodore 64 screenshots, that's a Kickstarter: it's a book and it's got Commodore 64 screenshots in it. Back in Time Live—levels of abstraction. SIDology—levels of abstraction. Fortunately, though, we're pitching to a really knowledgeable audience who are absolutely into this stuff.

This new one I'm working on, Project Hubbard, is probably the last Kickstarter I'll ever do. It is a monster of a project, and builds on pretty much everything else I've done, all the people I've met. The concept is something like a premix album. Imagine that all of Rob's SIDs were actually covers, SID covers of an album he'd done in 1979 as an experimental synth artist. So on the original he'd be throwing in, like funk guitars, Jeff Wayne and Kraftwerk … So you basically get a really eclectic album, the kind of album they would've done in 1979 when they were completely at ease with having a funk band in one corner and a guy playing a Moog in the other.

That idea appealed to Rob. I mean the SID … it was the way that Rob programmed it that made it sound unique to Rob. So if you take that idea back, and imagine what he would have done to his Moogs and Odysseys and whatnot, that's what this is. But … the only person who can go back and make that album is Rob. So we're essentially creating an alternate reality, an alternative Rob history, with this mythical 1979 album, fake reviews from Melody Maker, and an eighties picture disk.

I would've bought the fuck out of Rob Hubbard's album back then. Kickstarter lets me sell the idea to other people like me. It's weird-ass, but it's fun. I think it's all about that; it's all about fun really.[32]

Fun. That, surely is part of chip music's appeal. There's an old Steve Martin routine in which he advocates giving out banjos in place of welfare cheques, and getting world leaders to play *Foggy Mountain Breakdown* at summits; the rolling, jolly sound of the banjo would contribute more to the well-being of humanity than any amount of politicking and social subsidy.[33] Chiptune has something of that quality about it. Even tracks that proclaim a degree of melancholy in their title, like gwEm's *Tune 4 My Broken Atari*, can't help but put a smile on your face. It's a fun, upbeat sound, the sort of music that you can't help but warm to. It's the sound of childhood.

'There's nothing else that sounds quite like it, and there's nothing else that, specifically gamers of that time, that can make them feel quite so nostalgic', says journalist Aoife Wilson. 'It's really cool. There's something about chiptune music in particular that is just quite energetic. It just evokes feelings of my childhood, where you just want to get up and do stuff. [It's like a] sugar rush ... [the] excitement of a simpler time, maybe'.[34]

That sound, though, is not just the sound of nostalgia, although, for sure, those square waves provide a direct link to a time in all of our lives when life was simpler; a time before we get ground down by the pressures of life when all that really mattered was whether or not we would get through Eugene's Lair with all of our lives intact.[35] That retro sound places chiptune on a musical timeline that pulls in influences from video gaming, from film, from television, and from youth culture.

'With our video game music, we influenced the rave scene of 10 years later', Ben Daglish says.

> So a lot of the electronica that came out in the nineties was by kids who were listening to our stuff in the eighties. I mean, obviously, they'd grown up listening to a lot of the stuff that we were listening to as well, you know, like Kraftwerk and Jean Michel Jarre and Yellow Magic Orchestra and all those electronic pioneers, as it were. But we had our part to play in that, me and Martin and Rob. And so I think that then carried on, part of a continuum.
>
> The rave, electronica scene certainly had an influence on the hip-hop scene of the 2000s, and all of that has had an influence on the sort of chip music that people are producing today. Every generation rediscovers what the previous generation was doing and all the rest of it, you know? I grew up listening to sixties and seventies rock and all of that sort of stuff, and it all came out in my game music, but expressed through the creative lens of the SID chip. The nineties electronic scene took some of those ideas and did exactly the same thing, and what we're seeing with chip music now is that same process, but drawing on a broader musical palette. It's cool, but it's what kids have always done, you know? Play with older sounds and musical ideas and make them their own.[36]

Creatively, the limitations of chiptune can be very liberating. While virtual studio technology, the modelling of classic recording studio hardware in cheap, accessible software, has brought all of us the sort of creative options and capabilities that, even 15 years ago, were confined to the likes of Abbey Road or Capitol, it also brings a form of creative block, the tyranny of choice. Creative procrastination frequently kicks in when I sit in front of Cubase and load up virtual instruments and effects. The sheer choice is overwhelming, and rather than jump in and make, the temptation is to explore the multitude of presets and options, just in case the perfect sound that might make a track is hiding in the next menu along. It is just as Devo sang, 'Freedom of choice is what you got. Freedom from choice is what you want'.[37]

That is what chiptune can provide. With simple, raw waveforms, limited polyphony, and few options for dynamic articulation, chip musicians have no option but to go right back to the very basics and address the fundamentals that make music engaging and entertaining. There is nowhere for half-formed ideas or weak arrangements to hide. Chiptune is electronic music in its most fundamental state; it is about simple ideas expressed well.

Above all else, though, chiptune is cool. In 2003, when Malcolm McLaren declared 8-bit to be the new punk, he recognised that same lo-fi, DIY aesthetic, that sense of the outsider looking in scornfully at what youth culture had become. Just as punk raised a defiant middle finger to the worst excesses of prog and glam rock, 8-bit and its associated lo-fi subculture stands in stark contrast to the overproduced sound of much of today's commercial music. Little wonder, then, that one of the most popular slogans around the scene is 'Fuck Pro-Tools'. For those who wear that particular T-shirt, the future of music is square.

Acknowledgements

Writing a book is a long and at times lonely process, but it's one that depends on the generosity and goodwill of a number of people.

It's often said that you should never meet your heroes, but for me, meeting my chip-heroes has been a wonderfully life-affirming process. I have managed to catch up with many of those who, to my 11-year-old self, were video game music colossi, or who today are doing weird and interesting things with the sort of obsolete technology to which I have a slightly obsessive and nostalgic bond. Without exception, they have all been utterly delightful.

My gratitude, then, extends to all of the interviewees who took the time to speak to me and offer such a range of fascinating perspectives on music, performing, and technology. Some, however, went way beyond what might be reasonably expected of a contributor. In some cases, I was patiently indulged as the topic of conversation meandered onto Chick Corea, Professor Longhair, or different approaches to learning French. In others, I was warmly invited into homes and introduced to families. I have been made dozens of mugs of tea and shown secret 'geek closets' full of cannibalized SID chips, hacked circuit boards, and partially soldered Eurorack kits. Thank you to all who contributed, but special thanks must go to Chris Abbott; Michael Cox; Ben Daglish; Dr Rob Hubbard; Mark Lesser; Chris Nash; and Paul Soulsby.

My colleague Adam Sampson, a fellow musician and expert coder, responded with good grace and surprising speed when I sent him code to debug late at night and lent me endless bits of vintage hardware to tinker with and photograph. Danielle Morgan did likewise when I sent her digital recordings of some very long and rambling conversations to transcribe. She did a wonderful job.

Oliver Wittchow, whose English, even when under the influence of a heavy head cold, was streets ahead of my stilted German, showed me some top secret developments of his Nanoloop cartridges, but then, in what was possibly a strategic master stroke, introduced me to the finest beer that Hamburg has to offer so that I would immediately forget what I had just seen.

Radek Rudnicki, an experimental textural composer, met me for a fascinating chat and a tour of his studio in York just days after falling from a rock face and being airlifted to hospital. Radek I'm relieved you emerged from it all without any lasting damage.

Thank you to Grant Orchard and Sue Goffe of Studio AKA in Soho, who very kindly let me invade their production space so that I could ask dumb questions about Hey Duggee. I got a real kick out of talking 'toons with you, and my kids love Duggee even more now that they know their dad has actually met him.

Mark 'TDK' Knight, a form of nomenclature I later learned was imposed by iTunes and doesn't sit all that comfortably with the man himself, was perhaps the most indulgent of all. Not only did he feed me delicious homemade flapjacks throughout the course of an afternoon and early evening but also he postponed a family meal for more than two hours while we reminisced about tracking, the early demoscene, and gigging with a violin in a rough Bristol pub.

Gareth 'gwEm' Morris went out of his way to make sure that I was able to safely negotiate the London Tube, something that I confess induces a palpable level of anxiety in me. He travelled with me all the way from St. Paul's to join me and my cousin, Craig, who always managed to find me a bed for the night when I was in the South East, for authentic Thai noodles and some not-so-authentic Belgian beer in the back room of a pub in Ealing.

Timis Stamatiadis and Chris Evans, two very accomplished and accommodating photographers, have very patiently worked with me to create images that capture something of the spirit and presence of the computer hardware that lies behind the chiptune story, while my colleague Ryan Locke, who will Photoshop for cake, very kindly helped with editing whenever I asked. Timis, in particular, has proven to me just how multifaceted digital photographers need to be these days, managing most of our sessions remotely and at times swapping out and resoldering components on vintage games consoles that were very definitely past their best.

To my editor, Norm Hirschy, thank you for being no more than an email away and for your encouragement and patience. Most of all, thank you for giving me the time and space I needed to find my voice, and for encouraging me to tell this very personal story in the way I have. Nobody would have read any of these words without your generosity and expertise.

Mum and Dad, thank you for your endless patience and for encouraging me to stick with piano lessons when I couldn't see the point. Thank you also for encouraging Santa to leave a Spectrum+ under the Christmas tree in 1984. I'm delighted to be able to show that all of those hours spent poking at the keyboards of various Spectrums and Commodores has paid off. Dad, I wish you were still here to see the result. I think you would have enjoyed reading it.

As a counterpoint to all the worry and angst that fuels the writing of a book, my family have provided both light relief and an earthy, Scottish sense of perspective. Wee Kenny and Iona, thank you for introducing me to Duggee, and for making me stop and play when I needed to. Shonagh, thank you for your patience. I love you all.

And finally, hello to Jason Isaacs.

Notes

INTRODUCTION

1. Hey Duggee plays out several wonderfully nuanced pop culture references that work, like this, on multiple levels. One of my favourites involves a take-off of Francis Ford Coppola's *Apocalypse Now*.
2. Interview with the author, Studio AKA, London, October 2015.
3. See, for example, Lowey & Prince.
4. The origin of this simile is unclear, and in some form or other it has been attributed to many individuals over the years. However, in this form, the first print citation seems to come from the September/October 1979 issue of *Time Barrier Express*: 'All quick, very natural, and captured on vinyl. It's so hard to explain on paper, you'll just have to find the records and listen for yourself (because I truly believe—honest—that writing about music is, as Martin Mull put it, like dancing about architecture)'.
5. See, for example, Bennett.
6. For non-Finnish speakers, Suominen will be something of a challenge, but it is well worth the effort.
7. This approach is reviewed in Gilroy.
8. Ruggill & McAllister, pp. 70–71.
9. This notion is discussed more fully in Graham.
10. Boden, p. 95.
11. The 'music store' sequence begins at approximately 01:02:22.
12. Dixon provides a detailed exploration of the analogous story of how technological progress curtailed a very powerful mode of stylized filmic storytelling.
13. Alberts & Oldenziel present an excellent overview of the related subcultures that collectively make up the digital underground; Granzian, pp. 127–152, presents a musical perspective.
14. The July 1985 issue of *Your Commodore* explicitly references chip music on its contents page (see 'The Well-Tempered 64'), while Herman 1985 suggests that the term was one of many in use at the time.
15. Enders presents an interesting extended overview of this process of virtualization.
16. Available at http://speedoflight.ironmaiden.com.
17. The interview can be heard on episode 18 of Richard Herring's *Leicester Square Theatre Podcast*, https://soundcloud.com/britishcomedyguide/richard-herring-lst-podcast-18-stephen-fry. Anon. (2013). "Stephen Fry reveals he attempted suicide in 2012." BBC News. Published 6 June, http://www.bbc.co.uk/news/entertainment-arts-22782913.
18. See Herring for a full account of the story.

CHAPTER 1

1. O'Keefe, p. 57.
2. Bowman, Kowert, & Ferguson.
3. The early stages of exploratory research are outlined in an internal research report by the MIT computing group. See Dennis, Kerllenevich, & Levy.
4. Graetz.
5. Ibid.
6. Levy, p. 16.
7. Detail of the code can be found in the PDP-1 Maintenance Manual, pp. 5–22–5–23, available at https://archive.org/stream/bitsavers_decpdp1F17_28841238/F17_PDP1Maint_1962#page/n123/mode/2up.
8. Roads 1980.
9. Markoff.
10. Lowood.
11. *Video Game Invasion.*
12. Guins, p. 58.
13. Kent, p. 42.
14. Ibid., p. 45.
15. Campbell-Kelly, p. 273.
16. Sullivan, pp. 23–26.
17. Wolf 2012, p. 65.
18. Bloom.
19. Anon. (2017). "Average Historic Price of RAM." *Statistic Brain.* http://www.statisticbrain.com/average-historic-price-of-ram/.
20. See Montfort & Bogost for a full account.
21. Hoggar, p. 475.
22. Roads 1996, p. 925.
23. Johnston, p. xiv.
24. Silbiger, p. 357.
25. GameSpot (2011). "Pitfall Classic Postmortem With David Crane Panel at GDC 2011 (Atari 2600)." YouTube. Published on 7 March. https://www.youtube.com/watch?v=MBT1OK6VAIU. The anecdote about Pressure Cooker is approximately 52 minutes into the presentation.
26. Anon. (n.d.). "Quadrun." *AtariProtos.* http://www.atariprotos.com/2600/software/quadrun/quadrun.htm.
27. The Atari 'Family Tree' advertisement is archived, along with many others, at the Atari fan site, http://adtari.com/index.php/1/atari-2600.html.
28. Blakeman.
29. Kent, pp. 222–224.
30. Persons 1983b.
31. Persons 1983a.
32. Dillon 2011, p. 30.
33. Ibid., p. 74.
34. Herman 1994, p. 122.
35. Anon. (n.d.). "Atari Pokey Data Sheet." *POKEY CO12294.* http://krap.pl/mirrorz/atari/homepage.ntlworld.com/kryten_droid/Atari/800XL/atari_hw/pokey.htm.
36. N.S.
37. Loguidice & Barton, p. 122.
38. 'Supercharge a VCS and Load Up Games from Cassette Tapes' 1983.
39. Hubner & Kistner.
40. McCullaugh.
41. Dillon, 2010, p. 69.
42. Erickson, p. 623.

43. Crane, D. (2013). "IAM David Crane, creator of Pitfall! and co-founder of Activision." *Reddit*. Archived at https://www.reddit.com/r/IAmA/comments/yli88/iam_david_crane_creator_of_pit-fall_and_cofounder/.

44. Blakeman.

45. Montfort & Bogost, p. 112.

46. Blakeman.

47. 'What the Hell Happened?' 1998.

48. Montfort & Bogost, pp. 66–79.

49. Goodman.

50. 'What the Hell Happened?' 1998.

51. Ibid.

52. Dillon 2011, p. 73.

53. Anon. (1983). "Atari Parts are Dumped." *New York Times*. Published 28 September. https://www.nytimes.com/1983/09/28/business/atari-parts-are-dumped.html. Santos, F. (2013). "Hunting for an E.T. Castoff in a Most Terrestrial Place." *New York Times*. Published 17 June. https://www.nytimes.com/2013/06/18/us/hunting-for-an-et-castoff-in-a-most-terrestrial-place.html.

CHAPTER 2

1. Original leaflet: Anon. (1978). *MK14 Standard Micro Computer Kit*. Cambridge, UK: Science of Cambridge. Reproduced in full in: Fogarty, L. (ed.) (2005). *ZX Shed: Retro Spectrum Action*. Issue 1, pp. 24–25. *Internet Archive*. Published 28 May 2013. https://archive.org/details/ZXShed_Issue_01_2005_ZXShed.

2. Anon. (1978). *A Simple Tape Interface for the MK14*. Cambridge, UK: Science of Cambridge. Archived at: Anon. (n.d.), A Simple Tape Interface for the MK14, *Centre for Computing History*. http://www.computinghistory.org.uk/det/8413/MK14-Manual-update-Tape-Interface/.

3. Berk.

4. Tomkins.

5. Zombieboy's VHS Vault. (2016). "The Mighty Micro Episode 1 The coming of the microprocessor (VHS Capture)." *YouTube*. Published 1 July. https://youtu.be/WiiQrLMqsm8?list=PL13dwmxpaKl5JJyC4L09uf_PFXkn6FlGA.

6. Radcliffe.

7. Blyth.

8. A complete scan of the user manual is available at https://archive.org/details/ZON_X-81_1982_Bi-Pak_GB.

9. Gazzard explores the emergence of the Acorn/BBC partnership in detail.

10. Smith 2011.

11. See chapter 8 of Sinclair Research Ltd. 1982b.

12. Released in the United Kingdom in 1981, *The Birdie Song* by the Tweets reached number 2 in the charts.

13. Although initially released by Gershon Kingsley on his 1969 album *Music to Moog By*, it was the instrumental band Hot Butter's 1972 cover that became an international hit.

14. Written by Harry Akst and Benny Davis, *Baby Face* was published in 1926 and became a hit for Jan Garber later that year. Even in the mid-1980s, it would still have been subject to copyright law in the United Kingdom.

15. *Blaze Away* was written by Abe Holzmann in 1901 and remains the work for which he is best known.

16. *The Washington Post* was composed by John Philip Sousa in 1889 for the newspaper's essay contest awards ceremony. It remains a very popular marching band standard.

17. Also known as *60 Seconds to What*, the fatalistic organ and trumpet theme can be heard during the showdown with Tomaso in the church and recapitulates to accompany the final showdown in *For a Few Dollars More*, the middle chapter of Sergio Leone's trilogy *Man with No Name*.

18. Interview with the author, Matlock, December 2015.
19. Stein, p. 144.
20. Interview with the author, Matlock, December 2015.
21. Xenakis.
22. Robindoré.
23. Einstein & Infeld, pp. 262–263.
24. See Warren, chapter 6, for a discussion of the range and limits of the effect.
25. Smith's interview is included in the extras on the DVD release of the documentary feature *From Bedrooms to Billions*.
26. Sandy White recounts this story on a Q & A page on his personal website, http://sandywhite.co.uk/fun/visitors/visitors3.htm.
27. Arguably, Deus Ex Machina was the first indie art game. Croucher, who composed the music and arranged the recording sessions, combined his synth-based rock and a cast that included Ian Dury, Jon Pertwee, Donna Bailey, and Frankie Howerd. Together, the narrative, the aesthetic, and the cast place it alongside other urban dystopias from the 1970s, including Lindsay Anderson's classics *If . . .* and *O Lucky Man!*
28. This was originally posted by Alexander on his personal web page, http://www.atowers.u-net.com/mark/spectrum/spectrum.htm; it has since gone offline.
29. Follin 1987.
30. 'Code Britannia: Tim Follin' 2015.
31. Ibid.
32. "Computer Game Music—The Rock 'n Roll Years" 2013.
33. Wilkins, p. 13.
34. This was originally posted by Alexander on his personal web page, http://www.atowers.u-net.com/mark/spectrum/spectrum.htm; it has since gone offline.
35. 'Sinclair Stakes His Hopes on Blue Skies' 1986.

CHAPTER 3

1. The very best explanations of the Commodore 64 graphics modes can be found in the detailed programming guides that were released early in its life. Platt or Falconer both give a good introduction.
2. In the United Kingdom, Zzap!64 and Crash, respectively, catered for the Commodore 64 and ZX Spectrum gaming markets. Both titles were published by Newsfield Publications, and with a young journalistic team writing for a predominantly teen, male audience, the magazines thrived on good-natured, though sometimes acerbic, platform rivalry. Archives of these magazines can be found at http://www.zzap64.co.uk. and www.crashonline.org.uk.
3. Montfort, p. 218.
4. O'Regan, p. 59.
5. Valéry.
6. 'Calculator Maker Integrates Downwards' 1976.
7. Isaacson 2011, pp. 72–73.
8. Wolf, p. 85.
9. Laing, p. 975.
10. King 2010, p. 95.
11. 'New Developments from Commodore' 1980.
12. Herzog.
13. Williams.
14. Finkel.
15. Wallich.
16. Bagnall, p. 235.
17. Wallich.
18. Ibid.
19. Ibid.
20. Dillon 2015, p. 9.

21. Interview with the author, Matlock, December 2015.
22. *Commodore 64 User's Guide* 1982.
23. The technical information below is collated from Appendix O: 6581 Sound Interface Device (SID) Chip Specifications, in *Commodore 64 Programmer's Reference Guide* 1982.
24. See Russ, chapter 2.
25. Kennedy, p. 99.
26. Roads 1996, p. 220.
27. Russ, p. 159.
28. Reid.
29. Wallich.
30. Varga.
31. Interview with the author, Matlock, December 2015.
32. Interview with the author, London, July 2016.
33. "Hip Hop: We Do the Spectrum Bop" 1987.
34. Ibid.
35. New Order sold over 3 million copies of the 12-inch single 'Blue Monday' back in 1983, making it one of those rare tracks that balanced commercial appeal and musical innovation. The bouncing bass came from a Moog Source, sequenced using a Powertran sequencer that had been built by band member Bernard Sumner.
36. Lazy Jones uses a four-bar hook from Fade to Grey, which can be heard approximately 34 seconds into the original track with the lyric 'One man on a lonely platform'.
37. Lazy Jones, of course, loses the orchestral strings, disco backbeat, and funk guitar riffs of Page's disco mix but keeps the four-bar theme.
38. Nena's 1983 hit was undeniably the perfect musical accompaniment for a level titled '99 Red Balloons', but the music has crossed over for use in a number of other television shows and video games, including *Grand Theft Auto: Vice City*; *Gran Turismo 3: A-Spec*; *Donkey Konga*, and *Just Dance 2014*.
39. Anon. (n.d.). "ZOMBIE NATION." *Official Charts*. http://www.officialcharts.com/artist/7627/zombie%20nation/.
40. Interview with the author, London, July 2016.
41. Ibid.
42. This section is based on an extended long-form interview with the author, Matlock, December 2015.
43. Interview with the author, London, July 2016.
44. This section is based on an extended long-form interview with the author, Hull, December 2015.
45. Sanchez.
46. Dance.
47. Ibid.
48. Rydeen is one of those tracks that particularly influenced early chiptune. It crops up in several video games of the early 1980s, including Sega's *Super Locomotive* (1982), Rabbit Software's *Trooper Truck* (1983), and Superior Software's *Stryker's Run* (1986).
49. Additional background and a description of Hughes's Freeload system can be found on his personal website, http://www.pauliehughes.com/page3/page3.html.
50. In fact, in several cases, as with Mastertronic's *Night Racer* (1988) and *Rockford* (1988), for example, the gameplay of Invade-a-Load was arguably more entertaining than the main feature!
51. Interview with the author, Hull, December 2015.
52. Interview with the author, Nottingham, June 2017.
53. *From Bedrooms to Billions*.
54. Interview with the author, Hull, December 2015.
55. Wallström n.d.
56. Interview with the author, Hull, December 2015.
57. Vogel, p. 425.
58. Kinder, p. 90.
59. Ferrell & Keizer.

60. Stanton, p. 85.
61. Maher, p. 254.
62. Wallich.
63. Ibid.

CHAPTER 4

 1. Mace 1983.
 2. Hasegawa, p. 19.
 3. Sloan, p. 2.
 4. Houze, p. 159.
 5. Carter, p. 46.
 6. Sloan, pp. 64–65.
 7. Gorges & Yamazaki present some commentary on Nintendo's Blocks and the relationship with Lego.
 8. Sheff, pp. 22–23.
 9. Altice, p. 366.
10. Kohler & Yoshida, p. 27.
11. Gorges & Yamazaki, pp. 184–186.
12. Loguidice & Barton, p. 140.
13. Dillon 2011, p. 23.
14. Ryan 2013b, pp. 14–16.
15. Ibid., p. 21.
16. Paumgarten.
17. Firestone, p. 67.
18. Altice, p. 12.
19. Quotation from Takano 1995; translation commissioned by Nathan Altice, author of *I Am Error*.
20. Quotation from Takano 1994.
21. Wolf 2008, p. 115.
22. Ibid., p. 116.
23. Altice, p. 95.
24. Loguidice & Barton, p. 143.
25. Greg Lake's *Lucky Man* is just one example of this sort of prog rock lead voicing. You don't need to delve too deeply into Emerson, Lake and Palmer's back catalogue, or indeed that of any of the synth-infused supergroups who were active in the 1970s, to hear the square wave cutting through a dense mix to carry the lead line. Nonetheless, Emerson, Lake and Palmer were particularly influential, and Lucky Man was one of the first tracks to feature Keith Emerson's new Moog synth as a solo instrument in this way, something that can be explored further in Pinch & Trocco 2004 (see p. 248). As such, this particular track is perhaps the one that established the square-wave-as-soaring-lead voicing.
26. Roads 1996, p. 293.
27. There is not a great deal of official documentation about the NES APU. The information presented here has been reverse-engineered: tested and then corroborated through the homebrew and hacking communities.
28. See, for example, Kefauver & Patschke, pp. 59–61, for an overview of delta modulation.
29. Altice, p. 260.
30. Nintendo Family BASIC was released as a collaborative venture with Hudson Soft and the Sharp Corporation. The software cartridge came bundled with a branded computer keyboard, whose colour scheme matched that of the Famicom, and an instructional textbook. An external cassette recorder was required to save programs.
31. Kohler.
32. Ibid.
33. Otero.
34. Iwata.
35. Otero.

36. Iwata.
37. Kohler.
38. Iwata.
39. Schartmann, p. 86.
40. Kohler.
41. Gudmunson.
42. Tenzer & Roeder, p. 166.
43. Hopkins, pp. 19–20.
44. Vincent presents a very interesting exploration of funk, from both cultural and musicological perspectives.
45. Schartmann, p. 56.
46. McAlpine, Bett, & Scanlan.
47. See Collins, pp. 45–47, for an overview of the SNES sound system.

CHAPTER 5
1. Vail, p. 72.
2. Stewart.
3. Carlos's *Switched on Bach* remains a seminal album. It played a key role in popularizing the sound of the Moog synthesizer in popular music and in 1970 won three Grammy Awards: Best Classical Album, Best Classical Performance—Instrumental Soloist or Soloists (With or Without Orchestra), and Best Engineered Classical Recording.
4. The original series of articles, titled ETI 3600/4600 International Music Synthesizers, relating to the construction of the synthesizer can be found in Rivers, C. (ed.), *Electronics Today International*, October 1973: 25–31; December 1973: 74–79; January 1974: 50–54; February 1974: 58–60; March 1974: 76–78; April 1974: 66–69; July 1974: 69–72, 109; March 1975: 41–42; April 1975: 74–76; May 1975: 62–65, and August 1975: 51–55.
5. Dean, p. 62.
6. This quote is taken from 'Fairlight: The Whole Story' 1996 and is endorsed by Peter Vogel.
7. The original broadcast is available to view on YouTube, https://www.youtube.com/watch?v=dCu0NyZauzY&t=32s.
8. Vail, p. 73.
9. See Roads 1996, pp. 667–668.
10. 'Fairlight: The Whole Story' 1996.
11. The UK's Office for National Statistics, the executive office of the UK Statistics Authority, lists the average house price in the United Kingdom at £24,000 throughout the period 1980–1982.
12. 'Fairlight: The Whole Story' 1996.
13. An archive of Commodore adverts is available at http://www.commodore.ca/commodore-gallery/commodore-videos-tv-and-radio-adverts/.
14. Cox.
15. Wood & Abbott.
16. My translation of Ludwig.
17. Wood & Abbott.
18. Hülsbeck 1986b.
19. Hülsbeck 1986a.
20. Jazzcat.
21. Wallström 2004.
22. Ibid.
23. Wood & Abbott.
24. Goldberg & Vendel, p. 198.
25. Mace 1985a.
26. Maher, p. 14.
27. Hubner & Kistner.
28. Stilphen.

29. 'Jay Miner: The Father of the Amiga' 1988.
30. Goldberg & Vendel, p. 387.
31. Loguidice & Barton, p. 156.
32. Bagnall, p. 398.
33. Augenbraun & Greenley, pp. 3, 258–259.
34. Maher, pp. 17–19.
35. Ibid., p. 37.
36. Nelson. The interview appears in full on the cover-mounted disk, with an extract printed on p. 9.
37. Mace 1984.
38. Hoban.
39. Dorfman.
40. Mace 1986.
41. Maher, p. 180.
42. See, for example, Mace 1985b, to see how the battle lines were drawn up between the two machines from the very beginning.
43. Gantz.
44. Wright.
45. *Creator* was functionally similar to *Notator*, which was released in 1988. The developer changed its name from C-Lab to Emagic, and released *Notator Logic* in 1993. The company was purchased in 2002 by Apple, which has continued to develop Logic into the current version, *Logic X*.
46. *Pro 16* was Steinberg's first software sequencer product on the Commodore 64. The company released *Pro 12* on the ST, and then *Pro 24* on the ST and Amiga, but it was on the ST that the package really took hold and developed into Cubase. Steinberg was sold to the US firm Pinnacle Systems in 2003 and then was acquired by Yamaha in 2004, which continues to develop the Steinberg line of products.
47. 'Editors' Choice Awards' 1986.
48. Webster.
49. Interview with the author, Leamington Spa, October 2015.
50. See, for example, Csikszentmihalyi for a detailed study of the flow phenomenon.
51. Interview with the author, Bristol, June 2016.
52. Interview with the author, London, October 2016.
53. Interview with the author, Leamington Spa, October 2015.
54. Interview with the author, Leamington Spa, October 2015.
55. Magic of Nah-Kolor.
56. Interview with the author, Leamington Spa, October 2015.
57. The story of the emergence of the Internet is a fascinating one but, sadly, one that is beyond the scope of this book. I recommend several well-written histories that chart its emergence from dial-up BBSs, Fidonet, and academic and military networks, including Ryan 2013a and Goggin & McLelland.
58. Interview with the author, London, October 2015.
59. Interview with the author, Leamington Spa, October 2015.
60. Anarchy.
61. Interview with the author, Leamington Spa, October 2015.
62. The demo in question is almost certainly *I've Got the Power* by Alcatraz, released in 1991. The original Amiga image file is available for download at Pouët.net. Published 27 April 2004 available at http://www.pouet.net/prod.php?which=9574.
63. Evans & Lord.
64. Stud Brothers.
65. In fact, Some Justice was the second 'single of the week' in that week's *Melody Maker*. The first was their remix of Eon's *Basket Case*.
66. Andy Rea's ZX81 soundtracker, ZXBeta.p, can be downloaded from http://www.sinclairzxworld.com/viewtopic.php?f=6&t=556.

67. The notion of authenticity in music has resurfaced many times in connection with popular music but particularly so with punk, where authentic self-expression was perhaps more important than anything. Sabin, pp. 82–83, very neatly sets out the idea of 'authentic punk' and explores the challenges this raises in relation to the music later in his book. Barker & Taylor discuss authenticity and the problems that arise from it more broadly in relation to rock and pop. Harker is another excellent book that very clearly exposes how problematic it is to define and apply authenticity as a value judgement about music.
68. Polymeropoulou.
69. More information about the specifications of the SwinSID can be found at http://www.swinkels.tvtom.pl/swinsid/. The specifications of the Papilio can be found at http://papilio.cc.
70. Interview with the author, Edinburgh, March 2016.
71. Hood, pp. 21–22.
72. Interview with the author, Leamington Spa, October 2015.
73. Interview with the author, London, October 2015.
74. Interview with the author, Hamburg, November 2015.
75. Interview with the author, Bristol, June 2016.

CHAPTER 6
1. Hogan.
2. Freiberger provides a good overview of the Homebrew Club, while chapter 10 of Levy provides additional detail and insights from club members.
3. Isaacson 2015, p. 310.
4. Levy, p. 8.
5. Dompier.
6. Ibid.
7. Doornbusch.
8. In fact, Arthur C. Clarke witnessed the IBM demonstration and referenced it in his 1968 novel, 2001: A Space Odyssey. Since then, the piece and that context have entered the realm of popular folklore, most recently appearing on the big screen in the 2014 biopic *The Theory of Everything*, as Professor Stephen Hawking explores the synthetic voice of his text-to-speech synthesizer.
9. 'Altair … on the Road' 1975.
10. Gates, 1975a.
11. Armer.
12. Campbell-Kelly, p. 29.
13. Pugh is a very thoroughly researched and readable account of IBM's rise from a manufacturer of automated punched card machines in the late nineteenth century through to its position as the dominant player in computer systems in the middle of the twentieth.
14. Smith 1983.
15. Mapstone.
16. Akera, p. 263.
17. Weiss, pp. 191–192, in a chapter titled 'U.S. versus IBM: An Exercise in Futility?,' presents a collated timeline of the US v. IBM antitrust lawsuit.
18. Moore.
19. Levy, p. 192–193.
20. See Gates 1975b and Gates 1975c. A 'Second and Final Letter' (Gates 1976) highlights the 'innumerable replies' he received about 'controversy raised by [his first] letter'.
21. Coleman, p. 4.
22. Campbell-Kelly explores in detail the transition of the computer from industrial tool to domestic entertainment platform.
23. Similarly, *From Bedrooms to Billions* is a very thorough exploration of the emergence of the UK video games industry, in the words of those who were involved at all stages.
24. Coleman, pp. 1–2.

25. Dalzell, p. 229.
26. Interview with the author, Leamington Spa, October 2015.
27. Levy, p. 392.
28. McFadden.
29. Kowalski.
30. Craig, p. 61.
31. Schwartz.
32. Smart.
33. Wallström, 2005.
34. Borzyskowski.
35. Reunanen.
36. Vuorinen.
37. This account is collated from an online conversation and Wallström 2013.
38. Anon. (n.d.). "Our history." *The Gathering.* http://archive.gathering.org/tg14/en/information/what-is-TG/our-history/.
39. Interview with the author, Matlock, December 2015.
40. Interview with the author, London, October 2015.
41. The full performance can be viewed at http://www.linusakesson.net/music/variation18/index.php.
42. Interview with the author, Leamington Spa, October 2015.

CHAPTER 7

1. Pascoe.
2. In the patent application, dated July 31, 1979, Klose references an unnamed article in *Electronics*, March 4, p. 44, as inspiration for Auto Race.
3. The US patent for Auto Race, US 4162792 A, is available on Google Patents, https://www.google.com/patents/US4162792A.
4. Email interview with the author, September 2015.
5. Mattel, p. 2.
6. Baer, p. 171.
7. Ibid., pp. 172–173.
8. Crigger.
9. Inoue, p. 125.
10. The Game & Watch series of LCD handhelds—some 60 titles in all—were produced by Nintendo between 1980 and 1991. They were phenomenally successful and were published, according to Makoto Kano in an interview with Satoru Iwata, in April 2010—the root of all Nintendo's handheld gaming systems (see Iwata).
11. Yokoi's D-Pad controller has gone on to become so ubiquitous that it's difficult to imagine how we used to play. In 2007, Nintendo was awarded an Emmy by the National Academy of Television Arts & Sciences in recognition of 'the technological achievement of the D-pad, which radically changed how people interact with their video games and, by extension, their televisions' (Nintendo press release, 12 January 2007).
12. Part of an interview between Gunpei Yokoi and Yukihito Morikawa of developer MuuMuu, carried out in 1997 just before Yokoi's death. The full interview, translated by shmuplations, can be read at http://shmuplations.com/yokoi/.
13. Red Bull Music Academy. (2014). "Hip Tanaka Lecture (Tokyo 2014) | Red Bull Music Academy." *YouTube.* Published 22 November. https://www.youtube.com/watch?v=F7J5GlE3YLQ.
14. Hoad.
15. As detailed at http://www.officialcharts.com/artist/28121/doctor-spin/.
16. Tetris was a mainstream musical hit and featured on the UK chart show *Top of the Pops*, showing viewers the bizarre spectacle of five tetrimino-clad dancers grooving in front of a light show and an outsize backdrop of the original Game Boy cart.
17. In fact, the Game Boy Camera was used professionally. It was used to create images for Neil Young's album *Silver and Gold.* Its claim to be the world's smallest digital camera featured in the *Guinness Book of World Records* (1999), p. 172. London, UK: Guinness Publishing.

18. This section is based on an extended long-form interview carried out by the author with Oliver Wittchow in Hamburg, November 2015.

19. Kotlinski wrote a paper on Amiga music programs as part of a course on media between technology and culture at the Royal Institute of Technology in Stockholm in 2003; this was revised and translated into English.

20. Yamaha published a brief history of the QY series of Walkstations online as part of its *Yamaha Synth 40th Anniversary* corporate celebrations in 2014 https://uk.yamaha.com/en/products/contents/music_production/synth_40th/history/column/qy_series/index.html.

21. 'Nintendo Music' 2005.

22. Gabe Hayward. (2009). "Lo-Tek Resistance: Episode One—Capitol Hill." *YouTube*. Published 26 April. https://www.youtube.com/watch?v=w4fnHvvlcNM.

23. *Reformat the Planet*.

24. Wanderley & Depalle discusses exactly the notion that gestural information often signals the emotional intent of the performer or other nonfunctional aspects of performance.

25. My own article (2016) explores this issue and draws a comparison to drive- and fly-by-wire systems. In that respect, making music with technology providing both the front-end control interface and back-end tone generation is akin to performing-by-wire.

26. Hunt & Kirk.

27. See, for example, Nagashima.

28. Tanaka 2000.

29. Santi, p. 120.

30. In Cage, for example, the performer is instructed to 'determine position and size of mutes by experiment'.

31. Pinch & Trocco 2012, p. 258.

32. Ibid., p. 260.

33. Evans, p. 16.

34. Bussy, p. 21.

35. McLaren.

36. See Morris, 2004.

37. Interview with the author, London, October 2015.

38. Interview with the author, Hamburg, November 2015.

39. Totillo.

40. Doody.

41. Interview with the author, Leamington Spa, October 2015.

42. The rest of this section is based on an extended long-form interview with the author, Edinburgh, March 2016.

43. Now discontinued, the MIDINES cartridge was produced by Wayfar and sold through their website, www.wayfar.net, for $99.

44. Interview with the author, London, October 2015.

45. Ibid.

46. Interview with the author, Hamburg, November 2015.

47. Details of Wittchow's MIDI connector can be found at http://www.nanoloop.com/midi/index.html.

48. The source code for ArduinoBoy can be found at https://github.com/trash80/Arduinoboy.

49. Details of the MSSIAH cartridge can be found at http://www.mssiah.com.

50. 'Spectrum Music' 2005.

51. *Sinclair ZX Spectrum Basic Programming*, chapter 19.

52. Email interview with the author, June 2016.

53. Details of the Spectranet Ethernet card for the ZX Spectrum can be found at http://spectrum.alioth.net/doc/index.php/Main_Page.

54. Westcott's performance was held at Geek Out!, held at the Museum of the History of Science, Oxford, December 6, 2014.

55. Email interview with the author, June 2016.

56. Noble.

57. See Ellsworth (2012).
58. See Åkesson.

CHAPTER 8

1. Shepherd, p. 599.
2. See Gaunt & Kay.
3. Tschmuck is an excellent study of the rise of the recording industry. In particular, chapters 2–4 explore the emergence of recording technology and the reification of performances.
4. Marshall, pp. 32–34.
5. See, for example, Horn.
6. Gudmundsson, Lindberg, Michelsen, & Weisenthaut.
7. King, 2016, p. 94.
8. Fox.
9. Ensminger, p. 156.
10. See O'Connor for a thorough exploration of punk's influence on the emergence of homegrown and independent labels.
11. Hesmondhalgh.
12. Berners-Lee & Fischetti present a very thorough overview of the birth of the web, from Berners-Lee's initial work on hypertext through to a prototype system in 1990 and its subsequent public launch.
13. Sundell.
14. At 44.1 kHz and in stereo, a 16-bit sample stream will require 16 x 44,100 x 2 x 60 = 8,4672,000 bits of storage per minute, which equates to approximately 10.09 MB.
15. HVSC Admin Team.
16. Dawes.
17. HVSC Admin Team.
18. Interview with the author, London, July 2016.
19. Jones, p. 47.
20. Horton's project website: http://kevtris.org/Projects/hardnes/.
21. Akumu's NSF Archive: http://akumunsf.good-evil.net/dir.php.
22. Outlined in the 'microinfo/micromusic-concept' section in the main website, http://micromusic.net.
23. 'Nintendo Music'.
24. Interview with the author, London, October 2015.
25. Outlined in the 'microinfo/micromusic FAQs' section in the main website, http://micromusic.net.
26. Interview with the author, London, October 2015.
27. Espenscheid, pp. 45–50.
28. Interview with the author, London, October 2015.
29. Interview with the author, Edinburgh, March 2016.
30. *Reformat the Planet*.
31. Paoletta.
32. For more about the philosophy and practice of circuit bending, see Ghazala.
33. Swimm.
34. PC Plus.
35. Turner.
36. The excellent feature documentary *Reformat the Planet* includes footage of the 2006 Blip Festival. Additional footage of performances from that and other Blip Festivals can be found on YouTube.
37. Johnson.
38. Interview with the author, London, October 2015.
39. The name translates literally as 'end boss', a reference to the end-of-level bad guy in many video games.
40. Saunders, p. 256.
41. Murrell, Spencer, & McFarlane, pp. 127–128.

42. Townley.
43. Daniel, p. 65.
44. Torres, p. 242.
45. Stolzoff, pp. 52–54.
46. Moskowitz, pp. 278–279.
47. Welsh.
48. Website: http://www.jahtari.org.
49. Magni.
50. Gleichmar.
51. 'Silent Vinyl: Buying Records without a Record Player' 2016.
52. Email interview with author, September 2015.
53. Cohen.
54. Kreps 2007.
55. This was originally posted by Reznor on the official website, http://ghosts.nin.com/main/more_info, on March 2, 2008. This site has since gone offline.
56. Kreps 2008.
57. Interview with the author, Leamington Spa, October 2015.

CHAPTER 9

1. See Morris & Hartas for an introduction to the art and practice of machinima.
2. A sample from the show appears on the Mr. Bungle album between 'Love Is a Fist' and 'Dead Goon'. See http://www.bunglefever.com/faq.html.
3. Jahdi.
4. Some of Mr. Bungle's live performances from this time are available on YouTube.
5. Anon. (1995). "Mr. Bungle Setlist: December 27, 1989 Guerneville (CA), River Theatre." *CV Database*. http://www.negele.org/cvdb2/index.php?id=623.
6. Kregor & Kregor, p. 1, present an extract from a letter by Liszt to Count Géza Gichy in which he claims to have 'basically invented' transcription.
7. Sylvester.
8. Payne.
9. Schone.
10. Anon. (n.d.). "FAQ." *Minibosses*. http://minibosses.com/faq.htm.
11. Schone.
12. McNamara.
13. Sellers, p. 60.
14. Peralta & Peralta.
15. Turow, p. 554.
16. 'Buckner & Garcia: Biography' n.d.
17. Sellers, pp. 60–61.
18. Penn.
19. Raw, p. 45.
20. Mangram.
21. MacFarlane.
22. Wallström.
23. Dance.
24. The SID tune information list is part of the HVSC: http://www.hvsc.de/download/C64Music/DOCUMENTS/STIL.txt.
25. Stensdal, my translation.
26. *While My Guitar Gently Beeps.*
27. Ibid.
28. Interview with the author, Matlock, December 2015.
29. Stensdal, my translation.
30. *While My Guitar Gently Beeps.*

31. This and the following section are based on an extended long-form interview with the author, London, July 2016.
32. Interview with the author, Matlock, December 2015.
33. Interview with the author, Leamington Spa, October 2015.
34. Interview with the author, Matlock, December 2015.
35. Interview with the author, London, July 2016.
36. Interview with the author, Matlock, December 2015.
37. Interview with the author, London, July 2016.
38. Ibid.
39. Rowell, p. 52.
40. Hearsum & Inglis, p. 484.
41. Burgess & Green, p. 129.
42. With nearly 500 million copies sold across all platforms, Tetris beats its next nearest rival, *Minecraft*, by around 4:1.
43. See http://www.kungfurecords.com/artists.php?artist=Ozma.
44. Smooth McGroove. (2012). "Tetris—Theme 'A' Acapella." *YouTube*. Published 2 September. https://www.youtube.com/watch?v=PV06M-Gqxgg.
45. Tamburro.
46. Calvert.
47. Video Game Pianist. (2007). "Super Mario Medley." *YouTube*. Published 19 March. https://www.youtube.com/watch?v=dFZki6TcY4w.
48. Leung.
49. Simakis.
50. Interview with the author, Leamington Spa, October 2015.
51. Menotti.
52. 'Fetishising Busyness'.
53. Carlsson.
54. Interview with the author, Edinburgh, March 2016.
55. Beverage.
56. More information about the Plogue plug-in suite can be found at https://www.plogue.com/products/chipsounds/.
57. The blog: http://ploguechipsounds.blogspot.co.uk.
58. More information about the synth is available at http://soulsbysynths.com/atmegatron/.
59. This section is based on an interview with the author, London, July 2016.
60. Interview with the author, Hamburg, November 2015.
61. Some additional information is available at https://www.elektron.se/legacy-products/.
62. Jared-IGN.
63. For more information see http://www.ucapps.de/midibox_sid.html.
64. Anon. (n.d.). "sammichSID [MIDIbox]." *MIDIbox*. http://www.midibox.org/dokuwiki/doku.php?id=sammichsid.
65. http://twisted-electrons.com/product/therapsid/.
66. https://teenage.engineering/products/po.

CHAPTER 10
1. Interview with the author, London, October 2015.
2. Wolinsky.
3. Ubisoft 2010.
4. Goldstein.
5. McMahon.
6. Ibid.
7. Ibid.
8. Ibid.
9. Knowles.

10. Gottshalk.

11. Sale.

12. *Click On.*

13. Ibid.

14. Melissinos & O'Rourke, the publication that accompanied the exhibition, gives a good flavour of the event and provides some discussion of 8-bit artwork and music as art.

15. Barron.

16. O'Brien.

17. More information on George's role, a collaboration between the Victoria and Albert Museum and Abertay University, can be found at http://www.vam.ac.uk/content/articles/g/game-designer-resident-sophia-george/.

18. Majors.

19. Actor David Hayman utters these lines as Malcolm McLaren in Alex Cox's 1986 film *Sid and Nancy.*

20. Lydon's adverts for Country Life butter made national headlines. See, for example, Sweney.

21. Wilkinson.

22. Interview with the author, Leamington Spa, October 2015.

23. Nintendo Game Boy cartridge.

24. Dunn.

25. Timbalandrips.

26. Suni.

27. *Elliot in the Morning,* 2007.

28. Byrne.

29. Kernel Records Oy v. Timothy Mosley, 659 F.3rd 1294 (11th Cir. 2012).

30. Ibid.

31. Interview with the author, London, October 2015.

32. Interview with the author, London, July 2016.

33. The routine can be heard towards the end of the third track on Martin's debut stand-up album, *Let's Get Small* (Warner Bros., 1977).

34. *While My Guitar Gently Beeps.*

35. For what seemed like an eternity, this level on Manic Miner proved my undoing. Even today, having completed the game many times, I feel a sense of foreboding until I am past.

36. Interview with the author, Matlock, December 2015.

37. From *Freedom of Choice* (Warner Bros., 1980).

Glossary

1-bit music A collection of methods focused on creating music using 1-bit sound devices. See also *beeper* and *pulse-width modulation*.

2A03/2A07 The NTSC and PAL variants of the microprocessor at the heart of Nintendo's NES and Famicom consoles. The chip contained a modified 6502 processor and the consoles' audio processing unit.

6502 An 8-bit microprocessor, designed and manufactured by MOS Technology; variants of the processor were used in the Commodore 64 and several other computing platforms in the late 1970s and early 1980s.

6507 A cheaper, slightly feature-restricted version of MOS Technology's 6502; the 8-bit 6507 was used in the Atari VCS.

8-bit music A term that is often used synonymously with 'chiptune'.

algorithm A defined process or set of rules that is used by a computer to carry out an operation or calculation or to solve a problem.

Amiga A 16-bit computer platform released by Commodore in the mid-1980s as a successor to its popular C64.

amplitude envelope A time-varying signal that is superimposed on an audio signal to provide an amplitude contour.

arduino An open-source customizable microcontroller board.

arpeggiator A hardware device or algorithm that takes the notes of a block chord and generates note patterns using them. Arpeggiators have been a common feature of electronic music since the 1970s.

assembly language A low-level programming language that was commonly used to write video games on 8-bit systems.

attack-decay-sustain-release (ADSR) A common form of amplitude enveloping that became popular during the 'golden era' of analogue synthesis in the 1970s; ADSRs offer independent control over the duration of the attack, decay and release portions of a sound, and the level of the sustain portion.

Atari ST A 16-bit computer platform released by Atari in the mid-1980s as a direct rival to Commodore's Amiga.

Atari VCS An 8-bit home cartridge-based video game console.

Audio Processing Unit (APU) The programmable sound generator from the Nintendo Famicom and NES. This was embedded in the console's main CPU and offered five dedicated channels: two pulse channels; a triangle channel; a noise channel, and a delta-modulation sample playback channel.

AY-3-8910 A family of three-voice programmable sound generators from General Instruments that offered 4-bit volume controls and a single envelope generator. Variants of the chip appeared in the Spectrum 128 and Atari ST.

BASIC A high-level interpreted programming language that uses familiar English words as commands. The name is an acronym from Beginners All-Purpose Symbolic Instruction Code.

beeper A low-resolution electronic device that is capable of emitting simple electronic tones, or beeps. Music written on these devices, such as that for the original ZX Spectrum or PC speaker, is often called beeper music.

binary impulse A binary waveform constructed of a single positive bit followed by zeroes.

binary waveform A sound signal that is formatted as a series of discrete chunks of binary data, that is, as a sequence of ones and zeroes.

bit depth The bit depth of a signal corresponds to the resolution at which it has been sampled. In the case of digital audio, this usually refers to the number of bits of data that are used to sample the amplitude of the signal.

BITLive A high-profile UK chiptune festival that celebrates video game themes, particularly those of the Commodore 64, and combines performances of live video game covers and electronic performance.

bitpop A style of music that combines the lo-fi sound of chip music with contemporary pop sounds.

bulletin board system (BBS) A dial-up service, common in the 1980s, that served as an online repository for information.

C64 An 8-bit microcomputer platform based around the MOS 6510 process, a variant of the 6502. With a reported 17 million sales across its lifetime, the Commodore C64 remains the bestselling home computer in history.

cathode ray tube (CRT) display CRT displays form an image by firing electrons at a phosphorescent screen. The electrons are bent by an array of electromagnets so that the electrons sweep across the screen, forming the image a line at a time.

central processing unit (CPU) The 'brain' of a computer; the hardware that carries out the main logical operations of a computer system.

chiptune Lo-fi electronic music written using, or in the style of, programmable sound generators, typically from 8-bit computing platforms and video game consoles.

circuit bending The creative chance-based customization of electronic circuits, often those in low-cost electronic devices like effects pedals and children's toys, to create new sound generators and digital effectors.

coin-op A coin-operated video game cabinet.

compiler A computer program that converts instructions from a higher-level language like BASIC into machine code so that they can be read and executed more efficiently.

compo A contraction of 'competition'; compos are typically held at demoparties to allow participants to compete with others and showcase their technical and creative virtuosity.

conversion Similar in concept to a movie adaptation, a video game conversion involved redeveloping a video game from one platform onto another. Often, differences in hardware would require concessions to be made in graphics, sound, or gameplay, and the quality of a conversion would often be judged on how faithfully the developers had recreated the original gaming experience.

cracking Removing the copy protection from a piece of commercial software.

cracktro A portmanteau term from 'crack' and 'intro'; a cracktro is a compact program that combines elaborate graphical effects and chiptunes to be executed as a piece of cracked software loads.

delta modulation A 1-bit sound sampling method that encodes digital audio as a series of difference (delta) signals, either positive (1) or negative (0), from the previous sample.

demo A stand-alone piece of machine-based audiovisual art that is normally generated procedurally in real time.

demoparty A physical gathering of demosceners, often structured around coding events, competitions, and performance.

demoscene A distributed online community of technical artists who create and share demos.

digital audio workstation (DAW) A combination of hardware and software that is designed to aid the process of recording, editing, and producing audio files.

digital-to-analogue converter A device that converts a digital signal, such as a digital audio file, to an analogue signal.

diskmag An electronic magazine-style publication, normally distributed on floppy disk, that combined articles, best-of lists, competitions, graphics, music, and demos.

divide-down synthesis A method of generating frequency tables for a synthesis system by successively dividing the frequency of a master clock.

erasable/programmable read-only memory (EPROM) A type of read-only memory whose contents can be erased by exposure to ultraviolet light and then reprogrammed.

fakebit Writing music in the chiptune style, but with a process of composition that is divorced from the original hardware platforms.

Famicom An 8-bit cartridge-based video game console. It was the first released by Nintendo and was extremely successful in its home market.

fastloader A software utility, often incorporated into video game titles, that reduces the time it takes to load files from floppy disk or compact cassette.

filter A frequency-dependent amplifier that can either boost or cut the amplitude of a sound in different regions of its frequency spectrum.

flip-screen A method of providing transitions between screens or levels in video games that was particularly common in platform games during the 8-bit era; screens were redrawn as opposed to having the game world scroll continuously.

framebuffer An area of RAM that contains a complete image of the screen display that is updated multiples times each second to drive a video display.

Game Boy An 8-bit handheld console manufactured by Nintendo, with swappable cartridges and a four-colour greyscale LCD display.

granular synthesis An approach to sound synthesis that deconstructs sounds into tiny sound atoms or grains and then redistributes them to create new sounds.

hacking Exploring every possible aspect of a computer system just for the pleasure of understanding all of its intricacies in detail.

hard syncing A form of synthesis that generates complex and unusual waveforms by retriggering simple waveforms in response to an external sync source.

homebrew Software created by enthusiasts and/or amateur developers; also used in the name of one of the first home computer clubs in California in the mid-1970s.

impulse response The output of a dynamic system when it is fed a short, high-bandwidth signal, or impulse, as an input.

Krautrock A catch-all term to describe the experimental rock and electropop that emerged from Germany in the late 1960s and early 1970s.

leet A contraction of 'elite'; the informal but exclusive language of hacking culture. It substitutes combinations of numbers and letters to form alternate expressions of words and phrases.

linear feedback shift register (LFSR) A simple computing device that generates its next input as a linear function of its current state; commonly used to generate pseudorandom sequences of numbers and noise signals.

loader Used particularly on Commodore C64 cassette games, loaders were short programs that loaded and executed while the main game was loading. Like demos, typically they would display graphics and play music, although some would allow the user to play additional games or remix music while waiting.

low-frequency oscillator (LFO) An infrasonic (normally sub-20 Hz) time-varying electronic signal that is commonly used as a modulation source in analogue or digital sound synthesis.

machine code monitor A piece of software that allows the user to view and modify memory registers.

micromusic Term used in the 1980s to describe music written on microcomputers that became the title of a netlabel and an online chip music community in the 1990s.

MOD A compact music file format used in soundtracking that combined sample and music data.

modscene A geographically-distributed community of electronic music practitioners and consumers who shared music via MOD files on floppy disk and bulletin board systems.

musicdisk A packaged collection of music files, often accompanied by liner notes and graphics and distributed on floppy disk.

music driver A section of code, normally written in low-level assembly, that is designed to read music data and convert them to time-critical commands to the sound hardware.

musique concrète A form of experimental music constructed from edited fragments of recorded sounds.

netlabel A record label that distributes music as digital audio files via the Internet. Netlabels are often themed around a particular style of music and are often, though not exclusively, noncommercial.

New Romanticism A pop culture movement, characterized by a flamboyant and often androgynous or gender-bending sense of style and synth-pop sound, that grew out of the club scene in London and Birmingham in the early 1980s.

Nintendocore A style of music focused on playing rocked-up live arrangements of classic Nintendo NES soundtracks.

Nintendo Entertainment System (NES) An 8-bit cartridge-based video game console; essentially a repackaged Famicom for the international market.

nondiegetic music Traditionally, diegetic music in film and theatre is music that forms part of the story world; in other words, music whose source is visible or implied. Nondiegetic music, by contrast, originates from outside of the story world and would normally include incidental music or underscore. Broadly speaking, these concepts are translatable to video gaming.

nonmaskable interrupt A hardware-level interrupt: the highest priority of interrupt, which is capable of interrupting all software and nonvital hardware devices in a system; normally reserved for serious system errors or failures but often co-opted by 8-bit composers to achieve effects like sample playback.

note (or voice) stealing Digital tone generators are only capable of playing back a finite number of simultaneous voices. Once this limit is reached, one or more voices must be muted (stolen) before any new voices can be introduced. Typically, software or hardware algorithms will prioritize voices to minimize the impact of note stealing on playback.

NSF A file format for ripped NES music files.

NTSC Named for the National Television System Committee; an encoding system used in analogue television broadcast systems based around 525 vertical scanlines at 30 frames per second. It was mainly used in North America and Japan.

Paula The stereo sound chip from Commodore's Amiga. It is capable of four-channel 8-bit sample playback.

PEEK A BASIC command that allows a user to read the contents of a memory register; see POKE.

phase-alternating line (PAL) system An encoding system used in analogue television broadcast systems based around 625 vertical scanlines at 25 frames per second. It was used widely in Europe, Africa, Australasia, and parts of South America.

phasing An audio effect in which multiple copies of a signal are overlaid and slowly phase-modulated so that they gradually come in and out of phase with one another, creating a pulsing sound.

POKE A BASIC command that allows a user to write data directly to a memory register.

programmable sound generator (PSG) A user-programmable sound chip that synthesizes sound using simple waveforms—typically square, sawtooth, and triangle waves—and noise.

progressive rock A style of rock music that originated in the United Kingdom and the United States in the late 1960s and early 1970s and that brought together high and low culture, often fusing high concepts—'big ideas' that could be expressed succinctly, yet had tremendous reach and popular appeal—with technology, complex narratives, classical themes, flamboyant stagecraft, and virtuosic technique.

PSID A file format for ripped C64 music that packages up a player routine and the music data.

pulse-code modulation (PCM) The most commonly used method of representing sampled analogue signals, in which the analogue signal is sampled at regular intervals (the sample rate) and quantized to the nearest digital value as determined by the bit depth. This is the standard form of digital audio.

pulse width modulation (PWM) A form of synthesis that modulates the period of a pulse wave to synthesize dynamic tones. The technique was used extensively on the ZX Spectrum to generate multiple musical voices and effects.

punk An aggressive, countercultural movement that combined a DIY ethos with notions of anarchy and authentic self-expression. Punk combines fashion, art, music, and poetry.

racing the beam On the Atari VCS, the process of balancing the CPU load between game code and generating the display in real time, one scanline at a time.

radio frequency modulator A device that converts audiovisual signals from electronic devices, such as consoles and home computers, into a format that can be handled by a television receiver.

random access memory (RAM) A form of computer data storage that can be both read from and written to.

read-only memory (ROM) A form of computer data storage that can only be read from.

register A CPU memory storage location.

resonance An effect that originated in analogue filter designs that caused the filter to resonate and chime at frequencies close to its centre frequency and in this way artificially amplifying those frequencies. The effect is easily avoidable using modern digital filter designs, but many modern filters incorporate it as a controllable effect.

ring modulation A form of synthesis, related to amplitude modulation, that generates new tones by generating sideband frequencies around the harmonics of a source signal. The technique is named for the ring structure of diodes that are used to create analogue ring modulation circuits.

ripping The process of extracting a music driver and the associated music data from video game code.

sample In digital audio terminology, 'sample' can refer to the process of digitizing an analogue signal; the single chunk of digital data that is used to capture amplitude when an analogue signal is sampled; or the complete digital audio file that results.

shell voicing Used commonly when comping, or accompanying, in jazz, shell voicings strip complex chords to their simplest form, normally a third and a seventh. This approach allows players a great deal of flexibility, both in terms of maintaining a sense of harmonic movement and in reharmonizing familiar material.

SIDMetal A style of music that combines the lo-fi sound of the Commodore's SID chip with heavy, distorted guitars and driving percussion.

SidStation A hardware synthesizer, manufactured by Swedish company Elektron, that used the Commodore's SID chip as its main sound source.

Sound Interface Device (SID) The PSG in Commodore's C64. Designed by Bob Yannes as a full synthesizer-on-a-chip, the SID was the most advanced PSG on any of the 8-bit platforms.

Soundmonitor A music sequencer for the Commodore C64 that presented music data alphanumerically in three vertically scrolling tracks. This was the inspiration for soundtracker programs.

soundtracker A music sequencer that combines sample playback or synthesis for sound generation and a pattern-based layout for editing song data. This has become the dominant, though not the only, interface for chip music making.

Television Interface Adaptor (TIA) The combination display chip and sound generator from the Atari VCS.

vamping In music, improvising a repeating rhythmic or harmonic pattern on a chord sequence, often as a holding pattern or an accompaniment to an intro.

vibrato As a synthesis effect, modulating the frequency of a signal to add dynamic movement.

virtual (or implied) polyphony A series of compositional or musical arrangement techniques that are intended to create the perceptual effect of two or more musical voices where there is actually only one.

Z80 The 8-bit microprocessor, designed and manufactured by Zilog, that was used in the Sinclair ZX Spectrum, the Game Boy, and several other consoles and arcade machines.

ZX Spectrum An 8-bit microcomputer based around a Zilog Z80 CPU. The ZX Spectrum was the leading home computer platform in the United Kingdom in the early 1980s. A modified design was sold in the United States as the Timex Sinclair 2048.

References

PRINT AND ONLINE

Akera, A. (2006). *Calculating a Natural World: Scientists, Engineers, and Computers during the Rise of U.S. Cold War Research*. Cambridge, MA: MIT Press.

Åkesson, L. (2010). "The Chipophone," *Linus Akesson*. http://www.linusakesson.net/chipophone/.

Alberts, G., & Oldenziel, R. (2014). *Hacking Europe: From Computer Cultures to Demoscenes*. London: Springer Verlag.

"Altair ... on the Road." (1975). *Computer Notes*, 1(2): 1.

Altice, N. (2015). *I Am Error: The Nintendo Family Computer/Entertainment System Platform*. Cambridge, MA: MIT Press.

Anarchy. (1991). *Benson Pack 56*. http://janeway.exotica.org.uk/release.php?id=12565.

Anon. (n.d.). "SID Tune Information List." *High Voltage SID Collection*. http://www.hvsc.de/download/C64Music/DOCUMENTS/STIL.txt.

Armer, P. (1980). "SHARE—A Eulogy to Cooperative Effort." *IEEE Annals of the History of Computing*, 2(2): 122–129.

Augenbraun, J., & Greenley, L. (1991). *Amiga Hardware Reference Manual*. Reading, MA: Addison-Wesley.

Bach, J. S. (1867). *Toccata and Fugue in D Minor*. Rust, W. (ed.). Leipzig: Breitkopf und Härtel.

Bach, J. S. (1879). *Violin Partita No. 2 in D Minor*. Dörffel, A. (ed). Leipzig: Breitkopf und Härtel.

Bach, J. S. (2005). *The Well-Tempered Clavier: 48 Preludes and Fugues: Complete Books I and II for Piano*. New York: Schirmer.

Baer, R. H. (2005). *Videogames: In the Beginning*. Springfield, NJ: Rolenta Press.

Bagnall, B. (2006). *On the Edge: The Spectacular Rise and Fall of Commodore*. Winnipeg: Variant Press.

Barker, H., & Taylor, Y. (2008). *Faking It: The Quest for Authenticity in Popular Music*. London: Faber.

Barron, C. (2012). "Smithsonian Museum Explores the Art of Gaming." *Washington Post*, April 27. https://www.washingtonpost.com/lifestyle/kidspost/smithsonian-museum-explores-the-art-of-gaming/2012/04/26/gIQAUGYsjT_story.html.

Beethoven, L. von. (1802). *Piano Sonata No. 14, Op. 27 No. 2, 'Moonlight'*. 1st ed. Vienna: Gio. Cappi e Comp.

Beethoven, L. von. (1867). *Für Elise*. 1st ed. Nohl, L. (ed.). Stuttgart: J. G. Cotta.

Bennett, A. (2005). "Virtual Subculture? Youth, Identity and the Internet." In Bennett, A., and Kahn-Harris, K. (eds.), *After Subculture: Critical Studies in Contemporary Youth Culture*. Basingstoke, UK: Palgrave Macmillan, pp. 162–172.

Benvenutti, D. A. (2011). *Atari 2600 Frequency and Tuning Chart*. Academic Computer Club Umeå University. http://www.acc.umu.se/~tjoppen/files/vcs/Atari%202600%20Frequency%20And%20Tuning%20 Chart%20v1.1%20%28PDF%20FULL%20DOCUMENT%29.pdf.

Berk, A. (1979). "MK14 Review." *Practical Electronics*, May: 50.

Berners-Lee, T., & Fischetti, M. (2011). *Weaving the Web: The Original Design and Ultimate Destiny of the World Wide Web by Its Inventor*. New York: Harper Business.

Beverage. (2013). *Chiptune v. Fakebit: Does It Really Matter*. https://www.reddit.com/r/chiptunes/comments/19plo6/chiptune_v_fakebit_does_it_really_matter/.

Bizet, G. (1877). *Carmen*. 1st ed. Paris: Choudens Pére et Fils.

Blakeman, M. C. (1983). "The Music Man: Ed Bogas Breaks the Video Game Sound Barrier." *Video Games*, 2(2): 18–20.

Blargg. (2004). *NES APU Sound Hardware Reference*. Slack.net. http://www.slack.net/~ant/nes-emu/apu_ref.txt.

Bloom, S. (1982). "From Cutoffs to Pinstripes." *Video Games*, 1(3): 37–50.

Blyth, T. (1981). "Computing for the Masses? Constructing a British Culture of Computing in the Home." In Tatnall, A. (ed.), *Reflections on the History of Computing: Preserving Memories and Sharing Stories*. Heidelberg: Springer, pp. 231–242.

Boden, M. (1990). *The Creative Mind: Myths and Mechanisms*. London: Weidenfield and Nicholson.

Borzyskowski, G. (1996). "The Hacker Demo Scene and Its Cultural Artefacts." In *Cybermind Conference 1996*, Perth Australia. pp. 1–23.

Bowman, N. D., Kowert, R., & Ferguson, C. J. (2016). "The Impact of Video Game Play on Human (and Orc) Creativity." In Green, G., & Kaufman, J. C. (eds.), *Video Games and Creativity*. Waltham, MA: Academic Press, pp. 41–62.

"Buckner & Garcia: Biography." (n.d.). *Billboard*. http://www.billboard.com/artist/298482/buckner-garcia/biography.

Burgess, J., & Green, J. (2009). *YouTube: Online Video and Participatory Culture*. Cambridge: Polity Press.

Burton, C., & Bowness, A. (2015). *Ben Daglish BIT Brighton 2015 Interview (Preview)*. c64audio. Published 1 March. https://www.youtube.com/watch?v=qhv6U8Wm0GY.

Bussy, P. (2006). *Kraftwerk: Man, Machine and Music*. London: SAF.

Byrne, F. (2009). "Nelly Furtado, Timbaland Sued for Plagiarism." *New Musical Express*. Published 17 June. http://www.nme.com/news/music/timbaland-11-1307562.

Cage, J. (1940). *Bacchanale for Prepared Piano*. Leipzig, Germany: Edition Peters.

"Calculator Maker Integrates Downwards." (1976). *New Scientist*, 71(1017): 541.

Calvert, D. (2014). "Ninterview: Smooth McGroove on a Life in Game Music." *Nintendo Life*. Published 7 March. http://www.nintendolife.com/news/2014/03/ninterview_smooth_mcgroove_on_a_life_in_game_music.

Campbell-Kelly, M. (2004). *From Airline Reservations to Sonic the Hedgehog: A History of the Software Industry*. Cambridge, MA: MIT Press.

Carlsson, A. (2009). "The Forgotten Pioneers of Creative Hacking and Social Networking—Introducing the Demoscene." In Cubitt, S., & Thomas, P. (eds.), *Re:live: Media Art Histories 2009 Conference Proceedings*. Melbourne, Australia: The University of Melbourne & Victorian College of the Arts and Music, pp. 16–20.

Carter, D. M. (2011). *Money Games: Profiting from the Convergence of Sports and Entertainment*. Stanford, CA: Stanford Business.

Chopin, F. (1879). *Marche Funèbre, Op. 72*. Scholtz, H. (ed.). Leipzig: C. F. Peters.

"Code Britannia: Tim Follin." (2015). *Eurogamer*, January 2. http://www.eurogamer.net/articles/2014-01-02-code-britannia-tim-follin.

Cohen, J. (2007). "Nine Inch Nails Celebrates Free Agent Status." *Billboard*. Published 8 October. http://www.billboard.com/articles/news/1048419/nine-inch-nails-celebrates-free-agent-status.

Coleman, E. G. (2013). *Coding Freedom: The Ethics and Aesthetics of Hacking*. Princeton: Princeton University Press.

Collins, K. (2008). *Game Sound: An Introduction to the History, Theory, and Practice of Video Game Music and Sound Design*. Cambridge, MA: MIT Press.

Collins, K. (2014). "A History of Handheld and Mobile Video Game Sound." In Gopinath, S., & Stanyek, J. (eds.), *The Oxford Handbook of Mobile Music Studies*, vol. 2. New York: Oxford University Press, pp. 383–401.

Commodore 64 Programmer's Reference Guide. (1982). Carmel, IN: Commodore Business Machines and Howard W. Sams.

Commodore 64 User's Guide. (1982). Carmel, IN: Commodore Business Machines and Howard W. Sams.

Cox, K. (1984). "Keyboard Strikes Sour Note." *TPUG Magazine*, 11: 9.

Craig, P. (2006). *Software Piracy Exposed*. Rockland, MA: Syngress.

Crigger, L. (2007). "Searching for Gunei Yokoi." *Escapist*. Published 25 December. http://www.escapistmagazine.com/articles/view/video-games/issues/issue_129/2744-Searching-for-Gunpei-Yokoi.

Csikszentmihalyi, M. (2009). *Flow: The Psychology of Optimal Experience*. New York: Harper Row.

Dacre, H. (1892). *Daisy Bell (Bicycle Built for Two)*. Sydney: J. Albert.

Dalzell, T. (2010). *Flappers 2 Rappers: American Youth Slang*. Mineola, NY: Dover.

Dance, J. (1996). "Martin Galway Interview! (Part 1)." *Commodore Zone*, 6: 6–9.

Daniel, Y. (2011). *Caribbean and Atlantic Diaspora Dance Igniting Citizenship*. Urbana: University of Illinois Press.

Dawes, A. (2004). "Play It Again SID." *Retro Gamer*, 4: 28–34.

Dean, R. T. (2011). *The Oxford Handbook of Computer Music*. New York: Oxford University Press.

Dennis, J. B., Kerllenevich, N., & Levy, R. J. "XXXI. COMPUTER RESEARCH." *Quarterly Progress Report*, 76: 359–360. https://dspace.mit.edu/bitstream/handle/1721.1/54074/RLE_QPR_076_XXXI.pdf

Dillon, R. (2010). *On the Way to Fun: An Emotion-Based Approach to Successful Game Design*. Natick, MA: A. K. Peters.

Dillon, R. (2011). *The Golden Age of Video Games: The Birth of a Multi-billion Dollar Industry*. Natick, MA: A. K. Peters.

Dillon, R. (2015). *Ready: A Commodore 64 Retrospective*. Singapore: Springer Singapore.

Dixon, W. W. (2015). *Black and White Cinema: A Short History*. New Brunswick, NJ: Rutgers University Press.

Dompier, S. (1976). "Music of a Sort." *Dr. Dobb's Journal of Computer Calisthenics and Orthodontia*, 1(2): 6–7.

Donovan, T., & Garriott, R. (2010). *Replay: The History of Video Games*. Lewes, East Sussex, UK: Yellow Ant.

Doody, D. (2012). *Interview: Chipzel*. The Arcade. Published 1 November. http://www.the-arcade.ie/2012/11/interview-chipzel/

Doornbusch, P. (2009). "A Chronology of Computer Music and Related Events." In Dean, R. (ed.), *The Oxford Handbook of Computer Music*. New York: Oxford University Press, pp. 554–582.

Dorfman, D. (1985). "Commodore's Dive." *New York Magazine*, 18(19): 16–18.

Dunn, J. (2005). "Robocop or Ariston?" *Ocean Experience*. Published 24 February. http://oceanexp.proboards.com/thread/404/robocop-ariston.

"Editors' Choice Awards." (1986). *Amiga World*, 2(6): 74–75.

Einstein, A., & Infeld, L. (1938). *The Evolution of Physics*. New York: Simon and Schuster.

Ellsworth, J. (2012). "[Jeri Ellsworth] on making her c64 bass keytar." *Hackaday*. http://hackaday.com/2012/07/09/jeri-ellsworth-on-making-her-c64-bass-keytar/.

Enders, B. (2017). "From Idiophone to Touchpad. The Technological Development to the Virtual Musical Instrument." In Bovermann, T., de Campo, A., Egermann, H., Hardjowirogo, S.-I., & Weinzierl, S. (eds.) *Musical Instruments in the 21st Century*. Singapore: Springer Singapore, pp. 45–58.

Ensminger, D. A. (2016). *The Politics of Punk: Protest and Revolt from the Streets*. Lanham, MD: Rowman and Littlefield.

Erickson, H. (2005). *Television Cartoon Shows*. Jefferson, NC: McFarland.

Espenschied, D. (2004). "Cool Cool Cool." In *The Microbuilder Community Construction Kit Book*. http://microbuilder.com/docs/book/microbuilder_book_r3_07-Cool_cool_cool.pdf.

Evans, M., & Lord, G. (1992). "Hitting the Big Time." *Amiga Format*, 37: 24–26.

Evans, R. (2008). *Remember the 80s: Now That's What I Call Nostalgia*. London, UK: Anova.

Everest, F. G. (1982). *BI-PAK ZON X-81 Programmable Sound Generator Instruction Manual*. Ware, UK: BI-PAK.

Falconer, P. (1984). *Commodore 64 Sound & Graphics*. Tring: Melbourne House.

Ferrell, K., & Keizer, G. (1988). "Conversations: Epyx Grows with David Morse." *Compute!*, September: 10–11.

Finkel, A. (1981). *VIC 20 Programmer's Reference Guide*. Carmel, IN: Commodore Business Machines and Howard W. Sams.

Firestone, M. (2011). *Nintendo: The Company and Its Founders*. Edina, MN: ABDO.

Follin, T. (1987). "Program Pitstop: Star Tip 2." *Your Sinclair*, 20: 57.

Fox, K. J. (1987). "Real Punks and Pretenders: The Social Organization of a Counterculture." *Journal of Contemporary Ethnography*, 16(3): 344–370.

Freiberger, P. (1982). "History of Microcomputing, Part 1: Homebrew Club." *Infoworld*, 4(7): 13–14, 17.

Gantz, J. (1986). "Tech Street: Home Computers Will Survive If They Make It into Businesses." *Infoworld*, 8(50): 37.

Gates, B. (1975a). "Software Contest Winners Announced." *Computer Notes*, 1(2): 1.

Gates, B. (1975b). "An Open Letter to Hobbyists." *Computer Notes*, 1(9): 3.

Gates, B. (1975c). *Homebrew Computer Club Newsletter*, 2(1): 2.

Gates, B. (1976). "A Second and Final Letter" *Computer Notes*, 1(11): 5.

Gaunt, S., & Kay, S. (2003). *The Troubadours: An Introduction*. Cambridge: Cambridge University Press.

Gazzard, A. (2016). *Now the Chips Are Down: The BBC Micro*. Cambridge, MA: MIT Press.

Ghazala, Q. R. (2004). "The Folk Music of Chance Electronics: Circuit-Bending the Modern Coconut." *Leonardo Music Journal*, 14: 97–104.

Gilroy, P. (1993). *The Black Atlantic: Modernity and Double-Consciousness*. Cambridge, MA: Harvard University Press.

Gleichmar, J. (2012). *Theory v.3.0. Jahtari*. http://jahtari.org/archive/main/theory.htm.

Goggin, G., & McLelland, M. J. (2017). *The Routledge Companion to Global Internet Histories*. New York: Routledge.

Goldberg, M., & Vendel, C. (2012). *Atari Inc.: Business Is Fun*. Carmel, NY: Syzygy.

Goldstein, H. (2011). "Scott Pilgrim vs. the World: Game Review." *IGN*. http://uk.ign.com/articles/2010/08/25/scott-pilgrim-vs-the-world-game-review.

Goodman, D. (1983). Pac-Mania. *Creative Computing Video & Arcade Games*, 1(1): 125.

Gorges, F., & Yamazaki, I. (2010). *The History of Nintendo: 1889–1980*. Triel-Sur-Seine, France: Pix'n Love.

Goriunova, O. (2012). *Art Platforms and Cultural Production on the Internet*. New York: Routledge.

Gottshalk, K. (2008). "Tristan Perich". *Wire*, 297: 18.

Graetz, J. M. (1981). "The Origin of Spacewar." *Creative Computing*, August: 56–67.

Graham, P. (2004). *Hackers & Painters: Big Ideas from the Computer Age*. Sebastopol, CA: O'Reilly Media.

Grazian, D. (2013). "Digital Underground: Musical Spaces and Microscenes in the Post-industrial City." In Holt, F., & Wergin, C. (eds.), *Musical Performance and the Changing City: Post-industrial Contexts in Europe and the United States*. New York: Routledge, pp. 127–151.

Grieg, E. (1888). *Peer Gynt Suite. No. 1, Op. 46*. Leipzig: Edition Peters.

Gudmundsson, G., Lindberg, U., Michelsen, M., & Weisenthaut, H. (2002). "Brit Crit: Turning Points in British Rock Criticism, 1960–1990." In Jones, S. (ed.), *Pop Music and the Press*. Philadelphia: Temple University Press, pp. 41–64.

Gudmunson, C. (2011). "Zelda Past and Future: An Interview with Koji Kondo and Eiji Aonuma." *Games Radar*. Published 9 November. http://www.gamesradar.com/zelda-past-and-future-interview-koji-kondo-and-eiji-aonuma/.

Guins, R. (2014). *Game After: A Cultural Study of Video Game Afterlife*. Cambridge, MA: MIT Press.

Harker, D. (1985). *Fakesong: The Manufacture of British "Folksong" 1700 to the Present Day*. Milton Keynes, UK: Open University Press.

Hasegawa, Y. (2010). *Rediscovering Japanese Business Leadership: 12 Japanese Managers and the Companies They're Leading to New Growth*. Singapore: Wiley.

Hearsum, P., & Inglis, I. (2015). "The Emancipation of Music Video: YouTube and the Cultural Politics of Supply and Demand." In Richardson, J. (ed.), *The Oxford Handbook of New Audiovisual Aesthetics*. Oxford: Oxford University Press, pp. 483–500.

Herman, G. (1985). *Micro Music for the Commodore 64 and BBC Computer*. London: Macmillan.

Herman, L. (1994). *Phoenix: The Fall & Rise of Home Videogames*. 2nd ed. Union, NJ: Rolenta Press.

Herring, R. (2012). "Never Try to Impress the People You Most Admire in Life." *Metro*. Published 22 October. http://metro.co.uk/2012/10/22/richard-herring-never-try-to-impress-the-people-you-most-admire-in-life-606030/.

Herzog, M. (1988). *David Anthony Kraft's Comics Interview*, 54: 41–51.

Hesmondhalgh, D. (1999). "Indie: The Institutional Politics and Aesthetics of a Popular Music Genre." *Cultural Studies*, 13(1): 34–61.

"Hip Hop: We Do the Spectrum Bop." (1987). *Sinclair User*, 65: 32–33.

Hjelm, T. (2009). *Nerdy Nights Sound*. http://nintendoage.com/forum/messageview.cfm?catid= 22& threadid=22484.

Hoad, P. (2014). "Tetris: How We Made the Addictive Computer Game." *Guardian*, June 2. https://www.theguardian.com/culture/2014/jun/02/how-we-made-tetris.

Hoban, P. (1985). "Looks Great, Manny, but Will It Sell?" *New York Magazine*, 18(30): 15.

Hogan, T. (1981). "From Zero to a Billion in Five Years." *Infoworld*, 3(17): 6.

Hoggar, S. G. (2006). *Mathematics of Digital Images: Creation, Compression, Restoration, Recognition*. Cambridge: Cambridge University Press.

Holzmann, A. (1901). *Blaze Away*. New York: Feist and Frankenthaler.

Hood, B. M. (2009). *Supersense: From Superstition to Religion—The Brain Science of Belief*. London: Constable.

Hopkins, C. (2015). *Chiptune Music: An Exploration of Compositional Techniques as Found in Sunsoft Games for the Nintendo Entertainment System and Famicom from 1988–1992*. New York: Five Towns College.

Horn, A. (2009). *Juke Box Britain: Americanisation and Youth Culture, 1945–60*. Manchester, UK: Manchester University Press.

Houze, R. (2016). *New Mythologies in Design and Culture: Reading Signs and Symbols in the Visual Landscape*. New York: Bloomsbury Academic.

Hubner, J., & Kistner, W. F. (1983). "What Went Wrong at Atari?" *Infoworld*, 5(48): 151–158.

Hülsbeck, C. (1986a). "Musik ... Wie noch nie." *64-er*, 10: 51, 53–64.

Hülsbeck, C. (1986b). "Über den Wolken." *64-er*, 6: 173–176.

Hunt, A., & Kirk, R. (2000). "Mapping Strategies for Musical Performance-Trends in Gestural Control of Music." In Wanderley, M., & Battier, M. (eds.), *Trends in Gestural Control of Music*. Paris: Institut de Recherche et Coordination Acoustique Musique, pp. 231–258.

HVSC Admin Team. (2007). *The High Voltage SID Collection: [1–2] The HVSC Project*. http://www.hvsc.de/info.htm.

Inoue, O. (2010). *Nintendo Magic: Winning the Videogame Wars*. New York: Vertical.

Isaacson, W. (2011). *Steve Jobs*. New York: Simon and Schuster.

Isaacson, W. (2015). *The Innovators: How a Group of Inventors, Hackers, Geniuses and Geeks Created the Digital Revolution*. London: Simon and Schuster.

Iwata, S. (2010). "Iwata Asks: Vol. 5—Original Super Mario Developers. *Nintendo UK*." https://www.nintendo.co.uk/Iwata-Asks/Super-Mario-Bros-25th-Anniversary/Vol-5-Original-Super-Mario-Developers/2-The-New-Guys-Too-/2-The-New-Guys-Too--212791.html.

Jahdi, R. (2014). "In Praise of Mr. Bungle: America's Greatest Gonzo-Metallers, and Mike Patton's Best Band." *Fact*, August 1. http://www.factmag.com/2014/08/01/in-praise-of-mr-bungle-gonzo-metal-at-its-finest-and-still-mike-pattons-greatest-band/.

Jared-IGN. (2013). "An Interview with Machinae Supremacy's Robert Stjärnström." *IGN*, September7.http://uk.ign.com/blogs/jared-ign/2013/09/07/an-interview-with-machinae-supremacys-robert-stjarnstrom.

"Jay Miner: The Father of the Amiga." (1988). *Amiga User International*, 2(6): 20–21, 64.

Jazzcat. (2002). "Interview with Thomas Detert." *Vandalism News no. 37*. Published 13 January. http://www.atlantis-prophecy.org/recollection/?load=interviews&id_interview=173.

Johnson, J. (2006). "Blip Festival: 8-Bit Is Enough." *Wired*. Published 3 December. https://www.wired.com/2006/12/blip_festival_8/.

Johnston, B. (2007). *"Maximum Clarity" and Other Writings on Music*. Urbana: University of Illinois Press.

Jones, S. E. (2008). *The Meaning of Video Games: Gaming and Textual Strategies*. New York: Routledge.

Kefauver, A. P., & Patschke, D. (2007). *Fundamentals of Digital Audio*. Madison, WI: A-R Editions.

Kennedy, V. (2013). *Strange Brew: Metaphors of Magic and Science in Rock Music*. Newcastle upon Tyne, UK: Cambridge Scholars.

Kent, S. L. (2001). *The Ultimate History of Video Games from Pong to Pokemon: The Story behind the Craze That Touched Our Lives and Changed the World*. Roseville, CA: Prima.

Kinder, M. (1993). *Playing with Power in Movies, Television, and Video Games: From Muppet Babies to Teenage Mutant Ninja Turtles*. Berkeley: University of California Press.

King, E. (2010). *Free for All: The Internet's Transformation of Journalism*. Evanston, IL: Northwestern University Press.

King, M. (2016). *Men, Masculinity and the Beatles*. New York: Routledge.

Knowles, J. (2010). "How Computer Games Are Creating New Art and Music." *BBC News*. Published 9 June. http://www.bbc.co.uk/news/10260769.

Koenig, H. (n.d.). *The Post Horn Galop*. London: Musical Bouquet.

Kohler, C. (2007). "VGL: Koji Kondo Interview." *Wired*. Published 11 March. https://www.wired.com/2007/03/vgl_koji_kondo_/.

Kohler, C., & Yoshida, S. (2016). *Power-up: How Japanese Video Games Gave the World an Extra Life*. Mineola, NY: Dover.

Kotlinski, J. (2009). *Amiga Music Programs 1986–1995*. Goto80.com. http://goto80.blipp.com/wp-content/themes/goto80/datafoder/kotlinski%20%282009%29%20amiga%20music%20programs%2086-95.pdf.

Kowalski, G. (1985). "A Mickey Mouse Protection." *Hardcore Computist*, 25: 5.

Kregor, J., & Kregor, J. (2010). *Liszt as Transcriber*. New York: Cambridge University Press.

Kreps, D. (2007). "Nine Inch Nails' Trent Reznor Slams Records Labels for Sorry State of the Industry." *Rolling Stone*, May 14. http://www.rollingstone.com/music/news/nine-inch-nails-trent-reznor-slams-records-labels-for-sorry-state-of-the-industry-20070514.

Kreps, D. (2008). "Nine Inch Nails' 'Ghosts I–IV' Makes Trent Reznor a Millionaire." *Rolling Stone*, March 13. http://www.rollingstone.com/music/news/nine-inch-nails-ghosts-i-iv-makes-trent-reznor-an-instant-millionaire-20080313.

Laing, G. (2004). *Digital Retro*. Alameda, CA: SYBEX.

Leung, M. (n.d.). *Biography*. VideoGame Pianist. http://videogamepianist.com/biography/.

Levy, S. (2010). *Hackers: Heroes of the Computer Revolution—25th Anniversary Edition*. Sebastopol, CA: O'Reilly Media.

Liszt, F. (1876). *Danse Macabre, Op. 40 (Saint-Saëns, Camille)*. Paris: Durand, Schoenwerk.

Loguidice, B., & Barton, M. (2014). *Vintage Game Consoles: An Inside Look at Apple, Atari, Commodore, Nintendo, and the Greatest Gaming Platforms of All Time*. New York: Focal Press.

Lowey, I., & Prince, S. (2014). *The Graphic Art of the Underground: A Countercultural History*. London: Bloomsbury.

Lowood, H. (2009). "Videogames in Computer Space: The Complex History of Pong." *IEEE Annals of the History of Computing*, 31(3): 5–19.

Ludwig, B. (2012). "Der C64 war mein Mädchen: Heimcomputer machte Kasseler erfolgreich." *HNA*. Published 12 January. https://www.hna.de/kassel/der-c64-mein-maedchen-heimcomputer-machte-kasseler-erfolgreich-1560815.html.

MacDonald, I. (2003). *The People's Music*. London: Pimlico.

Mace, S. (1983). "Jack Tramiel Buys Atari." *InfoWorld*, 6(31): 11.

Mace, S. (1984). "Atari's Creditors Confer." *Infoworld*, 6(38): 14.

Mace, S. (1985a). "Amiga Shown with PC Option." *Infoworld*, 7(31): 23–26.

Mace, S. (1985b). "Christmas Contenders." *Infoworld*, 7(48): 27–28.

Mace, S. (1986). "Commodore Dodges Financial Bullet." *Infoworld*, 8(9): 3.

MacFarlane, K. (2011). "Frankie Goes to Hollywood & Gets There behind the 'Wheel' of a Classic Commodore 64." *Pop Matters*. Published 10 January. http://www.popmatters.com/column/134877-frankie-goes-to-hollywood-commodore-64-ocean-software-1985/.

Magic of Nah-Kolor. (n.d.). *Portrait: 4-Mat of Orb & Ate Bit*. http://hugi.scene.org/online/hugi36/hugi%2036%20-%20demoscene%20interviews%20magic%20portrait%204-mat%20of%20orb%20&%20ate%20bit.htm.

Magni, E. (2012). "Interview: Jahtari." *United Reggae*, January 22. http://unitedreggae.com/articles/n825/012212/interview-jahtari.

Maher, J. (2012). *The Future Was Here: The Commodore Amiga*. Cambridge, MA: MIT Press.

Majors, D. (2012). "Artist of the Chiptunes Genre Featured at Unblurred." *Pittsburgh Post-Gazette*, June 2. http://www.post-gazette.com/ae/music/2012/06/01/Artist-of-the-chiptunes-genre-featured-at-Unblurred/stories/201206010264.

Mangram, L. (1986). "Merely Mangram." *Crash*, 26: 14.

Mapstone, R. (1980). *An Interview with R. Blair Smith*. Charles Babbage Institute, Center for the History of Information Processing, University of Minnesota. https://conservancy.umn.edu/bitstream/handle/11299/107637/oh034rbs.pdf?sequence=1.

Markoff, J. (2002). "A Long Time Ago, in a Lab Far Away …" *New York Times,* February 28. http://www.nytimes.com/2002/02/28/technology/a-long-time-ago-in-a-lab-far-away.html.

Marshall, L. (2014). *The International Recording Industries*. London: Routledge.

Mattel. (1976). *Auto Race Game Instructions*. Hawthorne, CA: Mattel Electronics.

McAlpine, K. (2016). "BitBox!: A Case Study Interface for Teaching Real-Time Adaptive Music Composition for Video Games." *Journal of Music, Technology and Education*, 9(2): 191–208.

McAlpine, K., Bett, M., & Scanlan, J. (2009). "Approaches to Creating Real-Time Adaptive Music in Interactive Entertainment: A Musical Perspective." In *Proceedings of the AES*. New York: Audio Engineering Society. http://www.aes.org/e-lib/browse.cfm?elib=15168.

McCullaugh, J. (1982). "ActiVision: It's All in the Game." *Billboard*, June 19: 15.

McFadden, M. M. (1987). "Antique Soft Key for Frogger." *Computist*, 41: 28–29.

McLaren, M. (2003). "8-Bit Punk." *Wired*, 11(11). https://www.wired.com/2003/11/mclaren/.

McMahon, J. (2010). "Edgar Wright: Why the Scott Pilgrim Soundtrack Matters As Much As the Movie." *Guardian*, August 18. https://www.theguardian.com/music/2010/aug/18/edgar-wright-scott-pilgrim-soundtrack.

McNamara, J. (2008). "Shotfest 2 Featuring the Minibosses at Yucca Tap Room." *Phoenix New Times*. Published 14 April. http://www.phoenixnewtimes.com/music/shotfest-2-featuring-the-minibosses-at-yucca-tap-room-6593511.

Melissinos, C., & O'Rourke, P. (2013). *The Art of Video Games: From Pac-Man to Mass Effect*. New York: Welcome Book.

Menotti, G. (2009). "Executable Cinema: Demos, Screensavers and Videogames as Audiovisual Formats." In Cubitt, S., & Thomas, P. (eds.), *Re:live: Media Art Histories 2009 Conference Proceedings*. Melbourne, Australia: The University of Melbourne & Victorian College of the Arts and Music, pp. 109–113.

Miner, J. (1983). *Computer Design*, 22(1–3): 159.

Montfort, N. (2014). *10 PRINT CHR$(205.5 RND(1)) GOTO 10*. Cambridge, MA: MIT Press.

Montfort, N., & Bogost, I. (2009). *Racing the Beam: The Atari Video Computer System*. Cambridge, MA: MIT Press.

Moore, F. (1975). "It's a Hobby." *Homebrew Computer Club Newsletter*, 4: 1.

Morris, G. (2004). "Open Letter to Malcolm McLaren by gwEm." *Micromusic.net*. http://micromusic.net/public_letter_gwEm.html.

Morris, D., & Hartas, L. (2005). *Machinima: The Complete Guide to Making Animated Movies in 3D Virtual Environments*. Lewes, UK: Ilex.

Moskowitz, D. (2006). *Caribbean Popular Music: An Encyclopaedia of Reggae, Mento, Ska, Rock Steady, and Dancehall*. Westport, CT: Greenwood Press.

Mozart, W. A. (1883). *Eine kleine Nachtmusik, K. 525*. Leipzig: Breitkopf und Härtel.

Mozart, W. A. (n.d.). *Piano Sonata No. 11 in A major, K. 331/300i*. 1st ed. Vienna: Artaria.

Murrell, N. S., Spencer, W. D., & McFarlane, A. A. (1998). *Chanting Down Babylon: The Rastafari Reader.* Philadelphia: Temple University Press.

Nagashima, Y. (1998). "Biosensorfusion: New Interfaces for Interactive Multimedia Art." In Simoni, M, Conference Chair (ed.), *Proceedings of the International Computer Music Conference.* Ann Arbor, MI: University of Michigan and the ICMA, pp. 129–132.

Nelson, M. (1993). "The Jay Miner Interview." *Amiga User International*, March: Coverdisk.

"New Developments from Commodore." (1980). *Byte*, 5(4): 115.

Noble, M. (2012). "This Atari 2600 Chiptune Guitar Rocks Like It's 1977." *PC World.* Published 2 January. http://www.pcworld.com/article/247169/this_atari_2600_chiptune_guitar_rocks_like_its_1977. html.

Nova, N. (2014). *8-Bit Reggae: Collision and Creolization.* Paris: Near Future Laboratory and Volumique.

N.S. (1983). "Atari 5200—First Impressions." *Popular Mechanics*, April: 84.

O'Brien, J. (2012). "Video Game Art Gets the Gallery Treatment." *BBC News.* Published 16 March. http://www.bbc.co.uk/news/magazine-17373879.

O'Connor, A. (2008). *Punk Record Labels and the Struggle for Autonomy: The Emergence of DIY.* Lanham, MD: Lexington Books.

O'Keefe, N. (2008). *Software Games in the Danish Experience Economy.* Frederiksberg, Denmark: Imagine—Creative Industries Research, Copenhagen Business School.

O'Regan, G. (2015). *Pillars of Computing: A Compendium of Select, Pivotal Technology Firms.* Cham, Switzerland : Springer.

Otero, J. (2014). "A Music Trivia Tour with Nintendo's Koji Kondo." *IGN*, December 10. http://uk.ign.com/articles/2014/12/10/a-music-trivia-tour-with-nintendos-koji-kondo.

Paoletta, M. (2002). "Nü-Electro Sound Emerges." *Billboard*, 27 July: 1, 66.

Pascoe, R. D. (1975). "Electronic Wheel of Fortune: Simulates Mechanical Game." *Popular Electronics Magazine*, October: 69–70.

Paul, L. J. (2014). "For the Love of Chiptune." In Collins, K., Kapralos, B., & Tessler, H. (eds.), *The Oxford Handbook of Interactive Audio.* New York: Oxford University Press, pp. 507–530.

Paumgarten, N. (2010). "Master of Play." *New Yorker*, 86: 41–86.

Payne, W. B. (2006). "Nintendo Rock: Nostalgia or Sound of the Future." *Harvard Crimson*, February 14. http://www.thecrimson.com/article/2006/2/14/nintendo-rock-nostalgia-or-sound-of/.

PC Plus. (2010). "Inside the World of the Chiptune Artists." *Techradar.* Published 28 November. http://www.techradar.com/news/audio/inside-the-world-of-the-chiptune-artists-909471/2.

Penn, G. (1985). "Hyper Sports." *Zzap64!*, 5: 14.

Peralta, L., & Peralta, N. (2006). "Pac-Man Fever! An Interview with Buckner and Garcia." *Jawbone*, 117. http://jawboneradio.blogspot.co.uk/2006/06/jawbone-117-pac-man-fever-interview.html.

Persons, D. (1983a). "Dig Dug." *Video Games*, 2(2): 56.

Persons, D. (1983b). "Q*Bert." *Video Games*, 2(3): 65–66.

Pinch, T., & Trocco, F. (2004). *Analog Days: The Invention and Impact of the Moog Synthesizer.* Cambridge, MA: Harvard University Press, pp. 254–264.

Pinch, T., & Trocco, F. (2012). "Shaping the Synthesizer." In Sterne, J. (ed.), *The Sound Studies Reader.* New York: Routledge.

Platt, C. (1984). *Graphics Guide to the COMMODORE 64.* Berkeley: Sybex.

Polymeropoulou, M. (2014). "Chipmusic, Fakebit and the Discourse of Authenticity in the Chipscene." *WiderScreen.* Published 1 February. http://widerscreen.fi/assets/polymeropoulou-wider-1-2-2014. pdf.

Pugh, E. W. (1996). *Building IBM: Shaping an Industry and Its Technology.* Cambridge, MA: MIT Press.

Rachmaninov, S. (1934). *Rhapsody on a Theme of Paganini, Op. 43.* London: Boosey and Hawkes.

Radcliffe, J. (1983). *Towards Computer Literacy: The BBC Computer Literacy Project; 1979–1983.* London: British Broadcasting Corporation.

Raw, L. (2009). *The Ridley Scott Encyclopedia.* Lanham, MD: Scarecrow Press.

Reid, G. (1999). "Synth Secrets: Part 7, Envelopes, Gates & Triggers." *Sound on Sound*, November: 128–134.

Remix64.com. (2013). *Computer Game Music—The Rock 'n Roll Years.* Remix64.com http://www.remix64.com/articles/computer-game-music-the-rock-n-roll-years.html.

Reunanen, M. (2014). "How Those Crackers Became Us Demosceners." *WiderScreen*, 1–2. http://widerscreen.fi/numerot/2014-1-2/crackers-became-us-demosceners/.

Roads, C. (1980). "Interview with Max Mathews." *Computer Music Journal*, 4(4): 15–22.

Roads, C. (1996). *The Computer Music Tutorial*. Cambridge, MA: MIT Press.

Robindoré, B. (1996). "Eskhaté Ereuna: Extending the Limits of Musical Thought—Comments on and by Iannis Xenakis." *Computer Music Journal*, 20(4): 11–16.

Rosas, J. (N.d.). *Sobre las Olas: Über den Wellen. Vals pour Piano*. Leipzig: Musik-Verlags-Anstalt Rudolf Pawliska.

Rowell, R. (2011). *YouTube: The Company and Its Founders*. Edina, MN: ABDO.

Ruggill, J. E., & McAllister, K. S. (2011). *Gaming Matters: Art, Science, Magic, and the Computer Game Medium*. Tuscaloosa: University of Alabama Press.

Russ, M. (2013). *Sound Synthesis and Sampling*. New York: Focal Press.

Ryan, J. (2013a). *A History of the Internet and the Digital Future*. London: Reaktion Books.

Ryan, J. (2013b). *Super Mario: How Nintendo Conquered America*. London: Portfolio.

Sabin, R. (2003). *Punk Rock, So What?: The Cultural Legacy of Punk*. London: Routledge.

Sale, T. (n.d.). *Colossus—The Rebuild Story*. National Museum of Computing. http://www.tnmoc.org/colossus-rebuild-story.

Sanchez, C. (2003). *Interview with Martin Galway*. Remix64.com. http://www.remix64.com/interviews/interview-martin-galway-by-claudio-sanchez.html.

Santi, M. (2010). *Improvisation: Between Technique and Spontaneity*. Newcastle upon Tyne, UK: Cambridge Scholars.

Saunders, N. J. (2005). *Peoples of the Caribbean: An Encyclopaedia of Archaeology and Traditional Culture*. Santa Barbara, CA: ABC-CLIO.

Schartmann, A. (2015). *Super Mario Bros*. New York: Bloomsbury Academic.

Schone, M. (2004). "The Cartridge Family." *Spin*, 20(9): 82–86.

Schwartz, M. (2008). "The Trolls among Us." *New York Times Magazine*, August 3: 24.

Science of Cambridge. (1978a). *A Simple Tape Interface for the MK14*. Cambridge: Science of Cambridge.

Science of Cambridge. (1978b). *MK14 Standard Micro Computer Kit*. Cambridge: Science of Cambridge.

Sellers, J. (2001). *Arcade Fever: The Fan's Guide to the Golden Age of Video Games*. Philadelphia: Running Press.

Sheff, D. (1999). *Game Over: How Nintendo Conquered the World*. Wilton, CT: GamePress.

Shepherd, J. (2003). *Continuum Encyclopaedia of Popular Music of the World*. Pt. 1. *Media, Industry, Society*. Vol. 1. London: Continuum.

Shmuplations. (2015). "Console gaming then and now: A fascinating 1997 interview with Nintendo's legendary Gunpei Yokoi." Techradar. Published 10 July. https://www.techspot.com/news/61318-console-gaming-now-fascinating-1997-interview-nintendo-legendary.html.

Silbiger, A. (2004). *Keyboard Music before 1700*. London: Routledge.

"Silent Vinyl: Buying Records without a Record Player." (2016). *BBC News*. Published 14 April. http://www.bbc.co.uk/news/entertainment-arts-36040746.

Simakis, A. (2006). "Pianist Makes Name as Game Virtuoso." *Sun Journal*. Published 25 March. www.sunjournal.com/node/178544.

Sinclair Research Ltd. (1982a). *ZX Spectrum BASIC Programming Manual*. Cambridge: Sinclair Research Ltd.

Sinclair Research Ltd. (1982b). *ZX Spectrum Introductory Booklet*. Cambridge: Sinclair Research Ltd.

"Sinclair Stakes His Hopes on Blue Skies." (1986). *New Scientist*, 110(1503): 32.

Sloan, D. (2011). *Playing to Wiin: Nintendo and the Video Game Industry's Greatest Comeback*. Singapore: Wiley.

Slocum, P. (2003). *Atari 2600 Music and Sound Programming Guide*. http://www.qotile.net/files/2600_music_guide.txt.

Smart, J. (1988). "'ILLEGAL' presents the OLD 64 LEGENDS!: Cracking 1982–1985." *Illegal*, 30. http://csdb.dk/release/?id=6304.

Smith, R. B. (1983). "The IBM 701—Marketing and Customer Relations." *IEEE Annals of the History of Computing*, 5(2): 170–172.

Smith, T. (2011). "The BBC Micro Turns 30: The 8-Bit 1980s Dream Machine." *Register*, November 30. http://www.theregister.co.uk/2011/11/30/bbc_micro_model_b_30th_anniversary/?page=4.

Sousa, J. P. (n.d.). *The Washington Post*. New York: Carl Fischer.

South, P. (1985). "The Well-Tempered 64." *Your Commodore*, no. 10: 86–87.

Stanton, R. (2015). *A Brief History of Video Games: From Atari to Xbox One*. London: Robinson.

Stein, L. (1962). *Anthology of Musical Forms*. Evanston, IL: Summy-Birchard.

Stensdal, K. (2007). "Commodore 64-melodier hitter på YouTube." *ComputerWorld*. Published 10 September. https://www.computerworld.dk/art/41324/commodore-64-melodier-hitter-paa-youtube.

Stewart, Andy. (2005). Name behind the Name: Bruce Jackson—Apogee, Jands, Lake Technology." *Audio Technology Special*, 40: 49–53.

Stilphen, S. (2006). "Interview with Larry Kaplan." *DP Interviews*. http://www.digitpress.com/library/interviews/interview_larry_kaplan.html.

Stolzoff, N. C. (2002). *Wake the Town and Tell the People: Dancehall Culture in Jamaica*. Durham, NC: Duke University Press.

Strauss, J. (n.d.). *An der schönen blauen Donau, Op. 314*. Leipzig: Breitkopf und Härtel.

Strauss, J. (n.d.). *Radetzky March, Op. 228*. 1st ed. Vienna: Haslinger.

Stud Brothers. (1992). "Singles." *Melody Maker*, June 6: 29.

Sullivan, G. (1983). *Screen Play: The Story of Video Games*. New York: F. Warne.

Suni, J. (2002). "Acidjazzed Evening." *Vandalism News*, 39. http://www.pouet.net/prod.php?which=37478.

Sundell, P. H. (n.d.). *CCS64—A Commodore 64 Emulator*. http://www.ccs64.com.

Suominen, J. (2013). "Kieltäydyn määrittelemästä digitaalista kulttuuria—eli miten muuttuvalle tutkimuskohteelle ja tieteenalalle luodaan jatkuvuutta" [I refuse to define digital culture—how to build continuity for a changing subject and field of study]. *WiderScreen*, 2(3). http://widerscreen.fi/numerot/2013-2-3/kieltaydyn-maarittelemasta-digitaalista-kulttuuria/.

"Supercharge a VCS and Load Up Games from Cassette Tapes." (1983). *Computer and Video Games*, 21: 20–21.

Sweney, M. (2008). "Sex Pistols Singer John Lydon Flies the Flag for Butter in TV Ad." *Guardian*, October 1. https://www.theguardian.com/media/2008/oct/01/advertising.television.

Swimm, P. (2011). *Pulsewave's Fifth Anniversary | 04.30.2011*. http://pulsewave.org/nyc/pulsewaves-fifth-anniversary-04-30-2011/.

Sylvester, N. (2005). "The Advantage." *Pitchfork*. Published 6 February. http://pitchfork.com/features/interview/5955-the-advantage/.

Tanaka, H. (2014). *Hip Tanaka (RBMA Tokyo 2014 Lecture)*. https://www.youtube.com/watch?v=F7J5GlE3YLQ.

Takano, M. (1994). "How the Famicom Was Born—Part 7: Deciding on the Specs." *Nikkei Electronics*, December 19. Translation from a 3 October 2008 reprint of the original by Glitterberri. http://www.glitterberri.com/developer-interviews/how-the-famicom-was-born/deciding-on-the-specs/.

Takano, M. (1995). "How the Famicom Was Born—Part 8: Synonymous with the Domestic Game Console." *Nikkei Electronics*, January 16. Translation by Glitterberri. http://www.glitterberri.com/developer-interviews/how-the-famicom-was-born/synonymous-with-the-domestic-game-console/.

Tamburro, P. (2013). "Interview: Smooth McGroove on Becoming YouTube Famous." *Crave*. Published 30 September. http://www.craveonline.com/entertainment/579091-interview-smooth-mcgroove-on-becoming-youtube-famous/.

Tanaka, A. (2000). "Musical Performance Practice on Sensor-Based Instruments." In Wanderley, M., & Battier, M. (eds.), *Trends in Gestural Control of Music*. Paris: Institut de Recherche et Coordination Acoustique Musique, pp. 389–405.

Tenzer, M., & Roeder, J. B. (2011). *Analytical and Cross-cultural Studies in World Music*. New York: Oxford University Press.

Timbalandrips. (2007). *Producer Timbaland Rips Song from Finnish Musician?* https://www.youtube.com/watch?v=M4KX7SkDe4Q.

Tingen, P. (1996). "Fairlight the Whole Story." *Audio Media*, January. London: Intent Media London, pp. 48–55.

Tomkins, S. (2011). "ZX81: Small Black Box of Computing Desire." *BBC News*. Published 11 March. http://www.bbc.co.uk/news/magazine-12703674.

Tonelli, C. (2014). "The Chiptuning of the World: Game Boys, Imagined Travel, and Musical Meaning." In Gopinath, S., & Stanyek, J. (eds.), *The Oxford Handbook of Mobile Music Studies*, vol. 2. New York: Oxford University Press, pp. 402–426.

Torres, G. (2013). *Encyclopaedia of Latin American Popular Music*. Santa Barbara, CA: ABC-CLIO.

Totillo, S. (2009). "The Chiptunes Band That Might Just Break Through." *Kotaku*. Published 28 May. http://kotaku.com/5272206/the-chiptunes-band-that-just-might-break-through.

Townley, E. (1976). "Jazz, Blues and U.S. Railroads." *Storyville*, 68: 55–58.

Tschmuck, P. (2014). *Creativity and Innovation in the Music Industry*. Berlin: Springer Berlin.

Turner, G. (2006). *International Chiptune Resistance: Attendance Is Imperative*. The New GAMER. http://www.thenewgamer.com/content/journals/g_turner/2006/03/international_chiptune_resistance_attendance_is_imperative.

Turow, J. (2008). *Media Today: An Introduction to Mass Communication*. New York: Taylor and Francis.

Vail, M. (2014). *The Synthesizer: A Comprehensive Guide to Understanding, Programming, Playing, and Recording The Ultimate Electronic Music Instrument*. New York: Oxford University Press.

Valéry, N. (1975). "Coming of Age in the Calculator Business." *New Scientist* (Calculator Supp.), 68(975): ii–iv.

Varga, A. (1996). *Email Interview with Bob Yannes*. SID in-depth information site. http://sid.kubarth.com/articles/interview_bob_yannes.html.

Vincent, R. (1996). *Funk: The Music, the People and the Rhythm of the One*. New York: St. Martins Griffin.

Vogel, H. L. (2015). *Entertainment Industry Economics: A Guide for Financial Analysis*. New York: Cambridge University Press.

Vuorinen, J. (2007). "Ethical Codes in the Digital World: Comparisons of the Proprietary, the Open/Free and the Cracker System." *Ethics and Information Technology* 9(1): 27–38.

Wagner, R. (n.d.). *Die Walküre*. Mainz: B. Schott's Söhne.

Wallich, P. (1985). "Design Case History: The Commodore 64." *IEEE Spectrum*, March: 48–58.

Wallström, A. (2004). *Twenty Questions with Markus Schneider*. C64.com. http://www.c64.com/scene_display_interview.php?interview=135.

Wallström, A. (2005). *Twenty Questions with OTD/JEDI2001*. C64.com. http://www.c64.com/scene_display_interview.php?interview=178.

Wallström, A. (2013). *Twenty Questions with HBH*. C64.com. http://www.c64.com/scene_display_interview.php?interview=260.

Wallström, A. (n.d.). *Interview with Martin Galway*. C64.com. http://www.c64.com/interviews/galway_part_2.html.

Wanderley, M. M., & Depalle, P. (2004). "Gestural Control of Sound Synthesis." *Proceedings of the IEEE*, 92(4): 632–644.

Warren, R. M. (1982). *Auditory Perception: A New Synthesis*. New York: Pergamon Press.

Webster, B. (1986). "Product of the Month: Instant Music." *Byte*, 11(13): 308–310.

Weiss, E. A. (1987). *Computer Science Reader: Selections from ABACUS*. New York: Springer.

Welsh, S. L. (2001). "The Literatures of Trinidad and Jamaica." In Arnold, A. J. (ed.), *A History of Literature in the Caribbean*, vol. 2, *English- and Dutch-Speaking Countries*. Amsterdam: John Benjamins, pp. 69–96.

"What the Hell Happened?" (1998). *Next Generation Magazine*, 40: 41.

Wilkins, C. (2014). *The Story of the Spectrum in Pixels*. Kenilworth, UK: Fusion Retro Books.

Wilkinson, M. (2009). "John Lydon: 'PiL Reunion Tour Funded by Country Life Butter Adverts.'" *New Musical Express*. Published 12 November. http://www.nme.com/news/music/public-image-ltd-35-1310100.

Williams, G. (1981). "The Commodore Vic 20 Microcomputer: A Low-Cost, High-Performance Consumer Computer." *Byte* 6(5): 46–64.

Wolf, M. J. P. (2008). *The Video Game Explosion: A History from Pong to Playstation and Beyond*. Westport, CT: Greenwood Press.

Wolf, M. J. P. (2012). *Before the Crash: Early Video Game History*. Detroit: Wayne State University Press.

Wolinsky, D. (2011). "8-Bit Punks Anamanaguchi beyond the Side-Scrollers." *A.V. Club*. Published 18 July. http://www.avclub.com/article/8-bit-punks-anamanaguchi-beyond-the-side-scrollers-58886.

Wood, D., & Abbott, R. (2016). "Chris Huelsbeck Interview." *Retro Hour Podcast*, ep. 27 Published 8 July. https://theretrohour.com/the-retro-hour-episode-27-chris-huelsbeck-interview/.

Wright, G. (1989). "How Many Is a Million?" *AmigaWorld*, 5(6): 6.

Xenakis, I. (1971). *Formalized Music*. Bloomington: Indiana University Press.

BROADCAST, FILM, AND SOUND RECORDINGS

2001: A Space Odyssey. (1968). Dir. Stanley Kubrick. USA: MGM.

Akst, H. (1961). "Baby Face." From Jan Garber and His Orchestra: *Everybody Dance*. USA: Decca.

Applegate, M. (2009). *Obsolete?* https://pixelh8.bandcamp.com/album/obsolete.

Bach, J. S. (1980). "Toccata." From Sky: *Sky 2*. UK: Ariola.

Belousova, S. "Tetris." From *Player Piano Volume 1*. https://www.playerpianomusic.com/store.

Benites, B., Garrett, J., & Toni, C. (1990). "The Power." From Snap!: *World Power*. Germany: Logic Records.

Berry, M. (1985). *Everyone's a Wally*. UK: Micro-Gen.

Bill & Ted's Excellent Adventure. (1989). Dir. Stephen Herek. USA: Interscope Communications and Nelson Entertainment.

Bruce, J., & Clapton, E. (1967). "Sunshine of Your Love." From Cream: *Disraeli Gears*. UK: Reaction.

Buckner, J., & Garcia, G. (1982a). "Do the Donkey Kong." From *Pac-Man Fever*. USA: Columbia/CBS Records.

Buckner, J., & Garcia, G. (1982b). "Pac-Man Fever." From *Pac-Man Fever*. USA: Columbia/CBS Records.

Byrd, H. R. (1953). *Tipitina*. USA: Atlantic.

Canned Feud. (1951). Dir. Isadore Freleng. USA: Warner Bros. Pictures and Vitaphone Corp.

Carlos, W. (1982). "Tron Scherzo." From *Tron (Original Motion Picture Soundtrack)*. USA: CBS.

Click On. (2009). Presented by Simon Cox. UK: BBC Radio 4, first broadcast March16.

Close Encounters of the Third Kind. (1977). Dir. Steven Spielberg. USA: EMI Films.

Currie, B., Payne, C., & Ure, M. (1980). "Fade to Grey." From Visage: *Visage*. UK: Polydor.

Davis, M. (1970). *Bitches Brew*. USA: Columbia.

Deeco. (2010). "Famalam." From Jme: *Blam!* UK: Boy Better Know.

Douglas, A. (2000). "Who Let the Dogs Out?" From Baha Men: *Who Let the Dogs Out*. USA: S-Curve Records.

Eliott in the Morning. (2007). Presenter Eliott Segal. USA: WWDC-FM, first broadcast February 2.

Europe in 8 Bits. (2013). Dir. J. Gandía. Spain: Turanga Films.

Fahrenkrog-Petersen, U. (1983). "99 Luftballons." From Nena: *Nena*, Germany: CBS.

"Fetishising Busyness." *Oliver Burkeman Is Busy*. (2016). Presented by Oliver Burkeman. UK: BBC Radio 4, first broadcast September 13.

From Bedrooms to Billions. (2014). Dir. Anthony Caulfield and Nicola Caulfield. UK: Independent.

Furtado, N., Mosley, T., & Hills, N. (2007). "Do It." From Nelly Furtado: *Loose*. USA: Geffen.

Gill, P., Johnson, H., Nash, B., & O'Toole, M. (1983a). "Relax." From Frankie Goes to Hollywood: *Welcome to the Pleasuredome*. UK: ZTT.

Gill, P., Johnson, H., Nash, B., & O'Toole, M. (1983b). "Welcome to the Pleasuredome." From Frankie Goes to Hollywood: *Welcome to the Pleasuredome*. UK: ZTT.

Guaraldi, V. (1965). "Linus and Lucy." From The Vince Guaraldi Trio: *A Charlie Brown Christmas*. USA: Fantasy.

Hadaway, H. (1981). *The Birdie Song*. UK: PRT.

Hammer, J. (1985a). "Chase (Instrumental)." From *Miami Vice Soundtrack*. USA: MCA Records.

Hammer, J. (1985b). "Miami Vice Theme." From *Miami Vice Soundtrack*. USA: MCA Records.

Hansen, B. (2005). "Girl." From Beck: *Guero*. UK: Interscope.

Heckle and Jeckle. (1946). Dir. P. Terry. USA: Terrytoons.

Holmes, R. (1971). "Groovin' for Mr. G." From *Comin' on Home*. USA: Blue Note.

Hütter, R., & Schneider, F. (2003). "Vitamin." From Kraftwerk: *Tour de France Soundtracks*. Germany: EMI.

Jackson, E., & Langmaid, B. (2009). *Bulletproof*. UK: Polydor.

Jacobs, M. W. (1950). "Evans Shuffle." From Muddy Waters: *Louisiana Blues*. USA: Chess.

"The Jam Badge." *Hey Duggee*. (2015). Dir. Grant Orchard. UK: British Broadcasting Corporation, first broadcast January 20.

Jarre, J. M. (1978). "Equinoxe 5." From *Equinoxe*. France: Disques Dreyfus.

Jarre, J. M. (1981a). "Magnetic Fields 1." From *Magnetic Fields*. France: Disques Dreyfus.

Jarre, J. M. (1981b). "Magnetic Fields 2." From *Magnetic Fields*. France: Disques Dreyfus.

Jarre, J. M. (1986). *Rendez-Vous*. France: Disques Dreyfus.

King, G., & Guissani, C. (1991). *Some Justice*. UK: Urban Shakedown.

Kingsley, G. (1972). "Popcorn." From Hot Butter: *Hot Butter*. USA: Musicor.

Knight, M. (2012). *Reawakening*. https://marktdkknight.bandcamp.com/album/reawakening.

Koshiro, Y. (2015). *Streets of Rage*. UK: Data Discs.

Kraftwerk. (1973). *Ralf & Florian*. Germany: Philips.

Lake, G. (1970). "Lucky Man." From Emerson, Lake and Palmer: *Emerson, Lake and Palmer*. UK: Manticore.

Lennon, J. (1969). *Give Peace a Chance*. UK: Apple.

Lennon, J., & McCartney, P. (1967). "The Fool on the Hill." From The Beatles: *Magical Mystery Tour*. UK: Parlophone.

Lennon, J., & McCartney, P. (1968). *Lady Madonna*. UK: Parlophone.

Lloyd Webber, A., & Wright, N. (1992). *Tetris*. UK: Polydor.

Lytle, J. (1998). "A.M. 180." From Grandaddy: *Under the Western Freeway*. USA: Will.

Mancini, H. (1956). "Peter Gunn." From *The Music from Peter Gunn*. USA: RCA Victor.

Martin, S. (1977). *Let's Get Small*. USA: Warner Bros.

Michael, G., & Ridgeley, A. (1984). "Careless Whisper." From Wham!: *Make It Big*. UK: Epic.

The Mighty Micro. (1979). Dir. Lawrence Moore. UK: ITV. First broadcast October 29.

Moroder, G. (1984). "Ivory Tower." From Limahl: *NeverEnding Story*. UK: EMI.

Morricone, E. (1969). *Metti, Una Sera a Cena*. Italy: Cinevox.

Morricone, E. (2004). "La Resa Dei Conti." From *For a Few Dollars More*. UK: RCA, BMG.

Morris, G. (2001). "Tune 4 My Broken Atari". https://gwem.bandcamp.com/track/tune-4-my-broken-atari-original.

Mothersbaugh, M., & Casale, G. "Freedom of Choice." From Devo: *Freedom of Choice*. USA: Warner Bros.

New Order. (1983). *Blue Monday*. UK: Factory.

Nine Inch Nails. (2008). *Ghosts I–IV*. USA: Null Corporation.

"Nintendo Music." (2005). *Chiptunes*. Presented by M. Sharples. Produced by D. Stowell. UK: Flat Four Radio.

Ozma. (2001). "Korobeiniki." From *The Doubble Donkey Disk*. USA: Kung Fu Records.

Page, J., & Plant, R. (1971). "Stairway to Heaven." From Led Zeppelin: *Led Zeppelin IV*. USA: Atlantic.

Papathanassiou, E. (1981). "Chariots of Fire." From Vangelis: *Chariots of Fire*. UK: Polydor.

Papathanassiou, E. (1993). *Blade Runner*. USA: Atlantic Records.

Passalacqua, E., & Prezioso, A. (1991). *Tetris*. Italy: Daily Music.

Perich, T. (2005). *1-Bit Music*. USA: Cantaloupe Music.

Powerglove. (2005). *Tetris* (Themes B and C). From *Total Pwnage*. USA: Independent.

The Prisoner. (1967). Dir. P. McGoohan, P. Jackson, D. Chaffey, & D. Tomblin. UK: ITV, first broadcast September 6.

Race for Your Life, Charlie Brown. (1977). Dir. B. Melendez & P. Roman. USA: Charles M. Schulz Creative Associates.

Raiders of the Lost Ark. (1981). Dir. S. Spielberg. USA: Lucasfilm Ltd.

Reformat the Planet. (2008). Dir. Paul Owens. USA: 2 Player Productions.

Rollerball. (1975). Dir. Norman Jewison. USA: MGM Studios.

Schumann, W. (1953). *Dragnet: Main Theme*. Performance by Ray Anthony and His Orchestra. USA: Capitol.

Sebert, K., Dr. Luke, & Blanco, B. (2009). "TiK ToK." From Kesha: *Animal*. USA: RCA.

Sid and Nancy. (1986). Dir. Alex Cox. UK: Initial Pictures.

Simmonds, M. (2010). *Decades*. https://4mat.bandcamp.com/album/decades.

Smith, A., & Dickinson, B. (2015). "Speed of Light." From Iron Maiden: *Book of Souls*. UK: Parlophone/BMG.

"Spectrum Music." (2005). *Chiptunes.* Presented by M. Sharples. Produced by D. Stowell. UK: Flat Four Radio.

Takahashi, Y. (1979). "Rydeen." From Yellow Magic Orchestra: *Solid State Survivor.* Japan: Alfa Records.

Taylor, R. (1986). "A Kind of Magic." From Queen: *A Kind of Magic.* UK: EMI.

Tchaikovsky, P. I., & Fowley, K. (1962). *Nut Rocker.* USA: Rendezvous.

The Beatles. (1966). *Revolver.* UK: Parlophone.

The Beatles. (1967). *Magical Mystery Tour.* UK: Parlophone.

The Beatles. (1967). *Sgt. Pepper's Lonely Hearts Club Band.* UK: Parlophone.

The Beatles. (1968). *The White Album.* UK: Apple.

The Blue Collars. (1998). "Tetris." From *It's Casual.* USA: Yawn Records.

Tron. (1982). Dir. Steven Lisberger. USA: Walt Disney Productions.

Various artists. (1998). *Back in Time.* UK: C64Audio.com.

Various artists. (2002). *Nanoloop 1.0.* Germany: Disco Bruit.

Various artists. (2010). *Scott Pilgrim vs. the World: Original Motion Picture Soundtrack.* USA: ABKCO Records.

Video Game Invasion: The History of a Global Obsession. (2004). Dir. David Carr and David Comtois. USA: Beantown Productions, first broadcast March 21.

While My Guitar Gently Beeps. (2016). Presented by Issy Suttie. UK: BBC Radio 4, first broadcast June 7.

The Wild Bunch. (1969). Dir. Sam Peckinpah. USA: Warner Bros-Seven Arts.

Williams, J. (1975). "Main Title (Theme from Jaws)." From *Jaws (Music from the Original Motion Picture Soundtrack).* USA: MCA Records.

Williams, J. (1977). "Cantina Band." From John Williams & the London Symphony Orchestra: *Star Wars Original Motion Picture Soundtrack.* USA: 20th Century Records.

Williams, J. (1978). "Close Encounters of the Third Kind." From Gene Page: *Close Encounters.* USA: Arista.

Wittchow, O. (1999). *Nanoloop.* Germany: XXC3.

Wolf, P., & Wolf, I. (1986). "Who's Johnny." From El DeBarge: *El DeBarge.* USA: Gordy.

Xenakis, I. (2004). "Analogique A et B (Three Excerpts)." From Curtis Roads: *Microsound.* USA: MIT Press.

Yellow Magic Orchestra. (1978). "Computer Game: Theme from the Circus." From *Yellow Magic Orchestra.* Japan: Alfa Records.

Zombie Nation. (1999). *Kernkraft 400.* Germany: Drehscheibe.

SOFTWARE

Alcorn, A. (1975). *Touch Me.* [Coin-op] USA: Atari.

Alderton, N. (1983). *Chuckie Egg.* [ZX Spectrum] UK: Elite.

Alexander, M. (1985). *Wham! The Music Box.* [ZX Spectrum] UK: Melbourne House.

Amstar Electronics. (1980). *Phoenix.* [Coin-op] Japan: Taito.

Arens, A. (1987). *TurboPlus.* [Commodore 64] Germany: Kingsoft.

Atari. (1981). *Pac-Man.* [Commodore VIC-20] USA: Atari Inc.

Atari. (1982a). *Super Breakout.* [Atari 5200] USA: Atari Inc.

Atari. (1982b). *Video Cube.* [Atari VCS] USA: Atari Inc.

Atarisoft. (1984). *Pole Position.* [Atari VCS] USA: Datasoft.

Aubrey-Jones, D. (1984). *Ghostbusters.* [ZX Spectrum] UK: Activision Inc.

Aubrey-Jones, D. (1985). *Death Star Interceptor.* [ZX Spectrum] UK: System 3 Software Ltd.

Baer, R., & Morrison, H. (1978). *Simon.* USA: Milton Bradley.

Bit-Corp. (1982). *Open Sesame.* [Atari VCS] Taiwan: Bit-Corp.

Beuken, B., & Thorpe, F. D. (1985). *Yie Ar Kung Fu.* [ZX Spectrum] UK: Imagine Software Ltd.

Bowkett, R. (1985). *Dynamite Dan.* [ZX Spectrum] UK: Mirrorsoft Ltd.

Brooker, C. (1985). *One Man and His Droid.* [Commodore 64] UK: Mastertronic.

Brown, G. (1986). *Deluxe Music Construction Set.* [Commodore Amiga] USA: Electronic Arts.

Bullet-Proof Software. (1989). *Tetris.* [Nintendo Game Boy] Japan: Nintendo.

Bunn, P. (1984). *Shoot the Rapids.* [Commodore 64] USA: New Generation Software.

Burczynski, J. (1992). *Soundtracker.* [ZX Spectrum 128] Poland: Pentagram.

Butler, C. (1985a). *Commando.* [Commodore 64] UK: Elite Systems.

Butler, C. (1985b). *Hyper Circuit*. [Commodore 64] UK: Alligata Software.

Campbell, R. (1986). *Instant Music*. [Commodore Amiga] USA: Electronic Arts.

Canvas. (1986a). *Highlander*. [Commodore 64] UK: Ocean.

Canvas. (1986b). *Miami Vice*. [Commodore 64] UK: Ocean.

Carter, D. (1985). *Rockman*. [Commodore 64] UK: Mastertronic Ltd.

Caswell, D. (1982). *Escape from the Mindmaster*. [Atari VCS] USA: Starpath.

CDS Microsystems. (1984). *Timebomb*. [ZX Spectrum] UK: CDS Microsystems.

Chapman, S. (1985). *Wizardry*. [Commodore 64] UK: The Edge.

C-Lab. (1987). *Creator*. [Atari ST] Germany: C-Lab.

Collier, D. (1985a). *Daley Thompson's Decathlon*. [Commodore 64] UK: Ocean.

Collier, D. (1985b). *Yie Ar Kung Fu*. [Commodore 64] UK: Imagine.

Commodore. (1983). *Music Composer*. [Commodore 64] USA: Commodore.

Crane, D. (1982). *Pitfall!*. [Atari VCS] USA: Activision.

Crane, D. (1984). *Pitfall II: Lost Caverns*. [Atari VCS] USA: Activision.

Croucher, M., & Stagg, A. (1984). *Deus ex Machina*. [ZX Spectrum] UK: Automata UK Ltd.

Darling, R. (1985). *Master of Magic*. [Commodore 64] UK: Mastertronic Added Dimension.

Data East. (1990). *Bad Dudes*. [Nintendo NES] Japan: Data East.

Davis, W., & Lee, J. (1982). *Q*bert*. [Coin-op] USA: Gottlieb.

Denton Designs. (1989). *Frankie Goes to Hollywood*. [Commodore 64] UK: Ocean.

EA Canada. (2012). *NHL 13*. USA: EA Sports.

Edwards, K. (1983). *Atomic Protector*. [BBC Micro] UK: Optima.

English, E. (1982). *Frogger*. [Atari VCS] USA: Parker Brothers.

English, E. (1983). *Mr. Do!* [Atari VCS] USA: Coleco.

Equinox. (1990). *ST Soundtracker*. [Atari ST] http://www.pouet.net/prod.php?which=13335.

Evans, M. (1983). *3D Monster Maze*. [ZX81] UK: New Generation Software.

Exidy. (1981). *Venture*. [Coin-op] USA: Exidy.

Fasoulas, S. (1987). *Delta*. [Commodore 64] UK: Thalamus Ltd.

Follin, M. (1985). *Subterranean Stryker*. [ZX Spectrum] UK: Insight Software.

Follin, M., Wilson, M., & Gough, P. (1985a). *Star Firebirds*. [ZX Spectrum] UK: Insight Software.

Follin, M., Wilson, M., & Gough, P. (1985b). *Vectron*. [ZX Spectrum] UK: Insight Software.

Follis, G., & Carter, R. (1986a). *Sweevo's Whirled*. [ZX Spectrum] UK: Gargoyle Games.

Follis, G., & Carter, R. (1986b). *Sweevo's World*. [ZX Spectrum] UK: Gargoyle Games.

Frye, T. (1982). *Pac-Man*. [Atari VCS] USA: Atari Inc.

Fulop, R. (1982). *Demon Attack*. [Atari VCS] USA: Imagic.

George, S. (2014). *The Strawberry Thief*. [iOS]. London: Victoria and Albert Museum.

Hal Laboratory. (1981). *Jelly Monsters*. [Commodore VIC-20] Japan: HAL Laboratory.

Hampton, D. (1983). *Q*Bert*. [Atari VCS] USA: Atari Inc.

Hamre, L., Hamre, A., Vahsen, S., & Johnsrud, R. (1990). *ProTracker*. [Commodore Amiga] http://www.pouet.net/prod.php?which=48005.

Harrap, P. (1985). *Monty on the Run*. [Commodore 64] UK: Gremlin Graphics Software Ltd.

Harrap, P., & Hollingworth, S. (1987). *Auf Wiedersehen, Monty*. [Commodore 64] UK: Gremlin Graphics.

Harvey, C. (1986). *Bomb Jack*. [Commodore 64] UK: Elite.

Hinsley, C. (1984). *Pyjamarama*. [ZX Spectrum] UK: Micro-Gen.

Hinsley, C., & Strudwick, N. (1985). *Everyone's a Wally*. [ZX Spectrum] UK: Micro-Gen.

Hogue, B. (1982). *Miner 2049er*. [Atari VCS] USA: Big Five Software.

Ilyin, N. (1983). *Crossbow*. [Coin-op] USA: Exidy.

Irem Corp. (1983). *Moon Patrol*. [Commodore VIC-20] USA: Atari Inc.

Iwaniec, M. (1998). *Nerdtracker ii*. [MS-DOS] http://nesdev.com/nt2/.

Iwata, Y. (1990). *Gremlins 2: The New Batch*. [Nintendo NES] Japan: Sunsoft.

Iwatani, T. (1980). *Pac-Man*. [Coin-op] Japan: Namco.

Iwatani, T. (1983). *Pole Position*. [Coin-op] Japan: Namco.

Jangeborg, B., & Wilkes, J. (1985). *Fairlight*. [ZX Spectrum] UK: The Edge.

Jennings, P. (1978). *Microchess*. [Apple II] Canada: Personal Software.

Jones, C., & Williams, T. (1984a). *Fahrenheit 3000*. [ZX Spectrum] UK: Perfection Software.

Jones, C., & Williams, T. (1984b). *Turtle Timewarp*. [ZX Spectrum] UK: Perfection Software.

Jsr. (2005). *FamiTracker*. [Windows] http://famitracker.com.

Kerry, C., Dooley, C., Hollingworth, S., Harrap, P., Holmes, G., Kerry, S., & Duroe, M. (1987). *Thing Bounces Back*. [ZX Spectrum] UK: Gremlin Graphics Software Ltd.

Kinnunen, T. (1989). *MED*. [Commodore Amiga] UK: RBF Software.

Kinnunen, T. (1991). *OctaMED*. [Commodore Amiga] UK: RBF Software.

Kitamura, A. (1988). *Mega Man 2*. [Nintendo NES] Japan: Capcom.

Kitchen, G. (1983). *Pressure Cooker*. [Atari VCS] USA: Activision.

Kitchen, G. (1991). *The Simpsons: Bart vs. the Space Mutants*. [Atari VCS] USA: Acclaim Entertainment.

Konami. (1984). *Hyper Sports*. [Coin-op] Japan: Konami.

Kotlinski, J. (2000). *Little Sound DJ*. [Nintendo Game Boy]

Landrum, S. (1982a). *Communist Mutants from Space*. [Atari VCS] USA: Starpath.

Landrum, S. (1982b). *Dragonstomper*. [Atari VCS] USA: Starpath.

Landrum, S. (1982c). *The Official Frogger*. [Atari VCS] USA: Starpath.

Larsson, D. (2015). *SIDTracker64*. [iOS] http://sidtracker64.com.

Lesser, M. (1976). *Auto Race*. USA: Mattel.

Lesser, M. (1977). *Football*. USA: Mattel.

Livewire. (1984). *Carry on Laughing*. [Commodore 64] USA: Livewire.

MacLean, A. (1987). *International Karate*. [Commodore 64] UK: System 3.

Macrae, D. B. (1983a). *Pole Position*. [Atari VCS] USA: Atari Inc.

Macrae, D. B. (1983b). *Dig Dug*. [Atari VCS] USA: Atari, Inc.

Marsden, S., & Cooke, D. (1984). *Technician Ted*. [ZX Spectrum] UK: Hewson Consultants Ltd.

Mastertronic. (1985). *Action Biker*. [Commodore 64] UK: Mastertronic.

Maurer, R. (1980). *Space Invaders*. [Atari VCS] USA: Atari Inc.

Mayer, S., Decuir, J., Kaplan, L., & Wagner, L. (1977). *Combat*. [Atari VCS] USA: Atari Inc.

McGhie, B. (1982). *Rabbit Transit*. [Atari VCS] USA: Starpath.

McNeil, A. (1980). *Berzerk*. [Coin-op] USA: Stern Electronics Inc.

Meegan, J. (1987). *Short Circuit*. [Commodore 64] UK: Ocean.

Mello, E. (1982). *Donkey Kong*. [ColecoVision] USA: Coleco.

Melon Dezign. (1992). *Humantarget*. [Commodore Amiga] Sweden: Melon Dezign.

Mika, M. (2002). *Berzerk Voice Enhanced*. [Atari VCS] USA: Independent.

Miki, K. (1985). *Ice Climber*. [Nintendo NES] Japan: Nintendo.

Miyamoto, S. (1981). *Donkey Kong*. [Coin-op] Japan: Nintendo.

Miyamoto, S. (1984). *ExciteBike*. [Nintendo NES] Japan: Nintendo.

Miyamoto, S. (1985). *Super Mario Bros.* [Nintendo NES] Japan: Nintendo.

Miyamoto, S. (1988). *Super Mario Bros. 3.* [Nintendo NES] Japan: Nintendo.

Miyamoto, S. (1990). *F-Zero*. [Nintendo SNES] Japan: Nintendo.

Miyamoto, S., & Tezuka, T. (1984). *Devil World*. [Nintendo NES] Japan: Nintendo.

Miyamoto, S., & Tezuka, T. (1987). *The Legend of Zelda*. [Nintendo NES] Japan: Nintendo.

Miyamoto, S., & Yokoi, G. (1983). *Mario Bros.* [Coin-op] Japan: Nintendo.

Morris, G. (2005a). *maxYMiser*. [Atari ST] http://www.pouet.net/prod.php?which=18831.

Morris, G. (2005b). *Phatt Demo*. [Atari ST] http://www.pouet.net/prod.php?which=16261.

Nakamura, K. (1986). *Dragon Warrior*. [Nintendo NES] Japan: Nintendo.

Namco. (1982). *Dig Dug*. [Coin-op] Japan: Namco.

Namco. (1983). *Pac-Man*. [Commodore VIC-20] USA: Atari.

Narihiro, T. (1985). *Gyromite*. [Nintendo NES] Japan: Nintendo.

Nash, C. (2004). *reViSiT*. [VST] https://revisit.info.

Niitani, M. (1988). *Guardian Legend*. [Nintendo NES] Japan: Nintendo.

Nintendo. (1974). *Wild Gunman*. [Coin-op] Japan: Nintendo.

Nintendo. (1979). *Radar Scope*. [Coin-op] Japan: Nintendo.

Nintendo. (1984). *Clu Clu Land*. [Nintendo NES] Japan: Nintendo.

Nintendo. (1998). *Game Boy Camera*. [Nintendo Game Boy] Japan: Nintendo.

Nishikado, T. (1978). *Space Invaders*. [Coin-op] Japan: Taito Corp.

Obarski, K. (1987). *Ultimate Soundtracker*. [Commodore Amiga] Germany: EAS.

Ocean. (1988). *Robocop*. [Nintendo Game Boy] UK: Ocean.

Öörni, L. (2003). *GoatTracker*. [MacOS] http://www.sidmusic.org/goattracker/mac/.

Owens, P., & Smith, J. (1985). *Daley Thompson's Supertest*. [ZX Spectrum 128] UK: Ocean.

Palmer, G. (1977). *Basic Math*. [Atari VCS] USA: Atari Inc.

Perry, D. (1985). *Herbert's Dummy Run*. [ZX Spectrum] UK: Micro-Gen.

Plogue. (2009). *Chipsounds*. [VST]. Canada: Plogue.

Pomfret, T., & Barna, B. (1985). *Hunchback II: Quasimodo's Revenge*. [Commodore 64] UK: Ocean.

QuelleSoft. (1986). *Helikopter JAGD*. [Commodore 64] UK: Ocean.

Richardson, M. (1986a). *Thanatos*. [ZX Spectrum] UK: Durrell Software Ltd.

Richardson, M. (1986b). *Turbo Esprit*. [ZX Spectrum] UK: Durrell Software Ltd.

Roberts, C. (1992). *Wing Commander*. [Commodore Amiga] USA: Origin Systems.

Rogers, M. (1985). *Thing on a Spring*. [Commodore 64] UK: Gremlin Graphics.

Rosen, B. (1983). *Arcade Insanity*. [Apple II] USA: Avant Garde.

Sakai, T. (1992). *Gimmick!*. [Nintendo Famicom] Japan: Sunsoft.

Sawano, K. (1979). *Galaxians*. [Coin-op] Japan: Namco.

Scorpio. (1998). *Octalyser*. [Atari ST]

SDL. (1989). *Music X*. [Commodore Amiga] UK: SDL.

Sega. (1982). *Zaxxon*. [Coin-op] Japan: Sega.

Sensible Software. (1986). *Parallax*. [Commodore 64] UK: Ocean.

SFX. (1984). *Music Maker*. [Commodore 64] UK: Commodore.

Silva, D. (1985). *Deluxe Paint*. [Commodore Amiga] USA: Electronic Arts.

Simko, J., Danhof, D., & Decker, M. (1984). *Track & Field*. [Commodore 64] USA: Atarisoft.

Sinclair, J. (1984). *Jouste*. [Commodore 64] UK: IJK Software.

Slocum, P. (2002). *Synthcart*. [Atari VCS] https://www.atariage.com/store/index.php?l=product_detail&p=101.

Smith, J. (1979). *Microvision*. [Console] USA: Milton Bradley.

Smith, J. (1985). *Hyper Sports*. [Commodore 64] UK: Imagine.

Smith, J. (1986). *Cobra*. [Commodore 64] UK: Ocean.

Smith, K. (1984). *The Wild Bunch*. [ZX Spectrum] UK: Firebird Software Ltd.

Smith, M. (1983a). *Manic Miner*. [ZX Spectrum] UK: Bug Byte.

Smith, M. (1983b). *Styx*. [ZX Spectrum] UK: Bug Byte.

Smith, M. (1984). *Jet Set Willy*. [ZX Spectrum] UK: Software Projects.

Software Creations. (1986). *Agent X*. [ZX Spectrum] UK: Mastertronic Ltd.

Software Creations. (1987a). *Bubble Bobble*. [ZX Spectrum 128] UK: Firebird Software Ltd.

Software Creations. (1987b). *The Sentinel*. [ZX Spectrum] UK: Firebird Software Ltd.

Software Creations. (1988a). *Bionic Commando*. [ZX Spectrum 128] UK: Go!

Software Creations. (1988b). *Black Lamp*. [ZX Spectrum] UK: Firebird Software Ltd.

Software Creations. (1989). *Ghouls 'n' Ghosts*. [ZX Spectrum 128] UK: US Gold Ltd.

Software Creations. (1990). *Silver Surfer*. [Nintendo NES] UK: Arcadia Systems.

Spectrum Holobyte. (1987). *Tetris*. [Apple II] USA: Sphere Inc.

Stamper, T., & Stamper, C. *Knight Lore*. [ZX Spectrum] UK: Ultimate Play the Game.

Steel, A., Pearce, S., & Bolton, D. (1985). *Theatre Europe*. [Commodore 64] UK: Personal Software Services.

Steinberg, K. (1984). *Pro 16*. [Commodore 64] Germany: Steinberg.

Stewart, B. (1981). *Asteroids*. [Atari VCS] USA: Atari, Inc.

Stodart, A., & Foster, I. (1985). *Blade Runner*. [Commodore 64] UK: CRL Group.

Sundell, P. H. (2008). *CCS64*. [Windows] http://ccs64.com.

Taito. (1987). *Operation Wolf*. [Coin-op] Japan: Taito.

Taito. (1988). *The New Zealand Story*. [Coin-op] Japan: Taito.

Takeda, G., & Miyamoto, S. (1980). *Space Firebird*. [Coin-op] Japan: Nintendo.

Takeda, G., & Wada, M. (1984). *Punch-Out!!* [Coin-op] Japan: Nintendo.

Tanaka, H. (1985). *Stack Up*. [Nintendo NES] Japan: Nintendo.

Tejedor, I. R., & Aguilar, P. S. (1987). *Game Over*. [Commodore 64] UK: Imagine Software.

Tezuka, T. (1993). *Super Mario All-Stars*. [Nintendo SNES] Japan: Nintendo.

The Radical Tubes. (1987). *Chronos*. [ZX Spectrum] UK: Mastertronic Ltd.

Titus Software. (1991). *The Blues Brothers*. [Commodore Amiga] France: Titus Software.

Toms, K. (1982). *Football Manager*. [ZX Spectrum] UK: Addictive Games Ltd.

Toone, B., Holmes, G., Green, A., Lloyd, T., & Duroe, M. (1987). *Krakout*. [ZX Spectrum] UK: Gremlin Graphics Software Ltd.

Tsuruta, M., & Ueda, K. (1984). *Bomb Jack*. [Coin-op] Japan: Tehkan.

Tufvesson, P., & Berkeman, A. (1989). *NoiseTracker*. [Commodore Amiga] http://www.pouet.net/prod.php?which=13360.

Turner, N., & Dobbis, R. (1982). *Snoopy and the Red Baron*. [Atari VCS] USA: Atari Inc.

Ubisoft. (2010). *Scott Pilgrim vs. the World: The Game*. [Sony Playstation 3 and Microsoft Xbox 360] France: Ubisoft.

Ueda, K. (1982). *Mr. Do!* [Coin-op] Japan: Universal Entertainment Corp.

Universal Entertainment Corp. (1984). *Mr Do's Wild Ride*. [Coin-op] Japan: Universal Entertainment Corp.

Valeau, E., & Ivey, H. (1977). *Circus*. [Coin-op] USA: Exidy.

Wainwright, R. (1982). *Piper*. [Commodore 64] USA: Abacus Software.

Wainwright, R. (1983). *Synthy 64*. [Commodore 64] USA: Abacus Software.

Ward, M. W. (1983). *Pheenix*. [ZX Spectrum] UK: Megadoo Software.

Weatherburn, I., Butler, S., & Gray, F. (1985). *The Neverending Story*. [ZX Spectrum 128] UK: Ocean.

Wetherill, S., Salmon, P., & Walker, A. (1985). *Robin of the Wood*. [ZX Spectrum 128] UK: Odin Computer Graphics Ltd.

White, S., & Sutherland, A. (1983). *Ant Attack*. [ZX Spectrum] UK: Quicksilva Ltd.

White, S., & Sutherland, A. (1984). *Zombie Zombie*. [ZX Spectrum] UK: Quicksilva Ltd.

Whittaker, D. (1984). *Lazy Jones*. [Commodore 64] UK: Terminal Software.

Wittchow, O. (1999). *Nanoloop*. [Nintendo Game Boy]

Woita, S. (1983). *Quadrun*. [Atari VCS] USA: Atari Inc.

Woods, J. (1984). *Kong Strikes Back!*. [Commodore 64] UK: Ocean.

Wray, W. (1982). *Invaders*. [ZX Spectrum] UK: Artic Computing Ltd.

Yokoi, G. (1980). *Ball*. [Game & Watch] Japan: Nintendo.

Yokoi, G. (1982). *Donkey Kong*. [Game & Watch] Japan: Nintendo.

Yokoi, G. (1984). *Duck Hunt*. [Nintendo NES] Japan: Nintendo.

Zilec-Zenitone. (1982). *Check Man*. [Coin-op] USA: Zilec-Zenitone.

Index

CPSIA information can be obtained
at www.ICGtesting.com
Printed in the USA
BVHW050002210319
543285BV00002B/4/P

9 780190 4